Fall '13

MW00445850

CITIZENS AND SPORTSMEN

FIGURE 0.1. Map of Chile. Image courtesy of the U.S. Central Intelligence Agency.

CITIZENS AND SPORTSMEN

FÚTBOL AND POLITICS IN TWENTIETH-CENTURY CHILE

BRENDA ELSEY

University of Texas Press | Austin

Requests for permission to reproduce material from this work should be sent to:
Permissions
University of Texas Press
P.O. Box 7819
Austin, TX 78713-7819
www.utexas.edu/utpress/about/bpermission.html

∞ The paper used in this book meets the minimum requirements of ANSI/NISO Z39.48-1992
(R1997) (Permanence of Paper).

LIBRARY OF CONGRESS CATALOGING-IN-PUBLICATION DATA

Elsey, Brenda.
  Citizens and sportsmen : fútbol and politics in twentieth-century Chile / Brenda Elsey.
    p.   cm.
  Includes bibliographical references and index.
  ISBN 978-0-292-74393-9
  1. Soccer—Chile.   2. Soccer—Political aspects—Chile.   3. Nationalism and sports—
Chile.   I. Title.
  GV944.C5E57 2011
  796.3340983—dc22

                                                                  2011001182

First paperback printing, 2012

CONTENTS

FIGURE 0.2.   Neighborhoods of Santiago, Chile, 2009. Cartography by Bill Nelson.

ACKNOWLEDGMENTS

Financial support for this project came from a variety of institutions, including the American Association of University Women, the American Popular Culture Association, Hofstra University's Faculty Research and Development Fund, the Social Science Research Council, Stony Brook University, the Tinker Foundation, and the University of Florida library. I sincerely appreciate the staff of these organizations.

My interest in Latin American history began in graduate school. The teachers and graduate students at Stony Brook University created an ideal learning environment. Professors Javier Auyero, Brooke Larson, Nancy Tomes, Barbara Weinstein, and Kathleen Wilson taught rigorous seminars. I continue to draw upon their insights. I would also like to thank Pablo Piccato at Columbia University for his suggestions on this project in its early stages. My advisement team, lead by Thomas Miller Klubock, also included Paul Gootenberg and Temma Kaplan. I cannot adequately express my appreciation for the time they invested in my professional and personal development. I hope that my work, now and in the future, does justice to their efforts. Fellow graduate students Ernesto Capello, Yvonne Falabella, Enrique Garguín, Hernán Pruden, Ana Julia Ramírez, Hernán Sorgentini, and Jessica Stites have enriched my graduate and postgraduate life. Finally, I would like to thank Samuel Martland, Patrick Barr-Melej, Margaret Power, and Eric Zolov for their collegiality and comments on my work.

In Chile, I was warmly received by the historians at *oficios varios*, including Juan Pablo Barros, Jorge Iturriaga, Alberto Harambour, Marcos Fernández, and Daniel Palma. I would like to thank them for their advice and friendship. I especially appreciate the insights of Jorge Iturriaga into Chilean football. Consuelo Figueroa, a great historian and feminist, has been a wonderful friend. Francisca Piracés and Claudia Jería provided research assistance. Cristián Muñoz Funck, an encyclopedia of Chilean sports, generously shared his knowledge. Finally, I would like to thank the Palestro Foundation and the staff members at the National Library in Santiago, who assisted in the research for this book.

At Hofstra University, my colleagues in the History Department, the Latin American and Caribbean Studies program, and the Women's Studies program have been supportive. In particular, Johan Ahr, Sally Charnow, Michael D'Innocenzo, Simon Doubleday, Carolyn Eisenberg, Louis Kern, James Levy, Stanislao Pugliese, Mario Ruiz, Yuki Terazawa, John Walsh, and Susan Yohn have created a supportive environment for junior faculty. Outside my department, Zilkia Janer, Benita Sampedro, Karyn Valerius, and Dan Varisco have been good colleagues. Finally, I would like to thank the many Hofstra students who have enriched my teaching experience.

Two anonymous readers guided the revisions of the book manuscript. Their suggestions were invaluable. I owe the second reviewer special thanks for an additional report on the revisions. Their reports were examples of how the review process can become pedagogical. Furthermore, I would like to express my gratitude to Theresa May, my editor at the University of Texas Press. Ms. May was encouraging, efficient, and straightforward. I have appreciated her professionalism throughout the publishing process. In addition, Lynne Chapman and Kaila Wyllys at UT Press were helpful with the preparation of the manuscript. Finally, I am grateful to Kip Keller for his detailed copyediting.

It sounds cliché to mention the difficulty of accounting for the personal relationships that contribute to one's work, until faced with the task. Over the years, Jyoti Rai and Christina Stolz have been wonderful additions to our family, and I cherish their friendship. The Barbosa-Jiménez, Cimino-Rothman, Damm, Ellard-Simpson, and Toner families make life in Queens fun. There are a few friendships that have weathered every storm imaginable, including those I share with J. Edward Durrett, Alyssa Getz, and John Grob. I draw upon the laughs and inspiration you have given me more frequently than you can imagine. J. Edward, I thank you for sticking by me through thick and very thin. I would also like to acknowledge the Denny, Elsey, Espinoza, Hart, Piracés, Smith, Steele (especially Katlyn, James, and Ryan), Thorsby, and Thompson families for their love over the years. I deeply appreciate the support of my fathers, Don Elsey and Michael Steele. My grandmother, Jean Elsey, has always encouraged my interest in history and the world. Although they will not be able to read this, Bill Brown, Pauline Brown, Raymond Elsey, and Shirley Steele were wonderful grandparents. My mother, Joan, merits special mention, not only for vetting nearly all my ideas, but also for being my best friend.

Maya and Luna, I love you. You have given me immeasurable happiness. I promise to write other books so I can dedicate them to you. This one I owe to your father. Enrique, between us, hope springs eternal. I hope this very public pronouncement of love conveys the sincerity with which it is written. ¡*Valiente!*

CITIZENS AND SPORTSMEN

INTRODUCTION

Some people think football is a matter of life and death . . .
I can assure them it is much more serious than that.

—*Bill Shankly*

Fútbol, or soccer as it is called in the United States, is the most popular sport in the world. Millions schedule their lives and build identities around a relatively simple struggle between two teams for the control of a ball. The mechanics of the game have changed little over the past hundred years. Its audience, on the other hand, has expanded enormously. Market forces, globalization, and communications technology have fueled football's transformation into a mass spectacle. Twentieth-century thinkers grappled with the significance of the popularity of sports. Many asked, "What do sports distract us from?" George Bernard Shaw concluded that sports served as an outlet for men's resentment toward their wives. His contemporary George Orwell went further, arguing that sports were a form of modern warfare; Sigmund Freud suggested that they were a sublimated expression of sexuality; and still others have viewed sports as a detour from class struggle. These writers recognized sports as an important feature of modern society. However, they assumed that sports acted as a diversion from serious matters. This book takes the opposite tack, asking, "What do sports attract participants to?" By approaching football as "what really happens" rather than as a byproduct of something else, this study takes a fresh look at life in twentieth-century Chile.

The commodification of football accompanied its growth in popularity and shaped its political significance. This commercialism is on display during the World Cup tournament. Every four years, the Cup encourages audience members to feel a common bond with one another. Spectators are surrounded by athletic prowess, nationalist rhetoric, and advertisements that appeal to supposedly universal values. More than a billion people follow the tournament on television, radio, computers, and mobile telephones as well as in stadiums. It is so uniquely popular that scientists

and psychologists see the event as an opportunity to study human development.[1] Furthermore, a barrage of documentaries, films, television series,
and mainstream books have utilized football to comment on globalization.
Despite the sport's global appeal, this book uses a local case study of football and focuses on its less commercial subjects. *Citizens and Sportsmen*
tells the story of amateur football players whose dedication to civic engagement had long-term political significance in Chile. The book traces the
history of organizations formed by those who loved the "beautiful game."
It focuses on clubs, iconography, stories, and relationships that surround
football rather than on the technical development of the sport.

Given the ubiquity of football in much of Latin America, it may surprise
readers that few academic histories of the sport exist. Even fewer focus on
its relevance to politics in the region. In part, this stems from the assumption that football serves only nationalist and authoritarian interests. One
important historian of the region claimed that its "chief significance has
been its use by the elite to bolster official ideology and to channel social
energy in ways compatible with prevailing social values."[2] Anthropologists
and sociologists have been less dismissive, especially in their attention to
different forms of spectatorship and consumption.[3] While questioning the
assumption that popular culture merely reproduces existing inequalities,
this study demonstrates the conservative nature of professional football.
The process of commercialization reinforced values that underpinned the
stark disparities in Chile. Yet a historical approach provides a complex
picture of football's relationship to politics by explaining its context, con-
tingency, and change over time.

Citizens and Sportsmen argues that amateur football clubs integrated
working-class men into urban politics, connected them to political parties,
and served as venues of political critique.[4] In the spaces of civic associations, working- and middle-class men debated the dominant paradigms of
democracy and citizenship. They claimed that their labor and creativity entitled them to full political participation. Through their activities,
they expanded the terms of political discourse. In challenging the limits
of formal politics, civic associations energized the very institutions they
criticized. Once firmly rooted in popular culture, the narrative of Chilean
democracy created a unifying message that shaped a sense of involvement
in the political process. Although many of the club directors in this book
would not have characterized their work as political, it is the task of the
historian to build such a case. As Michel Foucault described historical

analysis, "People know what they do; they frequently know why they do what they do; but what they don't know is what what they do does."[5]

During much of the twentieth century, Chile's political system maintained a high degree of stability and democratic representation in comparison to the rest of Latin America, making it possible to examine football and politics over a long period.[6] Thus, *Citizens and Sportsmen* contributes to recent literature on civil society and democracy, an area of study reinvigorated by the transitions from authoritarian regimes in Latin America and Eastern Europe in the 1990s.[7] Leading social scientists, including Robert Putnam and Charles Tilly, have argued for the importance of voluntary organizations in creating democratic societies that connect citizens to the state.[8] However, many of the studies inspired by the democratic transitions of the early 1990s marginalize the role of popular culture.[9] This is a notable absence, given that people frequently form civic associations to share their passion for theater, dance, and sports. In contrast to scholarship in the social sciences, culture and language figure prominently in the work of literary scholars. Yet the process by which cultural forms, icons, and representations influence formal politics remains murky. Much of the work in cultural studies or literary criticism in the Southern Cone (Argentina, Chile, Uruguay, and Paraguay) analyzes popular culture during the authoritarian regimes and the transitions to democracy of the 1970s and 1980s. Yet without long-term historical analysis, authoritarianism appears as an anomaly, apart from society.

In *Citizens and Sportsmen*, I approach football as a cultural practice as well as a set of relationships, or a "field."[10] This field served as a meeting point between individuals and institutions as well as between the material and symbolic. I define political participation broadly as the engagement of individuals and groups with the governing of their lives. *Citizens and Sportsmen* joins a small but expanding group of monographs in Latin American history that examine civic engagement through the study of voluntary associations.[11] Their interest derives, at least in part, from contemporary dissatisfaction with the quality of democracy. Transitions to democracy in Chile, Argentina, and Brazil failed to alleviate social inequalities. Further, some argue that new democratic systems provide legitimacy for the neoliberal policies implemented during the dictatorships of the 1970s and 1980s. Finally, while current political systems allow for more participation than was possible under the authoritarian regimes, voter turnout and party membership have declined.

In the social sciences and the humanities, scholarship related to civic associations frequently analyzes formal political institutions at the macro level, bracketing local dynamics in the analyses of political change. Through attention to the circulation of ideas about citizenship at the local level, this book highlights the dynamic relationship between local and national politics. In Chile, working-class men and women were incorporated into municipal politics before they played a role at the national level. Although municipalities were strapped for cash and municipal posts did not offer a clear path to national political careers, candidates fiercely campaigned for local office.[12] It is safe to assume that prestige and recognition attracted candidates. Furthermore, discourses that stressed an obligation to engage in community service encouraged citizens' participation in local politics. Over the course of the twentieth century, an ideal of civic engagement became central to amateur sports organizations. For amateur sportsmen, political activity was rooted in the local context, at the neighborhood level. Football clubs took pride in the relationships they fostered with religious organizations, labor unions, and political parties. The capability of football clubs to express the concerns of citizens to authorities depended upon these relationships.

The concept of a "public sphere" brought together research concerned with the role of civic associations in the expansion of citizenship and democratic practices. In *The Structural Transformation of the Public Sphere*, Jürgen Habermas argued that urban coffeehouses, newspapers, and salons created spaces for discussion that served as cornerstones of modern democracies.[13] Historians have sought to identify the conditions that enabled the creation, expansion, and maintenance of the public sphere. Moreover, feminist scholarship has reworked the concept to account for the exclusionary nature of the public sphere.[14] For example, women's marginalization from football clubs was not incidental, but was a central component of their popularity and constitutive of the limits between public and private. The debates over these topics demonstrate that the correlation between democracy and civic associations is not a foregone conclusion. In certain contexts, civic associations have limited political discussions.[15]

Studies in Latin America have questioned the value of the public sphere for the region's history. The pioneering works of Hilda Sábato and Carlos Forment illustrate that the model of liberal democracy has not been able to account for the types of democratic practices in Latin America.[16] Sábato argued that a public sphere emerged in nineteenth-century Buenos Aires despite the lack of a stable liberal democracy. She traced the emergence of democratic practices, though not through the ballot box, examining the effervescence of clubs, mutual aid societies, and immigrant organizations. Furthermore, she traced the development of skills necessary for democratic practices—for example, petition writing—within these organizations. In the Chilean case, football clubs provided similar opportunities and acted as intermediaries between local governments, state agencies, political parties, and citizens.[17] In a similar vein, Forment demonstrated that in the nineteenth century, Latin Americans practiced a form of everyday democracy in guilds, religious associations, and mutual aid societies. Moreover, Forment concluded that in the case of Mexico and Peru, citizens formed democratic organizations apart from and often in opposition to formal political institutions. In Chile, a rich network of civic associations emerged among the traditional elites as well as among artisans and workers.[18]

Football clubs in Chile developed strong relations with political institutions. Members defined themselves as political subjects even when formally excluded from electoral participation.[19] Scholars have noted the particularly strong connection between local politics and center-left political parties. One analysis concluded that "center and left parties were driven by a desire to control the state and its resources in order to realize their distinct ideological objectives. To achieve those objectives, they pursued primarily directive and clientelistic linkages with constituents in the local political arena."[20] *Citizens and Sportsmen* offers a bottom-up perspective that challenges the unidirectionality of this relationship. Clubs actively pursued relations with local politicians in order to shape policy and resource distribution. As in neighboring Peru and Argentina, direct action and organization, not only voting, were key forms of political expression. Relative to its neighbors, fewer obstacles existed to electoral participation in Chile. Yet the political system still excluded much of the population. Legislation rescinded property requirements for voting in 1874, although the literacy clause remained until the 1920s. Furthermore, corruption, especially the *cohecho*, or vote buying, was prevalent in the countryside and, to a lesser extent, in cities. Finally, women could not vote in municipal elections until 1935 and in national races until 1949. Although strikes, protests, and actions of voluntary organizations provided forums where marginalized citizens could express their political views, formal political channels also provided important benefits.[21] Football clubs did not, however, adopt a unified political ideology. After the emergence of professionalism in the 1930s, divisions arose between professional and amateur clubs over their approaches to politics. The market for football created a strong incentive for professionals to adopt politically "neutral" positions. In the 1950s and 1960s, professional football clubs attacked their amateur counterparts for their ties to leftist parties. Amateurs, for their part, criticized the impact of market logic on football.

Football clubs played an important role in the secularization of public life. The idealized public sphere is a secular space; however, this was never entirely true in Chile.[22] Studies of Latin American associational life have argued that a strong notion of civic Catholicism emerged in the nineteenth century.[23] Sports clubs had distant relations with religious organizations, and nearly all of their statutes prohibited religious discussion within clubs. While we cannot assume this prohibition was enforced, evidence shows that clubs rarely focused on the spiritual concerns of their members. Despite the attempts of Catholic leaders to organize leagues, they did not become a major force within football. It is unclear why, but by the 1920s, Church leaders had turned their focus away from football to promote what they termed "healthier sports," such as basketball. In all probability, the secularism of sports clubs was part of their allure. The separation of sports clubs from religious organizations further segregated women's and men's social activities. Women took an active part in church-based groups, while men abandoned these groups beginning in the mid-1800s.[24]

Citizens and Sportsmen argues that Chileans' belief in their democratic tradition shaped their popular culture. The notion that Chileans were exceptionally democratic became a cornerstone of their national identity in the first part of the twentieth century. The reality of this democracy sparked debate across disciplines and generations. Nevertheless, popular groups drew upon this belief to bolster their claims to public resources. This discourse reconciled the exclusive nature of the political system with efforts to build an inclusive national identity.[25] Explanations of Chile's democratic character emphasized the cultural traits of the upper and lower classes. Diplomats, scientists, and popular writers created the image of a democratic Chile both within and outside the country. Ángel Floro Costa, a Uruguayan scientist and lawyer, declared in 1899, "Chile is the only republican nation that has preserved itself . . . It is governed by an intelligent, renewable, and progressive aristocracy, similar to the English aristocracy."[26] British diplomat James Bryce compared Chileans to the English also because, in his view, they were both "intensely political."[27] In praising Chilean elections, Bryce observed, "Chile is also the only South American state which takes so enlightened an interest in its electoral machinery as to have devised and applied a good while ago a system of proportional representation which seems to give satisfaction, and certainly deserves the study of scientific students in other countries."[28] International observers frequently noted the importance of political parties; for example, William Anderson Smith concluded, "The Chileno is nothing if not a politician, but mainly in the sense of being a violent partisan."[29] Although the rhetoric of Chile's democracy obscured the enduring inequalities within the country, it also encouraged popular organizations to engage with the political system in order to resolve the problems of their communities.

APPROACHES, CONTRIBUTIONS, AND SOURCES

The attempt to define politics and culture in a way that retains their analytical value reveals striking differences among academics. The "cultural turn" or "linguistic turn" in the social sciences involved an understanding of culture and language as productive of, rather than caused by, social, political, and economic structures.[30] However, many within political science, sociology, and history continued to disagree about the constitutive role of culture. Scholars interested in change and agency often felt uncomfortable with criticism of normative values like liberty and justice and of the coherency of subjects, such as women.[31] In conceptualizing this book, I have found Pierre Bourdieu's approach to politics and culture, which emphasizes practice, useful.[32] For Bourdieu, culture is expressive, performative, and productive of social relations. People practice culture when they express their worldviews through any number of actions, including speaking, writing, dancing, praying, and playing football. Clearly, social structures create limits to these expressions; however, literary theorists caution against the view of culture as a mirror of society. A more apt analogy may be to carnival mirrors that distort, change, and rearrange things "as they really are."[33] Bourdieu's emphasis on practice and relations avoided traditional binary categorizations of culture such as high or low, resistant or dominant, or derivative or productive (of social class).

Politics, though inseparable from culture, can be thought of as an overlapping set of practices intended to control power relations. Anthony Giddens, among others in political science, distinguishes between broad and narrow definitions of politics, the first being related to the governmental decisions of a state, and the latter to "any modes of decision-making which are concerned with settling debates or conflicts where opposing interests or values clash."[34] These types of politics frequently intersect in civic associations and popular culture. An inherent problem with defining politics is that the project itself is a political one. As J. Peter Euben explained, writers often lapse into definitions of politics based on who is doing it (often elite men) and where it is being done (in Congress rather than the home).[35] In this sense, feminist historiography has shown the inadequacy of a definition of politics that fails to account for the interconnectedness of the public and private, the distribution of power according to gender hierarchies, and the role of gender in the creation of social class and definitions of citizenship.[36]

Throughout the twentieth century, football clubs in Chile worked to include leisure and recreation in political agendas. In *Citizens and Sportsmen*, I have been especially interested in drawing out the connections among the daily practices of clubs, ideas about bodily habits, and broader political dispositions. It has revealed a fascinating process whereby club members' utilization of institutional channels (petitions to agencies, parties, and legislators) politicized football in a way that did not occur in neighboring countries. This politicization of football became part of a struggle between leftists and conservatives, who accused the former of "making politics" everywhere. Conservative parties characterized their efforts to give the Church authority over culture as a moral rather than a political stance. This supposed "apoliticism" became a staple of conservative rhetoric. At times, the book paints an overly political picture of Chilean football clubs, in the sense that many players probably drifted in and out of clubs after playing a few *pichangas*, or pick-up games, and certainly did not always agree with the politics of the club leadership. The protagonists of this book, therefore, are those members that connected clubs to a broader political agenda.

The history of the Chilean democratic tradition has generated controversy in part because of its mobilization in contemporary political debate. Coupled with the praise for neoliberalism, the rhetoric of Chilean "exceptionalism" has undermined the work of feminists and labor unions to address inequalities.[37] Taking an opposite position, some have argued that the stability of the Chilean state depended upon the marginalization of women, indigenous groups, and agricultural workers.[38] From the perspective of the Mapuche, Chile's largest indigenous group, for example, the dictatorship of Augusto Pinochet could be seen "less as a fundamental rupture of the democratic order than a resumption of a previous status quo."[39] Tomás Moulian, a prominent Chilean sociologist, argued that the integration of political parties representing the working class, the regularity

of elections, and the role of the state as the leader of economic modernization duped Chileans into believing they were democratically governed.[40]
At times, this view conceptualized politics as a zero-sum game, in which
gains for one social group necessarily involve a loss for another. This book
is sensitive to the importance of state violence and exclusivity throughout
the twentieth century. However, this line of inquiry does not account for
the significance of the discourse of democratic exceptionalism in Chilean
history. Nor does it explore how people shaped, contested, and accepted
this aspect of national identity.

By the mid-twentieth century, the notion that Chileans were democratic had become widely accepted. This book traces how the discourse
of democracy shaped the everyday interactions and self-presentation of
football clubs. The argument, in its simplest form, is that this narrative
of democracy engaged everyday people in politics, encouraged political
tolerance, and was skillfully used by working-class organizations to make
demands on elected officials. Certain interpretations of Antonio Gramsci's
concept of hegemony would characterize this integration as a way of
cementing workers' participation in their own domination.[41] However,
amateur criticisms of the ruling elite and political activities went beyond
the "acceptable dissent" of successful hegemony, which is why the military
dictatorships of Carlos Ibáñez in the 1920s and Augusto Pinochet in the
1970s and 1980s targeted these associations. Moreover, amateur football
clubs created discourses that championed working-class players, civic
commitments, and political militancy.

The relationship between club members' attitudes, capacities, and habits and the civil associations to which they belonged is a central preoccupation of this book. In recent years, historians have taken an interest in the
exercise of power on bodies through habitual practices.[42] Historians have
developed a more nuanced view of gender, seeing it as an ever-changing
process that undergirds the power of nation-states, economic relations,
and patriarchal violence toward women. As Pierre Bourdieu explained,
"The body believes in what it plays at: it weeps if it mimes grief. It does
not represent what it performs, it does not memorize the past, it *enacts* the
past, bringing it back to life."[43] For gender and citizenship, football was a
key venue for the production of images of male power, the creation of an
aesthetic archetype of the masculine body, and the reinforcement of men's
dominance as active political agents.

This book outlines contesting versions of masculinity among football
clubs and their change over time. It shows that the "crisis in masculinity"

perpetually expounded by politicians, doctors, state agencies, and journalists was not a dominant discourse among working-class men. This "crisis" of masculinity implied that femininity was an unproblematic and biologically stable category.[44] In Chile, these crises portrayed middle- and upper-class men as being in a vulnerable position despite their firm control of political, economic, and social power throughout the century. These "crises" were also connected with the efforts of corporate managers and the state to promote a disciplined, domesticated masculine ideal that would curb working-class men's radicalism.[45] While a preoccupation with heterosexuality and virility among working-class clubs was important to social relationships, it did not necessarily translate into further exclusion of women.[46]

Interest in gender history has inspired an impressive series of investigations in Latin American studies that question accepted colonial and national political narratives.[47] Although the focus on football means that this study is primarily concerned with male actors, I have included a consideration of women and an analysis of femininity throughout. In this vein, Karin Rosemblatt's book *Gendered Compromises* has provided an important template. Rosemblatt's work showed the centrality of ideas about masculinity in shaping policies and also contributed to the historiography on the emergence of a mestizo identity, putatively a mix of Indian and European ancestry, which was central to the construction of Chilean national identity. The Chilean case has been virtually left out of the regional literature on race and ethnicity in the 1990s.[48] Unlike Brazil and Argentina, for example, Chile never embraced the notion of a multiethnic nation. Instead, the model of Chile as a homogeneous mestizo nation with an ever-distant indigenous past became dominant. While perhaps they precluded certain forms of biological determinism, transnational racial ideologies intersected with local beliefs to shape the boundaries of political inclusion.

The research for this study is based upon virtually unexamined records, chiefly club documents, neighborhood publications, and sports magazines. The creation of a narrative for this book was a process of interpreting these disparate records. Textual analysis is only a window on what type of information passed between actors in what must have been lively exchanges.[49] Petitions from clubs to their representatives, as they appeared in newspapers or congressional records, enabled the investigation to explore the strategies of clubs and the language in which they couched their demands. I also relied upon histories commissioned by football clubs as well as the autobiographies of sportsmen, housed in the National

Library, in order to trace changes in clubs and the narratives of football. Clubs' statutes, bylaws, and annual reports provided information about their structure over time, their practices, and the ways in which members defined the clubs' purposes.

The task of mapping relationships between football clubs and other civic associations, unions, political parties, and state agencies required a review of the records of other organizations. For example, newsletters of immigrant societies were useful in understanding the role of football clubs within immigrant communities and their relationship to volunteer firefighting units, charities, and dance clubs. To trace the ways in which political parties interacted with sports clubs, I examined the records of party congresses, newspapers, and pamphlets. Comic strips, songs, and commemorative books provided materials that helped me analyze the representation of social hierarchies and citizenship in sports literature. In many cases, I have interpreted silences as data. For example, clubs touted their inclusiveness; however, their practices precluded the participation of women. Images and textual representations circulated among footballers in the clubhouse, through media, and at games. As these images circulated, they took on an air of truthfulness and legitimacy. Oral histories provided insight into the significance of clubs for participants, although my efforts to conduct interviews were only marginally successful.[50]

STRUCTURE

Citizens and Sportsmen begins by drawing a sociohistorical map of early football clubs, shedding light on their political practices, their relationship to reform movements, and urban leisure in general. The efforts of industrialists and politicians to remake the habits of workers through strict control of time, space, and health reforms fueled the dissemination of football throughout the Southern Cone. Patrons who founded clubs sought opportunities to create class harmony. In Chapter One, I argue that the ways in which football clubs narrated historical events and petitioned government agencies supported the legitimacy of the Chilean state as an increasing presence in cultural life. Upper-class football directors created family allegories within football organizations that approximated the ones used to oppose labor organizations. Working-class players' bodies became involved in a relationship conceived of as both voluntary and pleasurable to their patrons. Good performance on the field translated into economic benefits, social status, and travel opportunities. Alternative vehicles for participation, such as the Workers' Football Association, provided leadership opportunities for working-class players, connected them to the nascent leftist press, and challenged their political exclusion. In this way, football organizations shaped class identity in the urban milieu.

The second chapter, "The Massive, Modern, and Marginalized in Football of the 1920s," takes a fresh look at the populist military dictatorship of Carlos Ibáñez through the lens of football clubs. During his dictatorship, new practices of spectatorship in stadiums and clubs challenged the authority of the military government, which had promised to bring order and modernity to the cities. Certain clubs attempted to discredit the claims that the military had intervened to preserve democracy. Moreover, members utilized football clubs as a means to maintain party structure and continue union organization in the midst of increased repression. Throughout the decade, the relationship between football clubs and political parties intensified. With the birth of mass culture, technological and marketing developments meant that popular culture became more profit oriented, widespread, and accessible. Leisure activities defined the urban experience and created narratives that framed the way spectators understood their lives. Finally, new urban spaces, including stadiums, movie houses, dance halls, and restaurants, democratized entertainment.

Chapter Three, "'The White Elephant': The National Stadium, Populism, and the Popular Front, 1933–1942," analyzes the construction of the National Stadium, a turning point in the relationship between popular culture, civic associations, and politics. In previous studies of this period in Latin American history, popular culture was often portrayed as a handmaiden of populism. This chapter questions that characterization by examining football clubs in the 1930s and their efforts to shape the policies of the Popular Front. I argue that strong party identification and pluralism prevented football from becoming a populist tool. The mobilization of clubs against what they perceived to be President Arturo Alessandri's attempt to gain their support through the stadium also contributed to the formation of an antipopulist discourse. A critical public, led by amateur clubs, accused state agencies of corruption and wasteful spending during the stadium-building project. Debates over how and for whose benefit the stadium was to be built took place in sports magazines, newspapers, cafés, and clubhouses across the country. Furthermore, the mobilization of amateur clubs in support of the center-left coalition, the Popular Front, challenged the notion of culture as an apolitical sphere. This affiliation reflected a deepening connection between amateur clubs, leftist parties, and unions.

The fourth chapter, "'The Latin Lions and Dogs of Constantinople': Immigrant Clubs, Ethnicity, and Racial Hierarchies in Football, 1920–1953," traces the racial discourses that circulated in the clubs themselves as well as in the popular literature and iconography surrounding football. It argues for the importance of these narratives in defining citizenship. Immigration and transnational flows of racial stereotypes intersected with local identities to shape notions of the body politic. Popular culture acted as one of the most fluid, quickly moving, and broadly disseminated media for the construction of political subjects. The distinct experiences of European and Middle Eastern immigrants in sports clubs shed light on how racial discourses shaped civic associations. Beginning in the 1920s, sports clubs acted as vehicles by which immigrant communities could maintain relations among themselves, promote positive images of their cultures, and gain access to political power. However, as the ideal of the urban mestizo became dominant by the 1950s, Arab Chileans found themselves permanently cast as "foreigners" in a way that excluded them from being considered full citizens in the political realm. Finally, this chapter demonstrates that an assumed racial homogeneity figured importantly in the discourse of democratic exceptionalism.

By the 1950s, amateur football clubs were among the largest and most politicized civic associations in Chile, taking an active role in squatter movements, labor disputes, and political campaigns. In the process, they created a magnetic icon of the popular barrio, or neighborhood, football player. This figure became a charismatic symbol of working-class ingenuity and class injustice. The political nature of the Chilean barrio hero distinguished it from similar figures in other parts of Latin America. Chapter Five, "'Because We Have Nothing . . .': The Radicalization of Amateurs and the World Cup of 1962," examines neighborhood football clubs' roles in squatter movements, labor disputes, and political campaigns. I argue that amateur clubs contributed to the radicalization of working-class neighborhoods. Moreover, these clubs created an ideal of masculinity based on physical labor, creativity, class solidarity, and political militancy. Finally, the boom in barrio football clubs became a centerpiece of the Chilean bid to host the World Cup of 1962. Preparations for the event shed light on how the Cold War shaped the divisions between amateur and professional clubs.

The political context of the 1960s created new opportunities and challenges for Chilean football clubs. Chapter Six, "The New Left, Popular Unity, and Football, 1963–1973," examines how the emergence of the New

Left and the youth culture in the 1960s related to the leftist Popular Unity
(Unidad Popular, or UP) government of Salvador Allende (1970–1973).
Despite the growth of the professional football industry, amateurs constituted an important base for political mobilization. Football clubs and other
civic associations provided resources to working-class neighborhoods
despite blockades, hoarding, and threats from paramilitaries. Moreover,
they organized public support for Allende's Popular Unity government.
The study of football clubs illustrates the importance of civic associations
in shaping and implementing the UP agenda. Enthusiasm for a new socialist culture that rejected materialism emerged among amateur clubs. At the
same time, commercialization of the sport reached a new apogee. Despite
the professionals' embraces of technological innovations that made it easier
for multinational corporations to reach consumers, they failed to co-opt
youthful rebellion and convince audiences to reconcile with authority.

The book ends with an epilogue that brings the story up to the present. On September 11, 1973, a group of military officers conducted a coup
against Allende. The bombardment of the presidential palace prompted
Allende's suicide and resulted in the death of many of his closest advisors.
Following the coup, the military launched a campaign of massive repression. This began an era of terror for leaders of the civic associations that
are the subject of this study. Since football clubs constituted important
public spaces, the junta sent police to make their presence felt in clubs
and playing fields. The military used large stadiums, celebrated by sportsmen as monuments to progress, as places to torture and detain prisoners.
The seventeen-year dictatorship of Augusto Pinochet dismantled civic
associations, squashed public debate, and destroyed long-standing connections between civil society and the state. Finally, this epilogue argues
that along with neoliberal economic reforms and mass consumerism, the
lack of civic associations has limited political discourse and contributed to
apathy among Chileans.

I began the research for this book at the headquarters of the National
Association of Amateur Football (Asociación Nacional de Fútbol Amateur,
or ANFA), nestled in the bohemian barrio of República in Santiago. In the
main social room, a group of older men stood conversing over tea. Young
women and men walked in and out of the building. A large photograph
of President Allende visiting the El Teniente mines hung over the room.
When I arrived in search of records, the vice president of the association
shrugged his shoulders and informed me that, sadly, the association had

none. He explained that in 1973, ANFA had destroyed all membership rosters and meeting minutes.[51] Many of the leaders had gone into hiding, ceased their activities, or been detained. While it is beyond the scope of this book to detail the history of football during the military dictatorship, it cannot ignore the events that began on September 11, 1973, including the torture and detention of prisoners in the National Stadium and the Estadio Chile, as well as the stories of young men and women sent from the barrio football fields to prison camps. No doubt, the Pinochet dictatorship, characterized by brutal violence, sought to destroy meaningful political participation. Much of what the protagonists of this book built was demolished, and they found themselves persecuted, often unsure which of their many civic affiliations had landed them in such trouble. Hopefully, this book can be of use to the *futbolistas* who seek to understand and shape the politics of the sport they love.

RAYANDO LA CANCHA—MARKING THE FIELD
Chilean Football, 1893–1919

1

The photograph on the next page, taken in 1893 of the Santiago Club, has been cited as the earliest image of Chilean footballers. These eleven figures, stoically posed, have been reproduced countless times to evoke nostalgia among fans. A few years after the photograph was taken, these players gathered in an elite café in the port city of Valparaíso to form the first national organization of football clubs. Throughout the twentieth century, this event would be wistfully remembered as the inaugural moment of football's "golden era," a time when the game was supposedly free from commercial and political interests.[1] The men in the photograph would likely have objected to such a harmonious characterization. They believed their generation desperately needed sports to alleviate the stress of class conflict, industrialization, and urbanization. Like many football clubs in the late 1800s, the Santiago Club was founded by British businessmen working in banking and mining. The British origins of football bolstered its reputation among Chileans who embraced "refined" European imports. Its rapid dissemination prompted one enthusiast in 1912 to declare, "The seeds planted by the Ramsays, Campbells, etc. have borne fruit. And our workers have founded sports institutions that have provided moments of solace . . . and moral regeneration."[2] Despite football's remarkable popularity, scholars have shown little interest in it, leaving much of this early history unexamined.

The relationship between popular culture and politics that emerged in this period shaped social struggles for decades. New forms of leisure, like football clubs, contributed to the organizational capacity of working- and middle-class men in the early 1900s.[3] The appeal of football brought together men from distinct political and class backgrounds. In this chapter, I argue that through their participation in football clubs, members learned

FIGURE 1.1.   Santiago Club, c. 1893. This photograph appeared in *Los Sports*, 13 February 1925. Image courtesy of Zig-Zag and the Colección Biblioteca Nacional Archivo, Santiago.

political skills, made claims to public space, and forged valuable social relationships. Largely excluded from the formal political system, members expressed their views in the language, iconography, and practices they developed within clubs. Moreover, football clubs helped a steady stream of migrants from mining and rural areas adapt to urban life and facilitated the transformation of regional cultural practices.

THE "SOCIAL QUESTION" AND FOOTBALL

Concern for how to resolve the "social question" connected football organizers, reform movements, and local politicians. The "social question" encompassed a series of debates about how to quell the demands of labor, control urban populations, and create a stable industrial workforce.[4] As in much of Latin America, a small group of families had monopolized political posts and land ownership in Chile beginning in the independence period. Workers' increased participation in labor unions and mutual aid societies worried traditional elites as well as foreign investors. In the football clubs they sponsored, upper-class patrons positioned themselves as benevolent patriarchs in relation to workers. Other employers characterized their company football clubs as horizontal fraternities. Both the paternal and fraternal narratives resembled those used to oppose labor unions. Workers who played for their employers became entangled in a relationship conceived of as voluntary and pleasurable.

The desires of upper-class patrons to mold workers' habits according to their labor needs dovetailed with those of the reform movements in Chile's largest cities, Santiago and Valparaíso. Reformers blamed workers' immorality for miserable urban conditions. They targeted alcoholism, gambling, indolence, and poor hygiene as the worst of these vices. Despite the disparaging image of workers put forward by reformers, a significant number of working- and middle-class people supported the movement. They hoped to alleviate common problems in their neighborhoods, including housing shortages and tainted food. Leaders of football clubs advocated the sport as a vehicle for the regeneration of workers. These ideas about working-class reform were not exclusive to Chile, but rather part of a broader, transnational current. Middle-class professionals, including physical-education teachers and "hygienists," played an important role in reform movements. In the early 1900s, they created new fields for their specialties, replete with conferences, professional journals, and educational credentials. As in Lima, Buenos Aires, and other Latin American cities, reform organizations in Santiago and Valparaíso eagerly sought scientific solutions to social problems.[5]

British immigrants living in affluent neighborhoods of Valparaíso formed the first football clubs in the 1880s, expressing a profound nostalgia for England's landscapes and social customs.[6] While many clubs emerged from within bank and mining offices, others arose from foreign-language schools. Europeans and elite Chileans arranged matches between the English-, German-, and French-speaking schools that their children attended. Chileans who attended these schools distinguished themselves by their European tastes and habits. Participation in football, cricket, and rugby marked the European pedigree of Creoles, who often picked up the sports during their education abroad.

In response to the popularity of football and other foreign cultural practices, salesmen imported sports equipment for specialty stores that catered to the urban elite. Several prominent founders of football clubs, such as Juan Ramsay, began businesses that imported such goods. No doubt the social relationships developed in clubs helped the owners of these businesses. The interest in foreign goods continued a long trend in which the market share of local artisans was slowly eroded. Since the early nineteenth century, Europeans had constituted the majority of Santiago's merchants.[7] Their advertisements presented European goods as both superior to local wares and capable of conferring sophistication and elegance.

British immigrants brought definite ideas of football's social value, which had already received attention in England. The sociologist Norbert Elias described the adoption of football there as part of a "civilizing process" in the nineteenth century whereby popular habits reflected new forms of self-control and social life became less violent. Football was part of a series of cultural practices that fulfilled the demands of the emergent centralized state, whose inner circles sought to monopolize violence.[8] Similarly, directors of state institutions in France, including schools and prisons, saw football as a way to instill time management in young workers and fill their unoccupied hours.[9] The founders of Chile's first clubs, who were quite aware of these processes, viewed such developments as positive. Despite the club founders' efforts to attract governmental support for football, the Chilean state made little effort to incorporate or mobilize sports organizations. In the first decade of the twentieth century, the state controlled workers through direct violence and repression rather than co-optation or integration.

The preservation of class privilege was important among the elite who founded football clubs. Notwithstanding their rivalries, Chile's first generation of footballers shared a class status as well as a vision of themselves as civic men. Elite British and Chilean sportsmen cultivated innumerable hobbies and joined scores of social, professional, and political clubs.[10] Sporting events provided them with important social forums. This clique of early footballers orchestrated participation in the London Olympics of 1896. The self-financed Chilean athletes were among the representatives from thirteen nations who competed in track and field events. Upon their return, members of this group concentrated their energy on mobilizing support for sports, particularly football, among politicians. They were convinced that class tensions in London had been significantly reduced as a result of frequent sports competitions among elite and popular teams.[11]

Chileans who founded the first football clubs typically belonged to one of the two dominant political parties, the Conservatives or the Liberals. In their discussions of the social question, both parties focused on workers' habits. Conservatives rejected explanations that blamed economic inequality or government negligence for urban squalor. Furthermore, they sought to empower the Catholic Church to oversee charity and relief projects in urban areas. Prominent Conservative bishop Rafael Edwards, who founded several football clubs, explained, "Discontent stems from more profound causes [than the price of goods], more serious ones that have their roots in the people's own habits."[12] Edwards mildly criticized industrialists for their unbridled economic ambition. He suggested their support for sports organizations could help prevent migrants from falling victim to the corrosive influences of the city. As in most reform rhetoric, migrants from the countryside were portrayed as naïve and easily lured into drinking, gambling, and card playing. Liberal Party members placed greater responsibility on the government and on business owners to help workers reform their habits, advocating public education rather than religious instruction as the best means of accomplishing that.

Football patrons claimed to be reaching out to workers, but their message of sobriety, time management, and physical discipline more likely spoke to fellow upper- and middle-class professionals. As one club director complained in 1907, "Outdoor sports appear to have widespread acceptance, judging by the publicity given to football matches in the daily press. . . . In reality they have [diffused] little, very little. A large percentage of the adult population does not practice sport of any type. And the rest are content with a football match that lasts a couple of hours each month or mounting a horse once every six months."[13] Commentary such as this highlights reformers' limited understanding of workers' lives and their leisure opportunities. Sports publications rarely considered the space, time, and economic constraints that workers faced. They decried physically idle workdays that were descriptive only of professional employment. Furthermore, their concerns with the deterioration of men's bodies caused by innovations like electric lighting and train travel, which were assumed to disrupt natural rhythms, related more to their own experiences than those of workers. Working-class clubs showed particular disdain for the temperance movement. The Anti-Alcoholism League, which urged football clubs to encourage sobriety among their members, found middle-class sportsmen more receptive to their message than their working-class counterparts.[14]

Alongside reformers and upper-class patrons, journalists played a crucial role in the dissemination of football. Sports journalists founded football clubs, created channels of communication between clubs, and articulated the relationship between football and class identity. Sports journalists throughout the Americas were in the process of defining their trade. Increased literacy and urbanization expanded the reading public. Enterprising writers raised public interest in football through the creation of rivalries. The earliest sports coverage was an extension of the society page, with long lists of the well-known families and politicians that could be seen at matches. *El Diario Ilustrado*'s description of the match between Santiago and Valparaíso in 1913 reads more like an account of a garden party. People arrived hours early to drink tea or have lunch with one another. Ladies showed off their latest fashions and arrived in automobiles with distinguished sportsmen. The writer described the beauty of the field in painstaking detail, its radiant green contrasted with the orderly white boundary lines. He claimed there could not have been less than seven thousand or eight thousand people, which "gave the sensation of a combat field in its glory day."[15] There were few opportunities to see so many people gathered in one place, apart from major protests and military parades. The increased attendance at matches, even if exaggerated, helped journalists persuade editors that sports news deserved its own section.[16] Sportswriters also encouraged sports clubs to use newspapers as bulletin boards for communicating with one another and to declare particular papers to be their "official" press organs. These declarations reflected the political sympathies of the clubs' members, or at least of those involved in deciding the clubs' affiliations.

RACE AND NATIONALISM IN FOOTBALL

While the British origins of Chilean football contributed to its rapid dissemination, local dynamics and politics shaped its social significance. Club leaders' preoccupation with class struggle became intertwined with anxieties over masculinity and *la raza chilena*, or the Chilean race. Sportsmen defined race in fluid and inconsistent ways, according to their perceptions of language, skin color, geography, and dress. However differently they understood la raza chilena, club founders agreed that it was in serious peril because of urbanization. As one club patron explained, "In modern times, more and more often men tend to live in the great urban centers. Industrialization and other conditions attract them to cities. In these [cities], man degenerates."[17] He blamed airborne germs, noxious fumes, tainted consumer goods, and artificial light as sources of general physical malaise, which he termed "racial degeneration."[18] Football club organizers drew upon fears of degeneration to argue for the urgency of promoting outdoor team sports.

Rivalries between Chile's largest cities, Valparaíso and Santiago, a mere sixty miles apart, spurred interest in football matches between them. Footballers commonly framed the rivalry between Valparaíso and Santiago as a competition between Anglo-Saxons and mestizos, respectively. Positive views of racial mixing between Native Americans and Europeans were relatively rare in the Andes during the postindependence period.[19] Although an affirmative discourse of *mestizaje*, or racial mixing, had not become dominant, sportsmen from Santiago selectively celebrated their indigenous heritage. They referred to themselves alternately as mestizo, Creole, American, or "half-Indian," as opposed to players from Valparaíso, whom they described as European or white. According to these football players, the mestizo character of Santiago represented a more "authentic" Chilean-ness. They claimed to derive primal strength from their Indian heritage and decisiveness from the Spanish.[20] The emergence of a more positive evaluation of Indians coincided with the conclusion of military campaigns against the Mapuche in southern Chile. Prominent founders of clubs depicted Indians as anachronistic and frequently referred to them as ancient ancestors. Physical-education pioneer and football club director Guillermo Martínez, for example, asked Chileans to be "better friends of our past, to revive many of the ancient indigenous exercises and games."[21] With their Indian heritage relegated safely to the past, Santiago clubs affirmed a mestizo identity as part of what legitimated their city's claim to represent the nation.

Footballers from Valparaíso boasted that their Anglo-Saxon "roots" distinguished them from mestizos as well as from Spaniards. They described their city as the most cosmopolitan in Chile and, at times, Latin America. In the pre–Panama Canal days, Valparaíso was an important international seaport along the route between the Atlantic and Pacific oceans. Chileans treasured the city's romantic aura, which was created by its chaotic streets, unique architecture, and nightlife. Despite Valparaíso's lack of physical regularity, sportsmen pointed to the city's newspapers, banks, and transportation system as evidence of its modernity. Chile did not experience the same influx of European immigrants as did Argentina, Brazil, or the United States in this period, but many public figures emphasized the port's European character.[22] A lawyer for British nitrate interests, Julio Zegers, compared the two cities in the following way: "Wealth in Santiago does not reflect the elegant simplicity of the serious and honest classes in Europe: it is a servile imitation of costumes and ornaments. In Valparaíso . . . the English spirit has prevailed, and the fashion is of a serious, distinguished, and attractive character."[23] Football clubs in Valparaíso associated their city's "English spirit" with their superior grasp of the game. For instance, clubs in Valparaíso wrote their rule books, constitutions, and hymns in English, which they claimed better preserved the qualities of football.[24]

Football clubs engaged in debates over race and national identity in the 1910s. As the national team became a widely recognized symbol, its performances sparked discussions of what constituted *chilenidad*, or Chileanness. Journalists publicized achievements in international competitions, such as the South American Cup, as benchmarks of Chile's progress. Sportswriters claimed that compared with their Argentinian or Peruvian counterparts, Chilean sportsmen were homogenous (of mixed Indian and European heritage). They boasted that this homogeneity produced a selfless playing style, and they criticized players whose height or weight deviated from what they deemed "average." Football club directors claimed that Chilean sportsmen were democratic as well as physically consistent. To establish this, football club directors drew upon historical examples from well-known democracies. For example, Guillermo Martínez stated, "In the matter of physical education, we are the Greeks of South America. Indeed, our Araucanians cultivated physical exercise with love."[25]

FIGURE 1.2.   Postcard featuring an arch dedicated to the British influence in Valparaíso. The arch was built in 1910 for the centennial celebrations of Chilean independence. Image courtesy of the Archivo Fotográfico Colección, Museo Histórico Archivo, Santiago.

The notion that Chile was primarily a mestizo nation was contested and had important implications for policy making. For example, the Conservative Party promoted foreign immigration as a way to settle "uninhabited" areas of the South, which created conflict with the indigenous populations that lived there. They justified land concessions to European immigrants because of their supposed racial desirability. In opposition to such policies, Nicolás Palacios wrote *La Raza Chilena*, first published in 1904. A middle-class physician, Palacios set out to prove that the Chilean racial mixture exhibited characteristics superior to those of any of the "pure" European races or other mixes in Latin America. Palacios argued that the Chilean middle class deserved the land titles and job opportunities being given to European immigrants. According to Palacios, the Chilean mestizos descended from a group of German Visigoths who had migrated to Spain centuries before colonization. Palacios claimed that these Visigoths mixed with "Araucanians" to create an ideal combination.[26] He used crime statistics and media reports to show that Chilean mestizos were less prone to violence than European immigrants. His ideas became important within the Radical and Liberal party circles as well as in popular discussions of race.

In addition, *La Raza Chilena* influenced physical-education teachers, who drew upon Palacios's theories when writing their curriculums.[27] In response to their concerns for the race, physical-education teachers formed a civic association, which they named the National Society for the Protection and Promotion of the Chilean Race. This association sought to empower sports clubs, physical-education teachers, and temperance societies.

Theories that viewed Chile's mestizaje as a positive development, like those of Nicolás Palacios, were based on a belief in the special nature of the Araucanian Indians. The heroic image of the Araucanians who resisted Spanish colonization surfaced frequently in club songs and iconography. Contemporary indigenous communities, especially the Mapuche of the south-central regions, were depicted as degenerate versions of their valiant ancestors. The positive portrayal of Indians in the distant past contrasted sharply with the image of the provinces as barbaric outposts. Sports journalists worried about the influx of people from the provinces to urban centers, often conflating the categories of workers and Indians. In their descriptions, "the provinces" became a shorthand designation for "violence" and "primitivism." Describing a brutal fight between a referee and player, one writer asked, "Do you think that the earlier paragraphs refer to a game played in Coquimbo or in the nitrate fields? They are incidents between the first teams of La Cruz and América of Valparaíso."[28] Another observer complained, "With horror and shame, we read telegrams from the provinces that day in and day out [report] on numerous crimes against person and property, in particular in the south of the republic."[29] Aggressive behavior was often perceived as a sign of masculine prowess; however, workers (especially miners and port workers) and Indians were depicted as having trouble controlling their violent behavior.

Caricatures of other nationalities served to create a unified image of Chileans within sports literature. Certain nations became emblematic of racial difference, especially those with large populations of African descent, such as Brazil and the United States. African American and Afro-Brazilian athletes were portrayed as grotesquely masculine, with exaggerated features. For example, the Chilean sporting press described boxer Jack Johnson as having a "bestial torso and a mouth glittering with gold," an excessive masculinity, and an "inexplicable, incredible, and absurd" attraction for women.[30] Sports literature attributed the talent of black athletes to the primal instincts they derived from their African heritage. One journalist referred to two separate "tribes" of black sportsmen: those who viewed Johnson's audacious behavior with shame and those who approved.[31] By describing Johnson and other African Americans as savage, Chilean sportsmen placed themselves in the categories of white and civilized.

The historian Gail Bederman has argued that the fear of and hostility toward Jack Johnson signaled an important juncture in the process of remaking "manhood" in the early twentieth century. Across the Americas, the belief that men had become "overcivilized" prompted sportsmen to place a greater value on virility than on self-restraint. Thus, for white men to recapture the aggressive instincts they had lost in their adaptation to modern life, they had to adopt some of the primitiveness of the black man.[32] Among Chilean sportsmen, the model of manly self-restraint coexisted with one of masculine dominance. Elite sportsmen championed the former more commonly, but neither held exclusive sway. Sports directors across the social spectrum shunned violence on the field as a showing of weakness and mobilized the model of the British gentleman as an icon of masculine self-restraint.[33] At the same time, these clubs began excursion programs that encouraged members to reconnect with nature and cultivate the "savage within."

At times, spontaneous events on the football field and respect for talent undermined racial stereotypes. The experiences of footballers who visited the provinces often contradicted the frightening media images of the hinterlands. As football gained a broader fan base and clubs became more organizationally savvy, teams toured outside Santiago regularly. Players sent lengthy updates that were printed in sports magazines and distributed in clubs. Through these reports and interviews, players created their own commentaries on the provinces. Often, players glowingly described the people and places they encountered. For instance, the northern port city of Coquimbo, stereotyped by mainstream media as a rugged frontier made dangerous by Indians, became known for its polite football players.

Sports club leaders and journalists put forward wildly different ideas of race. At times, they defined the Chilean race as all people within the national political borders; in other instances, they applied the term exclusively to mestizos; and in other moments, they extended the term *race* to include humans in the broadest sense. Furthermore, class markers certainly exerted a significant influence on perceptions of race. Despite sportswriters' claims that only talent mattered, they were determined to properly categorize players according to race. In the case of hurdle champion Juan Gálvez Rivas, writers described his face as "Japanese" and wondered why his friends called him "China man."[34] Although one article stated that Gálvez's race was of minor importance, a large headshot of his face appeared with a caption that again questioned whether he was Chinese. In another instance, a journalist marveled at the good looks of boxer Benjamin Zárate, "despite" his indigenous heritage. He elaborated that Zárate's features were "very agreeable," adding that "he looks more European than Chilean-Araucanian."[35] In Zárate's case, excellence in sports could "whiten" people's perception of him. The separation of European and Araucanian from Chilean in the article demonstrated the writer's assumption that Chileans were mestizo.

WORKERS' CLUBS

According to newspaper accounts, football's popularity among workers grew with surprising speed. In 1905, *El Mercurio* reported:

> Football has spread in truly gigantic proportions, primarily among the
> working class. All workers' circles and societies count among them one or

two teams that practice regularly. . . . Others, those more knowledgeable of the sport, have founded some clubs that at the same time serve as sports centers, mutual aid societies, and meeting places. In these clubs, an enviable harmony and camaraderie reigns. One of these clubs, "Chile-Argentina," has 120 active members, all very enthusiastic and good players. As soon as a worker arrives to Santiago looking to join one factory or another, "Chile-Argentina" offers him a place among players that arrived before him.[36]

Mutual aid societies were at the vanguard of working- and middle-class sports organizations. At the beginning of the twentieth century, mutual aid societies in urban Chile encompassed a wide range of ideologies, including anarchism and Social Christianity. Mutual aid societies across Latin America advocated the inclusion of working- and middle-class men in politics.[37] Their members pooled resources in order to acquire insurance, death benefits, education courses, and recreational resources. While historians have regarded these societies as "an important force in increasing the organizational capacity of Chilean workers," they have paid scant attention to the cultural activities of these associations.[38] This neglect stems in part from skepticism toward the political significance of mutual aid societies. Some historians have argued that mutual aid societies were composed of artisans who wanted to protect their own privileges rather than empower workers. Others have described the societies' quest for respectability as a disciplinary force that muted workers' radicalism. In Chile, the pursuit of respectability and the embrace of radicalism often came together, as in the anarchist resistance societies.

Football clubs were part of an emerging network of civic associations that shaped the creation of working-class identity in urban neighborhoods. The cultural activities of workers' organizations, including football, theater, and dance, challenged the claims of working-class depravity that were used to justify the political exclusion of workers. They also created secular spaces where men could discuss issues of common interest, such as job opportunities and local politics. Despite the notable efforts of clergymen like Bishop Edwards, clubs with relationships to parishes were in the minority. More commonly, clubs sprouted from neighborhoods and workplaces.

When working-class football clubs encountered difficulties finding space or resources, they began to seek the help of politicians. The Democratic and Radical parties, both ascendant parties of the middle class that hoped to incorporate workers, were most receptive to these requests.

In June 1906, for example, a group of boys contacted the Democratic Party to protest their treatment by a local military regiment. The boys had begun a pickup football game in Parque Cousiño, where they sold fruit. When the soldiers arrived, they demanded the boys abandon the field. After the boys refused, the soldiers proceeded to destroy their fruit, insult them, and beat them.[39] The Democratic Party helped the boys publicize their story and report the soldiers to the police. Fights over access to public space broke out frequently and often resulted in police intervention. According to workers' newspapers, the police unwaveringly supported the wealthier groups in these disputes.

The notion that football ought to be democratic and representative of "the people" was a common theme of early sportswriting in the working-class press. *La Reforma*, the official organ of the Democratic Party and later of the Socialist Workers' Party (Partido Obrero Socialista, or POS), connected football to class conflict. Editors of the paper, such as Luis Recabarren, were labor organizers who recognized that football clubs constituted an important part of working-class sociability. In 1906, the paper accused the "bourgeois" directors of the Football Association of Santiago of selecting players to represent the city based on their social class. One writer complained that the selection process was undemocratic, since "the Football Association of Santiago is composed almost entirely of young workers' clubs."[40] Regarding a match between the rival cities, one journalist commented, "Enthusiasm has not reached the worker sportsmen, because of the indifference with which they have been looked upon, while young men of social position have been placed on the team that will represent Santiago."[41] The paper also claimed that Santiago lost intercity matches to Valparaíso because of the association's practice of favoring wealthier but less talented players. *La Reforma* reasoned that because of their more difficult lives, workers possessed greater resilience and strength than elite sportsmen. They did not share the Conservative and Liberal newspapers' concern with the physical degeneration of the working class. Instead, *La Reforma* implied that luxurious tastes and easy lifestyles had feminized upper-class athletes.

Working-class associations emerged as a collective response to the discrimination that clubs experienced. Baldomero Loyola, a journalist for *La Reforma* who cofounded the Socialist Workers' Party with Luis Recabarren and Elías Lafertte, gathered twelve clubs to form the Asociación Obrera de Foot-Ball, or the Workers' Football Association.[42] This group consisted "exclusively of working-class clubs, to disaffiliate themselves with bourgeois ones."[43] Delegates held the association's first meeting in the offices of *La Reforma* in 1906, during which they elected a provisional directorate and drafted statutes. At a party the following week, club delegates nominated officers for president, vice president, treasurer, and secretary. A variety of clubs joined the Workers' Football Association, including printers' clubs (Benjamin Franklin FC and the Britannia Club), neighborhood clubs (Independencia FC), and clubs of municipal workers (Chile-Arjentina). Small Chile FC, a Catholic workers' club founded by Bishop Edwards, joined the association, but "ideological conflicts" resulted in the club's withdrawal after two seasons.[44]

The Workers' Football Association protested obstacles that working-class footballers faced in accessing public spaces. Among its first actions, the directorate wrote a letter to local authorities in defense of the football field in Cousiño Park, which was threatened by development projects. The letter urged Santiago's mayor to stop plans to transform the field "because this measure would harm a great number of football clubs, principally those composed of members of the working class."[45] The association condemned attempts of the Football Association of Santiago to deny popular clubs equal access to fields. They accused the elite directors of segregating the city along class lines. Citing the statutes of the Football Association of Santiago, which stipulated that matches be held in the most publicly accessible manner, workers' clubs denounced the scheduling of games far from popular neighborhoods.[46] The Workers' Football Association tried to circumvent the Football Association of Santiago and arrange fields for matches between workers' clubs. For example, many players for Club Chile-Arjentina worked for the municipality. These workers identified a number of uncultivated areas that could be transformed into football fields. The association appealed directly to the municipality, with occasional success, for permission to use these open spaces.

The Workers' Football Association drew upon the skills of its members in the printing industry to spread its ideas for democratically run organizations. They published an instructional pamphlet for workers who wanted to start clubs. The association also produced a short-lived sports magazine, *El Sportman*, in which it outlined football's benefits for workers. Writers for *El Sportman* believed that football helped combat the fatigue brought about by manual labor. The running and jumping required of players "strengthen[ed] their lungs, weakened by the hard and constant work of six days."[47] This contrasted sharply with elite publications, which emphasized modern men's lack of physical activity. *El Sportman* also advocated football for workers because it cost less to play than boxing or cycling, its closest competitors. And for spectators, football matches were much more affordable that the cinema or theater.[48] In addition, women and children usually received free admission to matches. Given the benefits of membership, which included access to lectures, club libraries, and social salons, club dues were quite reasonable.

The wave of labor agitation in 1906 and the fierce repression that followed, most brutally demonstrated in the Santa María de Iquique massacre in 1907, shaped the foundation of the Workers' Football Association. Association leaders hoped to forge solidarity among workers. For example, they organized a benefit for victims of the 1906 earthquake in Valparaíso. In publicity for the event, organizers emphasized that workers suffered disproportionately from the resulting dislocation, lost wages, and injuries. The Workers' Football Association planned the event at Cousiño Park, but just a few days before the tournament, leaders learned that another group had reserved the facilities. Association president José Flores grudgingly requested use of the fields at Club Hípico. Flores worried that club members would refuse to play at the club, which was known as an exclusive space for elite sportsmen. He appealed to their sense of solidarity with the victims in Valparaíso.[49]

Footballers designed clubs as cooperative, non-for-profit organizations governed by a general assembly and a board of directors. Umbrella organizations incorporated ten to twenty clubs and usually mirrored the basic club structure. A few notable differences distinguished the Workers' Football Association from others. First, the association limited membership to clubs of manual laborers or those who "worked with their hands."[50] Second, its statutes stipulated that membership not be limited by nationality. Most associations required club members to be Chilean nationals. This restriction, which barred Peruvians and Bolivians from the largest associations, was an important exclusion in the context of state-sanctioned violence against these immigrants. In the early 1900s, the state waged campaigns to "chileanize" those northern provinces involved in border disputes after the War of the Pacific (1879–1883), fought between Chile, Bolivia, and Peru. The statutes of the Workers' Football Association indicate that the members' identification with class superseded any sympathies they may have had for nativism. The association's statutes also differed from the norm in their detailed disciplinary measures, particularly regarding personal appearance. The association required players to be clean and dressed in laundered clothing that conformed to club colors. These rules indicate that the association was concerned with respectability to an extent that similar organizations were not. Moreover, these regulations overlapped with the focus of reformers on the supposedly poor hygiene of workers.

Among workers in mining, railroads, and new urban industries, football clubs formed quickly. In some cases, managers started clubs; in other instances, workers who had already started clubs sought patronage from bosses, although workers' clubs more commonly opted to maintain their autonomy from management. Conflicts often arose between independent workers' teams and those organized by companies. Company owners such as newspaper magnate Agustín Edwards hoped that sports would "smooth the rough relations between capital and labor, which are always provoked when guarding their respective interests."[51] Particular industries gained fame for the success of their football teams, especially print shops, paper mills, and butchers. The track champion Fernando Peralta was among the first "worker-sportsmen" to achieve distinction. Through word of mouth and newspaper reports, Peralta attracted hundreds of spectators to his competitions. Workers' clubs struggled to keep popular athletes in their ranks, a difficult task when company clubs could offer resources ranging from a modest travel budget to lucrative employment opportunities.

Despite businessmen's dreams of creating a more pliable workforce through football, participation in company-sponsored teams often strengthened workers' identification with one another. Rather than eradicating drinking, gambling, and fighting, football matches ritualized them. As the historian Thomas Klubock demonstrated in the case of the El Teniente copper mines, organized sports bolstered solidarity among workers and developed players' leadership skills.[52] In some cases, unions emerged from sports clubs, which served as a cover and as an organizing base.[53] Elías Lafertte, a national labor organizer and founder of the Chilean Communist Party, advocated the creation of sports clubs among workers. He recalled that in the early 1900s, "football teams were at heart extensions of parties and political tendencies."[54] It was in a football club that Lafertte first gained public-speaking experience and ran for elected office. Later, he helped organize a workers' philharmonic that served as a social center of sports, dance and theater.[55] Lafertte believed that workers gained important skills by writing statutes and constitutions, holding regular elections, and building headquarters for football clubs. These social centers offered spaces where workers could congregate and afforded their members a degree of protection from police repression.

Not all union and leftist party leaders shared Lafertte's enthusiasm for football. His mentor and fellow Socialist Workers' Party founder, Luis Recabarren, responded with ambivalence to the popularity of football among workers. Recabarren feared that sports promoted fanatical nationalism at worst, and at best aided in the dissemination of bourgeois values. During football matches held in honor of Chile's national holiday, he castigated working-class revelers for expressing solidarity with the bourgeoisie and the oligarchy.[56] British leftists of the era also scorned team sports as "bourgeois athletic competitions" and encouraged noncompetitive activities such as hiking.[57] These nature excursions attracted some workers, but were expensive and time consuming compared with football. Labor leaders worried that football, and sports more generally, did not develop workers' consciousnesses in the way that didactic theater did.[58]

Neighborhood football clubs, the most common type of working-class club, encouraged a connection between workplaces and communities. The International FC provides an example of how local, class, and gender identities intersected in barrio, or neighborhood, football teams. A group of railroad workers and their neighbors founded the International FC in the city of Concepción. Concepción was considered the gateway to Chile's southern provinces, known for resilient indigenous communities and coal mining. In 1903, players for the International FC joined a solidarity strike in support of stevedores in Valparaíso.[59] The wave of strike activity lasted throughout the year, and confrontations with state and company authorities left hundreds of workers dead or injured. The strikers' militancy contributed to their reputation as tough footballers with a rebellious spirit. In 1904, the International FC changed its name to Fernández Vial in honor of the admiral who served as an arbiter between company managers and the strikers. Admiral Fernández recommended that the state stop using military violence against the workers. Thereafter, Fernández Vial FC would be one of the most popular Chilean teams, and one very much associated with a combative working-class tradition.[60]

FOOTBALL, SCHOOLTEACHERS, AND PHYSICAL EDUCATION

Middle-class reformers and workers' clubs forged enduring relationships within football organizations. Middle-class club founders often belonged to centrist political parties, especially the Radical Party. To a lesser extent, they joined the more conservative Liberal and more radical Democratic parties. These middle-class professionals connected their political and sports activities. The middle class was a nebulous category in much of Latin America at the turn of the century. Its emergence in Chile stemmed from the expansion of the state and the growth of professional positions within it. Public-school teachers carved a role for themselves in reform movements as experts on working-class life. Their claim to understand workers reflected the thin line that separated them, geographically and economically, from the poor.[61] This expertise became part of the teachers' efforts to wrest control of the educational system from the Catholic Church. In this context, physical education arose as a secular response to the social question and a perceived urban health crisis. Middle- and working-class organizations shared a common belief in the ability of science and technology to overcome poverty. Writers for the leftist *La Reforma* complained, "Neither Congress nor the government has done anything for the poor classes. None of the methods of modern social progress that have been applied in European nations are yet known among us."[62] Physical-education teachers who set out to establish the discipline thought that scientific training could help condition workers' bodies for work and encourage sobriety.

Leading educators viewed football as a way to promote nationalism as well as improve the physical state of workers. In 1905, Domingo Villalobos, the director of the educational journal *La Revista de Instrucción Primaria*, put together standardized lesson plans for public schools. In the schemata he distributed to teachers, physical education fell under the category of natural sciences. As the introduction to the course material explained, "The gymnasium is like a second natural environment. It shapes and forms the bodies of the miners that go to the heart of the earth; of the sailors that carry our products to remote shores; of the soldiers that advance over the deserts and cordilleras."[63] Villalobos and his collaborators emphasized physical education's role in producing future citizens. Their lesson plans connected the shaping of workers' bodies with the protection of the nation, economically and militarily. The physical-education curriculum sought to strengthen Chileans' connection to nature, which urbanization supposedly endangered. Educators viewed this relationship as essential to the development of their students' patriotic impulses and moral fiber.

Physical-education instructors involved in reform movements focused on the improvement of public health and urban life. Many of these teachers worked in night schools, temperance societies, and other community groups. They hoped team sports could address "character defects such as cowardice, lack of initiative, and violence."[64] Their experiences in the classroom and the sensational press coverage of juvenile delinquency influenced teachers. Articles on working-class youth frequently characterized mothers employed outside the home as negligent and responsible for the rise in crime.[65] Physical-education teachers pointed out that team sports could provide supervision for children during the hours that parents worked. Many of these teachers lived in and around their students' neighborhoods and experienced the conditions of urban squalor firsthand. Their schools lacked adequate infrastructure; many were dirty, without bathrooms, and were located next to bars.[66] Reform-oriented teachers, less concerned with national defense, argued that sports could engage young people with community affairs.[67] More broadly, they connected this civic engagement with the future of Chilean democracy.[68]

Public-health crises galvanized footballers to become involved in international forums that addressed rapid urbanization in Latin America.[69] During the first Pan-American Scientific Congress, held in 1908 in Santiago, physical-education teachers sought to incorporate sports into plans to address cramped housing, epidemics, and other health hazards. The conference proceedings prompted the National Education Association to recommend that physical education be mandatory at each stage of schooling.[70] They drew on findings of nutritionists, economists, and medical specialists to advocate a "scientific" physical-education program. At the conference, Guillermo Martínez warned against the use of physical education to achieve military goals. He did not believe that scientific physical training was compatible with military needs. Instead, he urged sportsmen to see football clubs as "collectivities with soul."[71] He recommended that physical-education teachers work in the community to address students' malnutrition, alcohol and tobacco abuse, and illiteracy. Martínez was not the only physical-education instructor who wanted to connect the classroom with the community. For example, the Loma Blanca FC, a club of high school students, alumni, and teachers, organized a series of football matches in Santiago prisons in 1915. The club hoped these competitions would highlight football as an instrument of reform.

The medical field strongly influenced physical-education curricula in the early 1900s. In 1912, a group of sports club directors, educators, and physicians formed the Chilean Physical Education League. Led by the Swedish doctor Henrik Ling, this group intended to promote the physical education of both sexes in schools, clubs, and factories. The league believed that athletics could reduce outbreaks of contagious diseases and improve the health of urban youth.[72] Ling became a celebrity in Chile for his advocacy of exercise among women and for his recommendation that sports clubs include them. The league advised women that they could discover ways to overcome the "weakness" of their sex through sports rather than "the vulgar practices of feminism."[73] League directors pointed out that women's athletics were fashionable in "developed" countries, citing the growth of women's boxing in the United States.[74] Ling and his devotees traveled to northern Europe, promising to bring the most modern techniques to Chilean education.

Physical-education teachers played a leading role in standardizing the rules and regulations of football matches. In their estimation, instructors and coaches lacked adequate teaching materials. In 1912, Chile and Argentina became the first countries in the Americas to join the International Federation of Association Football (Fédération Internationale de Football Association, or FIFA), which demanded adherence to European rules. Throughout the 1910s, groups published pamphlets to disseminate the game's formal rules and proper playing etiquette. In 1917, referees Juan Livingstone and Alfred Betteley put together one of the most popular instructional books.[75] They explained, "Thousands of Chilean aficionados practice football, from one extreme of the republic to the other, but sadly, we doubt that even a small fraction of them know the basis of the rules, not from a lack of interest or preparation, but from the complete absence of a manual."[76] Livingstone and Betteley organized the Chilean Association of Football Referees, which they hoped would standardize penalties, rules, and acceptable behavior. Physical-education instructors hoped that expanded public-school programs would help the process of standardization. According to teachers, Chile's last-place finish in the South American Cup of 1916 further demonstrated the need for scientific training.[77]

A small but important minority of physical-education teachers felt that football should primarily complement the military training of young men. Many of these teachers and administrators came from a military background. This sector argued that physical education's highest goal was to train young men to "successfully defend the motherland."[78] These military-oriented instructors saw exercise as necessary preparation for warding off threats to the nation rather than as a way to alleviate the physical stresses of urban life. Militarist educators conflated "racial threats" to the individual body with threats to the nation. They warned that unless a young man exercised daily, "his blood would lose its purity and his muscles and organs in general would suffer the consequences."[79] Their descriptions characterized the male body as the defender of the nation. The nation, in turn, appeared vulnerable, passive, and female.

POLITICS AND FOOTBALL: THE NATIONAL SPORTS FEDERATION

The campaign to construct a national stadium illustrates the developing relationship between politics and football clubs. The National Sports Federation (FSN) represented one of the few organizations in Chile that boasted a multiclass membership. Its creation attests to the growth of clubs, the variety of political ideologies that circulated within them, and their connections to politicians. Although it is difficult to estimate the number of football club members, it is safe to assume that by 1910, membership numbered 3,000–4,000 in Santiago, 2,000–3,000 in Valparaíso, around 1,000 in the northern cities Iquique and Coquimbo, and around 500 in the southern cities Concepción and Temuco.[80] Through their participation in the FSN, working-class clubs made demands upon the state for recreational resources. In 1908, the inspector general of primary education, Felipe Casas Espínola, called an open meeting of sportsmen to form a national organization. Casas hoped this organization could build a grand sports stadium. The attendees voted to create the National Sports Federation. The FSN represented sportsmen from across the socioeconomic spectrum; however, the leaders of the FSN had powerful ties to the political establishment. The FSN's directors acted as lobbyists, meeting with sympathetic politicians and mobilizing various sports entities around the stadium project.

The FSN was among the first civic associations to petition for state intervention in culture. In this way, sportsmen contributed to a growing sentiment that the state had an obligation to provide public resources for recreation and to regulate social life. On May 20, 1909, the FSN organized its first public protest. Marchers included workers from the Arturo Prat Football Association, representatives of the National Education Association, and the wealthy congressman Jorge Matte Gormaz. Protestors marched through the streets of Santiago, demanding that the government support a national stadium, suspend taxes on sporting goods, and invest in public parks.[81] Approximately four thousand sportsmen began their demonstration at the office of the newspaper *El Mercurio*, where they attracted the attention of journalists and gathered more followers.[82] The marchers continued to the presidential residence, La Moneda, where they delivered a petition to President Pedro Montt and the ministers of public education, the armed forces, and industry. As they continued their march, they presented their petition to the mayor of Santiago, the municipality, the prefect of the police department, and the archbishop. In walking to these offices, marchers learned where these authorities were located and gained a basic understanding of their responsibilities. For members without a background in politics, the march provided a spatial orientation to the governmental bureaucracy. In this era, direct action by civic associations was typically met with violence from the police or military. The elite status of the organization's leadership and the professed "apolitical" nature of the protest surely buffered the marchers against the standard repression.

The FSN's campaign for a stadium appealed to the state's concerns for national defense and "racial health." FSN literature depicted Chile as a racially homogeneous nation of mestizos that incorporated the best of Europe and the Americas. Its propaganda presented the sports club as both an egalitarian fraternity and a microcosm of the nation. The FSN's appeal to racial unity hinged upon the distinction between the Chilean mestizo and the caricatured Indians of Peru and Bolivia. FSN leaders claimed that Chileans, unlike Peruvians or Bolivians, could take pride in "being one of the strongest and most virile races on the continent."[83] This emphasis on racial homogeneity and equality obscured social hierarchies among sportsmen. It encouraged members to think of themselves as connected with one another by a natural bond.

FSN members realized quickly that petitions and protests would not be enough to persuade the government to act on the stadium project. Instead, they needed to identify sympathetic politicians. Compared with the leaders of most civic associations that included popular groups, the FSN's directors had extensive economic and social resources. They arranged meetings with President Montt and the minister of education, Emiliano Figueroa. Although exactly what transpired at these meetings is unknown, the FSN leaders must have been discouraged. Soon after their audience with Montt and Figueroa, they organized a flurry of fund-raisers among members, including dances, bachelor parties, and raffles in support of the stadium. Inspired by these efforts, a wealthy member of the FSN donated land in 1910 for a national stadium in the northwestern neighborhood of Renca. The National Sports Federation relied upon its elite leadership to lobby politicians, but working- and middle-class members mobilized large assemblies, brought their message to neighborhoods, and gained the sup-port of popular football clubs.

Working-class clubs made use of their reputations to gain access to social and political circles otherwise closed to them. In turn, these clubs provided the FSN with symbolic capital, "commonly called prestige, reputation, renown."[84] Among football enthusiasts, this prestige was based upon a player's talent, popularity, and playing style. As the electorate and the number of political parties expanded, the FSN provided politicians a forum where it could attract votes, party adherents, and publicity.[85] The number of registered voters grew from 227,000 in 1894 to 598,000 in 1909.[86] The centrist Radical and Liberal parties took greatest advantage of this in the 1910s. Liberal congressman Jorge Matte Gormaz, for example, recognized the political benefits of affiliation with the FSN. Matte suc-cessfully ran for the presidency of the organization in 1915. His election reflected the success of the federation in attracting the attention of young politicians as well as its growing ambition. During his tenure, Matte engi-neered a closer relationship between sports organizations and the Liberal Party. The strong presence of reformist Liberals and Radicals, both with anticlerical agendas, marginalized the Catholic Church's role in football organizations.

As sports associations became sophisticated political actors, they targeted nodes of political power with greater precision. For instance, they shifted their lobbying efforts from ministers to congressional representatives and political parties. Leaders of the FSN held the Conservative Party responsible for stalling the national stadium project. Although the FSN had obtained land, it needed financial support to build the stadium. One club director commented, "The government is disposed to concede good land if the Congress will release the funds; the new deputies that join Congress, for their part, have promised to work at it, and we do not doubt that this will come to pass."[87] The "new deputies" they referred to came from the ascendant Radical and Liberal parties, which allied themselves in the 1910s against the Conservative Party. The Radical Party aspired to attract working- and middle-class adherents. It was particularly active in honing relationships with football clubs. This began in the late nineteenth century when Radical Party leaders founded Santiago National, one of Santiago's first football clubs, in the party's headquarters.[88] One way that football clubs expressed their political affiliations was through the election of honorary positions. For example, the Workers Football Association chose Santiago mayor Washington Bannen as its honorary president in

1915.[89] The first Radical to serve as mayor of the capital, Bannen owed his support to the many civic associations he had been involved with, including football clubs.[90]

Despite the highly exclusionary electoral system, FSN members still believed they could sway politicians with promises to "create votes."[91] Few Chileans participated in elections; women and the illiterate were formally excluded, and informal factors such as transportation problems and a lack of interest in voting contributed to low voter turnout. Yet it would be misguided to suggest that democracy in the 1910s was fictitious.[92] The suffrage law of 1874, which removed property requirements for voting, encouraged the development of party competition and the growth of new parties.[93] Competitive elections encouraged coalitions like the alliance of Liberals, Radicals, and Democrats that wrested control of Congress from Conservatives in 1915. Political parties reached out to popular sectors at conventions and local branches. The proliferation of popular-culture venues, like football clubs, created opportunities for parties to reach apolitical citizens.

Radical congressman Héctor Arancibia Laso mastered the art of mobilizing civic associations and popular culture to create multiclass alliances. Arancibia was a dedicated football player who first introduced the FSN's stadium project to Congress in 1912. He saw a political opportunity in cultivating strong relations between the Radical Party and Santiago's football clubs. To that end, he served as president of the Football Association of Santiago between 1914 and 1918 as well as a director of dozens of sports clubs. Arancibia declared that sports were "the only effective means to combat the physical and moral degeneration of the human races."[94] Instead of repressive laws against alcohol and gambling, Arancibia argued that government needed to promote positive habits. Arancibia drew a direct connection between physical well-being and the cultivation of active citizenship: "For the republic to function properly, it needs enlightened and vigorous citizens. If each individual in the republic knew how to read and write and was physically apt for work, the democratic ideal would be realized; citizens would be conscious of their rights, attentive to their duties, and tightly united by national symbol[s] to work for the prosperity and aggrandizement of the country."[95] For Arancibia, sports developed competent men with a sense of duty to the nation. In reference to the stadium project, he explained, "Every citizen has . . . to take possession of his duties and obligations and has the right to ask for the life conditions that will enable him [to fulfill them]."[96] For Arancibia, stadiums and other sports venues created conditions for the cultivation of citizenship.

The introduction of legislation pertaining to sports had the unintended consequence of educating club members in the mechanics of the political system. Football club members followed the congressional debates related to sports projects such as the national stadium. Sports magazines printed these legislative proceedings at length.[97] Readers of these transcripts became familiar with the rules of congressional debates, key politicians, and the scope of legislative authority. Many legislators rejected the notion that the state had a role in promoting sports and culture. While Arancibia was popular with sportsmen in Santiago, other politicians mocked his interest in sports. One congressman responded to an Arancibia speech about the national stadium, "This speech is appropriate for the awards ceremony in San Ignacio's gymnasium, not for the National Congress. More respect for legislative powers, colleague!"[98] Arancibia persisted, however, in supporting the campaigns of various sports organizations. Inspired by a trip that Chilean footballers took to Brazil, Arancibia again proposed funding for a national stadium in 1913. This time, Arancibia stressed the role that footballers could play as cultural ambassadors. Some football club members attended these legislative sessions to express support for Arancibia.

FIGURE 1.3.   The Radical Party politician Héctor Arancibia Laso (*seated on the rock*) at the construction site of Cerro San Cristóbal in Santiago, 1918. Image courtesy of the Digital and Photographic Archive, National Library of Chile, Santiago.

CLASS IDENTITY AND CONFLICT

Middle- and working-class football clubs appealed to local authorities for access to football fields, public facilities, and sanitation reform—interventions denied them at the national or regional level. In their petitions to mayors and city councils, workers' organizations expressed a growing sense of entitlement to recreation. Whereas labor unions in the United States and elsewhere incorporated sports as part of their agendas, Chilean labor organizations did not make the same effort.[99] This pushed popular clubs to look to political parties that could champion their cause. In addition to the Liberal and Radical parties, the smaller Democrat and Socialist Workers' parties offered clubs resources. As they used political channels to acquire support for their clubs, working- and middle-class footballers developed a language of rights concerning leisure.

While some praised the opportunities for cross-class relationships within football, a notable degree of conflict emerged in the 1910s. In 1912, the sports magazine *Sport i Actualidades* described football as having been "invaded by the working class."[100] As long as workers remained under the guidance of their patrons or allowed elite clubs to control associations, the cross-class alliances remained stable. When workers' clubs tried to assume leadership positions or dissented from decisions made by the directorates of umbrella organizations, elite clubs drew upon their greater professional expertise, economic resources, and "refined sense of the game" to retain control. Umbrella organizations like the FSN emphasized the need for elite leaders to properly instruct the masses in how to play football. One journalist explained, "Fortunately, there are enthusiasts in the large workshops and factories who act as preaching fathers, on a day to day basis, to inspire a love for sport among youth."[101] Juan Ramsay, the founder of the National Association of Referees and owner of the country's leading sports equipment store, credited business owners with developing a passion for football among workers.

For many working-class players, football demonstrated the fine character of members of their own ranks rather than their need for upper-class tutelage. The Workers' Football Association celebrated anecdotes of workers "passing" for elites on the field. One member commented, "On many occasions, we have seen confusion between the elegant gentleman and the humble and laboring worker, together toasting to the good end of athletic competitions and the prosperity of the workshop."[102] In an oft-repeated story, the working-class club El Royal refused to accept the Municipal Cup of 1908 by forfeit. The captain of El Royal considered a cup won without playing beneath his team and requested a rematch.[103] Different variations of these stories in which working- and middle-class athletes exhibited qualities ascribed to elite sportsmen circulated in newspapers and club materials. Club members viewed these stories as evidence that given equal conditions, workers exhibited the same moral convictions as elites.

Despite reformers' claims that football inculcated bourgeois values in workers, many elite sports clubs complained that workers damaged the sport. They accused workers of bringing violence, professionalism, drinking, and dangerous passions to football. One club director compared football matches unfavorably to a more truly elite sport, "In cycling tournaments, one notes more culture, the competitors do not protest, and the public is not accustomed to involve themselves in arguments or to invade the track."[104] The press paid particular attention to stories of violent confrontations during football matches. In 1915, a number of magazines and newspapers interviewed Guillermo Gúzman, a player whose leg had been broken in a game. They described the player who broke Gúzman's leg as an unrepentant fellow worker. Journalists framed this story as a cautionary tale about the violence that unguided masses brought to football.[105] In the midst of media attention, the Football Association of Santiago created a disciplinary committee to punish outbursts. In addition, it urged club directors to establish internal disciplinary measures for players. In the hopes of promoting football as a family activity and further reducing on-field violence, club directors offered free admission for women.[106] Directors and journalists then urged players to consider women's presence before drinking and brawling during matches. The Football Association of Santiago expected women's attendance to improve the conduct of their male family members.[107]

Elite club directors complained that the popular enthusiasm for football violated the ideal of the versatile sportsmen, who practiced a bit of every sport. According to purists, an amateur was "an 'all around sportsman' a mix of a bit of everything."[108] One writer complained that football's "incredible diffusion has been slowly consuming the existence of other sporting entertainments. . . . Today, football is the only thing that grabs the attention of youth, and the proof of this is the increasing number of institutions founded in Santiago, Valparaíso, and other cities."[109] The singular dedication of workers' clubs to football differed from the attitude of elite clubs, which offered myriad sports teams to their members. In the elite model of amateurism, workers' excess of passion demonstrated that they had not developed proper masculine comportment. Furthermore, elite clubs blamed this lack of proper masculine restraint on supposed racial characteristics. For example, one club director complained that mestizos did not have the "racial disposition" to appreciate the patience and tranquility of genteel sports such as cricket.[110]

Elite critics charged that in addition to workers' overly exuberant play and spectatorship, they violated the spirit of disinterested amateurism by seeking financial rewards for their talent. Although professional football leagues had existed in England since the 1880s, directors across Latin America railed against the possibility of allowing such "distasteful" concerns to influence the sport.[111] They created nostalgia for a British tradition that they imagined but had not observed. Even though they criticized popular players, elite club directors began to recruit them in the 1910s in hopes of improving their teams' performance. Talented working- and middle-class players lacked the resources to participate fully in elite clubs. Privately, directors helped these players purchase travel accommodations, uniforms, and club dues. They also arranged better work schedules and paid time off so that workers could rest before important matches. Physical-education teachers scoffed at the hypocrisy of elite clubs. Instructor Guillermo Martínez claimed, "The professional is a true leper of physical education. . . . Our sports societies have fought and will fight professionalism to the death."[112] Middle-class directors like Martínez criticized upper-class directors for injecting their personal business interests into football. He complained that owners of sports equipment stores and factories had bought their way into the directorate of the National Sports Federation.[113] In this way, teachers held both workers and upper-class sportsmen responsible for creating a profit motive within football organizations.

Working-class club leaders largely shared the ideal of amateurism with their middle- and upper-class counterparts. Workers who stayed with their neighborhood teams and rejected material incentives became local heroes. Próspero González was a well-known player who refused offers to join wealthy clubs. One journalist gushed, "Próspero is our highest example of sports' morality. Próspero has been and remains a modest man. As a worker who lives from day to day, how many times has he been tempted by a well-paid job or another, similar offer?"[114] In 1903, González had founded Arco Iris FC, which belonged to the Workers' Football Association and was the most popular club among fans in Santiago. His reputation for discipline challenged the stereotypes of the "overly passionate" working-class player. In interviews, González and other club members showed their acceptance of the British model of the bourgeois sportsman. This meant not complaining about the referees, avoiding physical altercations, and showing appreciation for talent on the opposing team.

For the working-class footballer, the body became a form of capital that could translate into economic benefits, social status, and other opportunities. Since there are not many records of working-class players' lives, it is difficult to ascertain the personal impact on them of joining wealthier clubs. In any case, the effect must have been notable, since football occupied more and more time in the lives of talented players.[115] The participation of players from across the class spectrum was often cited as evidence of goodwill and common ground between classes. Although mainstream journalists portrayed hierarchies within football as differences of culture rather than class, the daily practices of football clubs reflected important disparities. For example, working-class players typically served as directors in the neighborhood clubs, but in elite and company clubs, they did not run for elected positions. In typical company-team photographs, a stylishly suited representative of management, sometimes the company owner, stands above the uniformed players. Moreover, company owners received the game ball, trophies, and prize money.

Struggles over public space escalated throughout the 1910s in response to segregation in the cities. Workers' organizations presented increasingly stronger and more articulate demands for equal access to space, posing a threat to elites' control of facilities. Because of perpetual difficulties in obtaining fields, working-class clubs struggled to arrange tournaments and plan their seasons. The Workers' Football Association resented the monopolization of the best public parks, such as the centrally located Cousiño Park, by elite clubs, since they often owned private fields they could use instead. Although it was customary for sports organizations to grant other clubs free admission to events held in public parks, workers complained that wealthier clubs turned them away. Club directors complained that cyclists, in particular, discriminated against working-class footballers. They urged cyclists to show a sense of "fraternity" and sportsmanship by sharing fields with them.[116] Fights frequently broke out between athletes over rights to use these parks.

Despite the importance of class status for access to land, some efforts to revamp urban spaces involved cross-class collaborations. For example, football associations worked together to pressure the municipal government to improve facilities in the popular Quinta Normal and Cousiño parks. These efforts involved petitions, editorials, and meetings with the municipal authorities. In 1916, after a multiyear campaign, the municipality of Santiago announced it would install public bathrooms in Cousiño Park. One writer explained the benefits for working-class sportsmen: "Surely, few are more grateful than the multitude of athletes who regularly meet at the park, the majority of them scarce in resources . . . and coming from the miserable rooms of the *conventillo* [tenement]."[117] In addition to their activism on behalf of public parks, clubs collaborated on projects such as the conversion of abandoned municipal property into sports fields and the construction of municipal stadiums. Sportsmen connected the state's lack of support for sports with its usual negligence of the working class. One official complained, "In Chile, the sport [of football] is considered to be something of the workers; neither the government nor society promotes it."[118] Sportsmen looked with envy at the modern stadiums in Buenos Aires and Montevideo built by the municipal governments.

MILITARISM AND GENDER

Military sportsmen had constituted an important minority of footballers since the beginning of the century; however, in the late 1910s, they exerted greater influence in the clubs. This created an antagonistic environment for women and workers within football organizations. Militarism was the belief that the military was the chief protector of Chilean society. Militarists glorified war, military ritual, and history. The period between 1900 and 1907 witnessed an aggressive military response to workers' organizations, particularly in the regions of the North, which had the most active labor movements.[119] Historians like Gabriel Salazar have argued that it is significant that Marxism developed alongside the modern military and a new national culture. Marxism engaged working-class civic associations in a set of debates informed by a modernist worldview rather than the oppositional discourses of the nineteenth century.[120] In the wake of military brutality against workers, the Workers' Football Association would logically have viewed with disdain the idea that football be used as an adjunct to military training. Moreover, the inclusion of representatives from both labor-union and military clubs within the FSN must have sparked conflict. The outbreak of World War I bolstered the prestige of sports clubs with ties to the military.

The current of militarism within football circles furthered the exclusion of women from clubs. Militarists denounced the state of masculinity and took pride in their contributions to its rejuvenation, as one explained:

"The young effeminate playboy of yesterday has put aside his bad habits and been transformed into a vigorous and mature citizen."[121] Militarists classified susceptibility to women's charms as a vice on par with gambling and alcoholism. Furthermore, they understood military service to be a prerequisite of citizenship. For militarist sportsmen, clubs needed to be based on the model of the Chilean military, with a vertical hierarchy and the strict separation of men and women. This view put them at odds with those reformers and educators who advocated that clubs offer women's sports. Furthermore, military-oriented sportsmen exclusively celebrated the male body and its performance in sports contests. Describing a football match, one writer gushed, "It is beautiful to see the radiance in the bodies of our panting youth, the multiple colors of their uniforms, which appear as flags waving on a battlefield."[122] Women's bodies, on the other hand, were portrayed as static vessels in need of protection rather than cultivation.

Football club directors influenced by heightened nationalism and the growing prestige of the Chilean military formed Boy Scout troops that were affiliated with their clubs. The Boy Scouts became a fashionable organization among youth of all classes. However, only a few could afford the regular excursions, uniforms, and tools that the Boy Scouts required. Often, military authorities and teachers with military backgrounds were Boy Scout leaders. For example, the scouts elected General Arístedes Pinto Concha their president in 1915. In a statement to the press, the Boy Scouts boasted that Pinto had served as minister of war (in the first cabinet of President Barros Luco) and was a veteran of the War of the Pacific.[123] General Pinto and other veterans led their scout troops to famed battle sites, where they recounted their war experiences for the young men.

These types of leaders and excursions were not the only aspects of the Boy Scouts influenced by the military. The hierarchical structure of ranks, the uniforms, and the overwhelming number of rules mimicked military life as well. Leaders instructed the Boy Scouts to act as protectors of society. Scout literature, often published in football magazines, emphasized scouts' responsibility to "weaker" citizens, including women, children, and the elderly. Troop leaders wrote stories of Boy Scouts saving lives, often by pulling wandering girls or elderly men off railroad tracks just in time to avoid an oncoming train. Scout leaders believed that a strict regimen would inculcate self-discipline and a love of order. Scout literature outlined a list of daily tasks dedicated to improving personal health, including morning walks (with one's hands outside one's pockets, to avoid arousal), cold baths, sleeping with open windows, breathing through one's nose, exercise routines, and so on.[124] Leaders of scout troops and youth football clubs hoped to encourage the development of "proper" adolescent sexuality. Directors advised boys that the time spent away from girls while practicing sports or socializing in the clubhouse would prevent the buildup of sexual tension.

According to militarists, sex-segregated leisure was among sports' chief benefits. Officially, club statutes and regulations rarely prohibited women. Instead, the absence of women from football clubs was primarily due to the desire of insiders to create a male haven of sociability. Early on, women's groups fully understood the ramifications of their exclusion from sports. In 1908, the feminist publication *La Palanca* complained that men denied the women in their families the free time to play sports: "Man acquires the liberty to see, walk, read and learn from infancy. He is not obliged to waste his time and numb his spirit in Church; on the contrary, he is pushed . . . to the professions, to travel, and toward all sports."[125] Female teachers, such as Victoria Caviedes, asked that the National Education Association form mixed-sex clubs modeled on those that people had begun across the country, with fixed quotas, scheduled discussions, and athletic matches (she suggested tennis).[126] Feminists recognized the importance of sports for individual development. Moreover, they took an interest in clubs as secular social spheres where women could form relationships that would further their education and career opportunities.

Since the late nineteenth century, football clubs had debated the potential benefits of women's participation. The most common justification for excluding women was their supposed lack of interest in sports. Advocates countered that with encouragement, as had occurred in Europe and the United States, women enthusiastically took part in sports. Opponents countered that feminism, which they considered decidedly undesirable, had sparked the expansion of women's athletics abroad. Others explained that Chilean women were fundamentally different from women in the United States. One sportswriter explained, "The Latin woman does not demonstrate an inclination to abandon her ancient ways and is very limited . . . but the woman of northern Europe has taken up sports with much enthusiasm."[127] It is difficult to assess whether women might have wanted to participate in football clubs, but it is easy to identify the factors that would have discouraged them. Sportsmen commonly expressed disparaging opinions of female athletes. Many doubted that women had the self-control and discipline that sports required. They described the female body as complicated, mysterious, and unpredictable. Football clubs' notoriety for violence and drinking likely hindered women's participation. Young women in particular would have been vulnerable to charges of immorality. In addition, many working-class women would have had difficulty affording club dues. Widespread social norms as well as state policies reserved the role of the breadwinner for men and placed a higher priority on their leisure than on women's. Finally, magazines, health professionals, and educators warned women that participation in sports would damage their femininity, fertility, and charm.

Men viewed sports as an opportunity to display their masculinity, physical attractiveness, and sexual prowess in public. Footballers competed against one another for the admiration of their fellow men, but women were essential for the display of sex appeal. Young stars flaunted their relationships with women as a show of their masculine authority. As previously discussed, sportsmen followed the romantic exploits of celebrities like boxer Jack Johnson.[128] They also paid attention to women's reactions to sports. For example, in 1912, sportsmen discussed a study conducted by the magazine *Femina*, which claimed that most women found boxers unattractive. The women interviewed gave various reasons for their distaste: some found violence undesirable, whereas others commented that the sport caused scarring and facial disfigurement. In response to the study, one sportsman stated, "Though our virile vanity suffers, we are obliged to confess that the world . . . has seen nothing that survived the beautiful sex's disaffection." He chalked up women's disapproval to their resistance to modernity and frivolity: "Not being handsome or desirable, or trying to be handsome in the old-fashioned way, the fighters of the new struggle will never manage to win the enthusiasm of women."[129]

By the end of the 1910s, football had emerged as the most popular leisure activity in urban Chile. At a time when the formal political system included very few citizens, football organizations offered a vehicle by which working- and middle-class men could express political opinions, take part in campaigns, and assume leadership roles. A variety of gender, racial, and nationalist ideologies circulated in clubhouses. Elite directors mobilized the metaphor of the family to invoke unity among sportsmen. This fraternal harmony rested upon the exclusion of women and assumed a homogenous mestizo identity. Tensions flared, however, when working- and middle-class clubs clashed with those of the elite over access to public space.

The expansion of football clubs was tied to the growth of reform movements and urbanization. Journalists, physicians, and physical-education instructors created niches dedicated to sports within their professions.

They claimed that their expertise in physical fitness provided them with a unique perspective on the social question. Working-class clubs benefited from the resources that these professionals brought to clubs, associations, and leagues. In campaigns like the one to construct a national stadium, club members learned political skills such as how to organize demonstrations. Footballers with ties to reform organizations found themselves in competition with a growing sector of military sportsmen. This sector emphasized football's potential contribution to national defense rather than urban improvement. In the coming decade, conflicts among clubs over authoritarianism, modernization, and politics intensified.

THE MASSIVE, MODERN, AND MARGINALIZED
IN FOOTBALL OF THE 1920S

2

In the historical literature on Europe and the Americas, the 1920s appears
as a watershed decade. The experience of modernity and urbanization,
quintessentially transnational, has been viewed as the defining characteristic
of the period. Thus, London, Paris, New York, Buenos Aires, and Mexico
City all had their "Roaring Twenties." Dozens of other cities more peripheral
to economic and political power, including Quito, Calcutta, Santiago, and
Cairo, were also part of this process. Leisure activities defined the urban
experience and created narratives that framed the way spectators understood
their lives. New urban spaces, including stadiums, movie houses, dance
halls, and restaurants, democratized entertainment. This chapter analyzes
how local adaptations of mass culture shaped the political practices of the
state, civic associations, and political parties.

Football clubs participated in the struggle between military and civilian
political forces as well as in broader debates about authoritarianism and
democracy. The protagonists and terms of these struggles had long-
term significance.[1] Football clubs and other civic associations provided
vehicles by which working-class people, particularly in-country migrants,
could engage in local politics. Throughout the decade, the relationship
between football clubs and political parties intensified. The development
of a competitive, multiparty system meant that it was difficult for any one
political camp to control football. Moreover, the relationship between
culture and politics grew more intense as a result of politicians' interest in
popular culture. Finally, the notion that Chileans were particularly political
and democratic became further entrenched in popular culture. In 1923, the
minister of the interior explained, "Sports attract me as much as politics,
although many of my colleagues believe the latter is the favorite sport of the

Chilean people, given that they foment every type of combination."[2] The double meaning of the word *combination* referred to an organized play in football as well as to the political alliances that different parties were forced to make because of the competitive electoral process.

The debates about what constituted "authentic" Chilean culture were prompted by the enthusiastic embrace of transnational trends, like the Argentine tango and films from the United States.[3] Although the elite had sought foreign goods and fashions since the colonial period, new technologies enabled music, film, sports, clothing, and literature to travel faster and farther than before. Thus, mass culture emerged. Mass culture was not equivalent to popular culture, but was, rather, a diffusion and transformation of a variety of cultural expressions, many of which were popular. As much as mass culture catered to the feelings, desires, and perspectives of a broad audience, it produced them.

These cultural changes accompanied turbulent political developments, including the election of a putatively antioligarchic president in 1920, Arturo Alessandri. Alessandri's term was interrupted by a military coup led by Conservative officers, who were ousted themselves by a competing group of reformist officers. Colonel Carlos Ibáñez consolidated control over this clique and established a dictatorship. These events engendered reevaluations of national history that resuscitated authoritarian figures like Diego Portales and dovetailed with the rhetoric of military leaders who paradoxically suggested that a dictatorship was necessary to reinstitute democracy. The military junta promised, "In less time than you can imagine, we will have given the country a new organization and distinct spiritual direction. The task is difficult, painful, but necessary and we are accomplishing it through real justice, in this way establishing true democracy. Neither privilege nor fortune nor political position will figure whatsoever in our resolutions."[4] Within football clubs, voices that questioned the efficacy of the military government and its authoritarianism were less scrutinized than those in spheres defined as political.

Alongside changes in political discourse, this chapter analyzes new forms of spectatorship and structure in civic associations. Often violent and unruly, these practices challenged the military regime's attempts to create more orderly cities. The efforts of national football organizations to standardize statutes and attempts to modernize the sport, however, legitimated aspects of the Ibáñez dictatorship. The top echelon of clubs, increasingly controlled by entrepreneurs, recognized the spectator as a consumer and clubs as businesses. They supported Radical and Liberal party politicians who sought to organize football in a vertical structure. This putatively more efficient structure made it easier to implement professionalism and develop markets. Strangely enough, elite and working-class clubs allied in opposition to these changes, albeit for different reasons. Whereas patriarchal leaders like Juan Ramsay bemoaned the crass and uncharitable elements of professionalism, working-class clubs lamented the deterioration of civic commitment among the largest clubs. Workers' clubs embraced the antimaterialism and respectability of the bourgeois British model of amateurism.

PRESIDENT ALESSANDRI AND THE SOUTH AMERICAN CUP OF 1920

The urban environment that fostered mass culture also gave rise to mass politics, inaugurated by the presidential campaign of Arturo Alessandri in 1919. Alessandri was known as the "Lion of Tarapacá," a moniker that stemmed from his fiery antioligarchic rhetoric and a reference to the northern province he represented in the senate. Alessandri appealed to those who saw reform as necessary to end class antagonism. His supporters felt his election would ensure that the "social question" could be resolved in a parliamentary fashion. In reference to Alessandri's election, L. S. Rowe concluded in his address to the American Political Science Association, "Democracy has become the goal toward which the nations of the world are striving; it is difficult for us to picture the dismay, amounting almost to horror, which the term 'democracy' inspired a century ago."[5] Rowe overstated this consensus in Chile. The spectacle of mobilized masses and Alessandri's antioligarchic rhetoric convinced many that the country was headed toward revolution. Coalitions of political parties and civic associations coordinated much of the public display in support of Alessandri. Héctor Arancibia, the president of the Football Association of Santiago and Radical Party politician, acted as Alessandri's campaign manager. Arancibia arranged speaking opportunities and rallies for the candidate that mobilized thousands of sportsmen.

The largest football clubs had rosters in the thousands by the 1920s, making for impressive crowds during matches. New media, including a national sports magazine, Los Sports, allowed fans to follow idols from afar. Membership became a rite of passage for young men and shaped their life cycles thereafter. Clubs expanded by establishing bases in unions, churches, mutual aid societies, and night schools. Many analyses of football's mass

FIGURE 2.1.   Arturo Alessandri (*center, with the presidential sash*), c. 1920. At his left is future president Pedro Aguirre, top hat in hand. Image courtesy of the Archivo Fotográfico Colección, Museo Histórico Archivo, Santiago.

diffusion have attributed its popularity to the low investment the sport required.[6] This is an unsatisfactory conclusion, since other sports, like basketball and boxing, were also relatively inexpensive to organize. Public space was quite scarce in Santiago and Valparaíso, and this drove up the cost of renting land for fields. In addition, while informal play and match attendance cost relatively little, club dues represented a burden on the average family's entertainment budget.[7] In comparison with admission to movies or dance halls, club inscription fees were costly. However, membership offered a wide range of activities. Football clubs hosted vaudeville acts, dances, and choral groups. The largest clubhouses included libraries, dental clinics, and movie projectors. The sport's transnational character, the quality of club membership, and the opportunities for socializing explain its popularity better than the cost of equipment alone.

During Alessandri's campaign, Arancibia drew a parallel between the Conservatives' lack of interest in sport and their broader neglect of the popular classes. However, football organizers were disappointed with Alessandri's government once it was in office. During the tumultuous year of 1920, Chilean football directors were preparing to host the South American Cup in Valparaíso. In preparing for the tournament, many clubs felt cheated by Alessandri's lack of support. During the campaign season, Alessandri had promised to support the Chilean Football Federation's bid for the games. When funds did not arrive, the federation's directors nearly bankrupted the organization. Only a last-minute personal donation from Alessandri himself saved them from collapse.[8] For football clubs, this lack of government-provided funds was indicative of larger problems that Alessandri's government faced with a recalcitrant Congress. If Alessandri hoped his donation would place him in the position of a powerful and benign patron, that message was lost on football directors.[9] Until the final weeks before the tournament, delegates feared they would have to cancel the event.

Sportsmen used ideas about masculinity to comment upon Chilean football's international reputation during the South American Cup won by Uruguay. The cup had become the most important sports tournament on the continent, and Chilean sportsmen hoped to prove that their football had matured. They explained that in the past, Chile had been "a baby, easy to defeat."[10] Drawing upon gendered metaphors, sportsmen proclaimed that after twenty-five years of playing football, the Chilean team was ready to wear "long pants."[11] In addition, sports journalists predicted that the Chilean players' common mestizo identity would provide them with a physical advantage. It was their supposed homogeneity, compared with their neighbors' history of African, indigenous, and southern European influences, that supposedly unified the Chilean team.[12] Sportsmen viewed racial sameness as essential to developing the uniform style of play that "modern" or "scientific" football required. This style relied upon specific combinations and patterns instead of individual talent.

Chile's last-place finish shocked fans and club members. Footballers searched for flaws in the Chilean character to explain the failures of the national team. Luís Zegers, a football club director, explained that the Chileans' greatest defects were a lack of scientific training and their individualism. Zegers explained that the basis of a modern team was "the annulment of individualism . . . whereby [the player] is just one of the gears of the machine."[13] Zegers and other directors encouraged clubs to hire expert physical-education teachers from Europe to improve their footballers' techniques.

Sportsmen blamed the team's disappointing performance on government negligence, nebulous "racial deficiencies," and a lack of masculine aggression. President Alessandri faulted the Conservative Congress, which rejected budgets that had allotted money for sports facilities and training.

He dismissed suggestions that the Chilean race and its virility were lacking. In an interview with *Los Sports*, Alessandri insisted that sports journalists during the South American Cup had been correct: Chile was a racially homogenous, mestizo country: "The Araucanian race that populated this land in the era of the Spanish conquest was the strongest of all natives on the continent and also fought against the bravest and strongest Spanish captains, because only they would arrive to the most distant and impoverished of the discovered countries. From the struggle between these two races our people came forth, strong, vigorous, enduring, and virile."[14] According to Alessandri, sports and physical education were among the only methods to preserve this racial heritage. His version of history relegated the indigenous to a vanquished past, cutting ties to the indigenous communities that were petitioning his help in land struggles at that very moment. With the indigenous assimilated through war and romance, the undisciplined worker emerged as the new subject to be tamed. In sports publications, Alessandri promoted the plan he sent Congress to create "dry zones" and stadiums in carbon-mining areas of the South.[15]

FOOTBALL CLUBS AND CITY POLITICS

The Radical, Democratic, and Communist parties strengthened their ties to football clubs and other civic associations at the local level in the early 1920s. Connections to civic associations helped these parties, chiefly the Radicals, make gains in municipal elections. Local politics offered an entry point for newer parties. Luis Recabarren, for example, who had founded the Chilean Communist Party in 1922, envisioned municipal governments as the building blocks of a socialist state in Chile.[16] For the time being, however, municipalities were a mixed bag, their governments showing a strong representation by independents, Conservatives, and Liberals. Civic associations worked with municipal politicians to promote innovative projects, such as Mayor Rogelio Ugarte's Universidad Municipal del Trabajo (Municipal University of Labor), which was designed to provide free classes for workers through the local government.[17] Via these relationships and experiments, footballers came to see city politics as an accessible means of effecting change. For political parties, these collaborations were a method to recruit supporters.

Football clubs and other civic associations introduced migrants to urban opportunities. Migrants from the countryside generally arrived in the city after having experienced an even more closed and coercive political system than their urban counterparts.[18] Urban organizations, influenced by dramatic stereotypes of an archaic and barbaric countryside, hoped to integrate migrants into modern society. Literacy programs were important to workers' civic associations of all stripes. Literate workers could vote, but equally as important, they could participate in civic life and unions.

Local branches of the Radical Party, buoyed by their alliance with Alessandri's government, helped neighborhood football clubs construct headquarters and enlisted their cooperation in community-improvement initiatives. Youth branches of political parties, in particular, organized football players into clubs. For example, in Recoleta, north of Santiago's center, the Young Radicals formed Santiago Infantil FC in the branch offices of the party.[19] Upper echelons of the parties doled out favors to these affiliated clubs. Radical Pedro Aguirre Cerda, Alessandri's minister of the interior and a future president, offered land concessions to football clubs in order to create more fields.[20] He also donated prizes, medals, and cups for tournaments. While political parties developed practices of clientelism, it was often the clubs that took the initiative in these relationships. Well-connected clubs had set such a precedent in the early years of the century.

Relationships with political groups gave working- and middle-class clubs access to social and economic capital. Juvenil Obrero FC, one of the most popular clubs in the working-class Santiago neighborhood of Yungay, solicited the support of the local Radical Party.[21] West of Santiago's center, Yungay was among the first industrialized zones and was notorious for its polluted air and unsanitary living conditions. The Radicals offered footballers from Juvenil access to their offices, space in their bulletins, and sponsorship for tournaments. Clubs like Juvenil Obrero had become an important part of Yungay's reputation as a tough neighborhood. One of the ways that Juvenil Obrero helped build a sense of neighborhood identity was by playing in other parts of the city. During these matches, club members, their families, and fans lunched and traveled together.[22] Local politicians frequently attended these matches. The Radicals helped Juvenil Obrero acquire and furnish their clubhouse. Party donations allowed club members to create a library that included classics and, of course, several Radical Party pamphlets.[23] Furthermore, Radicals participated in the club's lecture series on hygiene and household economy.[24] At the neighborhood level, football clubs connected labor unions, local parties, and civic associations.

Clubs offered politicians their organizational capacity, access to an extensive social network, and connections to groups with positive reputations in the community. A telling example occurred in 1921 after Pedro

Aguirre's resignation as minister of interior and in response to the massacre of workers in the nitrate fields of San Gregorio. Héctor Arancibia, who agreed to replace him, subsequently mobilized sports clubs in the same way he had during the presidential campaign. In response to an acute economic downturn, thousands of unemployed miners streamed into Santiago. Newspapers sensationalized their arrival, depicting the miners as delinquent hordes. Arancibia created an emergency council to coordinate the delivery of food and other necessities to these miners and their families. He chose the intendant of Santiago (the appointed regional governor), directors of charity organizations, the prefect of police, and two representatives of the National Sports Federation to serve on the council, including Jorge Matte, who was the FSN president and minister of foreign affairs, and Leonardo Matus of the Workers' Football Association.[25] Matus connected the council to leaders of working-class neighborhoods who could help accommodate miners as well as coordinate relief efforts from their club headquarters. As the relationship between political parties and clubs developed, football directorships became a vehicle for middle- and working-class men to begin careers in local politics. For example, Matus, a physical-education teacher, later ran for Congress with support of the Radical Party. As treasurer of the Workers' Football Association, Matus had gained exposure in political circles as well as a good reputation among workers.

In spite of the deepening relationship between football clubs and political parties, sportsmen passionately argued that one of football's finest qualities was its independence from politics. Accusations that Arancibia used his connections with football clubs to further his political career were met with outrage. He responded, "How poorly those who do not know me, judge me. . . . For me, sport is as sacred as the principles of the Radical Party to which I belong. . . . I have not gathered a crowd of sportsmen for my reelection."[26] In 1923–1924, Congress refused to pass the social reform package of Alessandri, which sparked rumors of military intervention. Sportsmen remained even more committed to football's apolitical nature as party infighting and government stalemate discredited national politics. In 1924, the sportsmen of Valparaíso promoted the election of a "sportsman-councilman" named Eliseo 2ª Guerra, to serve in the city government. When a journalist asked Guerra, an independent, if he would accept the support of a political party, Guerra responded, "The sportsmen have been very zealous on that point. They are tired of seeing municipal authorities engulfed in politics, to which they dedicate all their time."[27]

Unions participated in neighborhood football associations like the Yungay Football Association. Football clubs based in unions strengthened the connection between the workplace and home life. In addition, workers recognized that they could form unions under the auspices of football clubs, and generally would be supported by management when they did so.[28] In the late 1910s, the Federation of Chilean Workers (Federación Obrera de Chile, or FOCH) formed a Sports Commission charged with the organization of union clubs. FOCH hoped that the football clubs would strengthen loyalty to the federation, integrate migrant workers into urban life, and provide sober entertainment.[29] Some Santiago neighborhoods embraced union clubs as being representative of the barrio—Barrio Franklin, for example, in the southern part of the city. There, the glassworkers union formed a football team that fans identified with the neighborhood. The football club provided the union with a safe organizational structure that it could use to defend itself against repression from the company and police.

Football clubs continued to play leadership roles in urban reform movements, as they had in the 1910s. In the mixed working- and middle-class neighborhood of Ñuñoa, footballers helped build one of Santiago's most ambitious community organizations. The Arrieta Foundation started as a night school for workers' children. In the early 1920s, a group of young men interested in football suggested that the foundation extend its curriculum to include physical education. The foundation proceeded to buy football fields where the club could hold matches. Within a few years, the recreation team developed such an extensive network of activities that they became a focal point of social life in Ñuñoa. Throughout the decade, the foundation expanded its projects to include a temperance group, an "economic barbershop," a dentist's office, and a recreation room.[30] Arrieta conceived of its spaces as educational and secular. This represented one of the few social organizations in the neighborhood without a relationship to a religious organization or charity.

"RADICAL" RESTRUCTURING OF FOOTBALL

A tension existed between the desire of Radical politicians to use the popularity of football clubs for their own ends and their efforts to circumscribe the clubs' activities. The growth of middle- and working-class participation, on the fields and in the stands, overwhelmed the first generation of organizers. The reform-minded patriarchs of football boasted of the cross-class collaboration within the sport. Their enthusiasm,

FIGURE 2.2.   By 1920, football had become ubiquitous in neighborhoods and schoolyards. Image courtesy of the Archivo Fotográfico Colección, Museo Histórico Archivo, Santiago.

however, hinged upon their expectation that an "enlightened" leadership would direct the participation of the lower classes. In an effort to control and modernize football, Radical party leaders embarked on a campaign to revamp its organization. The new structure created hierarchical inequalities that pushed workers' clubs to the periphery. Directors of the largest clubs voiced their frustration with the feuds between rival associations and the confusion surrounding the chain of command. This reached a panicked pitch in 1923 when FIFA (Fédération Internationale de Football Association), the international governing body of football, threatened to suspend Chile's affiliation unless the competing national organizations from Santiago and Valparaíso settled their disputes. Club directors as well as leading players urged the government to intervene in the conflict. These changes marginalized clubs that could not or would not comply, creating a boundary between recognized and independent bodies.

To prevent Chile's disaffiliation from FIFA, Héctor Arancibia convened a National Football Congress in 1923 and directed it to form a governing federation. The delegates hoped that the federation would be truly national in scope, and they made efforts to involve provincial associations. That autumn was a busy one for Arancibia, who was back in the senate at the height of the congressional deadlock over social reform legislation that Alessandri tried to pass. Assisted by a fellow Radical, Deputy Rafael Torreblanca, Arancibia set out to broker an agreement on where to locate football's national headquarters.[31] Radical Party politicians, entrepreneurial directors of Spanish and Italian clubs, and provincial delegates supported Santiago as the seat. Despite the protests of football's original patriarchs, like Juan Ramsay and J. H. Livingstone, the National Football Congress created the Chilean Football Federation, recognized by the government and based in the capital. This decision recognized the growing power of Santiago, which was tied to industry and state expansion, and further cemented the capital as the center of national organizations.

The congressional delegates designed a hierarchical structure for the federation that created vertical ranks of associations. In addition, they linked the number of allowable affiliated leagues and associations to the populations of the areas they represented. They pressured independent clubs and leagues to join the hierarchy at the appropriate level. For example, directors forced independent leagues in Santiago to become members of the Football Association of Santiago if they wanted to affiliate with the national federation. They also convinced deputies to pass a law requiring football organizations to apply for legal recognition through the national federation. This legal recognition was needed before clubs could accept donations, receive state support, or receive permits for events. Thus, the federation became the mediator between the government and football clubs. Many protested that workers' clubs and leagues could not afford the application fees. The directors of the football congress defended their position, claiming to act according to "principles of justice, democracy, respect for the statutes and bylaws and the well-known interests of sports."[32] However, independent and small organizations resented being forced to submit to the authority of unfamiliar associations.

Football organizations that had worked within a broad, self-defined vision, like Arrieta, complained that this new structure would confine their activities. Arancibia promised that the new federation would continue to promote reform projects and included a final resolution directing the federation to begin "educational and moral programs."[33] In his closing speech to the football congress, Arancibia urged footballers to create programs to eradicate illiteracy, alcoholism, and "social sicknesses," a reference to venereal diseases.[34] Finally, congress leaders stressed the importance of fostering a fraternal spirit among sportsmen and their institutions, which included establishing solidarity, economic cooperation, and mutualism. By mutualism, Arancibia referred to mutual aid societies of workers. By the 1920s, Arancibia's promotion of mutualism rather than unionism clearly positioned him to the right of the workers' movement. Despite the congress leaders' claims that they were promoting democracy, they established a clear hierarchy down to the club level, all of it overseen by powerful politicians.

As a result of the resolutions adopted by the football congress regarding statutes and bylaws, the internal structures of established clubs began to differ from their turn-of-the-century incarnations. Moreover, the regularity of schedules, the dissemination of results, and the star making of teams placed greater pressure on directors to produce winning results. While the first generation of footballers had played and participated in club management, both players and managers now faced greater time demands. By the 1920s, a directorship was something to pursue after a playing career ended, if at all. This division of labor was more pronounced in elite clubs, where players often came from a much lower socioeconomic background than average members. The role of the team captain changed as well. Whereas clubs in the 1910s chose captains based on experience, modernizers pushed for the captainship to be awarded to the most talented player. One director complained, "In Chile, they always designate as captain the one who is most distinguished by his capacity to talk. . . . The captain, before all, needs to possess a perfect understanding of the game, of each man's worth, and must rise above his men with a clear head to direct the action."[35] Rather than being a club leader, the captain was being confined to a role entirely centered on on-field performance.

Many working-class clubs chafed at the reforms initiated by the National Football Congress. The standardization of statutes, the elevated dues, and the need for legal recognition discouraged workers' clubs from joining the federation. Moreover, some established clubs, such as Chile-Arjentina FC, had difficulty conforming to the new disciplinary guidelines set down by the congress, which had implemented fees and suspensions for violent behavior. Chile-Arjentina, founded in 1903 by municipal workers in Santiago, developed a reputation for having violent rivalries with other workers' teams. These became so intense that the police investigated players on several occasions for acts of revenge committed days and even weeks following matches. According to the federation, clubs had to create effective disciplinary committees as well as to subject players to measures determined by their association. The federation sought recognition of the national government as football's official governing body and as the entity responsible for the distribution of state aid. This left organizations little choice but to seek affiliation with the federation. When workers' clubs complained that the revamped structure deepened inequalities among sportsmen, elite directors accused them of bringing politics into the sport.

Changes in club statutes influenced practices to the extent that sportsmen viewed these rules as legitimate reference points during club debates. Members often cited the statutes when organizing club elections, reviewing membership qualifications, and considering disciplinary measures. At other times, club practices blatantly disregarded the statutes. For example, the statutes prohibited discussions of religion and politics in the club. Yet candidates for political office regularly spoke at official club functions. Umbrella organizations enforced the rule inconsistently at best. In the federation and the Football Association of Santiago, directors often used the "no politics" rule to head off complaints of inequalities in football. When workers' delegates criticized the federation for selecting only elite athletes, who could pay their travel expenses, to represent Chile internationally, directors chastised them for violating the rule against political discussions.

A good example of this hypocritical stance toward the favorable treatment of elites can be seen in the attitude of writer and sports enthusiast Antonio Acevedo Hernández, who identified himself as a middle-class moderate. Acevedo agreed that privileging elite athletes jeopardized the democracy of sports. Democracy, for Acevedo, meant that every Chilean would be "a cultivator of sport, that there would not be a child or man in the republic who would not be able to run, jump, or swim. All would know the gymnasium; no one would drag along through life." However, he chastised working-class clubs for trying to create a "dictatorship of the proletariat" when they proposed that the federation pay for the travel of players abroad and determine dues according to clubs' budgets.[36]

The modernization of clubs' structures also increased their secular nature. Whereas teams sponsored by Catholic parishes and the YMCA had joined secular football associations in the 1910s, they broke away in the 1920s. The standardized regulations created at the National Football Congress of 1923 forbade discussions of religion in member clubs. In addition, many religious leaders wanted to discourage violence and drinking at matches. Religious groups organized separate "dry" tournaments, such as the Union of Young Catholic Centers, which included football clubs of forty-one different Catholic parishes in the Santiago and Valparaíso metropolitan areas.[37] Many religious clubs, particularly those sponsored by the YMCA, focused their efforts on downtrodden communities; these centers offered free medical examinations and courses in health and nutrition.[38] However, clubs based in religious communities remained segregated from the Football Association of Santiago until the later part of the 1930s.

The restructuring of football also changed the experiences of members who belonged to compliant clubs. The naming of clubs, the election of directors, and the selection of uniform colors and hymns constituted major events for members. In the past, these events often occurred spontaneously or piecemeal, even among Santiago's top clubs. The modernized statutes provided a detailed schedule for events, especially elections. Statutes stipulated in which newspapers and how far in advance elections needed to be announced. On any given day, dozens of football clubs in Santiago announced elections, changes in directors, and motions passed by assemblies, as well as bachelor parties and funerals. These formalities took on great importance in footballers' lives. Seemingly minute changes in a statute or a disciplinary case could spark passionate debate. José Pardo recalled a heated election in his adolescent football club, which was named Fantomas FC in homage to the hero of a detective movie that the neighborhood boys "went crazy for."[39] Years after becoming one of Santiago's most popular players, Pardo felt bitter over this election and his subsequent departure from the club.

Changes in formal regulations meant that the daily governance of clubs was less participatory and democratic. The federation argued that these changes would help avoid squabbling and tedious debates. The federation required that directorates present annual financial information. The revamped statutes legitimized some details of common bylaws, such as the categories of membership, which were divided into active, passive, auxiliary, and so on. Honorary membership was bestowed by a general vote in recognition of an admired member of the community. Statutes created a further category of membership for young men who played on teams in junior leagues, usually between the ages of twelve and seventeen. A few clubs created categories for women, who had the same status as boys younger than twelve.[40] This "inclusion" of women, according to directors, was meant to encourage their participation. One club leader explained, "The best women of the country will be the healthiest. The most beautiful women of our race are not the pallid, skinny ones that cover the sad anemia of their faces with the props of the actor [makeup]."[41] In practice directors did not implement any strategies to include women, and their formal categorization with children underscored their status in clubs.

As an unintended consequence, the centralization of football ensured that clubs of different social classes continued to play one another. For instance, in the Metropolitan League, the May 1st Club regularly faced Green Cross. The former, composed of members of an anarchist resistance society founded May 1, had been forced to transfer to the Metropolitan League because of the decay of the Workers' Football League and the Football Association of Santiago's consolidation of leagues. Green Cross was a team of the Santiago elite, among the first clubs in the city. Spanish star Juan Legarreta, himself from a fairly privileged team, explained, "Green Cross was the club of the posh of the capital. All of them arrived in cars, already dressed from their houses. They were magnificent, and when they faced confrontations, they also showed their boxing skills."[42] Players in the May 1st Club, led by the charismatic director Dr. Carlos Aguirre, were described by journalists as "workers every one, and of scarce economic resources.... Their effort to equip themselves from head to foot demonstrates their noble efforts."[43] Delegates from Green Cross and May 1st met in league and association meetings as well as in the bleachers and on the football fields.

THE COUNTRY AND THE CITY

As international competition became increasingly frequent and prestigious, sportsmen agonized over the poor performances of Chile's national football team. Their discussions related to broader political controversies surrounding migrant workers from the countryside. Mainstream publications, such as *Los Sports* and *El Mercurio*, accused workers of perpetrating violence and drinking during football matches. Sports publications assumed that these workers were migrants from the countryside. They caricatured migrants as racially distinct from urbanites and intellectually dull. Sportsmen assumed that life in the countryside was boring, impoverished, and isolated.[44] Despite these stereotypes, there is ample evidence that migrants invigorated barrio football during the 1920s. Their interest in forming clubs and attending matches energized the sport. In turn, football helped integrate migrants into local politics and urban life. Between 1885 and 1930, the population of Santiago increased by 205 percent, but the city's infrastructure could not keep pace.[45] Clubs became a vehicle for migrants to secure housing, employment, and companionship.

At the same time that middle- and upper-class writers were creating images of the countryside as backward, they praised its idyllic simplicity. Sportswriters envisioned the countryside as the source of national values and authentic masculinity. Beginning in the 1920s, clubs created programs to restore a connection to nature. Club Unión Española began an official branch of the club, the Explorers, to coordinate trips outside the city. The Explorers trekked into the southern forests and the northern deserts to "fight against that tendency of modern life that removes one from natural life and that ends in the moral and material decay of organisms due to the artificial habits this life, each day more divorced from nature, dictates."[46] This "back to nature" rhetoric criticized urban modernization projects such as the installation of street lighting throughout the city. Sportsmen complained that the expansion of transportation routes between the city's outskirts and center was responsible for the destruction of the countryside. In addition, club members feared that a loss of contact with nature feminized urban men. Clubs that traveled to competitions in the provinces brought back anecdotes of rustic life that raised interest in excursions. For club members, the physical challenge of travel offered opportunities to demonstrate skills that they defined as masculine, such as horseback riding and navigation. The football field represented an attempt to bring green space to the city.

Anxiety that the absence of contact with the natural world signified a loss of moral and physical well-being shaped the growth of *criollismo* in new forms of popular culture. Criollismo was a literary movement with roots in the early years of the century. Teachers, journalists, and other professionals, often of the Radical Party and reform movements, "sought to democratize the concepts of 'nation' and 'culture' by demonstrating the value of lower-class traditions and lifeways."[47] Praise of criollismo frequently accompanied diatribes against urban workers' supposedly poor hygiene and moral practices. Criollismo challenged the elite interpretation of the countryside, which saw the *huaso*, or Chilean cowboy, as insufferably backward and primitive. The figure of the huaso became popular in print and performance.[48] The huaso, accompanied by the sounds of traditional music, conjured up feelings of nostalgia among urban migrants. Nostalgia, as in Mexican boleros, was the "most modern" form through which urbanites expressed criticism of their experiences in the city.[49] At the same time, the image of the huaso contrasted with that of rebellious and organized workers in the cities.[50]

The desire of provincial football players to move to Santiago and Valparaíso was at odds with a romantic picture of life in rural Chile. Northern port cities like Coquimbo had been cradles of football, but by the 1920s, the southern provinces were producing a disproportionate amount of football talent.[51] The South was known for a significant Mapuche population, a prominent German immigrant community, and natural resources. The Liceo Temuco (the school of the poet Pablo Neruda) built a reputation as a factory of footballers, turning out many of Santiago's best players. Temuco's leagues became a second-tier extension of Santiago football, and players circulated between the cities. Although the practice was officially banned by the Chilean Football Federation, clubs lured migrant players to Santiago and Valparaíso with financial incentives. Directors of clubs who could offer jobs were often connected to the expanding state apparatus. For example, the president of Colo Colo, Carlos Concha, served as the general subtreasurer of Chile and subsequently as undersecretary of the Ministry of Finance during the Ibáñez regime.[52] Concha arranged positions within these government agencies for Colo Colo players who came from the provinces.

Sportsmen caricatured migrant footballers as lacking in technique or elegance but making up for it in "heart." Players often reinforced these stereotypes, emphasizing the resilience of their play and their economic hardships. César Alsina described himself as a humble southerner of "Iberian and Creole blood."[53] Alsina boasted that southern players possessed greater endurance than their Santiago counterparts, playing up to three games a day. His football training began in the Liceo Temuco, which recruited Alsina and other poor boys from his neighborhood. When interviewed, migrant players denied that clubs offered them money. Migrant players routinely cited family and work matters as the reasons for their migration to Santiago. Alsina and other migrant players avoided questions that could implicate their clubs in professionalism. Football fans felt an intimacy with players who had followed their own migratory trajectories and took pride in their hometowns.[54]

Santiago's top clubs, such as Badminton, developed a hierarchical system in which talented provincial footballers played but did not fully participate in the institution. (These clubs tended to be the ones that later successfully made the transition to professionalism.) This treatment often alienated players who had migrated to the city, particularly those who moved from a working-class club to an elite one. For example, a teacher of César Alsina encouraged him to try out for Badminton. He arrived in Santiago in 1925 and joined the club, which had a large contingent of military officers and upper-class members. After a few months, Alsina felt disappointed in the way other club members treated him. He found himself lost in Santiago without the rhythms of southern culture that had structured his life. He explained, "My time with Club Yellow-Black [Badminton] showed me the enormous difference between the atmosphere I had lived in in Temuco and what I would come to experience in the capital. In the South, I had felt more in touch with my comrades, unlike the coldness I encountered in Badminton."[55] In a similar pattern, Guillermo Cerda left Liceo Temuco to join Badminton around the same time as Alsina. He explained to journalists that despite the rich talent in Temuco, the school's impoverished condition meant that children used tennis balls instead of footballs.[56] By the time Cerda joined Badminton, nearly everyone he played with had come from his hometown. In contrast to Alsina, Cerda found Badminton a familiar space. Within a few years, migrants had changed the character of the club.

FOOTBALL UNDER THE IBÁÑEZ REGIME: THE RISE OF PROFESSIONALISM

The first years of Arturo Alessandri's administration disappointed many reformers who had supported his campaign. The economic crisis in the mining sectors brought about by the end of World War I worsened conditions for the poor. Unemployed miners and farmworkers who arrived to Santiago and Valparaíso in search of work were met with housing shortages, high food prices, and poor sanitation. In addition, Alessandri used the same violent and repressive tactics against strikers and labor organizations as his predecessors. A military coup that displaced Alessandri in 1924 was followed by a chaotic year of power struggle between legislators, Alessandri, and the military (itself divided). The military forced the legislature to adopt a labor code, social security, and workmen's compensation. A reformist cadre of officers wrested control from their superiors and imposed a new constitution (with Alessandri's contributions), which limited parliamentary power, secularized government agencies, and consecrated the state as a protector of workers' rights. Alessandri went in and out of self-exile during this period, but resigned when he realized that the military planned to stay in control. The oligarchy organized a resistance campaign to what it viewed

as a socialist coup, but could not count on enough popular or military support. At first, the coup was supported by many centrist and leftist groups.
The communist union paper *Justicia* responded, "The actions of the army
and navy have brought hopes of a return to normality and national restoration."[57] In the midst of these chaotic and putatively reformist changes in the
capital, the state continued its unabated repression of workers, especially in
mining areas.[58] In the winter of 1925, 600–800 striking nitrate workers in La
Coruña were killed by troops on the orders of Alessandri and his military
allies.[59]

From 1925 until 1931, following the departure of Alessandri, a group of
midranking officers, led by Colonel Carlos Ibáñez del Campo, constructed
a state bureaucracy that increased its presence in the daily life of Santiago.
A significant sector of middle-class reformers believed that Ibáñez could
stop the spread of communism and reinvigorate patriotism. He promoted
a group of middle-class technocrats, whom he claimed would streamline
the old bureaucracy and create an apolitical state.[60] The military regime
repressed workers' organizations, intellectuals, and leftists. Sports clubs
and other civic associations were divided over the Ibáñez regime's modernization projects as well as the value it placed on scientific expertise.

As discussed in the previous chapter, the model of the civic sportsman
competed with a militarized view of physical education. In the context of
World War I, the military's prestige grew. Sports magazines praised the
Chilean sportsmen who had volunteered for the war in Europe, regard-
less of which side they joined. Journalists portrayed the Italian, British,
French, and German immigrants who enlisted as heroic patriots. Military

FIGURE 2.3.   Improvement of trolley lines from the city center to north of downtown under
Ibáñez, 1927. Image courtesy of Chilectra.

language and metaphors influenced clubs' rhetoric. Their arguments for unity among sportsmen emphasized that they should not "battle" amongst themselves, but should instead work together as "soldiers of the sporting cause."[61] Increased activity from groups such as the Boy Scouts and military sports clubs contributed to the climate of militarization. After primary education became mandatory in 1920, the public education system played an even greater role in instilling respect for military accomplishments of the nineteenth century in the War of Independence, the War of the Pacific, and the Occupation of Araucanía. The law requiring primary schooling made physical education one of the three mandatory branches of public education and grouped gymnastic and military exercises together.[62]

Military sports clubs criticized the "sleeping government" for not recognizing the importance of sports in training young men who could serve in Chile's armed forces.[63] Just months before the military's assumption of power, one director described the mood of sportsmen as restless. He explained that they sought "to rid [themselves] of this damned Indian pacifism that we have inherited and to make our bodies and souls flourish in a dawn of physical regeneration that will make Chile a new Sparta."[64] He disdained Chile's indigenous past and hoped to construct a social order based on military models. A strict separation of gender roles played an important part in this vision. For these men in search of a "new Sparta," Chileans needed to follow European models and embrace modernization projects.

Sympathetic sportsmen, including significant sectors of the middle class, believed that only a forceful hand could implement social reform, take a hard line against leftist movements, and restore national honor. Civic associations looked optimistically on Ibáñez's budgetary increases for the public school system, which earmarked funds for the expansion of physical education.[65] As Ibáñez consolidated power, club directors began to fear that his agenda stood at odds with their view of sport as a tool for invigorating civic involvement. Moreover, they felt uncomfortable with the regime's increasing surveillance of clubs. The military government declared that it suspected all types of societies of being covers for communist organizations and used the newly organized military police, the Carabineros, to monitor them.[66] Almost immediately, the junta replaced civilian sports authorities with military personnel. The midlevel officers hoped to both exert tighter control over sports clubs and provide renewed support to clubs with military leaders and sympathies. As early as November 1924, prominent sportsmen such as Carlos Cariola, a playwright and the president of the Chilean Football Federation, reported that Chile's international reputation for democratic government had been injured. His description of the South American Cup in Uruguay emphasized this: "There is not enough money to reward the work of clarification, performed with conviction and patriotism by delegates and players in Argentina and Uruguay, regarding the true situation in Chile, which has been compared with that of Brazil. The government must promote football. Consulates are not enough, even though Héctor Mujica and Julio Maqueira are worth ten of them [that is, diplomats], to dispel the impression of dictatorship. These two talented diplomats need help and know-how to skillfully portray our just rebellion when asked how is Chile under a dictatorship."[67] Many sportsmen considered the military's intervention progressive and felt confident that a constitutional government would follow shortly.

Ibáñez quickly emerged as the leader of the military junta, which dissolved the power of municipal- and national-level government bodies. Before the coup, Ibáñez's contact with sports had been limited to connections through the cavalry school, but he was astute enough to recognize the political value of sports.[68] He arranged appearances at local matches and gave "spontaneous" speeches. Ibáñez carefully selected the teams he supported, and used his association with them to bolster his image as a man of the people. Ibáñez patronized clubs of the unions he had control of, such as Club Deportivo "Fábricas del Ejército." Workers for the army's munitions factory had founded the club, which thrived under the patronage of Ibáñez.[69] The factory's newspaper, *El Obrero Industrial*, in explicit collaboration with the government, advised workers to ignore criticisms of Ibáñez, whom it described as "a great citizen, called upon to unite the country."[70] Sportsmen from this factory claimed that unlike traditional politicians, Ibáñez had "pure" motives.[71]

Despite Ibáñez's rhetorical support of sports, his administration could not successfully incorporate sports organizations into the state apparatus. While certain sectors supported his regime, clubs remained tied to unions, civic associations, and political parties (especially the Radicals). Ibáñez had created the General Directorate of Physical Education, but it managed to finance sports projects only sporadically. The technocrats that Ibáñez appointed encountered resentment from sports organizations that preferred less interference in their representative bodies. Distrust in the democratic practices of the national legislature had not broken their confidence in the procedural efficacy of their associations. Ibáñez's support largely took the form of granting personal favors, much as had Alessandri's. For example, the boxer Sergio Ojeda recalled during preparations for the Amsterdam

Olympics of 1928 that the minister of finance rejected the Olympic Committee's request for state support. As a last-ditch effort, the athletes met with Ibáñez, who directed the minister to disburse the necessary funds immediately.[72] Ojeda, who later served as a congressman for Ibáñez's party, explained, "You can imagine the impression that I received from the president's behavior: just, executive, understanding of the problem."[73] These stories of personal favors that Ibáñez bestowed upon athletes circulated among sportsmen and served to build his image as a man of action who cut through bureaucratic channels.

As discussed in Chapter One, civic associations integrated men from the popular classes into politics through municipal channels. The military junta recognized the importance of municipal governments and their relationships with civic associations. Among its first acts, the regime dissolved the elected municipal councils of Santiago and Valparaíso, replacing them with appointed committees, or *juntas de vecinos*.[74] Through the juntas, Ibáñez supported projects that extended the reach of the government. He directed junta members to organize cultural projects in their jurisdictions. For example, the Military Junta of Providencia provided the seed money to create the new Sports Association of Providencia and quickly ensured its legal recognition.[75] The mayor of Providencia channeled money to the association and gave it privileged access to sports facilities in the Escuela de Carabineros (police school).[76] The association attracted clubs whose leagues suffered from financial troubles, and within a few years, it claimed to have fifty-six affiliated clubs with more than five thousand members.[77] Ibáñez exploited his relationship with the association, giving speeches during matches on the need to "fortify the race" through exercise.[78] In Providencia, the regime mobilized widespread support, in part because of its encouragement of suburban growth.[79]

The military's policies toward municipal governments alienated sports clubs that had formed relationships with local politicians. The Sports Association of Providencia's close relationship with the military government caused its delegates problems with the national organization. The Chilean Football Federation rejected the association's request for affiliation in 1927, citing unconventional accounting practices.[80] The association refused to discuss the charges in detail, but it appears that the federation disapproved of the inordinate amount of funding it received from the military authorities as well as its independent application for legal recognition. Association founder Arturo Torres denied that the junta had given it substantial funding, but the federation was not convinced. The

Association of Referees refused to officiate the Sports Association of Providencia's matches, apparently for the same reasons. By 1930, Torres was claiming that the Sports Association of Providencia no longer wanted affiliation with the federation, which, he alleged, could not control violence among its members.[81] In addition, delegates from the Football Association of Santiago complained that the Sports Association of Providencia had circumvented its authority by applying directly to the federation for membership. Equally disturbing was that the local military juntas appointed, rather than oversaw the election of, the directorate of the association.[82]

Discourses of modernity and order, championed by the junta, shaped debates among football clubs, particularly over the adoption of professionalism. Of all the sports entities, Colo Colo received the most attention from the Ibáñez regime. Directors of Colo Colo had promoted professionalism since the club's inception. They envisioned their club as the vanguard of "modern" football for the masses. Founded by a young group of players in 1925, Colo Colo claimed to bring a revolutionary spirit to the sport that would result in order and victory, not unlike the way Ibáñez described himself. Colo Colo began as a clique within the popular Club Magallanes. Magallanes, known as a club of teachers, attracted a middle-class membership. During the 1924 season, conflicts arose between a cadre of players, led by the charismatic David Arellano, and the directors of Magallanes. According to some witnesses, Arellano's clique protested that directors awarded the captainship of the football squad to players with seniority instead of talent. Other members recalled that the players demanded half of the admission revenues, which the directors flatly refused, since it would have constituted professionalism.[83] In Arellano's view, these antiquated practices prevented Chile from developing a world-class team, as Uruguay had done.[84] After a heated dispute at a general-assembly meeting, Arellano broke with Magallanes definitively, taking a dozen players with him.[85]

David Arellano and his supporters wanted to create a club that transcended neighborhood allegiances and represented the nation. Arellano, a physical-education teacher, studied European methods of play and believed in dedicating more time to athletic training. He hoped to import trainers who could provide guidance in physical development as well as strategic game planning. Arellano viewed the role of a coach, a novelty in Chilean football of the 1920s, as a central part of the game's evolution, and he planned to hire one for his new club.[86] As a figure, Arellano became an important part of Colo Colo's founding myth and its enduring popularity. Arellano was a sober young man, described as reserved by his teammates. He lived a quiet life in his mother's home. According to friends, Arellano rarely drank, never smoked, enjoyed singing choral music, and was not known to date.[87] Moreover, he was a talented player, known for making intelligent decisions on the field. Directors of Santiago's largest clubs, especially those from the European immigrant communities, characterized Arellano's stance on professionalism as progressive. Pro-government sportswriters expressed a feeling that the country was moving forward, led by Ibáñez's technocrats in government, European engineers, and *científicos*, or scientists, like Arellano in cultural affairs.

Football fans have debated for decades how Colo Colo achieved its reputation as the "authentic" Chilean club. Several founders recalled that the club wanted a name with a distinctively Chilean ring, and the term "colo colo" had two distinct meanings in Chilean culture.[88] First, Colo Colo was the name of a sixteenth-century cacique (indigenous chief) who won important victories over the Spanish. And according to popular myth, a colo colo was a creature that sucked blood from humans while they slept. Colo colos were described variously as rats, lizards, and mountain cats.[89] The club's success attracted fans and, at first, seemed to bear out Arellano's faith in scientific football. Some of the country's most talented players appeared on the original Colo Colo roster, contributing to its nearly unde-feated record during the first season. In addition, Colo Colo incorporated talented provincial players, who attracted their own fans. Even more impor-tantly, the club toured southern Chile, something rarely done. After their first season, the club traveled as far south as Chiloé, approximately seven hundred miles from Santiago.[90] The tour included many matches in small villages, to the delight of local fans.[91] Finally, in the spirit of the era, many found Colo Colo's identification with youth, modernity, and progress ap-pealing. The story of its origins as a rebellion against an antiquated, even if noble, Magallanes continues to charm fans.

Colo Colo's decision to travel throughout the Americas and Europe in 1927 was met with great enthusiasm. Club directors pitched the trip as a way to demonstrate the progress of Chilean football as well as an opportunity to learn the latest European techniques. Carlos Ibáñez helped finance the trip by channeling money to the club through the Ministry of Education. Ibáñez ensured that players received their salaries during their travels, justifying it with the claim that physical-education teachers could make professional observations of programs abroad.[92] Players complained that Ibáñez arranged these benefits on a case-by-case basis. For example, the teacher Togo Bascuñan received his salary for only three months of the tour, while the ministry paid other players for the full five months.[93] Journalists paid close attention to Colo Colo's trip, dubbing the players "the most efficient diplomats" sent abroad.[94] Players sent accounts of their travels to football clubs and the country's major newspapers. Led by the acclaimed playwright Carlos Cariola, footballers kept up regular communications with their fans. In 1929, Alberto Arellano, David's brother, published a book relating stories of the club's travels.[95]

An unfortunate event generated great sympathy for Colo Colo when David Arellano became ill during a match in Spain and died shortly thereafter. The public responded with outpourings that included Catholic masses and tournaments in memory of the young player. Clubs named in homage of Arellano sprang up throughout the country. Colo Colo adopted a black armband as part of its uniform, which it has maintained to date. The repatriation of Arellano's remains from Spain became a nationalist cause célèbre. The Democratic deputy Rafael Silva asked Congress to provide funds for the transfer. In addition, he requested a special pension for Arellano's mother.[96] Politicians not only championed the club's causes within Congress, but also tried to associate themselves with Colo Colo socially. Politicians invited returning players to luncheons, teas, and other events. In Congress, the Democratic Party, reformist and to the left of the Radical Party, criticized the military government as it praised the team. Congressman Silva distinguished between the patriotic "people" and the Ibáñez government. He alleged that the regime's neglect of Arellano reflected its general failure to support football, resulting in the Chilean team's poor showing at the 1928 Olympics.[97] The Liberal Party deputy Benigno Acuña expressed his disappointment that the military government had not intervened to prevent an embarrassing defeat by Portugal. He claimed that the success of Uruguayans, who won the gold medal, should have convinced the government to invest more in football, adding that the Uruguayans were of the same racial stock as Chileans, which demonstrated that blame lay with the government rather than biology.[98]

The first generation of football directors opposed the new developments in football epitomized by Colo Colo. They nostalgically recalled the nineteenth century as the glory days of amateurism. Juan Ramsay, who was a referee, an equipment importer, and a club patron, complained that football was deteriorating. Ramsay griped that players appeared late to matches, in poor condition (drunk, improperly attired, etc.), and lacked club loyalty.[99] Ramsay and many of his elite peers felt that football belonged within the realm of charity and ought to show the good instincts of the leading social class. They promoted the sport as an outlet for the working class, but only under the proper direction. Ramsay blamed poor players and upstart directors for introducing a vulgar profit motive into football. Ramsay's own business interests in the importation of foreign sports equipment may have been threatened by the growth of a new sector of leaders.

This assessment by Ramsay grossly misjudged the interest of working-class clubs in professionalism. First, only a handful of Santiago's clubs had the financial wherewithal to consider such a transition. At least in the press, working-class clubs embraced the personal conduct of amateurs and a commitment to a "fair game."[100] In addition, football clubs based in neighborhoods, unions, and schools had become more, not less, involved in community projects. These clubs cleaned up neighborhood spaces, built libraries, and joined with other groups in campaigns for the installation of water lines. For Ramsay, these projects constituted politics, not the charity that he advocated. He criticized directors for raising funds through admissions, concessions, and the sale of team paraphernalia. However, the Workers' Football Association, which was renamed the Workers' League following the hierarchy set up by the National Football Congress in 1923, requested only a donation for admissions to matches.[101] It collected funds from dues, contributions, and gate receipts at away games. Delegates of working-class and elite clubs consistently voted against the implementation of professionalism, in opposition to their middle-class counterparts. Working-class clubs suffered a talent drain when their top players transferred to high-paying clubs. While modest clubs thrived at the community level, they could not compete with the financial opportunities offered by clubs like Colo Colo. Workers' clubs such as Chile-Arjentina decayed as their best players left and their fans followed. Although the club had gained prestige with victories over well-financed competitors like Loma Blanca, as professionalism advanced, it had difficulty attracting supporters.

Fans did not share the reservations of football's elite about professionalism and star making. Radio broadcasts and magazines brought sports idols into Chilean homes. The magazine *Los Sports*, first published in 1923 by Zig-Zag, Chile's largest publishing house, created a new venue for sports journalists. The magazine featured full-page photographs of matches and lengthy interviews with players, heightening their profile throughout the country. Olympic silver medalist Manuel Plaza was among the first to experience this idol status. Plaza, a long-distance runner, sold newspapers on the streets of Santiago for a living.[102] As an adolescent, he began running for a small club named Atlético Centenario. Plaza changed clubs several times, though he denied being offered money by any of the clubs he represented. This is difficult to believe, given his dire economic circumstances. Plaza's fans boasted that "one of their own" had risen to the top of track and field. When Congress awarded Plaza a house for his success in international competition, photographs of his family were featured in the press for weeks. Plaza became a hero for working-class youth, who named clubs in his honor and swapped stories of meeting him.[103]

TROUBLE IN SPARTA: THE BIRTH OF THE BARRA

Just as Santiago football fans thwarted the attempts of the Ibáñez government to control social events in the city, they dashed the patriarchs' hopes of preserving football as they remembered it. For the older generation, the presence of rowdy fans defeated the educational mission of sports. A director of the elite club Santiago FC explained that indifference toward the score of a match showed a true love for sport. He boasted that players from his club "compete without ridiculous disappointment when they do not win and without pretentious vanity when success has crowned their efforts."[104] For Santiago FC's directors, control over emotions and stoicism in the face of defeat demonstrated a properly developed sportsmanship. These traits were central to their ideal of masculine comportment and the exercise of citizenship. Thus, too much emotion betrayed a lack of control.

A handful of clubs during the 1920s changed spectatorship in Santiago by constructing stadiums that held more than ten thousand spectators. Only a few, with bases in immigrant communities and the military, had the financial prosperity to acquire the capital for such projects. For example, Club Unión Española built Estadio Santa Laura in May 1923. It seated 22,000 people, dwarfing the capacity of other stadiums.[105] In 1928, Club Audax Italiano opened Estadio Italiano close to its Spanish rivals, which increased local interest in their matches. Stadiums brought together a larger number of spectators than any other forum. They provided spectators with a visual representation of themselves collected as a public. Stadium goers reported feeling excited and disconcerted at once. Stadiums produced a physical manifestation of the communities that sports fans already imagined themselves as belonging to. Stadium goers were brought together by similar interests and shared an experience shaped by unfolding events. They created participatory norms within the stadium, clapping, whistling, selling, fighting, singing, socializing, and so on.

Sports spectatorship joined an array of new leisure activities that fueled one another's popularity. Early cinema, for instance, contributed to an enthusiasm for sports and to making athletes into stars. Movie houses featured films of sports events, especially Chilean boxers' matches abroad. Boxing gained a wide following during this period, and many new clubs appeared throughout the country; however, the level of participation never approached that for football. As in the United States in this period, the cinema expanded women's options as spectators. Whereas some sporting events were considered too rowdy for women, there were less social restrictions on their attendance at movies. In addition, movies drew upon images of women in the city, becoming a way for audiences to understand changing gender roles.[106]

There existed a strong tension within sports circles between rhetorically encouraging women's participation in sports and maintaining practices that excluded them. The notion that gender roles were in the process of a major revision was pervasive in the 1920s. Historians have shown that women's increased visibility in new types of labor, especially manufacturing, prompted some groups to reinforce the female connection to the domestic sphere.[107] In supporting protective labor legislation, male-dominated trade unions, the Catholic Church, and elite charities created images of working-class women as victims of exploitative employers. While feminists looked skeptically upon the characterization of this decade as a watershed for women's equality, middle- and upper-class sportsmen believed that women's opportunities had expanded. They commented that sports lagged behind politics and labor as a means of women's advancement. One sportsman lamented, "While, in this era, women have independence and freedom of action, they have not managed to escape the ridiculous but strong claws of prejudice," which was "incubated by ignorance or antiquated customs."[108] Sportswriters who encouraged women's sports often explained that their participation was a benchmark of the country's modernity. Other articles advocated women's sports, especially tennis and cycling, but emphasized that boxing and wrestling were definitely not appropriate.[109] Alongside the formal advocacy of women's physical education, sportswriters and directors continued to ridicule and objectify women interested in sports. Regular cartoons lampooned women's vanity and lack of sports knowledge. Beginning in 1928, *Los Sports* began to publish full-page photographs of topless women in sporting activities. These features made a clear statement that men composed the magazine's readership and that sportswomen were objects to be gawked at. In addition, the perceived threat of violence at football matches would have discouraged participation by some women, especially those with children, in the sport.

While fans' disruptive behavior was not necessarily motivated by politics, social disorder was politically charged during the Ibáñez regime. The government dispatched the Carabineros to monitor fans.[110] The Carabineros confronted a new actor in football, one that disrupted any notion of public order, the *barra*. Barras, organized groups of fanatics, emerged in football matches around the late 1910s.[111] Early barras formed in the neighborhoods surrounding stadiums, such as Unión Española's Santa Laura. During matches, the *barristas* chanted, brought placards, sang hymns, and dressed in support of their team. Barras followed their teams throughout the city, fighting with opposing fans and storming fields when unhappy with referees. The latter activity often affected the outcome of matches. One observer complained that because of the barra, "women and children stay away from the games."[112] Directors of clubs discouraged their members from affiliating with the barras, but often found that the boundaries blurred between the club and the barra. Aristocratic clubs such as Santiago FC complained about the barras to the Chilean Football Federation and the press. It threatened to stop playing clubs with strong barras, including Unión Española and Colo Colo.

Stadiums presented a problem for crowd control because of the quantity and exuberance of the fans. Ibáñez dispatched undercover Carabineros to monitor crowds during matches. Sportsmen and fans complained that these policemen made unfair arrests.[113] Clubs objected that Carabineros dampened the spirit of spectators. Fans delighted in "outing" the plainclothes police officers and ridiculing them. Violent confrontations between barristas and the police became commonplace. Players also participated in violent brawls with each other, referees, and fans. Certain clubs' barras, such as Colo Colo's, became notorious for their aggressive behavior. For example, in November 1928, a match between Colo Colo and a team that represented the city of Talca erupted into violence.[114] During the first minutes, both squads threatened the referees, and the crowd followed suit. The police rushed onto the field several times during the first half, but they were unable to prevent further violence. At the half, the intendant of Talca visited the locker room and advised players to refrain from playing the rest of the game. The police warned him that they could not control the fans or the players. The Talca team left the field for good four minutes into the second period. The following day, the general director of physical education, Lieutenant Osvaldo Kolbach, sent memos to the intendant of

Santiago and the Chilean Football Federation to urge that severe sanctions be levied against both clubs.[115]

Football fans expressed their antipathy toward the police and the Ibáñez government during matches. In 1923, the Carabineros built Estadio Policial (Police Stadium), which had a capacity of ten thousand spectators. Located in a central, working-class community, the stadium was meant to be a community center. The police offered neighbors the use of a pool, football fields, and other facilities.[116] Relations with the surrounding neighborhood soured in the late 1920s when the government used the police to increase repression, targeting leftist newspapers and workers' meetings. Newspapers reported that fans began to attend the stadium with the intent of ridiculing the police team, Brigada Central. Footballers from San Pablo, an area of intense police surveillance, noticed that their fans reacted extra violently when their clubs played the police squad. The popular football player Carvajal explained that Brigada Central violated the norms of football by using its members' authority against opposing clubs (for example, by arresting "drunken" fans of their opponents).[117] Other accounts concurred: "[Brigada Central] imposed force, the strongest law, winning the hatred of the public."[118] In 1928, Brigada Central played an anticipated match against the popular Colo Colo. Despite a heavy police presence, the crowd showered abuse on Brigada players. They cheered every misfortune of the policemen, insulted them, and threw whatever they could find onto the field.[119] Soon, the club limited its schedule and renamed the stadium Fort Mapocho.[120]

During the period of increased repression, working-class football clubs suffered harassment and surveillance. Ibáñez openly aired his suspicion that all types of civic organizations encouraged communist subversion. Moreover, the regime's attack on municipal power also hurt workers' sports clubs, which had formed mutually beneficial relationships with local authorities. In particular, police shut down the meetings of clubs affiliated with unions or mutual aid societies. For example, dozens of clubs that regularly used the offices of the Federation of Railroad Workers were forced to find other venues.[121] This persecution contrasted with the experiences of clubs that had ties to the military government, such as Green Cross or Badminton.

Leaders of working-class clubs criticized Ibáñez's failure to implement social reform, his authoritarian style of government, and his modernization projects. Dr. Carlos Aguirre, the president of the popular May 1st Club, openly opposed the military's intervention in cultural affairs. Aguirre stated to the press that he saw no benefit to sports from military intervention in the government.[122] Aguirre's worries for the future of worker's clubs under a military regime were quickly realized. Independent workers' clubs struggled with direct repression by the police as well as a lack of access to government agencies.[123] Their applications for legal recognition were either rejected or ignored. The intendant of Santiago closely monitored clubs' petitions to stay open later on holidays, serve alcohol in their restaurants, and be given building permits.[124] Workers complained that the police interfered in their meetings and searched members on the basis of fictitious noise complaints. To stave off bankruptcy and avoid police harassment, some clubs joined kindred organizations. For example, Arauco FC, of Providencia, which had played with the Workers' League for over fifteen years, left to become part of the mutual aid society called September 18.[125]

In May 1929, the general director of physical education, Lieutenant Kolbach, stripped the Chilean Football Federation of its legal status, or *personalidad jurídica*. He then replaced the elected directorate with one chosen by the government.[126] This act drew widespread criticism; even *Los Sports*, published by the conservative Zig-Zag, scoffed at the government's lack of respect for the electoral procedures of sports associations.[127] Outrage reached a higher pitch, though it was still gentle, when the government proposed a law to raise the tax on ticket prices to sporting events to more than 20 percent, which sportsmen interpreted as a direct attack on small neighborhood clubs.[128] When the Chilean Football Federation petitioned and protested, Kolbach responded with language that echoed the military's broader agenda: "Without question, one of the causes of the politics and anarchy that have disgracefully reigned in sporting institutions has been the excessive number of directors and their eagerness to occupy positions of the highest order, for which they have carried out true political campaigns."[129] Kolbach's justification for the government's intervention demonized politics and negotiation.

The military government aggressively promoted its vision of sports and society through routine conferences and lectures. Magazines such as *Los Sports* hardly had any choice but to publish many of these. One such lecture, entitled "The Twenty-two Commandments of Hygiene and Their Observance," delivered by police Lieutenant Armando Mandujano, provides insight into how the military government perceived the role of physical education.[130] Mandujano explained: "Physical education, as it is understood and practiced today, habituates men to action, to work together: men come together, they connect; social classes disappear and are more level, much more than through exclusively intellectual culture. All intellectual education is capable of aristocratizing [*aristocrazar*] the spirit; physical education democratizes it."[131] In popular cultural magazines, representatives of the military laid out their claims to being more democratic. As Mandujano's statement above indicates, the officers responsible for sports exhibited a strong streak of anti-intellectualism. While influenced by the corporatist approaches of their European counterparts, the military government was unable to bring football organizations into its fold.[132]

The military government's rhetorical support for physical education and the cultivation of "hard bodies" contrasted with its failure to complete stadiums and other sports projects. The education budget was doubled between 1925 and 1930, and the Ministry of Public Education promised to increase funds for physical education further, but instructors complained that they saw little of the investment in their schools. Physical-education teachers and associations sought the help of military technocrats such as Major Alfredo Portales. Portales, the director of physical education, was typical of the young, middle-rank officers promoted during the Ibáñez regime. He had studied physical education in Europe and took a greater interest in the construction of gymnasiums like the ones he had observed in Sweden than the popular stadiums that sportsmen demanded. For Portales, physical education and sports were integral parts of military training. The regime created an entire department dedicated to the construction of stadiums and gymnasiums. However, few of Portales's projects materialized, a failure he blamed on financial constraints.[133] It appears likely that police and military athletics, particularly equestrian activities, absorbed much of the department's annual budget. In the area of physical education, marksmanship became mandatory in public schools, and the administration increased expenditures on guns and bullets. Representatives of the regime stressed that it was young men's civic duty to be able to shoot in order to defend the nation.[134]

NEW LEADERSHIP IN URBAN FOOTBALL (AND THE GOVERNMENT)

A new generation of middle- and working-class football directors kept football clubs thriving during the repression of the 1920s and the economic downturn of the early 1930s. These directors were less involved with reform movements and more rooted in neighborhoods and unions than their predecessors. In Santiago, the era of the workers' football club led by a patron–father figure came to an end. Community leaders such as Carlos Aguirre from the 1st of May Club took leadership positions in clubs and umbrella organizations. Leaders like Aguirre placed little stock in the potential of football to instill self-discipline. Aguirre expressed skepticism about the notion that football curbed alcoholism, pointing out that the players looked forward to drinking after a match, win or lose.[135] One physical-education teacher remarked, "They celebrate or cry by sucking down alcohol. Drunken sportsmen in the middle of their stupor look like all drunks, and go to the brothel . . . where they surely leave with tuberculosis or some gangrenous disease."[136]

The activities of football organizations during the economic crisis increased their importance in communities. Neighborhood sports clubs recruited unemployed men, temporarily waiving their dues. Directors hoped that membership would lift their spirits and expand their social connections, which were vital to their obtaining new jobs. Hence, neighborhood clubs became centers where unemployed and underemployed men gossiped, read the news, and played football. Neighborhood clubs held weekly benefit matches to raise funds for neighborhood food cooperatives, artisan unions, and impoverished families.[137] Not only barrio clubs but also high-profile football teams such as Colo Colo arranged fund-raisers.[138] For instance, Colo Colo played a combined team from the South to raise funds for the mutual aid society of printers, the Sociedad Unión de Tipógrafos.[139] Other footballers played benefit matches for themselves. In September 1931, the Liverpool Wanderers announced that they would play a group of unemployed workers from the North. The team from the North consisted "of players who have been working in the nitrate region but currently are unemployed, and for this reason, they take the greatest interest in this undertaking, since the admissions will go to their benefit."[140]

During the economic crisis, sports figured low on the agenda of labor unions and leftist parties. They did, however, formulate criticisms of the state of workers' health, which circulated among sports clubs. *La Justicia* blamed capitalists for encouraging alcoholism among workers in order to maintain a steady supply of "automatons, not thinking men."[141] The Communist Party formed its own version of the Boy Scouts, the Pioneers, which attempted to channel workers' enthusiasm for sports and outdoor recreation into the party structure. The group hoped to counteract the tendency of football to reinforce patriotic chauvinism rather than class or political solidarity. At the same time, leftist papers frequently expressed their concern for national honor. For example, *La Justicia*'s writers breathed a sigh of relief when the Chilean Football Federation withdrew from the South American Cup of 1926. They described the federation's decision as "lofty and patriotic," since Argentina and Uruguay would likely have badly beaten the Chilean team.[142]

Football tournaments connected working-class players within certain industries that crossed national boundaries. Railroad companies encouraged these matches and offered prizes, free rail passes, and lenient work schedules to players. They arranged free transportation for football clubs, which enabled workers to travel to matches in other regions and abroad.[143] In the North, where the borders between Chile, Bolivia, and Peru were still contested, witnesses remarked that workers' football matches were uniquely amicable. In reference to a match played between Chilean and Bolivian train workers in 1930, one observer noted, "There are no words to describe the enthusiasm and high spirit of fraternity developed on that day. Our neighbors [Bolivian players], who have a high concept of sport, gave proof of their gentility in every respect during this competition, not only the sportsmen, but also the authorities and the people in general."[144] In a region with a history of xenophobic violence toward Bolivians, often encouraged by Chilean state officials, this type of cordiality was most unusual. Right-wing radicals who sought to counter such sentiments formed civic associations that harassed Peruvians and Bolivians. Patriotic leagues had been formed in the early 1910s and, despite moments of decline, were promoted by local officials. In 1926, buoyed by the military's assumption of power, the leagues began to form sports associations.[145] These sports clubs were active from the extreme north, in Tacna and Tarapacá, to Valparaíso; however they did not integrate into the local associations or the Chilean Football Federation.

In their criticism of sports, leftists reserved their harshest words for boxing. Boxing achieved widespread popularity in the 1920s, and clubs sprang up rapidly, particularly in the provincial cities.[146] An anarchist newspaper from the northern port city of Iquique complained that boxing and horse races completely occupied workers' thoughts and conversations. Worse yet, the boxers, almost always of working-class origins, were treated like horses forced to race around a track.[147] Another anarchist paper, *Verba Roja*, described boxers as "bestial."[148] It observed that during boxing matches, "patriotism, decayed and misused, revives . . . and retains its dominion over the spirit of the masses."[149] Leftist writers often compared sporting events to those held during Roman times, with worker-sportsmen as modern analogues of the gladiators. The chauffeurs' union of Valparaíso criticized the waste of workers' energy in sports, claiming that it could be better used in more noble causes, such as stopping the adulteration of food or challenging the exploitative system of labor.[150] The union assumed that workers would have been busily working toward revolutionary causes if they had not been engaged in more frivolous activities. Conspicuous cases of capitalist paternalism in sports provided easy ammunition for these arguments.[151]

THE ADOPTION OF PROFESSIONALISM

In 1931, amidst a financial crisis, a well-organized opposition movement ousted Carlos Ibáñez's government. Political parties and other civic associations that had experienced repression buoyed quickly. Football organizations canceled activities in order to participate in the general strikes, but otherwise continued the season as planned. Footballers held elections on time, organized new community projects, and played games as scheduled. Chilean Football Federation directors showed uneasiness about the coming shift in political power. They presented an ambitious proposal to Congress that would have shifted responsibility for distributing revenue from the Alcohol Laws (which had been earmarked for sports) from the government to sports organizations. Sportsmen reasoned that their organizations showed greater stability than the government. However, legislators considered the project "utopian" and quickly dismissed any arguments that a civic association could better manage such funds than the government.[152]

The unity of football organizations collapsed quickly thereafter over the question of professionalism. Many of the clubs that pushed professionalization had benefited from their ties with the dictatorship. By the late 1920s, directors of clubs such as Colo Colo used their access to the press and their influence among sportsmen to publicize arguments in favor of professionalism. The discourse in favor of professionalism stressed its connection with modernity, the economic necessity of contracts to keep players on teams, and the rights of consumers to quality entertainment. During an economic depression, the notion that sportsmen should play football only for the sake of playing found few supporters. The acceptance of professionalism reflected the legitimacy that efficiency, international trends, and scientific expertise had attained. If the Ibáñez regime had been discredited among directors of these upper-echelon clubs, it was because the government could not make good on its promises to pursue these values, not because the directors rejected the values themselves.

It was common knowledge that Santiago's top clubs practiced clandestine professionalism. Fernando Larraín, a director of both Colo Colo and Magallanes, admitted that by the mid-1920s, clubs that could pay players often did. Colo Colo's recruitment of provincial players during its tours raised eyebrows, but the federation did not take disciplinary action. Colo Colo called the federation's stance against professionalism elitist, since many of the best footballers could not afford to play for the national team. Directors cited the example of Guillermo Saavedra, who had missed the South American Cup of 1920 because of financial troubles.[153] Directors frequently cast their arguments in nationalist rhetoric. They denied being motivated by economic incentives, insisting that they wanted only to improve Chile's standing internationally. Chile's poor football performance abroad jeopardized its reputation as a progressive and strong country, according to these directors. In bars, clubs, and sports pages, professionalism became a topic of public debate. The pro-professional camp claimed to represent "realist" views. Its argument rested on the supposed inevitability of professionalism. Led by Carlos Concha, the assistant treasurer of the republic, this group portrayed the current system of surreptitious professionalism as morally damaging. He complained that clubs presented falsified books to the federation and put players in the position of having to lie.[154]

Arguments for professionalism revealed a new concern with spectators as consumers. They made analogies to the ways in which businesses operated. For example, Larraín claimed that professionalism was necessary to create a stable workforce of football players. Clubs needed to secure players with contracts as they would workers in order to provide high-quality entertainment.[155] Clubs addressed fans as consumers who had certain rights and expectations. Colo Colo's delegate to the Chilean Football Federation, Waldo Sanhueza, reasoned that clubs could use legal agreements to demand more from players.[156] According to Sanhueza, Chilean clubs would face difficulties retaining talented footballers once the Argentine professional league consolidated (it had been created in 1931).[157] This argument was completely disingenuous, for immediately upon the sanctioning of professionalism, Sanhueza traveled to Argentina to scout players.

A group of directors, chiefly from either the most elite clubs or working-class clubs, strongly opposed professionalism. They warned that players would lose a sense of civic duty. A few players turned down professional contracts, in particular those who had well-paying or fulfilling work already. The popular *colocolino* (as players from Colo Colo were called) Eduardo Schneeberger rejected professionalism on the basis that it diminished camaraderie among players and the sense of belonging to a club.[158] In addition, the time professional play required would have infringed upon his duties in the Ministry of Land and Colonization. Opponents of professionalism claimed that it was not economically viable for even the most stable clubs. Taking into account the depressed economy and the clubs' internal finances, Jorge Bate, the president of Badminton's football club, warned that clubs lacked the financial capital to turn themselves into businesses. He worried that professionalism would lead to the death of many institutions that tried to turn professional. Bate also warned that salary expectations of players were impossibly high: "With the exception of Colo Colo, which has managed to put together some capital, and the Spanish and Italians, who have an economic base in the communities, the rest of the national clubs are gravely poor."[159] Colo Colo countered that any salary would be a considerable improvement for its players.[160] Bate's prediction proved accurate: except for a few standouts, players did not earn enough to dedicate themselves entirely to football until nearly a decade after professionalism began.

Provincial and workers' clubs were afraid that professionalism would create a tiered system, pushing clubs of modest means further from the center of power within football. They predicted that professional clubs would wield greater influence in the federation, at the expense of amateurs. They viewed this possibility as the imposition of a less democratic system upon football, in which a few clubs would determine the fate of thousands of amateurs. To placate provincial associations, the first professional league included five teams from Santiago, three from Valparaíso, one from Concepción, and one from Talca. They excluded the North entirely because of doubts about the depressed economy in the region. This configuration was short-lived. In June 1933, after months of squabbling, eight teams, all from Santiago, formed the first professional league. Only one, Morning Star, came from the Workers' League (and this was only partly true, since Morning Star was a merger between Small Star, a club from the Workers' League, and Santiago Morning, from the Metropolitan League).[161] Despite the debates among players over professionalism, the public responded with unabashed enthusiasm. The first professional games were well attended, and occurred without any form of protest by spectators over the adoption of professionalism.[162] Almost immediately, the grave predictions of amateur leaders became reality. Professionals sought to free themselves from the influence of amateurs in the Chilean Football Federation. To prevent a rift among footballers, the federation was forced to grant concessions to the professional league in exchange for its financial contributions.

Working- and middle-class clubs flourished at the community level, but found it increasingly difficult to survive in competition with the top echelon of clubs. In 1933, at the start of sanctioned professionalism, the Workers' League complained that its lack of stadiums, access to media, and connections to state agencies was pushing it to the brink of dissolution. It remained one of Santiago's largest football leagues and yet could not count on a single stadium to host matches. Professionalism divided football into two distinct camps. It pitted powerful businessmen who directed large clubs and had connections to the expanding state apparatus against provincial, barrio, and elite clubs. Workers' clubs, which would come to dominate amateur football, pinned their hopes for governmental support on local politicians. Professional clubs drifted between parties that held power, particularly connecting with the Radicals. Older elite clubs moved their headquarters to fancy neighborhoods in eastern Santiago, where their members lived. Like working-class amateurs, they remained skeptical of, and at times hostile to, the idea that professionalism served national interests.

By the end of the 1920s, football had become part of a popular culture that expanded with successive waves of migrants and new technologies. Furthermore, clubs played a high-profile role in their communities. The popularity of sports, cinema, and music opened opportunities to create markets. Transnational corporations like Paramount Studios and entrepreneurial businessmen hoped to orient popular culture to these consumer markets. Amateur clubs, participatory and nonprofit, offered a social setting in which members could enjoy leisure activities. In stadiums, fans created rituals that confounded the military government's attempts at order. Clubs had been vehicles for integrating their members into city politics, but they struggled during the Ibáñez years, when elected municipal governments were shut down, civic associations repressed, and political parties restricted. Despite government harassment and a modernization program that isolated independent clubs, football clubs broadened their role in their neighborhoods, helped integrate migrants into urban life, deepened their ties to unions, and provided opportunities to express political criticisms. The longtime relationships between political parties and football clubs hindered the sport's co-optation by the Ibáñez regime. Ibáñez and his supporters founded their own football organizations, such as the Football Association of Providencia, to disseminate their views. In particular, they argued that authoritarianism could provide reform more efficiently than parliamentary politics. Clubs at odds with the military regime stressed both its inability to fulfill its reformist promises and its antidemocratic nature. The struggle among football clubs over what constituted democratic practice continued during the construction of the National Stadium in the 1930s.

"THE WHITE ELEPHANT"

*The National Stadium, Populism, and
the Popular Front, 1933–1942*

3

At the inauguration of the National Stadium in December 1938, thousands of Chileans experienced a massive spectacle for the first time. Arturo Alessandri imagined the stadium as his administration's final triumph. Following the downfall of Carlos Ibáñez and the subsequent political turmoil, Alessandri had been reelected to the presidency in 1932. After another controversial term in office, he hoped the inauguration of the stadium would symbolize his legacy as a man of the people. To his dismay, players paraded toward the government's section with protest placards, armbands, and leftist chants. The booing and hissing of the crowd, approximately sixty-five thousand people, drowned out his speech. This chapter argues that the building of the National Stadium signified a crucial turning point in Chile in the relationship between popular culture, civic associations, and politics. The populist style that had worked for Alessandri in 1920 no longer swayed audiences in 1938, because of widespread discontent with the practices of his administration. A critical public emerged in the debates over the National Stadium.[1] In café discussions as well as in newspapers and neighborhood petitions, sports fans and organizers denounced state agencies as corrupt and inefficient. Sports club members condemned Alessandri's support of the stadium as a patently "populist" move.

By supporting new political coalitions, football clubs of the 1930s rejected the ideal of the sportsman removed from politics. Their hostility to Alessandri was equaled by their enthusiasm for the Popular Front. Center-left parties and labor organizations formed the Popular Front in 1936 as a response to the international threat of fascism as well as to the Comintern's strategies to address it. The centrist Radicals dominated the coalition, although they derived vital support from their promises to include Democrats, Socialists, and Communists in their government.

Popular Front propaganda positioned the coalition as the only means of maintaining Chilean democracy. The front's candidate, Pedro Aguirre Cerda, won the election just two months before the stadium's inauguration. Amateur footballers linked the Popular Front's rhetoric against the entrenched oligarchy to their own criticisms of the materialism and bullish power of the professional league.[2] Clubs participated in shaping Popular Front projects that they envisioned would provide healthy recreation in working- and middle-class communities.

Historical scholarship has been divided on the nature of the relationship between Popular Front governments and the working class. An important group of historians has argued that Popular Front governments attempted to co-opt working-class radicalism.[3] These studies demonstrate that the Popular Front—often referred to as Popular Fronts in recognition of their distinct administrations—created their programs in a manner that excluded women, the indigent, and agricultural workers. Most of this literature focuses on political parties, state agencies, and unions as the mediators between the Popular Front governments and workers. Often, the analysis takes a top-down perspective. This chapter looks at this relationship from the vantage point of civic associations, which, I argue, shaped participants' views on the coalition. Admittedly, this analysis focuses on a mostly urban perspective. The ways in which the first two popular front governments, led by Aguirre (1938–1941) and Juan Antonio Ríos (1942–1946), mobilized popular culture to promote their policies became a template for future political coalitions, especially the Popular Unity government of Salvador Allende (1970–1973). The tendency of the Radicals to promote increasingly conservative policies, which reached its apex with Gabriel González Videla's prohibition of the Communist Party in 1948, alienated many of the grassroots organizations that it needed in order to implement programs at the local level.

The Popular Front has been characterized as populist in reference to its attempts to mobilize broad sectors of the population around a nationalist and proindustrialist platform. The utility of the term "populism" has been much debated among social scientists, but its persistent presence in the secondary and primary literature makes it a difficult concept to avoid.[4] As the historian Alan Knight summarized, "Pronounced dead, buried, unlamented, with a stake through the heart, populism returns, like the living dead of Latin American politics, to haunt the sentient world, undeterred by the bright dawn of democracy and neoliberalism."[5] For Knight, populism can be described as a political style rather than an ideology, one that makes claims to a special rapport with "the people" and creates an "us and them" discourse. Populist programs tend to be reformist rather than revolutionary, and are assumed to be urban, although this has not always been the case. In the 1960s and 1970s, the social scientists Gino Germani and Ernesto Laclau identified a rough pattern in which populism emerges as a confrontational force, only to become institutionalized and dependent on state patronage, as happened with Peronism in Argentina and Cardenism in Mexico.[6] In the case of Chile, populist movements were muted by the gradual incorporation of working-class sectors into political parties and the electorate as well as by strong party identifications.

Popular culture usually lurks in these analyses as a handmaiden of populism. Especially in reference to European populist-fascist governments, popular culture appears as a necessary precursor of demagoguery. However, most of these studies spend little time exploring the relationship between politics and popular culture or demonstrating that it is an important piece of populism.[7] If, as Laclau claimed, "a class is hegemonic not so much to the extent that it is able to impose a uniform conception of the world on the rest of society, but to the extent that it can articulate different visions of the world in such a way that their potential antagonism is neutralized," popular culture must play some role in shaping those "visions of the world."[8] Mass culture emerged in the 1920s, reshaping and disseminating local popular culture through new technologies like the radio and print media. In the 1930s, civic associations mediated the relationship between populist politics and mass culture. This chapter argues that the actions of these civic associations, along with strong party affiliations, militated against the type of "one-man" populism that Ibáñez and Alessandri ultimately failed to establish. This contrasted sharply with the role of football in neighboring countries, most notably Argentina.[9]

THE STADIUM CAMPAIGN AND CONGRESSIONAL DEBATES

The campaign for a national stadium began with football clubs' first demands to Congress in 1909 and came to fruition in 1938. As the previous two chapters demonstrated, football clubs emerged rapidly in cities and developed increasing organizational capacity during these decades. Over the years the stadium acquired the nickname *elefante blanco*, or the "White Elephant." The nickname incorporated a variety of criticisms aimed at state officials in charge of the stadium project. The term expressed general skepticism about the project's size as well as the probability of its being built. It encompassed a critique of the government's financial improprieties, inefficiency, and clientelism. Club members gained a political education through the relationships they developed with political parties and politicians. In the 1910s and 1920s, the Radicals and middle-class professionals quickly incorporated support for football into reform projects, while right- and left-wing parties showed more ambivalence.

The rejuvenation of the Radical Party following the downfall of Carlos Ibáñez in 1931 gave clubs with ties to the party greater access to political channels and public resources. Footballers continued their campaigns for a national stadium with renewed hope that the change in government would bring results. In the presidential campaign of 1932, the first following the dictatorship, sportsmen succeeded in making the stadium an issue of at least symbolic importance. The Radical candidate Juan Esteban Montero criticized the military junta as well as his opponent, Alessandri, for their failure to construct the stadium. He quoted veteran party boss Arancibia: "A million men physically strong are worth more to a nation, despite their lack of a broad intellectual culture, than a million sickly, rickety literary weaklings."[10] Esteban defeated Alessandri, but was displaced in a brief Socialist coup led by military officer Marmaduke Grove. In 1932, Alessandri won the presidency again, on the promise of restoring civilian rule and constitutionality.

The adoption of professionalism in 1933 created a chasm between amateurs, who hoped the stadium would serve the need for physical education, and the professionals, who hoped that their matches would take priority. The process of professionalization increased and concentrated revenues for the Chilean Football Federation. This supported football clubs' efforts to lobby the government for the stadium. In addition to lobbying efforts at the national level, amateur clubs worked with other civic associations to garner the support of local authorities. Footballers used examples of European governments that had invested in sport to convince Alessandri of the stadium's importance for progress, nationalism, and modernization. In 1934, his administration began to push Congress for budgetary approval of the stadium project.

Despite the popularity of the project, many congressmen hesitated to support the stadium's construction. Provincial congressmen questioned the national character of a stadium that seemed to benefit Santiago alone. Like their counterparts in Santiago and Valparaíso, football clubs in cities like Iquique and Valdivia acted as powerful lobbying groups that actively participated in local politics.[11] Their deputies struggled to include benefits for sports in their jurisdictions within the budget for the national stadium. Other legislators argued that a stadium should not be built until the government funded better educational facilities. Whereas Deputy Arancibia had envisioned a harmonious, in fact necessary, relationship between citizenship and sports in the 1910s, some congressmen viewed them as practically antagonistic. In addition, funding the stadium would limit the availability of funds for sports facilities that could encourage exercise in places beyond the capital.

The Chilean Football Federation drew upon sexist stereotypes to caricature those who fought for educational funding as maternal men who would nurture Chileans into effeminacy. Their delegates belittled traits they associated with women, like sensitivity, as unnecessary and potentially detrimental to the development of civic virtues.[12] When describing the public benefits of stadiums, the federation assumed that men would be the primary beneficiaries. The stadiums already operational in Santiago served as sites for the performance of masculinity and sociability. Women entered the stadiums as vendors and fans, but the attractions were exclusively male in character. The pro-stadium legislators emphasized that sports developed masculine traits, including independence, initiative, and vigor, essential qualities for the ideal citizen.[13]

The Radical congressman and future president Juan Antonio Ríos led the congressional group that criticized the cost of the stadium in light of the scarce funds allotted to education. Ríos pointed out that the provinces lacked enough schools, since many had been closed for health violations. The emphasis on education, presented by Ríos, remained a mainstay of the Radical Party, whose slogan in the coming election would be, "To govern is to educate." Pro-stadium sportsmen criticized Ríos for what they considered his elitism.[14] Ríos accused congressmen of collaborating with sports clubs in a smear campaign against him. Furthermore, he complained that football clubs unfairly influenced politicians with promises to garner votes for their campaigns. Ríos portrayed himself as a voice for primary-school students who could not participate in this political lobbying. After weeks of wrangling, congressmen snubbed Ríos and passed the legislation to fund the National Stadium as well as provincial ones.

The congressional debates sparked a wave of activity among sports clubs that hoped their neighborhood would house the stadium. The participation of clubs in these public discussions highlights how they offered members a vehicle for direct participation in politics. Deputies read petitions aloud in Congress, and their speeches reached the public through newspapers, sports magazines, word of mouth, and radio. Petitions from Maipú and Renca offer two examples of the collaboration between football clubs, municipal governments, and civic associations. They also show the organizational capabilities that these clubs brought to their communities. Both neighborhoods, though peripheral to the metropolitan area, were in the midst of rapid urbanization. The Municipality of Maipú, a working- and middle-class neighborhood southwest of central Santiago, sent its petition to Congress in 1935.[15] Written by a local football club and neighborhood association, the petition highlighted the history of Maipú as a historic battleground during the War of Independence. Club members felt that a stadium in their community would offer a lesson in patriotism to all visitors. In impressive detail, the citizens of Maipú planned the construction of museums and cultural centers dedicated to Chilean independence around the stadium. With a clear sense of pride, the petition argued that in the metropolitan area, Maipú had the most beautiful views, the best climate, and the highest quality of air. As a further incentive, the municipality offered to donate the land and construct a train station. Though the residents of Maipú had persuaded their own congressman of their case and echoed the rhetoric of prostadium politicians, Radicals dismissed their arguments as "all very poor."[16]

Football clubs in Renca, northwest of the city's center, also lobbied for the stadium. President Sanfuentes had placed the first stone of a proposed national stadium in Renca in 1916 on land donated by a wealthy member of the National Sports Federation. Nearly twenty years later, that stone remained unaccompanied. The Socialist congressman Emilio Zapata, acting as Renca's advocate in Congress, presented a petition from the mayor and sportsmen.[17] Zapata represented a younger generation of leftist politicians who took a greater interest in promoting popular culture. These politicians articulated a critique of class relations that stadium advocates from other political parties had not raised. Zapata accused congressmen of unjustly favoring the elite neighborhoods where they lived. Opposing congressmen stated that Renca's lack of urban services, such as paved roads, should eliminate it from consideration. Zapata responded that the project would provide the investment Renca needed to establish these services. He predicted that Renca would be a central location for workers, since they had been pushed toward the city's periphery. Zapata added that the workers' sports tradition in Renca would enrich the stadium project.[18] Club Estrella de Bulnes helped draft the petition to Congress and served as an example of this tradition. The club's social seat included a library, sports facilities, and a salon, attesting to its organizational sophistication. Apart from its relationship to Zapata and the Socialist Party, Estrella de Bulnes worked with other community leaders to form the Democratic Group of Renca, which presented a separate petition to Congress. This petition contained a thorough history of the congressional debates about the stadium since the 1910s and included lengthy quotations from the pertinent sessions. The petition testified to the skills of the clubs in Renca.[19]

LOCAL POLITICS, URBAN SPACE, AND NEIGHBORHOOD CLUBS

Football leaders who had boasted of their organizations' nonpartisanship faced serious challenges in the 1930s. The emergence of a mass public aggravated these tensions. As discussed in Chapter Two, football fans had created novel rituals and spectacles in newly constructed stadiums during the 1920s. Spectators recognized themselves as a group, and one with the right to expression. Crowds attacked police, referees, and undercover officers, often with the encouragement of players. Chants and hymns antagonized clubs identified as political or class antagonists. From the perspective of some footballers, the growing popularity of leftist parties within working-class football clubs eroded the "neutrality" and openness of football. They considered visits of Conservative or Liberal congressman to a club as occasions for moral lectures, whereas they defined appearances by Communists as "political." The emergence of a small but significant National Socialist Movement in Chile further polarized sportsmen along political lines.[20]

As their relationships with political parties deepened, football club members began to connect their conflicts over public space to their political struggles. The troubles of Club Gladiadores, part of the Democratic Youth of Santiago, illustrate this process.[21] During the 1935 football season, the Gladiadores played a couple of times in Vitacura, a public field in a wealthy neighborhood of the same name. Clubs from all parts of Santiago used the field because of its proximity to transportation routes. On their third visit, the caretaker informed the Gladiadores that they could no longer use the field. The caretaker insinuated that his bosses disapproved of the club's affiliation with the Democratic Party.[22] After the incident, the Gladiadores discovered that other teams with bases in unions and political parties had been denied access to the field. They sent a letter of complaint to the local newspaper and also brought the issue to the Congress of Democratic Youth in November 1935. The young men of Gladiadores warned that these exclusionary practices would drive working-class youth from sports activities to the taverns. In addition, this injustice reflected a larger problem: the elite felt free to limit access to public spaces. With the collaboration of Councilman Guillermo Martínez and the Democratic Party, the Gladiadores acquired their own fields near the city's center. Martínez contributed municipal land and the materials for club members to build bleachers and locker rooms. The Gladiadores held a celebratory barbecue for the neighborhood with wine, meat, and empanadas.[23] This incident sheds light on the creation and re-creation of political difference that entered into daily social interactions.

Urban dwellers, like the club members of Gladiadores, witnessed the class boundaries of Santiago being redrawn. Commercial and administrative business began to dominate Santiago's center during the 1930s. The population flowed in several directions: the middle and working classes moved directly south (to San Miguel), north (to Conchalí and Renca), and west (to Quinta Normal and Barrancas/Pudahuel), while the upper-middle and upper classes moved east (to Providencia, Las Condes, and Ñuñoa). Housing, food, and other goods were more affordable outside the city's center.[24] Expanded urban transportation facilitated these demographic shifts. Despite the improvement of city utilities, most working- and middle-class communities lived without basic services. The creation of parks, sports fields, and other green spaces made the neighborhoods to the east of Santiago more attractive. For example, the extension of Parque Forrestal to the east beautified the route between Santiago's center and Providencia. Other neighborhoods had considerably less success in creating spaces for public recreation. The southern and western neighborhoods became increasingly strong bases of electoral support for the Popular Front.[25] Civic associations in these areas hoped the coalition would provide support for their efforts to build community infrastructure.

Neighborhood football clubs worked with municipalities, which had been rejuvenated since the end of the Ibáñez regime. Clubs with ties to centrist or leftist parties experienced less police harassment and surveillance than they had during the dictatorship. Furthermore, local media and business conditions had improved considerably since the early days of the Great Depression. As the city's growth pushed workers to the outskirts of Santiago, football clubs joined with other civic groups to obtain basic services. Clubs in these areas supported campaigns for drinking water, electricity, and paved roads. In turn, community leaders encouraged residents to support football clubs, which they saw as essential to building a safe, prosperous neighborhood. Footballers saw their clubs as bridges connecting distinct social groups. Residents of the neighborhood La Florida expected their football clubs to act as community organizers. La Florida was an agricultural community on the outskirts of southern Santiago. Residents arrived from urban areas of Santiago complained that La Florida lacked community activity. The local newspaper chastised football clubs for languishing and offered to help rejuvenate interest in them.[26] *La Voz de La Florida* publicized the events of local sports clubs and increased communication between clubs by giving directors space in the paper.

The experience of La Florida's Bellavista Football Club illustrates the importance of internal club practices and a club's role in the community. Furthermore, it highlights the earnest approach of members to their club. In 1937, the club suffered a crisis in leadership.[27] Club members of Bellavista worked a rigid agricultural schedule, with only Sundays and holidays free from work. The club treasurer, José Ginesta, collected dues either at meetings or around the football field during matches. Members accused Ginesta of failing to collect dues and accused the entire directorship of lax governance. The lack of revenue caused the club's dues to the Football Association of Santiago to fall into arrears. Concerned members consulted the statutes, which stipulated that a notarized letter from twenty members could force the president to resign. With the help of *La Voz de La Florida*, members publicized their petition to the football association. The newly elected secretary asked, "Are we not within the logic and duty of sportsmen to defend our beloved institution, the only place to play sports in this village, with the express mission of forming robust, vigorous, and resilient young men who will have the virility and capability to face all possible duties?"[28] The members' efforts showed their dedication to procedure and their affection for their club.

Neighborhood newspapers and bulletins show the degree of marginalization that women experienced in relation to local football clubs. Women collaborated with clubs in campaigns to equip their communities with public services, but did so through local parishes and other neighborhood associations, such as food cooperatives. Women's participation in neighborhood football clubs was frequently limited to family picnics, booster activities, and contests for things such as "Queen of the Spring Festival." In clubs such as Bellavista of La Florida, that particular competition operated as a mini beauty pageant in which the club members evaluated young women's beauty, homemaking attributes, and feminine qualities. These contests, which varied slightly, were popular among politically connected football clubs also. For example, the Democratic-affiliated Gladiadores elected a "Compañera Democrática," or Democratic Companion, instead of a queen; however, the evaluations of the women were based on the same criteria. The spring queen reigned during the season's dances and parades and kicked the first ball to open the football season.[29] While a few professional clubs formed women's sports sections in the 1930s, neighborhood clubs did not make significant efforts to recruit women. Instead, clubs included women in their activities when their attention would reinforce the performance of masculinity. Having the prettiest beauty queen or attracting a large female audience at matches added to the prestige of clubs. The public discourse around stadiums, the role of clubs in communities, and the government's actions was one assumed to occur exclusively among men.

In La Florida, clubs like Bellavista served as forums for discussions of governmental policies on sports. Debates over the construction of the National Stadium often treated the actions of the national and municipal governments similarly. At times, sportsmen in La Florida criticized the municipality for failing to build stadiums. They argued that the local and national governments were obligated to provide workers with access to sports facilities.[30] Furthermore, they argued that state intervention was not only obligatory but also necessary to ensure equal access to resources.

A small but significant minority of sportsmen in La Florida felt that local football clubs (including Bellavista) had become too political and should depend less on parties for resources. Their editorials accused these clubs of violating a set of "universal values" to which all true sportsmen adhered. These critics claimed that the political tendencies of clubs had begun to sully the "sacred terrain" of football.[31] The sanctity of football for these sportsmen rested on its universal appeal and ability to unite all men.

Club members criticized the state's presence in football when it meant police intervention. For example, the directors of Bellavista sent a letter to the local paper, the mayor's office, and the police department to complain about the police presence at a match between two La Florida clubs. The footballers noted that the teams were known for their clean play, and so the police presence was unnecessary. Spectators also protested that the assistant chief of police attended the match in uniform, which they found intimidating.[32] Club members assumed that their request to serve alcoholic drinks had prompted the attendance of the authorities. They defended

drinking during football matches as a perfectly normal part of football culture. They served alcohol, along with snacks, as part of fund-raising efforts.
Fans also signed the letters expressing discomfort with the presence of the
authorities.[33] While the directors of Bellavista and their fans viewed the
violence at matches as not rising to a level that required police interference,
it does not mean that violence was rare. Indeed, it was a common feature of
neighborhood matches. During a match between hacienda workers from
Deportiva Tarapacá and La Pintana in La Florida, fans threatened players
from both sides until they left the field. Fans claimed that Club La Pintana
had abused referees so badly that the team had difficulty finding any to officiate its matches.[34] Residents clearly preferred to work out their problems
without interference from authorities.

STADIUM CONSTRUCTION, PROFESSIONALS, AND THE CRITICS

Despite the rancorous debates over the National Stadium in the football
community and Congress, Alessandri remained confident of the popularity of the project. He had appointed a commission to oversee the stadium's
construction even before congressmen voted on the budget. Alessandri

FIGURE 3.1.   The National Stadium. Image courtesy of Chiledeportes, Santiago.

chose commission members from the Liberal Party, various ministries, and his own family (his nephew Guillermo Alessandri). Footballers drew parallels between Alessandri's authoritarian decisions regarding the National Stadium and his corrupt political practices more generally. Frustrated with the seemingly endless discussions of where to locate the stadium, Alessandri issued an executive order in January 1937 that decreed the site would be in Ñuñoa, directly adjacent to Alessandri family property (administered by Guillermo). Abruptly, stadium construction began the following month. Alessandri disappointed many sports and neighborhood organizations whose campaigns to house the stadium went back decades. Clubs complained that Ñuñoa had never been proposed in Congress and that Alessandri passed up choices accessible to the popular classes, such as Parque Cousiño or Quinta Normal.[35] Alessandri's decision to build on the property, named Lo Valdivieso, shocked the amateur sports community, in part because it required the destruction of one of the biggest sports complexes at the time, Campos de Sport de Ñuñoa. The Pontifical Catholic University owned the complex, which provided students and local residents with football fields, boxing rings, and a pool.

The commission awarded design and construction contracts to political insiders, many of whom had been part of the technocrats employed by Carlos Ibáñez, which generated further accusations of corruption and clientelism.[36] The commission, predictably, chose a design by one of its own members, the architect Ricardo Müller Hess. Müller had been a leader in his field, helping organize Chile's first National Congress of Architecture and Urbanism, in 1934, at a time when the subject of urban planning was taking on new importance. In addition, Müller had extensive experience in sports. He led the track and field delegation at the Olympics in Amsterdam in 1928 and in Berlin in 1936, where he personally surveyed the stadium constructed by Adolf Hitler, which inspired his design for Chile's National Stadium. Müller provided an efficient bridge between the architectural community, the government's commission, and sports organizations.

In addition to Müller, the architectural team included Aníbal Fuenteabla, a longtime participant in and patron of amateur football.[37] Fuentealba served as the director of the Badminton football club, a professional team with high-ranking political and military connections. Both Fuentealba and Müller belonged to the young professional class that had benefited from state patronage during the Ibáñez administration and continued to do so during Alessandri's second term. The committee chose the construction firm of Salinas and Fabres for the project. A top executive of the firm,

Claudio Vicuña Ossa, also served as the president of the professional football league.[38] These appointments fueled charges that committee members and their friends would profit handsomely from the stadium project.

Müller's design reflected aspirations for an orderly, well-planned city. He sought to invoke the monumental feeling of Berlin's Olympic Stadium, placing the seating back from the center.[39] The location of the stadium, in Ñuñoa, required the construction of large avenues to connect the stadium to the city's center. The neighborhood was distant from downtown. This allowed the stadium to become a world of its own, with a post office, telegraph lines, conference rooms, a library, a restaurant, an amphitheatre, and a tearoom. Despite growing disenchantment with Hitler's government, many Chileans took pride in a stadium modeled after one in Germany, which they associated with progress and modernity. Teams of engineers and architects became part of the government's entourage in Alessandri's last years. As with other massive urban projects, the National Stadium entailed the demolition of working-class neighborhoods. The government notified several thousand residents that they would have to abandon their homes, promising that plans to relocate them would be forthcoming.

As details of the stadium's construction unfolded, public criticism of the project became intertwined with disappointment in professionalism. From the selection of the commission to the scheduling of the stadium's first events, it became clear that professional clubs would have the greatest access to the stadium. The amateur association suggested that building smaller stadiums throughout Chile would be a better use of public funds and that professional clubs should be left to finance their own large venues. Professional clubs insisted that the national diffusion of football was their primary concern. Amateurs scoffed at this, given the number of foreign players in the professional ranks. In addition, most professional clubs had stopped investing in their youth leagues, signaling their plans to continue to import players, despite promises that these recruitments were only temporary. Government agencies in charge of sports found themselves embroiled in regular disputes between amateurs and professionals for resources. The relationship between amateurs and professionals worsened when the professional league passed a rule in 1937 that forbade their clubs from playing amateurs. Professional directors claimed that amateurs played too violently and that they could not afford the potential injuries to their players. In the discussions leading up to the passage of this rule, professional leaders portrayed amateur clubs as disorderly places of drinking and brawling.[40] Professional directors requested that the minister of labor inspect the legality of amateur sports clubs' headquarters and applications for government recognition. Amateurs felt that the professional directors exaggerated the violence in their leagues and, in fact, were afraid to lose to amateurs. Amateur directors challenged the masculinity of professionals, characterizing their fear of getting hurt as evidence they were delicate and effeminate.

Professional clubs used their financial clout to control the Chilean Football Federation. As professionalism became more commercial, amateur clubs leveled greater criticisms at the profit-driven clubs, especially Colo Colo. In 1936, an anti-barra formed in response to Colo Colo's dominance in the league. These antifans followed Colo Colo to each game and rooted against it. They petitioned other football clubs to refuse to play matches against it, though given Colo Colo's popularity, few teams were willing to do so.[41] Amateurs, particularly from the working class, began calling themselves "true" sportsmen in order to distinguish themselves from professionals. Some placed a positive value on their lack of resources, which they saw as a source of creativity. The talented amateur footballer Victor Alacchi, from Iquique, expressed this sentiment: "Professionalism does not attract me. I prefer to earn a living through my work and play for pleasure. . . . I think that professional players take a lot of care with their legs, and they do not shoot like the amateurs. They do not have the spirit or the enthusiasm of amateurs."[42] Alacchi complained that the federation unjustly chose only professionals for the national team.

Amateurs led the charge against the "White Elephant," as they nicknamed the stadium in conversations that took place in clubs, cafés, and bars. For many, the image of a white elephant represented the excessive expenditures of Alessandri's government in the construction of the stadium. The critics complained this expense was inexcusable, since Alessandri neglected to help working families. Alessandri's antioligarchic discourse during his 1919 campaign did not accompany an enduring commitment to change. During his second presidential term, he continued to repress labor and confer economic advantages on the elite. According to the sportswriter Jaime Drapkin, the term "white elephant" evoked a generalized critique of Alessandri's corrupt financial policies; it implied that Alessandri was a "spendthrift."[43] The famed football player Eduardo Símian concurred that "white elephant" referred to the excessive cost of the project and the government's continual expansion of its budget.[44] For the time, the amount of money spent on the National Stadium was enormous. Congress originally allotted three million pesos for construction; in the end, the materials alone cost twenty-three million pesos.[45] Star player Sergio Livingstone explained that the nickname meant "something that serves no purpose."[46] The popularity of the term came from its provocative imagery and its flexibility in signifying different things to different speakers. For his part, Alessandri interpreted the term as a reference to the stadium's majesty.

Critics of the government accused Alessandri of supporting the stadium only as an attempt to recover his popularity among the masses. Representatives of leftist parties drew comparisons between Alessandri and Benito Mussolini as leaders who used stadiums to provoke nationalist hysteria. Enthusiasm for the Popular Front among the working and middle classes intensified complaints about Alessandri's populist excess. The Radical Party–aligned newspaper *La Hora* asserted that the stadium did not "reflect the reality of a ragged and undernourished people who need to form hygienic habits and to have the right to fresh air and sun, far from the despicable hovels they rent from the government and the bourgeoisie."[47] On the eve of the stadium's inauguration, the Popular Front urged the public to remember Alessandri's violence against workers. Its members worried that the stadium would dazzle spectators and cause them to forget the abuses of Alessandri's government.[48] They likened the manner in which Alessandri built the stadium to the construction of the Colosseum in ancient Rome, and emphasized his antidemocratic character.[49] The Popular Front overestimated the capacity of Alessandri to woo sportsmen. After three decades of anticipation, amateurs were deflated by the manner in which the stadium was being constructed.

Disappointment with professionalism and the Alessandri administration strengthened the alliance between amateurs and the Popular Front parties. This shift reflected, at least in part, the inattention of the Liberal Party to amateur clubs. Radicals and, to a lesser extent, Socialists, Democrats, and Communists showed sympathy for amateurs who wanted the stadium to be a space for recreation, civic instruction, and physical education. The relationship between amateurs and center-left parties rested upon their shared hope for the construction of popular public spaces. Conservatives continued to garner many votes from the working and middle classes, but it was apparent that the Radical Party had increased its presence in cultural life by the 1930s. Even if Radical leaders came from affluent backgrounds, rhetorically they emphasized their role as political outsiders.

In contrast to amateurs, professional football clubs praised Alessandri's construction of the stadium as a crowning achievement. They focused on the nationalist sentiment the stadium inspired as well as on its similarity to those in other Latin American and European capitals. Professional directors declared that they would finally have a dignified place to play international matches. In turn, professional clubs emphasized their ability to generate revenue for the state through their use of the stadium.[50] Professionals argued that in this way, they would help support sports throughout Chile. While amateurs followed professional clubs intently and admired star athletes, they made clear distinctions between professionalism as a business and as a site of spectatorship.

THE ELECTIONS OF 1938 AND THE INAUGURATION

The elections of 1938 took place just two months before the inauguration of the National Stadium. The mainstream press prophesied an easy victory for Alessandri's handpicked replacement, his conservative minister of finance, Gustavo Ross. The Popular Front accused Ross of acting as an arm of the parasitic oligarchy. The Popular Front's campaign included a critique of class relations and promised better living conditions for workers, specifically for male breadwinners.[51] Various Popular Front candidates brought their message of a revitalized Chilean nation, one with greater industrial capacity and economic equity, to football clubs. The participating parties—the Democrats, Radicals, Communists, and Socialists, along with labor organizations—reached out to football clubs. Though the Conservatives and Liberals had fewer contacts in the clubs, they also appealed to sportsmen. They accused the Popular Front of fomenting Marxist agitation. Both sides tried to woo sportsmen with visits to matches, interviews with sports publications, and campaign promises of greater support for civic associations.

Gustavo Ross countered his reputation as a member of the oligarchy by pointing out that he played amateur football. He offered a photograph of his youth club to sports magazines such as *Crack*.[52] Just four days before the election, he granted the magazine an interview, which he hoped would prove the high priority he placed on sports. In addition, Ross signed a written declaration that promised he would, as president, create a Ministry of Sports. This far-fetched idea had circulated among sportsmen for decades, and in retrospect, it is difficult to believe that Ross genuinely meant to create this ministry. In his interview, Ross bemoaned Chilean football's failure to perform well in international tournaments and claimed that he would ensure that the national team acquired top trainers from abroad.[53] He appealed to Chileans' sense of national honor, presumably at stake in football matches. In neighborhoods with a significant Liberal Party presence, such as Providencia and Ñuñoa (where the stadium was being constructed), the party made great efforts to organize sportsmen around Ross. Ross attended several professional matches during the campaign; however, neither his party nor his close associates had the reach into the football community of the Popular Front parties.[54]

The Radical Party boss and longtime leader of the Football Association of Santiago, Héctor Arancibia, acted as a bridge between the Popular Front and football clubs. As president of the Popular Front, he defined the Radicals as a middle-class party that had united with workers to create a Chile that was not controlled by an "oligarchic caste."[55] His enthusiasm for sports and its civic benefits had changed little in the two decades since his first congressional speech in favor of the stadium. However, criticism of class inequalities now emerged more prominently in Arancibia's political discourse. In the 1938 campaign, he blamed the failure of Chilean football internationally on the fact that Chilean workers were "depressed and deformed from years of poverty and social pauperism."[56] Arancibia proposed the creation of local councils that would be responsible for the distribution of government monies for sport. Thus, the Popular Front promised amateurs greater financial autonomy. Arancibia argued that only amateurs should receive support from the state and that under no circumstances should professionals be given public resources.

Clubs, leagues, and associations organized a number of events in support of the Popular Front as the elections drew near.[57] Footballers who supported the Popular Front wrote editorials on sports during the campaign. They called the directors of professional clubs "dictators" and claimed that they were connected to the moneyed class, which rarely knew anything about football.[58] In turn, Popular Front publications heaped praise on amateur directors. Discussing the president of Patricio Lynch FC, Juan Goncalves, the Popular Front newspaper stated that he "demonstrate[d] an incredible enthusiasm for following the path of true proletarian culture and complete social democracy by teaching boys to understand their role as sportsmen and forming them into men who will create a better society."[59] The Popular Front urged club directors to set up libraries, artistic centers, and conference rooms.[60] Local clubs hardly needed encouragement; they had worked for years to establish these services.

The election of the Popular Front candidate Pedro Aguirre Cerda surprised many conservatives. After the elections, the amateur Football

Association of Santiago arranged for ten thousand affiliates to attend a ceremony in honor of the president-elect. Aguirre had been the vice president of the association at the time of his election. The association leaders remarked, "Aguirre Cerda leaves the directorate with lessons of discipline and culture."[61] The participation of Santiago's most popular clubs in events that supported the new president boosted his image among sportsmen. Well-respected football clubs affiliated with leftist political groups, such as May 1st and Eugenio Matte, lent public support to Aguirre, whom they affectionately called "the Indian." Nicknames gave an air of familiarity to the relationship between these workers' clubs and the Radical president. In substantiating Aguirre's claim to champion the working class, football clubs proved important allies. Their support did not necessarily translate into votes, but provided prestige and momentum. The working class's demonstration of support during Aguirre's process of congressional confirmation was central to his success at conveying this image.[62]

The preparation for the inauguration of the National Stadium sparked a flurry of activity in the sports community. Politicians from across the spectrum sought to capitalize on the event to create closer relationships with sports clubs.[63] National sports federations, in conjunction with Alessandri's committee, planned a week of inaugural events. They scheduled the opening day for December 3, 1938, with free admission to the public. The government distributed tickets through media, especially newspapers and radio, and sports clubs. The inaugural schedule promised to be truly spectacular. The ceremonies would open with a grand parade of legendary and contemporary sportsmen. Footballers would number about half of the estimated twelve thousand sportsmen in the parade. At the end of the parade, Alessandri and his ministers would give their speeches. Directly after the speeches would be gymnastic presentations, dancers, bands, scholastic athletes, and military processions of horses, motorcycles, and automobiles. Each day of the week after the inauguration would feature international competitions in a different sport.

The government decided that the day following the inauguration, Sunday, should feature an international football match. The professional league convinced the commission and pertinent ministries that one of their clubs should be given the prime slot. The government's committee decided upon Club Colo Colo despite protests from the current season's champion, Club Audax Italiano. The president of Colo Colo, Ernesto Blake, explained, "Colo Colo is traditionally the club of the *roto chileno* because it is seen as representative of his race and class, and because of this, he cries for its defeats and heartily celebrates its victories."[64] Literally meaning "broken," *roto* referred to peasants and workers. Although *roto* was used to praise Chilean soldiers and the poor, it was largely a derogatory term. Blake's statement was part of a campaign to produce an association between Colo Colo and workers, which Colo Colo often used to its marketing advantage. Colo Colo was Chile's most popular team, with high political connections and a strong barra to prove it. Its weekly radio show, *The Colo Colo Hour*, premiered earlier in 1938, with resounding success. Radio proved to be an intimate, powerful means to reach fans in their homes and local sports bars.

Audax Italiano's identity as an immigrant team, particularly one associated with fascism, worked against its bid to play the inaugural match.[65] After a failed coup attempt by Chile's National Socialist Movement, opponents of fascism became more vigilant in their efforts to stop its spread. Moreover, many politicians and fans felt uneasy about Audax's public support for Benito Mussolini. Directors of Audax had encouraged Alessandri to recognize Mussolini's "Italian Empire," which he did in 1936.[66] Despite their great performance on the field, Audax had to retire from many matches because of abusive crowds. Fans treated stadiums as sites where they could denounce clubs' affiliations with fascism. During the 1938 football season, Club Unión Española withdrew from the professional tournament because of public hostility.[67] Fans and other club members engaged in violent skirmishes with the supporters and players of both Audax and Unión Española, making specific reference to their political positions.

Amateurs took advantage of the publicity surrounding the inauguration of the stadium to call attention to their arguments with professionals. In November, the Football Association of Santiago, the country's largest amateur organization, announced to the Chilean Football Federation and the media that it would abstain from participating in the inaugural festivities. The amateurs announced that this abstention was in protest of the federation's negligence of youth football. Amateurs pointed out that even though support for youth clubs would produce better professional clubs in the future, these organizations received very little funding. The sixty-four clubs of the association scheduled to march in the parade unanimously agreed not to participate.[68] These clubs represented at least five thousand of the twelve thousand or so athletes scheduled to march, not to mention some of the most popular teams in Santiago. The federation, with help from the minister of education, quickly came up with the money promised to the youth leagues.[69]

The supervisory committee took steps to ensure the smooth procession of inaugural events in anticipation of problems with crowd control. Tensions ran high as Alessandri awaited the inauguration. In the waning months of his term, Alessandri's popularity had flagged. The week before the inauguration, the Chilean Football Federation held a meeting with clubs in order to forestall any chaotic or politically embarrassing events.[70] Only football clubs and associations specifically invited by the federation could participate in the inauguration. They were required to attend a dress rehearsal and several meetings with the federation's directors. The state newspaper *La Nación* ran stories that characterized Alessandri's visits to the stadium as bonding moments between the president and construction workers at the site.[71] Furthermore, the minister of education sent instructions to newspapers and to club headquarters to remind sportsmen of the parade's order. To encourage a disciplined parade, the Football Association of Santiago created prizes for its affiliates who made the best presentation. It hoped clubs would work on their uniforms, banners, organization, and the like.[72] Working-class clubs, particularly those from unions and neighborhood groups, participated in large numbers. The Club of Newsies (newspaper vendors) chose five hundred boxers, football players, and track stars to march in the parade, and railroad workers' clubs sent twice that many.[73]

The stadium brought together at least fifty thousand attendees in the stands and an additional twelve thousand in the parade (impossibly high figures in some newspapers reported that the crowd totaled one hundred thousand). This constituted perhaps the largest public spectacle in the nation's history. Sports fans waited with intense anticipation, offices closed early, and special transportation ran between the stadium and urban centers. Those who could not attend the match listened to the proceedings on the radio. Spectators reported feeling disconcerted, overwhelmed, and exhilarated by the size of the stadium. The number of attendees raised concerns about the structural stability of the stadium and the efficiency of the city's public transportation. The government's official paper, *La Nación*, urged transportation authorities to distribute a transportation map to the public and warn of long delays.[74] The newly constructed avenues that led the stadium as well as the sheer size of the complex awed many as they approached the inauguration.

Alessandri and his ministers used propaganda to instruct the audience in the proper forms of deference to the government during the inauguration. The official program gave credit to Alessandri for the construction of the stadium. It stated that his government had been "the constant and enthusiastic driving force behind the Stadium, in each moment, since the first steps were taken in August 1924."[75] By situating the origin of the stadium project in Alessandri's first term, the program erased the work of civic associations in intervening years. The program seamlessly connected Alessandri's first and second terms, as if the military intervention of the 1920s had never happened. Glowing captions accompanied the large black-and-white photographs of Alessandri on the program. The pamphlet emphasized that Alessandri had exclusively employed Chilean labor and materials in the stadium's construction. In essence, the inaugural program served as a storybook ending to Alessandri's presidency. The mainstream press published various histories of the stadium, usually disregarding the role of sportsmen, physical-education teachers, and neighborhood organizations in the project. *La Nación* claimed that in championing the stadium, Alessandri had won "the recognition of sportsmen throughout the country and all who understood the value of, and looked with sympathy upon, the defense and invigoration of the race."[76] Alessandri's version of the stadium's history had rendered those sportsmen passive recipients of his benevolence.

Many observers based their commentaries on the assumption that the stadium was a microcosm of the Chilean nation. By stressing the representativeness of the event, they overlooked the absence of provincial sportsmen, female athletes, and teams without legal recognition, all of whom found themselves unwelcome in the parade.[77] The inauguration of the National Stadium hardly included Valparaíso, Iquique, or Concepción, cities that boasted long-standing sporting traditions. In addition, Chileans outside Santiago who wanted to attend the event found it difficult to obtain tickets, which were distributed only in major cities, particularly Santiago and Valparaíso. The inauguration substantiated the concerns of provincial congressmen who feared that this would be a stadium for Santiago. A paltry example of participation from the provinces came from their military teams. For example, the minister of defense allowed players from a naval squad in Concepción to join the festivities, but the majority of teams without links to the government, political parties, or Santiago sports authorities sat out.[78]

On inauguration day, spectators began to arrive midmorning. By all accounts, the atmosphere in and around the stadium was electric. Just before the parade began at three, the loudspeakers announced the appearance of Alessandri and his ministers. To their surprise, the audience greeted them with boos, hisses, and loud insults that ended only as the national anthem began.[79] The crowd did not reserve its abuse for Alessandri alone. During the parade, the crowd ridiculed players from the football club of Guillermo Franke's construction firm. Franke had been at the center of a *cohecho*, or electoral bribe, scandal involving the conservative presidential candidate, Gustavo Ross.[80] Fans shouted insults, whistled, and threw food at the club members, criticizing their association with Ross.

In the first moments of the ceremony, spectators showered support on Club Deportivo Eugenio Matte. Amateur sportsmen from Eugenio Matte received thunderous applause as they approached Alessandri's podium with their fists raised, a symbol of their affiliation with the Socialist Party. A founder of the Socialist Party, Eugenio Matte taught at the night school for workers where approximately forty students began the football club. Alessandri sent Matte into exile on Easter Island after he had served as a minister during the short-lived socialist republic of Marmaduke Grove. Matte was elected senator in 1933, but died shortly thereafter, in 1934. Over the years, Club Eugenio Matte had created ties to the Socialist Party and the unions in Ñuñoa. Directors hoped that the club would help the community weather the economic depression and the feelings of hopelessness among the unemployed.[81] Alessandri did not hide his disgust at the wave of crowd approval that followed Club Eugenio Matte around its stadium lap.[82]

In the weeks following the inauguration, the actions of Club Eugenio Matte provoked distinct reactions. Many approved of the club's behavior; in fact, the Football Association of Santiago named it one of the best presenters, a clear show of support for the club's performance. Others were furious. The Conservative daily *El Diario Ilustrado* described the team's gesture as "a politically charged salute that had nothing to do with sports."[83] The newspapers' editors did not consider the speeches of the president, ministers, or congressmen to be unduly political. They complained that "the sporting family of Chile needs unity, common ideas, and an absolute separation from politics, because its infiltration will only achieve division among the youth."[84] Politics, for these journalists, was something that should be reserved for appropriate times. This view was directly opposed to the leftist parties' vision of a struggle against fascism in every sphere.

After the inaugural parade, the speakers began. The ministers in Alessandri's government described the importance of the stadium as a home for civic education. The minister of education, Guillermo Correa Fuenzalida, claimed that the stadium would develop the moral spirit of Chilean youth, as ancient stadiums had done for Greeks in Hellenic times. He likened the preservation of Greek democracy by active and healthy citizens to similar actions by the Chilean system. Contrary to the propaganda produced by Alessandri's committee, which portrayed the stadium as Alessandri's gift to the Chilean people, Correa stressed that the government had an obligation to construct recreational spaces. In another departure from the official rhetoric, he credited the highly developed civic conscience of Chile's sports community for the stadium's completion. According to Correa, this conscience provided the foundation of Chile's democratic traditions, which were unique in the region.[85]

Speakers marveled at the size of the stadium's audience and the experience of being able to observe and be observed for a full 360 degrees. The rector of the University of Chile, Juvenal Hernández, likened the stadium to a mirror in which Chileans could see their reflections, particularly their racial characteristics.[86] Hernández informed the crowd that a statue dedicated to the Araucanian Indians would soon be erected close to the entrance. He praised Chile's mixture of indigenous and European racial heritages, emphasizing that the stadium could help create a uniform culture. Hernández urged Chileans to look at the stadium as a school for gentlemanly manners where they could display their sense of cooperation and humility. He reminded audience members that they did not intend to cultivate "brute force" but "disciplined vigor."[87] Hernández's didactic speech generated little enthusiasm among spectators. His admonition that Chileans should show their gentility in the stadium already seemed unrealistic.

As Alessandri approached the microphone to give the final speech, the booing of the crowd intensified. Attendees recalled that they could not hear Alessandri's speech even a few aisles from the podium. Football player turned politician Eduardo Símian recalled that Alessandri received "a ridiculing as few [have experienced] in Chilean history."[88] Alessandri did not publish his speech, and many guessed that it was at least partly spontaneous. Those who accompanied Alessandri, who were among the few who could hear the speech in full, recalled that he concluded with the phrase, "Now I can die in peace."[89] The final line, whether Alessandri uttered it or not, was a poignant reminder of the confidence the once-popular president had in his relationship to the Chilean masses. In his later years, Alessandri insisted to friends that he received the warmest applause of his life at the stadium's inauguration.[90]

What occurred at the inauguration became contested in memory even a few hours after it happened. Politicians realized that the stadium was a new medium through which the Chilean public could be reached, but also one in which the Chilean public could reach them. According to the official press, the inauguration was an unqualified success. The state newspaper, *La Nación*, claimed the crowd responded to Alessandri's entrance with a "warm ovation."[91] Other newspapers attacked *La Nación* and *El Mercurio* for censoring the "truth" of the inauguration.[92] The journalists who covered the event marveled at the crowd's power to destroy and create idols. One witness reflected, "For [Alessandri] and the official world that accompanies him, the sports festival yesterday must have had a profoundly sad tone. Public opinion responded at times angrily and violently, and for those who, until they arrived, haughtily believed themselves to be directors of the people's will, the terrible hour of twilight came fatally forth."[93] The audience rendered the stadium a site of mass expression and interacted with performers—in this case, athletes—to create a spectacle charged with political criticism.

Given the history of football spectatorship in Santiago, the crowd's actions seem, even if not predictable, intelligible. Attendees, many of whom belonged to clubs and barras, drew upon stadium practices that football fans had created over the course of two decades. As discussed in the previous chapter, fans created rituals in the 1920s such as outing undercover police officers, showing support for politicians, and shouting chants that expressed pride in working-class identity. Crowds could punish clubs that fell out of favor, as evidenced by their attacks on Audax Italiano and Unión Española after their clubs declared their support for fascist governments. The National Stadium provided an expansive arena for this behavior, even if some of the more violent practices could not be translated to the larger venue. In addition, public discussions of the National Stadium had generated a series of criticisms of Alessandri's government. The crowd's responses also reflected the successful mobilization of the working- and middle-class clubs by the Popular Front. They testified to the long relationship between clubs and the Radical Party as well as to their ties to labor unions, Communists, and Socialists.

SPORTSMEN AND THE FIRST POPULAR FRONT GOVERNMENT

Amateur football clubs with ties to the Popular Front pushed the Socialist and Communist parties to reconsider their ambivalence toward sports. By engaging with these parties, football clubs broadened the social projects that they participated in. Amateur organizations pressured the Aguirre administration to fulfill the Popular Front's promise to make sports facilities more accessible to workers. One of the administration's first projects was to increase workers' and students' use of the National Stadium. The National Sports Council, made up of sports federations, worked with the new government to encourage average Chileans to participate in open sports at the stadium.[94] The stadium's administrator, Joaquín Orellana, urged physical-education instructors to bring their students to the stadium.[95] He stated that the true mission of the stadium was to improve the health of the common Chilean, "in defense of the race."[96] With the help of the minister of education, Orellana put together a plan to bus schoolchildren to the stadium for classes on sports ethics, exercise, and hygiene.

Despite the assurances of Alessandri, Aguirre, and the Chilean Football Federation that the stadium would support physical education, professional football clubs dominated the stadium's schedule. Economic interests sealed the close relationship between professional football and the National Stadium. Football clubs paid high fees to use the stadium; as a result of the sport's popularity, they provided the lion's share of the stadium's revenues. Even in the stadium's first year, football was the only sport that could regularly deliver a full crowd.[97] Pressured to offer more sports facilities and to increase revenue, the Aguirre government made plans to expand the stadium just two years after its inauguration.

Amateur clubs enthusiastically participated in the Aguirre government's initiatives to diffuse sports beyond Santiago and other urban enclaves. In response to criticism that government support focused on urban areas, the National Sports Council increased its efforts in the provinces. This dovetailed with the Popular Front's growing interest in the political mobilization of rural Chileans. Programs included the country's first Athletic Trainers Institute and a sports medicine program, organized by the Ministry of Education.[98] Sportsmen from Santiago volunteered to participate in the institute, which served rural physical-education teachers and sports organizations. One product of this effort was the widely distributed pamphlet *How to Play Football*, printed by the government in 1941. The pamphlet, which was distributed directly, advertised that the government would send free copies to any campesino, or rural resident, who sent a written request.[99] Dr. Carlos Aguirre, the president of the football club May 1st (affiliated with the Socialist Party) and the Chilean Association of Football Referees, prepared the pamphlet. It instructed potential players that football was a sport of gentlemen, played all over the world, and without distinctions between classes. The booklet explained that sports especially benefited the popular classes, instilling self-respect and social solidarity. It encouraged the reader to take the initiative and form a local football club.

The upsurge in municipal support, workers' increase in disposable income, however small, and the reduced threat of government repression fostered the growth of civic associations. Under the Popular Front administrations of Aguirre (1939–1941) and his successor, Juan Antonio Ríos Morales (1942–1946), the real wages of the working class rose significantly.[100] Certainly, extra cash and leisure time helped working- and middle-class club members pay dues, attend events, and participate in club governance. As municipalities regained some of the authority lost under the Ibáñez dictatorship, they had greater resources to offer local clubs. The distribution of funds to municipalities from the Alcohol Laws increased considerably during the first Popular Front period. In the early 1940s, more than half of the funds ended up in local sports councils, an impressive increase from the previous decades.[101]

This increase in revenue enabled municipalities with vibrant football communities, like San Miguel, to donate trophies, equipment, and clothing to local clubs.[102] The municipality opened its offices to the Football Association of San Miguel and worked with local clubs to lobby for support from the national government. By 1941, they had pooled enough funds to begin the construction of a municipal stadium. In Santiago proper, Socialist mayor Graciela Contreras de Schnake funded programs to diffuse sports among a greater number of residents. She approved the construction of playgrounds and community pools in working-class neighborhoods. Contreras also provided sports clubs with a mobile recruitment truck, equipped with a loudspeaker, that members could drive through communities during registration drives.[103]

The largest source of state funding for sports came from the Popular Front's Defense of the Race program. Aguirre's government formulated the program in 1939 with two central objectives. The first goal was to strengthen citizens' physical fitness through the diffusion of sports and recreation. A Pro Popular Sports Committee was formed, headed by a leading physical-education theorist, Joaquin Cabezas. The Communist and Socialist parties were particularly excited about the potential benefits of this program for disadvantaged students.[104] Second, the program intended to raise the "moral standard" of Chilean homes.[105] Rhetorically, the Defense of the Race divided the initiatives between the public and private spheres. The programs that sought to improve the physical condition of workers worked to get them into gymnasiums, stadiums, football fields, pools, and outdoor areas. The projects of moral improvement reached out to women in their homes, offering assistance in child rearing, household management, and family budgeting. Pedro Aguirre explained that the program had been prompted by the abysmal state of young men when they reported for their military service. The Defense of the Race contained a clear goal of creating disciplined families that would exemplify the values of sobriety, thriftiness, and hard work. The government created local sports councils in order to distribute the program's resources among popular organizations. The hope was that participation in sports could stimulate workers' self-worth and encourage them to occupy their leisure time in honest, educational ways.[106] Aguirre's administration stated that the projects would teach young men "to respect hierarchy and discipline."[107] The architects of the program assumed that organized recreation among workers would encourage men to participate in civic life and help them take advantage of their rights and duties. They assumed further that women would benefit in their roles within the family. Though a few women's sports clubs managed to squeeze some meager resources from the Defense of the Race, the program reinforced the traditional image of a male worker-sportsman who was active in the community and married to a modern homemaker-wife, who stayed within the confines of the home.

Football clubs saw the Defense of the Race program as an opportunity to promote the projects they had worked on for decades. They formed local "popular sports" committees in their communities. A citywide newspaper, *Deporte Popular*, published petitions from these committees and advertised their efforts to build new sports facilities.[108] These committees made the involvement of women a priority, creating a popular-sport Olympics that included as many women's as men's teams. Governmental agencies, particularly the Ministry of Health, headed by Salvador Allende, and the Ministry of Education, under Benjamín Claro, solicited the collaboration of sports organizations for these programs. That Claro also served as the president of the professional football club University of Chile strengthened the relationship between the ministry and the Chilean Football Federation. The Hogar Parque Cousiño, created in 1939, was one product of the collaboration between football clubs, municipalities, and state agencies. Local sports councils helped design this special section of the park, which included an indoor gymnasium, a restaurant, a theater, locker rooms, and a playground. Although some clubs complained that the Defense of the Race program "destroyed the traditionally democratic organization of sports," most conceded it fostered greater community involvement.[109]

The Aguirre government and the succeeding Popular Front administrations found it difficult to navigate the divisions between professionals and amateurs in the Chilean Football Federation. The federation lobbied the government to host the South American Cup in 1941, but then became embroiled in constant arguments over tournament preparations. The cup would commemorate the four hundredth anniversary of the discovery of Santiago by the Spanish, and disputes surrounding it revealed new trends in club participation and the relationship between football and the state.

This new relationship was marked by the efforts of professional clubs to create ties to ministries that would bypass both amateurs and the officials in charge of sports. As football became a bigger business, professionals limited their dealings with local governments. For example, the Central Association (as the Professional League began to call itself) held a benefit for the earthquake victims of 1939. (On January 24, a quake in south-central Chile killed fifty thousand people and injured sixty thousand.) Instead of organizing the tournament with local clubs, the professional clubs played against one another and sent the check directly to the minister of finance.[110] By the mid-1940s, amateur clubs were expressing disappointment with the Popular Front's ineptitude and its favoritism toward professionals.[111] However, it should be noted that among professionals, a few "old-timers"— for example, the founders of Colo Colo—attempted to preserve their "democratic and popular character" and avoid state dependency.[112] The government budget bore out amateurs' complaints about the underfunding of their organizations. While revenue from the Alcohol Laws nearly doubled between 1942 and 1943, the percentage that amateur sports clubs received declined dramatically.[113] This appeared grossly unjust to amateurs, who composed the vast majority of members of the federation: around 384,000 by 1945, compared with about 50,000 in professional clubs.[114]

The 1941 South American Cup highlighted changes in the relationship between players and directors, which had come to mirror that between employers and employees. Players took advantage of the publicity surrounding the cup to demand better pay and travel accommodations. That year, the players Oscar Sánchez and Domingo Sepúlveda started a union that threatened to withdraw the national team from the tournament. The Central Association acted quickly to offer most players enough money to abandon the idea and then promptly suspended the leaders for one year.[115] In response to players' demands, the directors of professional clubs countered that players often appeared at games "in deplorable physical condition, their faces showing the effects of alcohol or a sleepless night."[116] Directors tried to deflect attention from players' demands to their supposedly poor work ethic also.

LABOR UNIONS AND FOOTBALL

In the 1930s and 1940s, working-class clubs made up the majority of amateur football clubs. Those organizations multiplied in number, enriching the fabric of daily life in popular communities. Football players often understood their participation in union, neighborhood, and party clubs as seamless transitions throughout their life cycle. The experience of Mario Cubillos provides an example. The son of a stonecutter, he grew up on the outskirts of Santiago.[117] At the age of thirteen he joined an amateur club with his friends. They traveled by horse cart to play matches in other neighborhoods. Like other young men in working- and middle-class neighborhoods, they created football fields on abandoned lots and unused parcels of farmland. After football games, they celebrated by drinking wine, eating empanadas, and dancing the *cueca*. Cubillos's father agreed to give him five pesos a week, three of which he spent on club dues and the other two on sports magazines. For young Mario and his father, joining his neighborhood team was an important rite of passage and a source of understanding between them. In the early 1940s, Cubillos landed a job with the trolley company in Santiago's center, where he sought out the union football club. Cubillos recalled the transition to Santiago football as difficult. He noted that the players were more concerned with technique in comparison with the hardier rural footballers.[118] He remembered that certain unions gained a reputation for their violent play, such as the Bakers Union, whose players carried knives in their socks. Cubillos remembered that the barras caused major problems for union teams. Often, fans smoked marijuana during the matches and intimidated referees. Various professional clubs approached Cubillos, but he claimed that they lacked the camaraderie he had found in neighborhood and union teams.

As unions' memberships increased, so did the importance of their sports clubs as social organizations. Pedro Aguirre's administration made overtures to these clubs through the Ministry of Labor, which collaborated with unions to create the Sports Association of Unionized Workers.[119] Unionists had already begun to form associations by trade, such as the Football Association of Paperworkers, which included unionized workers

from paper factories throughout Santiago.[120] Local unions elected delegates to represent them in citywide associations as well as in national
meetings of the Federation of Workers' National Council of Workers'
Culture. Union leadership hoped to tie together the model sportsman
and unionist. This ideal man would be a productive worker, a good
compañero, and a civic leader.

Union clubs made efforts to create a stronger presence in the communities in which their members worked and often lived. They collaborated
with neighborhood teams to organize campaigns against violence and gambling in football. Disagreements over bets often resulted in brawls between
rival neighborhood clubs after matches.[121] The Popular Front urged union
clubs to take the leading role in campaigns to reduce violence. Together
with the Socialist and Communist parties, union leaders demanded recreational opportunities for workers in labor negotiations. Encouraged by the
Defense of the Race program's focus on popular sports, union clubs petitioned government agencies for help. In 1939, the Club of Newsies (newspaper vendors) began a campaign to provide low-cost housing at the beach
for workers' families. In his first month as minister of education, Rudecindo
Ortega received dozens of similar requests. Ortega's contribution of three
thousand pesos to the campaign of the Newsies inspired even more clubs
to petition him.[122]

Union sports clubs rivaled barrio clubs as neighborhood favorites,
particularly when the community was known for a certain type of industry.
For example, residents of the working-class Barrio Franklin turned out
weekly to support the Glassworkers Union Football Club. Begun in the
1920s, the club was part of the neighborhood's growth. Just south of the
city's center, Barrio Franklin housed glass factories. By the 1930s, the
football club had added basketball, cycling, and table tennis to its offerings.
As in many unions, the autonomy and influence of sports sections were
sources of tension. In the case of the Glassworkers Union, one member
explained that "the sports group, though dependent on the union, counted
upon a certain autonomy ... Although surely its membership was important
in numerical terms, among the formal concerns of the union, the group
occupied a secondary place."[123] Proper sports facilities and support for
sports clubs figured low on the list of union demands.

Regardless of its formal importance in the daily life of workers at the
National Glass Factory, the union team provided a source of endless conversation. Workers linked the characteristics of their club's style of play with

their trade. Moreover, participation in the football club integrated young workers in the workplace and its union. One glassworker explained that older union members commonly tried to help young workers by buying them a pair of overalls with union funds or inviting them to play football.[124] Sportsmen often felt increased self-assurance in the workplace when they were recogonized as good footballers. One player recalled the confidence he gained after joining the football team: "One day at the factory exit, I noticed that the guards were carefully searching the workers," to which he responded, "I am going to leave the factory with my bicycle and my football clothes. I did not allow them to mess with me. I said to the doorman: if you want to know what I take with me, I prefer to undress," which he proceeded to do.[125] Rather than be subjected to a physical search, this worker preferred leave naked. Workers often recounted stories that connected their talents as sportsmen with their rebellious spirit and refusal to be humiliated by their superiors on the job. Sportsmen linked this sense of control to their masculinity.

In the 1940s, it became commonplace for club directors to serve as union leaders. Sports introduced them to workers from all sections of a factory and developed leadership skills, and their athletic prowess often translated into symbolic capital.[126] Being a director of one of these sports clubs had benefits beyond the workplace. Union teams played clubs from other unions, neighborhoods, and regions. Although companies and national labor organizations emphasized sports as a way to instill discipline, matches between union clubs frequently involved drinking and violence.[127] The bonds forged in these rituals built solidarity among workers and boosted the unions' presence in daily life. Many football clubs that predated unions contributed to a fertile environment for labor organizing. For example, a group of metalworkers formed Club "Fundación Libertad" in 1915, fifteen years before their union was formed.[128] Union sports clubs also provided continuity to workers' organizations when government repression forced the closure of the unions, as happened during the Ibáñez regime.

During the late 1930s and early 1940s, leftist parties intensified their relationships with civic associations. Football clubs already identified with the Socialist Party hoped that their party's new leverage in the government would result in increased support for neighborhood projects. Party branches for the young increased their efforts to found clubs; for example, the young men of the United Socialist Youth founded a sports club in honor of the Mexican president Lázaro Cárdenas.[129] The Communist Party paid more attention to sports also, but was less enthusiastic about the Popular

Front. Communist leaders viewed the Defense of the Race program critically, referring to it as a "simple and costly bureaucratic tangle."[130] They
felt that the party apparatus could organize sports among the masses more
effectively than civic associations. Communist football clubs sought out the
unemployed, the underemployed, and otherwise exploited young workers.
The use of sports as a means of uniting Communist youth figured among
the top resolutions of the Youth Congress of 1940.[131] Instead of playing neighborhood or union teams, Communist clubs focused on playing
against one another. Communists held sports tournaments during large
congresses and party commemorations, such as the anniversary of founder
Luis Recabarren's death. Party sections formed clubs named in honor of
leaders, like the Santiago section, which named its club in honor of Elías
Lafertte.[132]

The appearance of the Communist newspaper *El Siglo* contributed to
the vivacity of football among leftists, particularly the youth sections. The
considerable space the paper dedicated to football attests to its importance
among Communists. In its first year of publication, writers for *El Siglo*
organized their own football club as well as sports tournaments among
affiliated clubs.[133] In the early 1940s, *El Siglo*'s sports pages promoted
amateurism and covered neighborhood sports more than any other
publication, including *Estadio*, the country's most popular sports magazine.
El Siglo copied practices of the mainstream press to build relationships
with clubs, such as offering advertising space to clubs that declared *El Siglo*
their official paper. It dismissed the national sports federations, advocating
exclusively local solutions to sportsmen's problems.[134] *El Siglo* argued that
local sports committees represented the only chance to start a genuine sports
movement of the masses. As the era's most important leftist publication,
El Siglo was the most important bridge between the party and the masses
of sports clubs in Santiago.

In its sports coverage, *El Siglo* differed from its mainstream counterparts in its criticism of class inequalities and its emphasis on the class
background of players. When it reported on professionals, it focused on their
families' socioeconomic position and political affiliation. *El Siglo* portrayed
the amateur worker-sportsman as the true model of masculine athleticism.
It gushed that in the football fields of poor neighborhoods, "manliness
and mastery of the ball originates."[135] *El Siglo* offered to help working-
class clubs eliminate corruption by printing the names of members found
guilty of wrongdoing and the charges against them, such as directors who
stole club funds. *El Siglo*'s anecdotes and editorials associated creativity,

masculinity, and talent with the working class. "Sopera" was an oft-repeated story of a boy known for his barefoot play. Several versions of Sopera circulated, but the general features remained constant.[136] Sopera's face was dirty, and his clothes ragged, but he was a great football player. His teammates called him Sopera, or soup bowl, because he was always hungry. Sopera was a restless young man, who played for three different clubs at any given time. No one in the neighborhood knew Sopera's real name, nor did they ever see him at school. Regardless, everyone held him in high esteem because of his behavior on the field. Suddenly, Sopera disappeared, but the story never explains what provoked his disappearance. The reader was left to assume that one of the various dangers confronting a poor boy must have befallen Sopera. El Siglo used these stories as fables to castigate the government and citizens alike for failing to appreciate the situation of poor youth.

As the sports clubs expanded their interests in the community, more of their members sought political office. Clubs had become respected actors in local civic life as well as bridges between members and other civic organizations. For example, an ex-footballer from Santiago National became a popular mayor of Iquique.[137] He drew upon his reputation as a football player to convince Iquiqueños of his honest character and bipartisanship. Under his authority, the municipality paid for the services of a Uruguayan trainer to coach its basketball team. He himself directed improvements to the municipal stadium and appointed sportsmen to municipal positions. Not only leftist parties encouraged sportsmen to enter politics. The ex-footballer Rafael Vives, of the Liberal Party, became mayor of the eastern neighborhood of Providencia. Vives mobilized his connections to sports clubs to gain favor for the Liberal Party in the community. Just weeks before elections to replace a deceased city councilman in 1941, Vives refurbished the defunct football fields of the municipal stadium in Providencia. He brought the candidate he supported for the city council, Conservative Carlos Barros, to the inauguration of the fields and accompanied him to various sports clubs to campaign.[138] Vives also donated municipal property to be used as a sports center and library for the football club Jorge V.[139] Jorge V, an elite club with ties to the British community, publicly supported Vives along with the Liberal and Conservative parties of Providencia.[140]

Amateur clubs worked with other civic associations to improve community life, particularly in peripheral areas. Populated by newcomers seeking employment in meat processing, metalworking, and domestic service, these neighborhoods lacked basic urban services. Club delegates collaborated on committees to improve sports facilities in the neighbor-hoods as well as to help them acquire trash pickup, street lighting, and transportation. These community activities gave rise to a coherent de-nouncement of the class inequality perpetuated by the state even as they engaged citizens with the agencies being criticized. The Unión Progreso Mutuo, a mutual aid society and football club from La Cisterna, started its own paper, which covered news of the working-class neighborhoods in the southern metropolitan area, including La Cisterna, San Miguel, and La Granja. These neighborhood bulletins facilitated community action among sportsmen. In San Miguel, the Committee for Popular Sports, com-posed of union, political, and neighborhood sports clubs, completed an extensive study of neighborhood sports needs and petitioned the mayor to take action.[141] The sportsmen of San Miguel explained that they did not need, nor want, large stadiums, where only spectatorship took place. They proposed a four-year plan, funded through the Defense of the Race program, in which San Miguel would be divided into four equal sections, each of which would construct sports centers equipped with a football field, basketball courts, tennis courts, boxing rings, and a social center. The clubhouses would include a library, a gymnasium, games, and conference rooms.[142] La Cisterna and other southern neighborhoods followed the example of San Miguel's Committee for Popular Sports. The collaboration of clubs across neighborhoods to pool resources and knowledge increased their effectiveness.

Despite the Popular Front's efforts to expand workers' access to parks, playgrounds, and sports facilities, professionals dominated many of the city's resources, especially the large sports venues. For example, the Central Association rented the Estadio Carabineros, which had been intended to provide recreational space for the crowded central district, for entire seasons. Amateurs accused professional clubs of using corrupt financial incentives to control the Chilean Football Federation. Frustrated with the demands of amateurs, professional clubs called for federation leaders who had "firm pants" and could take control of the situation.[143] Professional clubs invoked metaphors of the family to call for unity among their ranks. Directors from Club Magallanes, which had a vocal faction that preferred the club remain amateur, distributed materials that described the club as "a loving and caring father who sees all his sons grouped beside him, old and young. The old ones . . . will pass on the experience that comes from life's struggles, and this, joined with the energy and enthusiasm of youth, will form a splendid combination that yields exquisite fruit."[144] Directors employed these metaphors of family and fraternity to quell internal nostalgia for amateurism.

In the familial metaphor constructed by professional and amateur club directors, the mother appeared as an implied absence only. They presented the club as a space free from the constraints of home life, where women imposed demands. When a well-known player grudgingly admitted that he was engaged to be married, he explained, "It's true . . . but I am not going to abandon sports, which is a part of my life, because of it."[145] Men criticized other men for their attention to their families, and club members often portrayed marriage as a regrettable rite of passage. Intraclub matches pitted the married versus single footballers against one another. Bachelor parties were major club events in which all members were invited to help celebrate the bachelor's last "night of freedom." The growth of women's sections of sports clubs disrupted this space of reprieve. Initially, women's sports sections were formed independently of men's sections. Their events often showed a conscious effort to display the femininity of the participants. For example, the women's section of Colo Colo raised money for its basketball team by holding raffles in which women could win dolls, floral bouquets, and lipsticks.[146] Despite the growth in women's sports, football players and fans continued to view women as incapable of playing the national sport.

Entrepreneurs emerged as a dominant force on the directorates of professional clubs in the 1940s. The first generation of elite football patrons characterized this crop of leaders as the crass new rich. For this older clique, including Juan Ramsay and J. H. Livingstone, mass spectatorship and barras had ruined the decent reputation of the sport. Green Cross and Badminton were the only clubs of the traditional elite that remained in professional football. The wealthiest amateur clubs, such as the Prince of Wales Country Club, limited their scheduled matches to those against other clubs in the "upper neighborhoods" of the northeast. Publications targeted to the upper class, including *Aire Libre* and *Zig-Zag*, championed the value of sports to curb passions and produce all-around athletes, benefits at odds with popular practices. In these publications, announcements of elite football matches appeared next to those for polo tournaments, dog shows, the National Society of Agriculture (a powerful elite lobbying group), and mountain climbing.[147] In addition, these clubs, such as the ritzy International Sporting Club, whose members included the former president Juan Esteban Montero, bought large tracts of lands in the eastern parts of Santiago. These clubs created greater geographic divisions in the football community by abandoning the urban center for neighborhoods synonomous with privilege, such as Vitacura.

Physical-education teachers at the University of Chile and the Pontifical Catholic University opposed their clubs' transformations into business ventures in the 1940s. Many felt this transition was at odds with the mantra of the Popular Front: "to govern is to educate." Before professionalization, university students had formed clubs around their disciplines, and the university's top teams were drawn from these branches. In a letter to his colleagues, Professor Victor San Martín accused the University of Chile's administrators and their government collaborators of putting profits before education.[148] San Martín stated that physical education as a field rested upon the belief that regardless of class, political, or racial background, the masses needed sports to develop their physical fortitude. Without sports, working-class men would continue to act as slaves and be politically dependent upon others because they would lack forums where they could display their dignity and confidence. He used as an example the football player Guillermo Saavedra, who, he claimed, was among the last amateur sportsmen to have played purely disinterestedly.[149] San Martín praised Saavedra for rejecting professionalism. For many physical-education instructors, spectatorship was the chief evil that resulted from professionalism. Instead of cultivating their sports abilities, crowds indulged their aggressive instincts. San Martín criticized the government for allowing the National Stadium to be used for the profit of professional clubs. Alfred Betteley, a legendary footballer and referee, concurred with San Martín that professionalism perverted the democratic nature of football clubs. He claimed members of professional clubs voted for representatives, whereas amateur club members voted directly.[150] Physical-education teachers saw their hopes for a national stadium as one big classroom dashed. In the coming decades, they joined forces with amateur organizations.

In conclusion, political changes in the late 1930s, particularly the formation of the Popular Front coalition of center-left parties, mobilized sportsmen. The growth of union, neighborhood, and political clubs opened opportunities for active men in civic associations to assume leadership roles in their communities. Increasingly, clubs and political parties incorporated critiques of class relations into their assessments of sports in Chile. Arturo Alessandri and his administration's attempt to capitalize on the construction of the National Stadium reflected the failure of his populist style, honed in the 1920s. During construction of the stadium, clubs robustly criticized Alessandri's efforts to use sports as a tool. Thus, no single political figure or party managed to become the dominant influence over football clubs.

As professional football grew as an economic enterprise, amateur sportsmen came to view the sport as an extension of class hierarchies rather than as a site of equality. However, clubs drew upon the skills they learned in the campaigns for the National Stadium to energize state programs, especially the Defense of the Race, to channel support for recreational intitiaves in their communities. Club participation in campaigns for urban services increased the prestige of civic associations. In addition, members gained knowledge of state institutions. The public that had emerged around sports—in the pages of newspapers as well as in restaurants, factories, and stadiums—continued to expand. At the same time, the elite leadership, formerly in dialogue with working-class amateurs, withdrew from football organizations. In the coming years, the growth of sports businesses and political differences would further strain relations among club leaders. Although sportsmen expressed disappointment with the implementation of programs under the Popular Front, they served as a model for future administrations.

THE "LATIN LIONS" AND THE "DOGS OF CONSTANTINOPLE"

Immigrant Clubs, Ethnicity, and Racial Hierarchies in Football, 1920–1953

4

In 1962, the executive committee of the World Cup distributed a magazine throughout the world to attract visitors to Chile, the host country. State officials, businessmen, and leaders of civic associations offered basic facts, including population, area, and climate. In addition, the magazine informed the reader, just below the section on population density, about race: "White, of European heritage; without a population of color or mixes, the population is the most homogenous in the Americas."[1] The discourse that identified Chile as a nation of mestizos, of mixed European and Indian descent, was hegemonic by the 1960s. It is impossible to know for certain, at least with the available evidence, whether the committee affixed the label of whiteness to Chile out of genuine belief or a desire to impress foreign delegates—or for some other reason. In any case, this revision represented a broader trend of whitening the concept of mestizaje (in this case, out of existence) and homogenizing national identity. The notion of homogeneity became a key element in explanations of Chile's stability, democratic tradition, and political pluralism. Authors of the document knew that reality in Chile was more complicated than this description. The early 1960s witnessed renewed political struggles involving indigenous groups and demographic growth. Moreover, of the nine professional football clubs, three were immigrant teams: Audax Italiano, Unión Español, and Palestino. Arab Chileans figured prominently on the committee, including Nicolás Abumohor (treasurer), Amador Yarur, Raul Maffey, and Antonio Laban (directors).

This chapter traces the racial discourses that circulated in the popular press and in clubs, and that influenced the iconography surrounding football, and their relevance to politics. Transnational demographic flows and cultural stereotypes interacted with local identities in shaping ideas about race. Popular culture represents one of the most fluid, quickly moving, and broadly disseminated mediums for the building of these paradigms. The distinct experiences of European and Middle Eastern immigrants in sports clubs shed light on how race figured into national identity and definitions of citizenship. Moreover, this chapter analyzes the relationship between the participation of immigrant clubs in popular culture and their participation in politics. Since the 1920s, sports clubs had acted as vehicles that allowed immigrant communities to maintain relations among themselves, promote positive images of their cultures, and gain access to political power. Immigrant clubs followed a remarkably similar trajectory, whether founded by a dozen friends or large-scale business enterprises. As immigrant clubs, the most visible representations of their communities, professionalized, they became less connected to community members. With the increasingly dominant narrative of the raza chilena as mestizo, homogenous, and European, clubs of Spanish and Italian descent found it difficult to maintain their distinct ethnic identities, whereas Arab Chilean clubs found themselves defined as permanently foreign. The popular depiction of the Arab communities as foreign left Arab Chileans vulnerable to racist violence, political exclusion, and charges of imperialism.

The urban mestizo model became the basis for political projects, nationalist rhetoric, and citizenship.[2] In other countries, an archetype of mestizaje sometimes represented a more inclusive model of racial identity than the binary categories grounded in colonial law, but in the case of Chile, it limited the possibilities of ethnic claims in politics. As a projection of power from the urban center, it served the interests of state building. State agencies created policies based on a simplified citizen, ethnically homogenous and male. The participation of labor organizations, popular civic associations, and leftist parties in the construction of this narrative left little space within their agenda for the claims of Indians.

Across the Americas, dominant racial ideologies shifted from the biologically and environmentally based models of the 1910s to the culturally grounded (and more national-populist) paradigms of the post–World War II era. This shift was never complete or total; instead, biological and cultural definitions of race were used inconsistently and interchangeably. Ethnicity, the category much preferred by today's academics, was either employed as a classification within a race or else entirely effaced. Typically, it was used when referring to different indigenous groups. Ideas about gender and sexuality were inseparable from notions of race. Throughout the twentieth century, the male body served as the cornerstone of active, dynamic images of the Chilean race. Women's bodies were portrayed as vehicles for passing on racial traits. Practices of sexuality, labor divisions between men and women, and grooming differences were important in shaping categories and hierarchies of race.

Recent work on immigration in Latin America has focused on transnational flows between home and adopted countries. Much of it has centered on the impact of increased communication, economic ties, and transportation on migration patterns in the Americas.[3] This literature focuses on flows between "underdeveloped-developed" or "authoritarian-democratic" nations and the United States or Europe, the ultimate destinations.[4] The political impact of these immigration patterns is assessed by studying voting preferences or consumption patterns; however, a look at civic associations in Chile allows for a more nuanced understanding of the intersection between immigrants' cultural practices and their politics. Alejandro Portes, among others, has shown that social science studies of ethnic and race relations often bracket work on immigration.[5] This chapter uses football clubs as a means of studying the relationship between immigrants, "minorities," and the normative mestizo.[6]

This chapter has three distinct but interrelated objectives: first, to shed light on the social and cultural practices of immigrants in urban Chile; second, to assess the relationship between these practices and political participation; and finally, to put forward initial arguments about the role of popular culture in shaping attitudes toward race, ethnicity, and immigration. As discussed in Chapter Three, the 1940s have been considered the period in which a national-populist program was consolidated by the center-left parties in control of the state. A focus on civic associations and popular culture demonstrates how racial identity was shaped from below as much as from above.

There have been scattered attempts to record the experiences of immigrant groups in Chile, but nothing on the scale, for example, of the ethnography of the Chicago school.[7] The most visible immigrant groups in cities, the Spanish, Italian, and Arab communities, were economically successful and dispersed. There were no ghettos or even barrios specific to these groups in Santiago. German immigration, the subject of many conservative fantasies, was relatively small, but important. German influence on the Chilean frontiers resembled the civilizing influences Frederick Jackson Turner attributed to the U.S. frontier. While the state and conservative politicians perpetuated the idea that German farmers had shaped Chilean national identity, particularly linking it to the country's political stability, most immigrants lived in urban areas. References to immigrant groups, communities, and organizations hold the danger of portraying them as sharing a singular experience. Significant attention is paid in this chapter to the creation and re-creation of identities within these communities.[8] In addition, a study of the variety of debates within immigrant groups can offer a unique look at the process of integration, or lack thereof, in a society with strong social pressures for ethnic conformity.[9]

THE MESTIZO IDEAL, FOOTBALL, AND POLITICS

At the beginning of the twentieth century, state agencies promoted significantly different versions of the raza chilena than their counterparts did fifty years later. In the public school curriculum of 1905, the Department of Education instructed teachers that "two races exist in Chile: the primitive indigenous and the European conquerors."[10] The lesson plan went on to divide the Indians into three ethnic categories: Fueginos, Araucanos, and Changos. It dismissed the possibility of other groups being present in Chile, particularly Africans: "The African race is unknown. Black people do not prosper in our mild and temperate climate, and they die from lack of heat."[11]

As previous chapters have highlighted, a wide range of racial ideologies circulated among football clubs in the early twentieth century. "Himno de los Deportistas de Chile," the official hymn of the National Sports Federation, written in 1917 and used at least through the 1940s, began, "We are the sons of El Cid and the Aucas." This reflected the popularity of the idea that Chile was a mestizo nation. Frequently, race and nation were conflated in sports publications. Clubs used the rhetoric of racial degeneration also heard in temperance leagues, night schools, cooperatives, and other reform organizations. Modern work routines, technology, and urban development were targeted as causes of men's physical weakness. While reformers typically envisioned workers as those stricken by modernization, the despised sedentary lifestyle in fact characterized middle- and upper-class routines. Racial and regional stereotypes intersected in clubs' portrayal of their playing styles. Valparaíso sportsmen positioned their city as a European one, influenced by British and German bankers, whereas the capitalinos of Santiago claimed that their mixed-race background was more authentically Chilean. Clubs from both central cities portrayed the provinces to the north and south as savage territories populated by miners and Indians.

Throughout the 1930s and 1940s, national programs such as the Popular Front's Defense of the Race idealized a racially homogenous Chilean citizenry, a belief that became an important cornerstone of the nation's political stability.[12] Pedro Aguirre conflated the concept of the Chilean race and nation in his formulation of the Defense of the Race program and asserted that this racial unity could overcome political partisanship and class differences.[13] He referred to "the love of the race, the Chilean race . . . which we admire and love, despite the defects it may have, as we love our mothers and the flag."[14] While women may have protected or passed on racial characteristics, they were secondary subjects. In his speech, Aguirre formulated an image of the nation as a whole, afflicted not by a totalitarian Communism or class differences, but by sexually transmitted diseases, tuberculosis, alcoholism, and delinquency. The Defense of the Race program sought to create, through disciplined physical activity, more efficient workers, citizens, and able-bodied men for military duty. During the Cold War, this ideal remained entrenched in political rhetoric across the spectrum. Folklore projects of the 1960s and 1970s that sought to preserve indigenous culture assumed the existence of an unchanged set of practices, doing little to disrupt the dominant paradigm of Chilean urban mestizaje. Heidi Tinsman has shown that workers in the countryside had embraced this mestizo identity by the 1960s, but that their employers used the term "Indian" disparagingly to reinforce their power and class privilege.[15] Among the working class, *indio* could be used as an insult or a friendly gesture, depending on the context.

Chilean racial hierarchies have been less studied than those in neighboring Latin American countries, where racial minorities have been considered an important part of society. The Chilean case was virtually left out of the postrevisionist literature of the 1990s that set out to debunk myths such as racial democracy and to uncover ways in which perceived egalitarian race relations obscured hierarchies.[16] Chile differs from other Latin American countries, such as Brazil, in that its image as a multiethnic nation did not become dominant during the first half of the twentieth century. Some academic literature argues that mestizaje functioned as a site of creative subversion of racial essentialism. While perhaps mestizaje replaced certain forms of biological determinism, it rested upon a firm belief in the superiority of the European.[17] As Marisol de la Cadena has demonstrated in the case of Peru, the categories "European," "Indian," and "mestizo" were not fixed classifications but a malleable series of traits mobilized in daily life to exert power over others.[18] However, mestizaje never became a dominant, state-sanctioned ideology in Peru as it did in Chile. Partly, this shows the efficacy of the Chilean state at accruing power and marginalizing the claims of indigenous groups; however, the process was not entirely top down.

Anxieties over the Chilean race were firmly anchored in the social question and in challenges to elite authority in the 1910s and 1920s, to national-populist projects of the 1930s and 1940s, and to Cold War development paradigms in the 1950s and 1960s. Among sports clubs, these discussions were frequently prompted by the failure of the national football team. In the 1920s, sportswriters pushed for an understanding of Chile's losses that was more cultural than biological. Arguing that the superiority of teams from Argentina and Uruguay was due to training and not to racial factors, one director stated, "It is well known that there is hardly a difference of race, and if it existed, we would not be the Latins who are most notoriously inferior."[19] Throughout the era, sportswriters maintained a belief in Chileans' physical homogeneity and their potential to produce a great football team. Journalists and club directors determined that Chileans' homogeneity, in height and character, would enable them to overcome the Argentines through mathematically precise passes and teamwork.[20] After professionalization in the 1930s, some blamed the influx of foreign players for the national team's demise, since they disrupted the homogeneity of a team that would consist of all Chileans.[21] This continued through the 1950s as the success of Argentine and Brazilian football became more and more spectacular. Writers consoled fans that Chilean players were not flashy or individualistic but part of a team, in the tradition of the British gentleman.[22] While most footballers were willing to recognize indigenous influences on the Chilean national character, not all embraced it. One club leader explained, "Someone told us that in America we still could not see matches that compare [illegible] with Nordic culture, because we are very close to the Indian . . . Is this the fault of the Indian? We don't think so; in any case, we have advanced culturally enough to have defeated him with a little character and good effort."[23] Rather than a physical threat from belligerent Indians, it was the inner Indianness that this sportswriter viewed as necessary to dispose of.

Club Colo Colo's popularity was linked to its identity as an authentically working-class Chilean team. It paid homage to an indigenous past by creating an icon of the Mapuche leader Colo Colo, often emphasizing the respect and admiration that the Spanish had had for him. While the directors of Colo Colo freely borrowed from Mapuche practices, they did not recognize contemporary indigenous communities. Club leaders explained that the team's popularity was based upon the idea that all Chileans had a bit of Indian in them. The club's founder, Alberto Arellano, explained, "In honor of Colo Colo and its Araucanian legacy, during the first two years, our team gave a bouquet of *copihues* [Chilean bell flowers, the country's national flower] as a gift to the rival team."[24] The Mapuche had a variety of popular stories surrounding the history of colonization and the copihue. Yet Arellano referred to an "Araucanian legacy" rather than to a living tradition.

Among working-class clubs, the assumption that the proletarian mestizo was more Indian than his middle- and upper-class counterparts made the projects of reforming workers and improving the race almost indistinguishable from each other. One director enthusiastically saw the workers' practice of football as a step toward "recovery of the force and power symbolized in the descendents of Arauco."[25] Colo Colo's iconography was part of a broader trend to keep the image of an Indian apart from any specific community. Colo Colo's promotion of a mestizo Chilean identity that combined the unvanquished image of the Mapuche with a style of scientific, market-oriented football meshed well with Popular Front ideology. The club maintained particularly close ties with the Radical Party. Through the party, in which many Colo Colo directors held leadership positions, the club accessed resources of the state agency overseeing sports, the Consejo Nacional de Deportes, earning itself a good deal of resentment from other clubs in the process.[26]

Mestizaje was not embraced by Chilean elites at the turn of the century. As in other Latin American countries, Chilean elites advocated European immigration in order to help create a "whiter," more modern nation.[27] These projects assumed that racial mixing between Indians and Europeans had caused physical and mental deficiencies in workers, thus stalling industrial development. Elite consumption patterns reinforced notions of European cultural superiority.[28] In their property ownership, recreation, daily goods, and events, elites used consumption as a marker of citizenship. The association between consumption and citizenship was strengthened with the growth of disposable income, marketing, and the availability of goods throughout the first half of the twentieth century. As the middle and working classes gained greater access to mass culture, elites sought out goods and practices that could set them apart. Football was replaced by rugby, tennis, and skiing as the sports of choice among wealthy Chileans in the post–World War II period.

The revalorization and whitening of the mestizo was a project of middle-class writers such as Nicolás Palacios and Francisco Encina.[29] Rather than taking the view, prevalent in the nineteenth century, that considered mestizaje biologically dangerous or, at least, undesirable, Palacios and Encina argued that the special form of mestizaje in Chile produced an ideal individual. In their best-selling works, racial characteristics were passed on by men, that is, mestizos were predominantly European in character, since they had been fathered by a Germanic Spaniard. Women, in their narratives, only weakly contributed to the character of their children. This reexamination became part of a continent-wide effort to create a positive identity for Latin America, one that could provide the basis for strong national narratives.[30] Along with a growing sector of middle-class professionals, Palacios, a physician, resented unchecked European immigration. In his book *Raza Chilena*, Palacios drew on crime statistics, dubious historical research, and Darwinism to posit the superiority of the mestizo over foreign settlers. Like Encina, Palacios concluded, rather fantastically, that the Chilean mestizo was a product of the Araucanian Indians and German Visigoths (who had migrated to Spain centuries before colonization).

Racial theories such as those espoused by Palacios reinforced, and were informed by, a xenophobic tendency among labor organizations. Anti-imperialist critiques of Chilean capitalists, labor competition, and nationalist rhetoric fueled workers' animosity toward immigrants.[31] In the northern provinces, workers targeted Bolivian, Peruvian, and Chinese laborers. Workers' organizations characterized Peruvians and Bolivians as Indians who were lacking in solidarity and whose desperation drove down the value of work. The Chilean police and state agencies, while working to "Chileanize" the northern territories of Tacna and Arica, often sanctioned and participated in violence against these immigrant workers. These provinces were part of Chile's ongoing border dispute with Peru following the War of the Pacific. Racism toward Peruvians and Bolivians on the basis of their perceived Indianness implied that Chileans were closer to Europeans on a spectrum of racial makeup.

Working-class civic associations also expressed animosity toward Asian immigrants.[32] Their views of Asian immigrants demonstrate the importance of gender in perceptions of race and class. Chilean workers accused Asian immigrants, all of whom they assumed to be male, of stealing women's wages. Asian immigrants' masculinity was suspect because they worked in laundries and as cooks, jobs that fell into the category of women's labor.

Notions of proper masculinity were based on what type of labor a man performed and how he socialized.[33] Workers' publications bragged that Chilean men played sports, while Asians played games that lacked the same physical challenge and complexity. An anarchist periodical criticized the gaming habits of Chinese immigrants: "The gambling vice is doubly rooted among the Chinese compared with ourselves, the Americans, or the Europeans."[34] In its denigration of Asian immigrants, the paper positioned Chileans within the umbrella of Western culture. Workers' organizations pressured local politicians to limit Asian immigration, which they referred to as an "invasion" that jeopardized the "conservation of the race."[35] Journalists urged men to vigilantly protect women from sexual liaisons with Asians, which would damage the Chilean racial heritage.

Not all labor organizations promoted nativism; in fact, some considered nationalist arguments about race and immigration to be unnecessary divisions propagated by the oligarchy to prevent the formation of class consciousness. One union leader suspected that the government promoted sports as "a method to distract the people from their aspirations, so they value the Olympic Games, create sports fields, parks, etc."[36] Working-class football clubs in urban centers continued to lobby for state support based on their capacity to "uplift the race." Many workers' sports clubs understood racial uplift to mean not the amelioration of biological defects, but improvements in the living conditions of the working classes, such as sanitation in their neighborhoods, vacation time, and opportunities for exercise. Club leaders connected race to the general population's health rather than its ancestry.

In the popular press, including that produced by football clubs, migrant players from the countryside were depicted as racially distinct, less modern, and more indigenous than city folk. However, the ethnic identity of migrants remained a murky, undefined territory in clubs' public discussions. Given the steady waves of migration from the countryside to urban centers, there is a surprising absence of football clubs identified as migrant teams. This is especially notable because many of Chile's top football stars were migrants who attracted fans from their hometowns. Because migrants often moved to barrios that families from "back home" recommended, we can assume that many neighborhood teams were largely composed of migrants from particular regions. Unfortunately, very few football sources reveal specific connections between neighborhood clubs and provincial identities. However, we cannot conclude from a lack of evidence that clubs did not form around migrant identities or that participants did not recognize these identities as important factors in football clubs. It is plausible to assume that it was common knowledge among Santiago footballers that certain streets or uniform details signaled a provincial association.

Debates about race and nationality surfaced in anecdotes, game analyses, and jokes. Jokes about race and gender were rampant; clearly, editors thought that this type of humor appealed to a wide audience. International competition generated extensive commentaries on nationalism, gender, and race, particularly with regard to Chile's success or failure against other Latin American teams. The growing success of the Brazilian team complicated theories that Europeans had a superior physique for athletics. The Brazilian team's third-place finish in the 1938 World Cup sparked admiration in Latin America. Clubs portrayed the Afro-Brazilian players as excessively virile and strong because of their African heritage. When the Brazilian team visited, journalists reported on their eating habits and sleeping patterns with intense curiosity. These intimate details both satisfied and provoked the voyeurism of reading audiences.

As shown in Figure 4.1, Brazilian football players were depicted as children and exoticized through blackface.[37] To highlight the Brazilian players' African heritage, Chilean sportswriters referred to them as the "Kings of Gamba."[38] Footballers often joked that to improve their international performances, they needed to adopt some of the Brazilians' habits and African rituals. This humor hinged upon a belief in the fundamental racial difference between Chileans and Brazilians. As can also be seen in Figure 4.1, sportswriters racialized the practice of eating, suggesting that Chileans could not physically tolerate the *feijoada* (a hearty stew of beans, beef, pork, onions, and spices) and jerky diet of the Brazilian team. Instead, they recommended that footballers eat *porotos* (Chilean-grown beans) and drink red wine. In interviews with Brazilian stars, journalists considered their racial background of great importance. In an interview with the Brazilian captain Domingos Da Guia, one journalist summarized, "Da Guia is an awesome black man in every respect."[39]

Images of racial passing contributed to the creation of the normative, mestizo Chilean footballer. The comic strip *Cachupín*, a regular feature in *Estadio*, frequently employed racial stereotypes. The main character, Cachupín, is intended to represent a typical Chilean football fan and club member. Racial passing was a common event for Cachupín in the 1940s and 1950s. When he desires to join the Brazilian, Uruguayan, and Peruvian delegations during international competitions, Cachupín paints himself

FIGURE 4.1.   Caricatures of Brazilian football players implied similarities between Chileans and white Europeans. *Estadio*, 1945. Image courtesy of Zig-Zag.

black.[40] Instances of passing reinforced Cachupín's whiteness in comparison with his Latin American neighbors. A variety of sports publications homogenized *all* Brazilian football players as Afro-Brazilian and aligned *all* Chileans with whiteness. Frequently, Cachupín feels solidarity with other Latin Americans when faced with his wife's lack of understanding for his football passion. In Figure 4.2, the Brazilian player, again infantilized and in blackface, contrasts sharply with Cachupín and his wife, who are portrayed as mature adults. In this example, the joke turns on the suspicion of the wife, who unfairly attacks Cachupín, thinking he has been somewhere other than a football match.[41]

Popular beliefs about football's inherent fairness and egalitarianism precluded explicit discussions of racial hierarchies within clubs. Yet cartoons, anecdotes, and technical commentary on playing style were interwoven with strong messages about the whiteness of Chileans. While the cartoons in Figures 4.1 and 4.2 are not focused on scientific evidence of racial distinction, as images from the 1910s were, racial differences were still not viewed as malleable in the post–World War II period. In this way, popular culture contributed to the construction of a "commonsense" notion that Chileans were racially homogenous and distinct from peoples in neighboring Latin

FIGURE 4.2.   The friendly gesture of Brazilian players, depicted in blackface, is juxtaposed with Cachupín's suspicious wife. *Estadio*, 1945. Image courtesy of Zig-Zag.

American countries. Those defined as outside the raza chilena, including rural migrants, Indians, and Middle Eastern immigrants, risked losing out on the political and social capital that could be garnered through participation in civic associations. The dominant notion of mestizaje shaped how immigrant clubs defined themselves and made political claims. Immigrant organizations presented their communities as groups seamlessly united in the face of external threats and rewards.[42] Directors often argued that their communities were knit together by the essential traits of their race. But hard as they tried to foster the image of a fixed community, it was never a complete process. Global political changes derailed the unity of immigrant clubs in the 1940s and 1950s. In the case of Italian and Spanish clubs, fascism created deep divisions, whereas the rise of nationalism among Middle Eastern clubs threatened their organizations.

BRITISH, FRENCH, AND GERMAN FOOTBALL CLUBS

The involvement of immigrant clubs in Chile began as early as the sport's introduction by British visitors. By the 1910s, the Spanish, German, Italian, and French communities had founded sports clubs, several around cycling. As the popularity of football grew, these clubs voted to include the sport in their organizations. Drawing upon the resources of their communities, immigrant clubs expanded and maintained greater economic stability than any other type of club between the 1910s and 1960s. At times, educators and association directors worried that the popularity of Spanish and Italian clubs—or "Latin Lions," as they were often called—threatened the nationalist mission of football. Football clubs were centers of sociability that helped immigrants maintain connections to the homeland and build relationships with one another. Sportsmen from immigrant communities, like working- and middle-class footballers, gained access to political channels through their participation in clubs. Many directors became so successful at political networking that they formed core parts of commissions that advised governments on immigration policies.

Middle- and working-class sports clubs often structured their organizations around the pattern of mutual aid organizations and anarchist cultural groups, especially musical troupes. Immigrant clubs created variations on organizations in their countries of origin as well as those in their new communities, especially charity groups. European clubs that harnessed the patronage of the wealthiest members of their social circles wielded an inordinate amount of power in football leagues and associations. In football's early years, immigrant clubs shared the city's public spaces with other teams. For example, English Club, founded in 1906 by a mix of middle- and upper-class sportsmen, including A. W. Betteley, Duncan Jackson, and Alejandro Ramsay, played matches in the popular Parque Cousiño alongside and sometimes against clubs from the Workers' Football Association.[43] However, by the 1920s, urban development and the demands of a growing number of workers' clubs limited the availability of public space. Clubs followed their members who moved to exclusive northeastern neighborhoods. This spatial segregation gave many European clubs a distinctly upper-class character. If working- and middle-class immigrants wanted to join an expatriate club, they were unlikely to travel such a distance.

French, British, and German clubs distinguished themselves by not giving preferential treatment to football. They claimed that sports should cool passions, not provoke them. British clubs abhorred professionalism, even though it had begun in the nineteenth century in England. Clubs built stadiums in their members' neighborhoods, especially Las Condes and Vitacura. Elite clubs, such as the Prince of Wales Country Club, continued to play football in the 1930s and 1940s, but exclusively with other clubs of its social status.[44] Over time, membership in European clubs such as the Prince of Wales Country Club and Club Stade Francais became sought-after markers of status, regardless of one's background. Thus, these clubs' identity came to be associated with class rather than ethnicity or nationality. By the 1940s, many Middle Eastern immigrants, including the Palestinian Sarqui and Yarur families, as well as Luis Lamas from the Zionist Federation, had purchased memberships in the British club.[45] World War II and the growing condemnation of Nazism lowered the status of the most prominent German club, Deutscher Sport Verein.[46]

UNIÓN ESPAÑOLA AND AUDAX ITALIANO

Unlike the British, French, and German clubs, the Italian and Spanish clubs remained in central Santiago. The most prominent Spanish sports organization, Club Unión Española, began as part of the Centro Democrático Español. In the 1890s, a group of young professionals, with the support of elite Spanish Chileans, created the Centro Democrático as a space for "cultural uplift" and social interaction. The center used a series of family metaphors to describe its mission. Founders explained that during the nineteenth century, there had been a long series of misunderstandings between Spain, and her "son," Chile. The center wanted to build a commercial and cultural brotherhood.[47] In these narratives, the bonds of brotherhood were only strengthened in the absence of the mother figure. One of the center's founders, Antonio de la Pridea, recalled, "In those years, a lot of Spanish immigrants came to Chile, especially workers, who helped the country make great progress. In Spain, they were accustomed to spend hours in cafés . . . and here, unfortunately, there was not one café, but taverns, where, in general, the continual experience of disgraceful things squashed the lively character of the race."[48] From its inception, the center was a political organization that hoped to influence the Chilean government's policies. According to the center's directors, Spanish immigration would help modernize Chile and enhance its racial makeup. To this end, volunteers provided free classes in grammar and personal economics for male newcomers.[49] Dances, family picnics, and sports provided opportunities for Spanish immigrants to interact with one another.

The center's sports clubs were in the vanguard of creating mass-consumer cultural practices, using magazines, club merchandise, and radio shows to build a following. By the 1920s, clubs were no longer hangouts for "young men who normally worked in Spanish-owned businesses and sought a diversion during parties"; rather, they had become serious enterprises.[50] Centro Democrático Español's cyclists merged with its footballers in 1923, forming the Unión Deportiva Española. The club's growth in membership and the financial opportunities apparent in sports spectatorship encouraged the club to construct its own stadium. To accomplish this, it called in a number of political favors. Directors had lent support to members who campaigned for political office. Besides organizing fund-raisers and publicity matches, they often gave candidates access to their members through speaking engagements. Relationships with local politicians helped the club acquire the property and permits needed to build Chile's largest stadium, the Estadio Santa Laura, in 1924. After a futile search for land, club member and politician Absalón Valencia offered a piece of his estate in the neighborhood of Independencia, which was just north of the city's center and had a long tradition of successful football clubs, at a discounted price. Valencia, a senator from the Democratic Liberal Party, had served as minister of public works during Alessandri's first presidency. Valencia served as bridge between inspectors from the ministry and the club. Moreover, the club received financial support from the Spanish embassy for the stadium project. Club directors recognized that they had a built-in fan base in Independencia. The club created a market for merchandise, tickets, and membership. A virulent barra formed around its football club. The stadium became such an important part of the neighborhood's identity that people began to call the area Barrio Santa Laura.

Despite its connection to a popular neighborhood, Club Unión Española was directed by a set of upper-class entrepreneurs who culti-vated a fan base by emphasizing that all Chileans were at least a little bit Spanish. Special attention, however, was paid to players seen as having a more direct relationship to Spain. Before Juan Legarreta, a star football player for Real de Irún, one of Spain's top clubs, immigrated to Chile, the directors of the center spread the rumor that he would play for their club. They stressed that Legarreta could bring the most modern and advanced techniques from Spain. They asked club members to help recruit him by arranging lodging and work. When he stepped off the train in Santiago's Mapocho Station, hundreds of members of Unión Española waited to greet him. Legarreta not only went on to become Unión's most popular player of the 1920s—one of the country's first true pop stars—but also served for decades on the club's directorate. Legarreta attributed his popularity to his Spanish background and considered the club crucial to the success of his shoe factory.[51]

In the early part of the century, Spanish immigrant organizations commemorated Christopher Columbus as an uncomplicated symbol of Hispanic ingenuity rather than as the leader of a violent colonization. However, center-left politicians questioned the progressive heritage of the Spanish. Although the "Spanish character" was criticized as violent and antidemocratic, leading to questions about the superiority of the Old World over the New, the Chilean indigenous heritage was not valorized by contrast.[52] The Unión Española continued to organize celebrations on 12 October to commemorate the "Day of the Race," the anniversary of

European arrival in the Americas. During these celebrations, the Centro Democrático Español presented the Spanish as part of a pan-Latin race that included Italians, French, and Portuguese. Roman Catholicism was a deeply embedded part of this Latin heritage, and the Spanish felt it was a great gift that the Old World had imparted upon the New. In their publicity for Day of the Race events, Spanish clubs reinforced the popular belief that Chile was predominantly Spanish.[53]

The rivalry between the Unión Española and Audax Italiano heightened the excitement surrounding both clubs. Like Unión, Audax originated from a social group, Centro Demócratico Italiano, founded in the 1890s. Many of the Italian immigrants who joined had been born or spent time in Argentina, Uruguay, and Brazil. They arrived in Chile with contacts and a good grasp of Spanish. These attributes enabled them to integrate into Chilean society with relative ease. Audax also recruited players from Italy, and the proximity of those players to the mother country gave them cultural cachet. In 1923, the Yacopponi brothers caused a sensation when they arrived from Livorno to play for Audax. Just as Legarreta had football contacts to help him start a factory, the Yacopponis used their connections in the football community to help them open a store in San Alfonso; for example, they received financing from Italian banks where many of the club directors held officer positions.[54] As with Unión Española and Spanish immigrants, Audax not the first or the only club to represent Italians in Chilean sports, but it was the most successful.[55] Audax built Estadio Italiano in 1927, within walking distance of Unión's Santa Laura, creating an intraneighborhood rivalry. Estadio Italiano held ten thousand spectators upon its completion, which ranked it among Santiago's largest venues.[56]

Although the directors of Audax and Unión came from the upper class, most of the players they recruited had humbler backgrounds. Juan Legarreta described the economic disparity between football clubs considered to be aristocratic, such as Green Cross, and the Italian and Spanish clubs.[57] The players of Unión traveled to matches via public transportation, whereas Green Cross members came in automobiles. In addition, many Audax and Unión players opted to live in Independencia, near the Unión stadium. Along with the excitement that matches generated, the stadium became a lively center of commerce: vendors sold sports merchandise, refreshments, magazines, and a wide range of other goods. Fans anticipated violence, particularly after the game's conclusion, which often spilled onto the adjacent streets.[58]

The power and prestige of Spanish and Italian clubs grew as their founders climbed the economic ladder. Many of the young men who joined football clubs in the 1910s and 1920s as middle-class professionals became high-ranking leaders in the business community. These directors used their business skills and connections to catapult their clubs into the professional ranks. Simón Martínez, for example, joined Ciclista Ibérico in 1912 soon after he arrived from Spain, and several years later he founded the football section of the club. He began as a midlevel clerk in the banking firm La Nueva España. By the time he became president of the Unión Español in the 1930s, he was a bank director. The Audax Italiano president Danti Lepori came from a middle-class family in Punta Arenas that had emigrated from Italy via Uruguay. Lepori participated in a wide range of social activities upon moving to Santiago, including Audax's football club, the volunteer firefighters, and the Red Cross. Like Martínez, he started as a midlevel bank officer and rose to become the president of Banco de Credito e Inversiones.[59] Entrepreneurial directors of immigrant clubs conducted membership drives, pushing the number of club members from 2,000 to 4,000 in the mid-1930s to 15,000 in the post–World War II era.[60] Membership in European sports clubs constituted a staple obligation even of businessmen who had no clear connection to an immigrant community.[61]

Audax's and Unión's headquarters in the city's center offered a wide array of services to members, including barbershops, medical clinics, and restaurants. Unión's secretariat also included a public telephone, legal aid, and a library with subscriptions to all the major newspapers and magazines in Chile and Spain.[62] Audax's headquarters provided members with a beautiful dance hall and a gymnasium. The club hosted weekly dances at which young people danced the tango and listened to jazz. Social dances and concerts generated profits for the clubs and were open to Santiago youth, members or not.[63] During the 1930s and 1940s, directors felt that the expansion of services warranted stricter entry requirements for members, greater regulation of members' activities, and higher dues than before.

In a city that could seem impersonal and harsh, the family image projected by immigrant football clubs attracted many members. Moreover, club narratives stressed the masculine qualities that members developed in the process of immigration, including independence, self-reliance, and ingenuity. These qualities were linked to the exercise of citizenship. That the founders of European clubs included numerous sets of brothers reinforced their image as a fraternity. The football player César Alsina left

Badminton for Unión Española because he perceived the latter as a family.[64] In the rhetoric deployed by immigrant clubs, the native country played the role of the absent, estranged mother in club songs and histories. Literature from immigrant clubs told a common story in which club members had moved away from the motherland like pioneers discovering a new land.

Many other football clubs looked with envy at the expansion of immigrant clubs. Resentment flared when immigrant clubs were accused of paying players before the implementation of professionalism. This charge frequently involved paying for players' passage from Europe and securing inordinately well-paid jobs for them.[65] In addition, many felt that the money brought to football associations by immigrant clubs gave them disproportionate power in Chilean football. Clubs accused immigrants of sacrificing the nationalist goals of football to the interests of their specific communities.

Dissatisfaction among fans, reinforced by the rhetoric of Popular Front officials, resulted in the "Chileanization" campaign of the 1940s.[66] Coaches concurred that without the full-time training demanded by professional clubs, players would not be able to compete on an international level. Under pressure from government officials and fans, professional clubs agreed to replace foreign-born players with Chileans.[67] Critics of clubs' use of foreign players borrowed from anti-imperialist political rhetoric to criticize the patriotism of clubs that employed them. Colo Colo, because of its popularity and its efforts to claim authentic Chilean-ness, received the harshest treatment. Directors who campaigned on promises to replace foreign players with Chileans rarely fulfilled expectations. To satisfy what it referred to as sentimental *socios* (members), Colo Colo implemented Chileanization in 1943, but after a disappointing season, it began to scout Argentinians the following year.[68] Audax Italiano, Unión Española, and Palestino maintained the program throughout the 1950s, perhaps because of the extra scrutiny given to immigrant clubs.[69]

Fascism, especially in relation to the Spanish Civil War, sparked divisions within clubs and pushed them to declare political positions. In part, this reflected the magnitude of the importance that events in Europe had for Chilean political parties. The directorate and membership of Unión Española split along political lines, as happened in its parent organization, the Centro Demócratico Español. After several years of tense conflicts within the club, the fascist faction won control. Eugenio García, a son of Spanish immigrants, recalled, "I played for Unión Española: first in baby football and later in the fourth special team. But Unión was ruined when it sent a salute to Franco during the Spanish Civil War. That, they could not do. That dissolved the union."[70] A similar split occurred in Audax, which lost nearly half its membership because of divisions over Mussolini's fascist state. Club members lamented the demise of their sports organizations and, in keeping with the family metaphor, termed it "fratricide." When they could manage, Unión and Audax continued their social activities. Audax continued to broadcast its radio show, *Radio Club Sportivo Audax Italiano*, which transmitted nightly news, music, and sports events from Italy. The pro-Mussolini bent of the show stirred significant controversy, as did club publications.[71]

With their harmonious family images destabilized by political differences among members, Spanish and Italian clubs used their publications to emphasize the clubs' roles as places of solace from the demands of work and family life. One Audax member explained that single men reveled in avoiding "a woman, club in hand, who waits behind the door . . . rolling her eyes when [her husband] arrives late, explaining to the imp [his wife] that he was praying in the church of the Carmelitas Descalzas [Discalced Carmelites] or was in Mass for the month of Maria—but without saying which Carmelita, or which Maria, he is talking about."[72] Paradoxically, fascism both endangered the fraternity of Audax and Unión and bolstered male authority in their communities. In the late 1930s, club publications promulgated increasingly negative images of the sportsman's wife, implying that men should unite against her presence. As exemplified by the quotation above, sports publications frequently encouraged male infidelity, sympathizing with adultery as an escape from a demanding wife. At the same time, the decline in membership provided clubs with incentives to open opportunities for women. Clubs categorized women's memberships with those of children, and rules prohibited women from athletic facilities, the bar, meetings, and elections.[73]

The rise of Italian and Spanish fascism caused some Chileans to question the principles of European culture. Public antipathy toward the Spanish and Italian communities increased, particularly after the outbreak of the Spanish Civil War and the consolidation of Chile's Popular Front in 1936. The antagonism of crowds toward Unión Española had become so violent by 1938 that the club's directors announced its departure from professional competition. One sportswriter explained, "They say that they have had it with the hostility of the public. True, the Spanish team has never been a crowd favorite, but in any case, the measure is extreme."[74] The withdrawal of the Spanish club adversely affected the finances of the professional league and the Chilean Football Federation. The league and the federation urged fans to stop their violent attacks on players, whom they were now eager to distance from their European heritage. Members of the Popular Front, on the other hand, encouraged fans to hold immigrant sports clubs responsible for their support of fascists. Popular Front supporters complained that Spanish immigrants abused the goodwill of the Chilean people by supporting Francisco Franco. They alerted the police and the press when the Falangists held meetings in Unión Española's Estadio Santa Laura. Supporters of the Popular Front announced that by allowing this, Unión was not an impartial bystander in the struggle between fascists and republicans.[75]

Football crowds also expressed anger toward Audax's support of Benito Mussolini.[76] During their matches, football fans booed, shouted insults, and threw things at Audax players. By 1938, Audax was threatening to drop out of the professional league unless the safety of its players could be guaranteed.[77] Audax maintained close ties to representatives of the Italian government and received funding from them for a number of the club's projects, such as the Scuola Italiana in the mid-1930s (the school taught language and history to children of Italian descent). The Italian government provided financial assistance for the publication of Audax's monthly bulletin. The bulletin served as an important source of communication within the community, announcing weddings, births, and other events. The publication also dedicated ample space to discussions of Mussolini's promotion of sports and complimentary articles about his regime.

Audax's publications reproduced fascist rhetoric that valorized Italy's Roman heritage and modern Italians' connection to what they called the "Latin race." At a club banquet, President Alberto Caffi passionately stated, "The blood that runs in our veins is the inheritance of ancient Rome, great in its power because its sons were great in spirit, mind, and muscle."[78] Directors of Audax encouraged their members to visit Italy under a fascist program to help the "sons of Italy" abroad reconnect with their Italian heritage.[79] Despite the popularity of fascism among some members of Audax, many in the Italian community objected to its support of Mussolini's government. Audax's parent organization, the Centro Democrático Italiano, severed relations with Audax completely. Members of Audax who disagreed with the club's position retreated to smaller Italian sports clubs or neighborhood clubs. Several of the club's directors resigned in protest of the club's politics.

Audax hoped to influence the Chilean government's policies toward Italy. Directors sent petitions, letters, and telegrams urging President Arturo Alessandri to recognize Mussolini and his *Imperio Italiano*. When Alessandri complied in 1936, Audax congratulated him for recognizing that he, like all Italians, descended "from the great common Mother."[80] Directors were frustrated by the lack of cohesion within their community. They complained that immigrants "still did not understand the pride of being a son of Italy, the cradle of arts, letters, and sciences, which disseminated its civilization throughout the world for a millennium."[81] Audax cultivated relationships with its counterparts in Buenos Aires and Montevideo who also praised Mussolini, especially his sports programs. They competed against these clubs to demonstrate their fascist loyalties. When Italian sports clubs in Buenos Aires accused Audax of offering only fainthearted support to the fascist cause, Audax denied it vehemently.[82] As proof of its loyalty to Mussolini's government, the club hosted extravagant celebrations on the anniversary of the Italian Empire in honor of Ambassador Marchi.

As fascism fell into disrepute during and after World War II, the Spanish and Italian football clubs faced the challenge of reuniting their communities. Chile's acceptance of Spanish refugees, the popularity of the Popular Front programs, and the growing energy of leftist parties in the country sapped the fascists' momentum. Unión Española's largest retrospective, *Bodas de Oro*, which celebrated fifty years of the club, lacked even cursory explanations of the divisions caused by the Spanish Civil War or the missing football season of 1938.[83] During the 1940s, Unión regrouped under the leadership of the community's economic elite. Entrepreneurs found an opportunity within this period of reconstruction to streamline football clubs into more profitable businesses, with the occasional support of state agencies. This new generation of directors looked at the huge revenues professional football was garnering in postwar Europe and tried to imitate its structure and management style. In the postwar period, Unión's directors focused on merchandising and building a brand image.

In the postwar climate, Audax and Unión downplayed their relationships to Europe and muted their claims to a superior racial legacy, instead emphasizing the variety of cultural contributions that their communities had made to Chile. They also made an effort to blend Chile's democratic tradition with the authoritarian nature of the Spanish state. Moreover, they tried to connect political characteristics with those in sports. Directors explained, "In the realm of politics, a people committed to discipline and the command of authority are much more democratic; these tendencies support rather than exclude each other. . . . In the realm of sports, there exists one of those apparent contradictions that is in reality nothing other than two concepts that mutually support and strengthen each other. It deals with the subjugation of the bodily spirit to the collectivity, to obedience, and to a social ideal, and with the personal spirit of distinction, originality, and eminence over the rest."[84] With this logic, Unión reconciled its support for the Chilean political system and Franco's dictatorship. Conservative politicians continued to strengthen their role in Unión; for example, Carlos Atienza, who was the secretary-general of the Liberal Party and a congressman, held a director's position for many years in the club.[85]

Audax and its partner organization, Stadio Italiano, which formed after professionalism, had a more difficult time recuperating from the divisions over fascism. Directors also complained that Italian Chileans did not show a commitment to maintaining their Italian-ness. Fears of assimilation surfaced frequently in club publications. One editorial warned, "The Italians of our land would not preserve any racial pride or unity if it were not for the diverse associations that have formed to promote these objectives and provide Italians with their own social seat. . . . Estadio Italiano is a necessary outgrowth of a stable organization that has supported the Italians of our capital."[86] This fear was reinforced by popular perceptions of a population decline in European immigrant communities.[87] One sports magazine concluded that the Italian community had decayed the most, since no "real" Italians lived in Chile any longer.[88]

Social events played a large part in maintaining interest in Spanish and Italian clubs. Weekly dances generated significant revenue, but perhaps more importantly, they energized the club atmosphere on weekend evenings.[89] For adolescents and young adults, the clubs offered opportunities to socialize with the opposite sex, often with parental encouragement. However, organizers complained that teens were often rowdy, sexually expressive, and violent. Chaperones at a dance held at Club Stadio Italiano criticized the sexuality expressed in fashionable dances. They described a spectacle of "screeching and sweaty youth, moving frantically to keep time with chords . . . [and] with their bewitched and idolatrous dances."[90] Parish authorities criticized teenagers for acting like Indians in a state of pre-Christian euphoria.

Despite the fame that professional football brought to clubs, most operated with financial losses. This strengthened their dependency on state support and wealthy directors. While club members grumbled that directors stole the profits or spent lavishly on foreign players, directors bankrolled many club activities. Fifteen years after the formation of the professional league, directors could not count on ticket revenues to pay for stadium projects and club travel. The amateur star Mario Cubillos, who was recruited by Audax, recalled, "I played four months as a trial. . . . They never paid me. One day, someone stole my watch in the locker room, and being quick tempered, I went to Solari, the president, who was also the head of Falabella, and I told him that I was leaving. I walked out and I did not go back. I thought: never again a professional team."[91] Solari, who ran Falabella, one of Chile's largest banks and department store chains, was typical in his approach to club players. Not surprisingly, two players from Audax and Unión, Domingo Sepúlveda and Oscar Sánchez, led the first attempts to form the Professional Football Players' Union.[92] The Professional League collaborated with Unión and Audax to suspend the players for one year. The head of the Professional League's disciplinary tribunal, Julio Ortuzar, wrote the decision. Ortuzar also served as a juvenile court judge in Santiago, which put state power behind the professional league's practices.[93]

MIDDLE EASTERN IMMIGRANT CLUBS

The history of Middle Eastern immigrant clubs illuminates how a dominant, racialized model of national identity shaped social relations and popular culture. Popular culture, as evidenced by publications, illustrations, and humor, perpetuated a belief that Middle Eastern immigrants could not assimilate to "Chilean culture" in the same way as Europeans. These clubs, founded in the 1910s and 1920s, were formed in response to discrimination, which ranged from physical violence to subtler forms of prejudice. Organizers hoped that sports clubs would help disseminate a positive image of their communities in Chilean society, one that ultimately could enable Middle Easterners' full participation in civic life. Moreover, sports directors created relationships with other social leaders through association meetings. Just as in European clubs, entrepreneurs had taken control of Middle Eastern organizations by the 1940s. However, these directors encountered more difficulty than their European counterparts in translating their economic prestige into cultural and political spheres. Their involvement in football clubs shaped, and was shaped by, the popular perception that Middle Eastern immigrants were all men of fortune, an impression derived from their uniquely terrible exploitation of Chilean workers. The dominant image of Chile as a homogenous nation forged of a heritage that was European and, to a lesser extent, indigenous created a permanently foreign status for Syrian, Lebanese, and Palestinian Chileans. Children and grandchildren of immigrants, who spoke Spanish exclusively and had never left the country, still found it difficult to establish themselves as Chilean.

Numerical estimates of Middle Eastern immigration to Chile differ drastically. Social scientists and government sources concur that immigration began in the 1880s from Syria, Palestine, and Lebanon and peaked in the first two decades of the twentieth century. The majority of immigrants identified themselves as Arab Christians and arrived with hopes of escaping the Ottoman Empire's military conscription and rule. One can imagine their disappointment when, upon arrival, they were called Turcos, or Turks.[94] Like their counterparts in Brazil, Middle Eastern immigrant associations in Chile did not necessarily embrace Spanish or "pan-Latin" Catholic culture. Many club directors admired British cultural and social institutions, which they claimed had greater influence in the Middle East than Latin ones. At the beginning of the century, the lines between "Arab" and "Jewish" immigrants from the Middle East were relatively blurry. The majority of Middle Eastern immigrants defined themselves as Arab, which included Jewish, Christian, and Muslim natives of Syria, Palestine, and Lebanon. The earliest sports clubs were overwhelmingly Christian; by the 1930s, Jewish and Muslim immigrants had formed separate clubs.[95] The partition of Palestine had provoked animosity between these groups by the 1950s. In addition, divisions between these immigrants were complicated by their disagreements over Chilean politics.

A range of writers on national identity, race, and immigration attacked Arab Chileans in the early twentieth century. In his influential book *Raza Chilena*, Nicolás Palacios exaggerated Arabic immigration and complained that "Turks" were "stealing" middle-class jobs.[96] The respected journalist Joaquín Edwards Bello wrote scathing editorials in *La Nación* that accused Arab businesses of unethical practices.[97] *El Mercurio*, which had the largest circulation in the country, printed some of the most hateful attacks, likening Arab immigrants to contagions. One editorial stated, "No matter whether they are Muslims or Buddhists, the issue is that they look and stink from afar, that all of them are dirtier than the dogs of Constantinople, and that they enter and leave this country with the liberty that those dogs enjoy in their own land."[98] The journalist suspected that Arab immigrants brought "some of the horrible and mysterious plagues of the Orient, such as the case of leprosy discovered a few days ago in Talcahuano."[99] By equating Arab immigrants with dogs and heightening fears that they brought illnesses from abroad, the writer dehumanized them and incited violence against them. The editorial reinforced representations of the "Orient" as an exotic site of disease, sexual deviance, and mystery.

Recent arrivals from Homs, in contemporary Syria, formed the first Arab Chilean organization, Juventud Homsiense, in 1913. The young founders hoped to counteract negative images of Arabs in the media and threats to their businesses. The police often ignored racist attacks on Arab-owned businesses, which included arson and theft.[100] The press, the attackers, and apologists justified the violence by claiming that Arabic business owners lacked ethics and did not have the right to profit from Chilean consumers. The founders of Juventud Homsiense saw social organization as a way to gain access to the political channels that could help improve their situation. They hoped to cultivate relations with municipal authorities in order to improve police protection in their communities. The antioligarchic rhetoric of Arturo Alessandri during the 1920 presidential campaign appealed to the Arab community and motivated Middle Eastern clubs to become involved in local politics.[101] When business owners posted signs of support for Alessandri, his opponents as well as his supporters ripped them down or broke windows, outraged at the immigrants' engagement with Chilean politics. Following the formation of Juventud Homsiense, Arab immigrants formed Syrian Orthodox societies, charities, and commercial associations. Arab immigrant clubs followed a trajectory similar to the one taken by European clubs. The first sports clubs established separate entities from the parent organizations in the 1920s. Club Deportivo Palestino followed this arc; it joined the professional football league and remains the most visible Arab immigrant organization.

Benedicto Chuaqui's memoirs, *Memorias de un Emigrante*, are a valuable repository of information about the founders of the first Arab Chilean organizations.[102] Chuaqui left Homs at the age of thirteen and settled with his grandfather in the working-class neighborhood of San Pablo, which was replete with lively commerce, a good number of brothels, and a vibrant popular culture. Chuaqui's neighbors gave him the nickname *turquito crespo* (roughly, "nappy little Turk"). During his first attempts at establishing a small shop, Chuaqui faced harassment from municipal agents (whom he eventually bribed) and theft from fellow merchants. In social situations, friends often felt sympathy for Chuaqui, lamenting, "What a shame that you are a Turk!" Chuaqui quickly learned Spanish and sought to participate in the thriving civic associations in Santiago. However, his sisters and aunts in Syria, worried that he would assimilate completely, begged him not to marry a Chilean. Chuaqui, wanting very much to blend in, sought out activities that afforded him the opportunity to improve his Spanish. As an adolescent, he joined a dance academy, but found that potential partners refused to dance with a "Turk." After his sister and her infant child died in a fire (intentionally set) in his store, Chuaqui and his friends founded a community newspaper to publicize cases of arson against immigrant businesses. He volunteered in the firefighting squad as a way to show his community's appreciation for its protection. Chuaqui believed that Chilean democracy would help Arab immigrants achieve full participation in their adopted country if only they made the proper effort to learn Chilean customs. His desire to participate in Chilean politics was representative of a segment of a particular generation. Later immigrants, who had a more well-developed sense of nationalism and a greater ability to stay connected with their countries of origin, looked critically on Chuaqui's advocacy of immersion.

While Chuaqui despised the racism he experienced, he also adopted popular prejudices toward groups he encountered in Santiago. Chuaqui's depiction of Indians concurred with the dominant representations of the indigenous in Chile. He called the Mapuche he hired to help with the newspaper "dumb, but loyal" and blamed his "indigenous blood" for his alcoholism.[103] Chuaqui proposed that Arab clubs participate as often as possible in national celebrations, including the Day of the Race. They were not invited to the tournaments of European immigrant clubs, but found a niche in games sponsored by the municipality. Directors of Arab clubs used history to challenge articles exalting Spanish racial purity. They reminded readers that during the eight hundred years of Moorish rule in Iberia, the Spanish and Arab races had intermingled. They also noted that Arab contributions to science were essential to the discovery of the Americas.[104]

Chuaqui and his social circle founded the Arab community's first sports organizations, Club Deportivo Palestino and Club Deportivo Sirio. Chuaqui explained that the goal of these clubs "was to distinguish Syrians and to defend them from the continual attacks in the press that denigrated our race, presenting it as savage, uncivilized, and immoral."[105] Chuaqui aspired to be as socially committed as possible, which he saw as the bedrock of citizenship. He focused on the cultural cooperation that associations could foster between Chileans and Arab immigrants. Syrian societies he founded were inclusive, encouraging anyone who wanted to join, regardless of nationality, language, sex, or religion.[106]

The tennis star and cofounder of Club Palestino, Elías Deik Lamas, recalled that their attempts to participate in the Chilean sports community were often met with hostility.[107] He remembered that a small circle of friends began to play football informally during their school years and eventually formed Club Palestino, taking their cue from other immigrant groups in Santiago. Deik recalled that most of the members were teenagers, so they joined the Santiago Football Association's Youth League of Honor, which they competed in between 1921 and 1923. To their surprise, competitors as well as spectators insulted their ethnicity and threatened physical violence against them. Deik diplomatically explained their withdrawal from the Santiago Football Association in 1923: "We abandoned those expeditions, since we thought our contenders showed a particular roughness in their play."[108] Deik added with pride, "Until that point, we remained undefeated." After dropping out of the Santiago Football Association, Club Palestino continued to play football informally with other Arab immigrant clubs as well as with students of the Catholic University. In place of football, Club Palestino focused on tennis, "considering it a sport less dangerous and more gentlemanly in its finest manifestations."[109] Deik criticized the treatment Palestino members had received from other football clubs and lauded the manners of tennis players. Through tennis, Deik and his fellow club members claimed a more refined understanding of British sports ethics, which were prized among elite Chilean sportsmen. They echoed upper-class disdain for football's rowdy spectatorship, pointing out that tennis fans exhibited a more masculine control of their emotions.

While Arabic sportsmen stressed the community's unity in its efforts to secure police protection, business loans, and political participation, a great deal of diversity characterized Arab immigrants. After the French and British divided the Ottoman territories at the end of World War I, nationalist divisions among Arab immigrants emerged with greater force. Although they collaborated in associations under the general category of "Arab," sportsmen split among themselves in the 1920s, creating Syrian, Palestinian, and Lebanese sports clubs. Palestinian dominance of the Arab immigrant community organizations sparked resentment from Syrian and Lebanese members. In addition, directors of Club Palestino were highly concerned with the loss of tradition and the dangers of integration, as was reflected in the club structure. Whereas Lebanese and Syrian clubs allowed other

Arab national groups or Chileans to join, Club Palestino's statutes limited the right to vote, hold office, or represent the club to Palestinians and their "direct descendents."[110] A lesser category of membership existed for those who had no familial affiliation to the Palestinian community.

Members of the social and sports club Sirio Palestino sought to position themselves as political subjects independent of appointed officials, explaining that they needed a voice "beyond those that represent us before the authorities of the country and immigrant community."[111] Rather than focus on the maintenance of its members' homeland traditions, Sirio Palestino wanted to forge relations with the Chilean intellectual and political set. Although Club Palestino and Sirio Palestino pursued political activities similar to those of Italian and Spanish clubs, the press denounced their activities. Like other civic associations in Santiago, they raised money for earthquake victims, lobbied the government to stop the passage of immigration limits in 1928, and sent Carlos Ibáñez a wedding gift. However, El Mercurio and other major dailies viewed these activities as an attempt by foreigners to control Chilean politics. In 1931, El Mercurio described the clubs' activities as electoral interference.[112] Sirio Palestino responded with a letter to the editors: "We consider the motivation for these statements a lamentable error. Many of our members hold Chilean citizenship, and many others, through their Chilean birth, have the right to participate in these activities. They have been confused with and considered foreigners; therefore, it was thought our community interfered in political struggles."[113]

To publicize the characteristics of its community, as well as to include it in the national demography, Club Palestino conducted a census of Arab immigrants in 1941. Studies of immigration in Latin America have argued against taking numbers from immigrant communities at face value. Regardless of its accuracy, the census reveals that club directors believed that the Palestinian community was twice as numerous as the next largest Arab population, the Syrians.[114] According to the census and qualitative accounts, Syrian and Lebanese immigrants integrated faster into Chilean society; they entered professions such as law and had higher rates of marriage to Chileans, whether of Arab descent or otherwise.[115] Despite the Palestinian directors' cautious approach to assimilation, Benedicto Chuaqui made his argument in the census, writing, "Our Chilean sons already have contracted an obligation with this land. They form part of the Chilean family. Their blood, heightened by the miracle of love, will be part of tomorrow's hopes, which Chile's future will depend upon."[116]

By the post–World War II era, directors of Middle Eastern clubs were frustrated that the commercial success of their ethnic cohort, particularly in the textile industry and banking, had not translated into political power. Alberto Yazigi, the president of the Círculo Árabe (a social club for Arab immigrants), believed the community needed what Bourdieu later termed "cultural and social capital." Yazigi argued that Arab immigrants needed to develop social relationships in order to integrate into political networks. While Arab Chileans moved in circles of high culture through their support of opera and their memberships in country clubs, they lacked a place in mass culture. Yazigi suggested that a pan-Arab sports organization, such as the Juventud Deportiva Árabe, could create a space for their community within popular culture.[117]

As with European sports directors, Arab Chilean leaders viewed political power as an essential way to influence state policy toward the Middle East. For example, the leaders of Palestino sent petitions, letters, and banquet invitations to the government of President Arturo Alessandri, pushing the administration to recognize Palestinian independence.[118] By the 1940s, leaders had broadened their ambitions, hoping to influence domestic policies and conditions as well. To help potential entrepreneurs and political candidates from their community, Arab civic associations collaborated to form a bank. The project grew out of the repeated experience of discriminatory practices by Chilean banks, which offered Arab Chileans unfair loan terms or rejected their applications for credit altogether. The sports director Juan Commandari hoped that the bank could help fund the capital projects of sports clubs as well as entrepreneurial and political ventures. Commandari hoped to halt the dispersion of second- and third-generation Arab Chileans. He lamented, "The sons of Arabs are distant, and many have never met the sons of our friends. Sport is a way to stimulate social interaction among the collectivity."[119] The emphasis on sons was not only a linguistic convention. Arab Chilean clubs conceptualized the role of women much as did other sports organizations. In the annual of Club Sirio Palestino, President Hafez Awad explained, "It is possible to live without the love of a woman, but it is not possible to live without the love of country. . . . A woman forgets us, leaves us, does not wait for our devotion; the patria does not forget, does not stop loving us, and does not despair of hoping for our affection and, more than this, our grandest sacrifices."[120]

Arab Chilean sportsmen hoped to create relationships among their members across the nation as well as with other ethnic clubs. Clubs

Deportivo Sirio and Deportivo Palestino developed rivalries in basket-ball with Club Israelita.[121] In the 1930s and early 1940s, Jewish and Arab sportsmen organized events with one another. They discussed how they faced similar prejudices. Common stereotypes depicted Jewish and Arab immigrants as being motivated solely by profit and lacking scruples in busi-ness. These stereotypes precluded the possibility of there being working-class Arab and Jewish Chileans. Although Arab and Jewish sports clubs declared their support for peaceful coexistence in the 1930s—stating, "We recognize Jews have the right to live and flourish in Palestine and feel the land is theirs"—the 1948 Arab-Israeli War damaged their relationship.[122] By the 1940s, Arabs' concerns with integration into Chilean politics had taken a backseat to their struggles against Zionism. In their efforts to deni-grate Zionists, Arab Chileans took an increasingly conservative stance in domestic politics. Headlines such as "In the United States they don't want Jews either" made Arab Chilean animosity toward the Jewish community clear.[123] In 1946, Arab Chileans premiered *El Mundo Árabe*, a radio show that took its name from a community newspaper. The radio program lasted only a year, and the newspaper accused Zionists of arranging its cancela-tion.[124] Arab Chileans also attempted to revive the link between commu-nism and Judaism as a way to convince center and right-wing politicians to support their anti-Zionist positions. Though community leaders insisted that their stances applied only to Zionism, their rhetoric often invoked anti-Semitism.[125]

Sports magazines, newspapers, and comic strips depicted Arab Chileans as parasitic. They caricatured Arab business leaders as voracious social climbers who built empires by exploiting Chilean workers and consumers. However, the history of Arab immigration contradicted this narrative. A significant number of wealthy Arab Chileans brought substantial wealth with them when they immigrated and then were further assisted by government contracts. Their story is distinct from a Horatio Alger tale of social mobility. In addition, it differs from what scholars have surmised about the Arab communities in Argentina and Brazil.[126] Anti-Arab rhetoric aimed at categorizing the immigrants as gaudy parvenus ignored the histories of families such as the Yarurs, who arrived to Chile with a fortune from Bolivia and Peru. In a similar vein, one descendent of a textile factory owner recalled, "My grandfather began his plant, Algodones Sumar, in 1941 and was a tough competitor of Yarur. He did not come to Chile, as some say, to make a fortune. He arrived at the Hotel Carrera with $750,000, which he invested in machinery."[127]

Sportsmen directed critiques of class privilege at immigrant teams from Europe, but showed particular disdain for Arab clubs, drawing upon racist images and assumptions. The popular weekly *Estadio* complained that the facilities of immigrant clubs, including those of Stade Francais, Audax Italiano, Unión Española, Club Palestino, and Estadio Sirio, were "all from the same mold: exclusive, closed, made for the solace of the moneyed men of our land."[128] The sportswriter went on to suggest that these facilities should be open to the general public when the clubs were not using them. Working-class amateurs resented the modern facilities of immigrant clubs. *Estadio* blamed the lack of appropriate sports facilities for the average Chilean on the monopoly of resources enjoyed by immigrant clubs. Sportsmen claimed that in cities such as Buenos Aires, the state had ensured more opportunities for "natives."[129] After Club Palestino entered the professional football association in 1952, one sportswriter complained, "Already they cannot live in peace with their *baisanos*. The best men of football are somewhat restless and waiting for an offer from Palestino. . . . They are arming the new rich of professional football."[130] (*"Baisanos"* was a term of mockery for the mispronunciation of *"paisanos,"* or fellow countrymen.) As anti-imperialist rhetoric intensified in the 1950s and 1960s, leftist parties and labor organizations questioned the civil rights of Arab Chilean businessmen. Sports coverage was less hostile than the coverage of labor conflicts, as in *El Siglo*, for example, even when the business and sports leader was the same person (such as Amador Yarur). Leaders of Club Palestino made overtures to sports journalists by, for example, organizing elegant luncheons every month for members of the press. As part of fund-raising campaigns, sports directors tried to convince Arab immigrants that sports clubs were a sound investment, both for financial returns and for their public relations value.[131]

The domination of civic associations by the wealthiest sector of Arab Chileans obscured the participation of many working- and middle-class members, particularly those with leftist political positions. The assumption that all Arab Chileans supported the Conservatives persisted despite the prominence of several directors with ties to leftist parties. For example, the director Sabino Aguad was a well-known supporter of Socialist Salvador Allende. Aguad's father arrived in Chile after fleeing Turkish army con-scription.[132] Aguad was born in Chile and raised in Barrio Recoleta. He recalled that he and his friends were fanatics of Colo Colo, Magallanes, and Unión Española. Aguad played basketball for the traveling team of Sport Juvenil Árabe while he was in law school. Instead of practicing law, Aguad decided to pursue a career as a sports trainer and director. As a sports director, he worked to improve relations among amateur and professional clubs, promoted women's integration, and built ties with political figures on the center-left. He served as president of the Chilean Olympic Committee several times, beginning with his appointment by the Christian Democrat Eduardo Frei. At a dinner in Aguad's honor, Salvador Allende joked, "I feel truly envious of my great friend Sabino, *compañero* of so many sports struggles throughout his life. He has been president twenty-two years, and I have been a candidate for eighteen."[133] After winning his presidential bid in 1970, Allende appointed Aguad director of the State Department of Sports. Aguad coordinated many of the Popular Unity projects, including exchanges with Cuba and the nationalization of the magazine *Estadio*.

Leaders of the Arab immigrant community who hoped to find a niche within popular culture for their organizations decided to participate in football once again in the mid-1940s. Amador Yarur, who was elected president of Club Deportivo Palestino for the first time in 1945, promised to enter Palestino in both the professional and amateur ranks of football.[134] A skilled businessman and son of textile entrepreneur Juan Yarur, Amador procured new investments for the club. Under his administration, Palestino gained national recognition, but the project of constructing a professional club alienated some of the club's rank-and-file members. In particular, the middle-class Lebanese and Syrian immigrants who had helped build the club lost their connection to Palestino. As part of the professionalization of Palestino's football club, Amador Yarur and his family planned the construction of an elaborate stadium complex. When Yarur encountered greater difficulty than he expected in raising the seed money, he complained that the older generation of Arab Chileans did not understand that the stadium facilities would be a good investment in the long term. Yarur lured star players, acquired a marketable logo, and advertised sports events. Despite his promise of quick profits, sportsmen from an earlier generation, including Emilio Deik and Benedicto Chuaqui, showed ambivalence about the project. They complained that professional football did not serve to encourage social interaction or civic participation among members.[135] Finally, older members failed to see how a professional team without players of Arab descent would improve the image of the community.[136]

Not only did directors of Palestino face objections from other community leaders in their efforts to create a professional squad, but other football directors also accused them of bribing officials and using other "dirty tactics."[137] Specifically, directors scrutinized the entrance of Palestino into the second division, from which they could climb into the Division of Honor. Other clubs complained that Palestino lacked a tradition of football and experience in professional sports. The director of Palestino's football team, Enrique Atal, admitted that he and other officers had called in numerous favors so that their team could enter the professional league. Moreover, Atal convinced friends with influence in the sports community, such as the journalist Carlos Arancibia, to campaign for Palestino. Amador Yarur's brother Jorge, a lawyer and director of the newspaper *Imparcial*, also helped convince football authorities to allow Palestino's entrance.[138] Jorge Yarur had been a longtime supporter of amateur clubs such as Fútbol Carioca and Stade Francais, which had allowed him to build a number of relationships with members of the Chilean Football Federation. Over the objections of many sportsmen both inside and outside the club, Palestino FC entered the professional league in time for the 1952 season. Sportswriters hinted that directors of Palestino had stolen the presidential election of 1952 for Carlos Ibáñez and would employ the same tactics in football.[139] Almost immediately, newspapers attacked Palestino for recruiting the Robledo brothers. The brothers came from a Chilean family living in Great Britain, where they played for Newcastle. When they announced their plans to return to Chile, every professional team tried to recruit them. However, fans and journalists criticized only Palestino for trying to "steal" the Robledos from Colo Colo, by using its ill-gotten gains.[140]

The same year that Palestino put together its first professional team, the Arab Chilean community became the subject of national controversy over its role in the government of Carlos Ibáñez. A number of community leaders had become closely tied to both Ibáñez's presidential campaign and the new Partido Agrario Laborista, a conservative party with regional roots, which provided a support base for Ibáñez. In addition to political scandals, labor disputes shaped sports publications' criticism of Palestino. In the early 1950s, the sports director Elías Musalén attempted to quash workers' demands at his textile firm, Musalén e Hijos. Workers complained that the company did not respect their right to unionize, intimidated noncompliant workers, and paid exploitative wages. Their arguments contained nationalist elements that focused on Musalén's "foreignness" and his "Arab Palestinian-Lebanese" descent. The workers demanded that the government deport Musalén to Palestine, without bothering to ask whether Musalén was in fact a Chilean citizen or not.[141] The workers' press acknowledged that the Musalén company had been in Chile for decades: "As we have stated, Elías Musalén is an Arab

Palestinian-Lebanese citizen, hence a foreigner, who has amassed an immense fortune in Chile with the ruthless exploitation of generations of textile workers. . . . He deserves nothing less than to be expelled from the country."[142]

As sports organizations more and more often elected directors of Middle Eastern descent during the 1960s, sports publications drew frequent parallels between their supposed corruption of both politics and sports, implying that a broad cultural conspiracy existed in the community.[143] One of the principal scandals of the Ibáñez administration (1952–1958) involved his economic minister, Rafael Tarud.[144] Congressmen accused Tarud of showing favoritism to the firms of Yarur and Kattan in the establishment of import-export quotas for cotton. Sports publications and directors argued that these companies received the highest quotas because they were the largest firms. Arab civic associations labeled the incident "political racism" and claimed that Jews and light-skinned immigrants did not face the same scrutiny. Moreover, they explained that Yarur's board of directors included none other than ex-president Arturo Alessandri.[145] Connections between Arab Chileans and these politicians only increased the Yarurs' unpopularity with working-class amateurs.[146] While some well-known community leaders had connections with conservative parties, especially the Partido Agrario Laborista, Arab Chileans integrated into politics across the right-left spectrum. For example, in the 1950s, Alejandro Chelen was elected to Congress from the Popular Socialist Party and two other Arab Chileans were elected from the Radical Party, Alfredo Nazar and Carlos Melej.[147]

Observers such as the political scientist Donald Bray argued that despite the Arab community's increased access to political channels under Ibáñez, it continued to lack social prestige corresponding to its economic status. Bray noted, "The political advances which Tarud and other Arab-Chileans achieved during the 1952–1958 Ibáñez government were a delayed counterpart to the economic gains which the group had made earlier. Ibañismo, divorced from established ideologies and socio-political traditions, was a non-exclusive banner under which Arab-Chileans found political opportunity. The struggle for social equality remains, and will not be won until Arab-Chileans do, indeed, figure prominently among the membership of the Club de la Unión."[148] Although never accepted by the traditional oligarchy, Arab immigrants appeared on the rosters of the Club de la Unión, a very exclusive social club, in the 1920s. Arab community leaders who obtained political posts did not hale from the wealthiest sector.

Rather, those who received posts combined experience in key industries with prominent service in civic associations. For example, Miguel Labán, the longtime sports director of Deportivo Sirio, became ambassador to Syria and Lebanon. Those who contended that Arabic politicians and businessmen followed Ibáñez solely because of his "outsider" status underestimated their collaboration with the traditional oligarchy. Businessmen typically contributed to more than one political campaign, including that of Socialist Salvador Allende. As one businessman explained, "Capitalists are obliged to be on good terms with everyone."[149]

The formation of Palestino's professional football club boosted enthusiasm among some club members, particularly young ones. Directors used the momentum to expand the club's social activities. In the year 1951 alone, Palestino held numerous conferences (on topics ranging from Chilean history to Oriental medicine), installed a movie theater, held Arab music concerts, and hosted political figures such as the Egyptian ambassador.[150] One sports fan gushed, "A new emotion has awakened in the local Arab collectivity. Never before has it felt more exuberance, a passion of this sort."[151] Observers noted that members packed into the salons of Club Palestino to mingle with their favorite players and discuss sports. After a successful season in 1953, Club Palestino toured Colombia, Ecuador, and Peru. Club directors hoped to represent Chile abroad and to express "how united we feel with this generous land."[152] In addition, they felt that a touring football club would challenge prejudices that Arab immigrants contributed only to commerce in Latin America. Seeking to dismantle another prejudice—that Arab immigrants were archaically sexist—directors urged female club members to take a greater interest in the team. When female turnout increased, one member reported happily that the stands included "not only a masculine public but also a lovely number of the feminine element of our community."[153] Several women's teams in Palestino, including basketball, elected women as coaches and directors in the 1950s.

Despite the efforts of directors to dispel prejudice, sports magazines continued to express resentment toward Arab Chileans in jokes, anecdotes, and editorials. They ascribed Spanish clubs' success to "ingenuity" and "hard work," but described Arab immigrants' success with words like "parasitic" and "new rich." The use of politicized terms such as "sultanic" had far-reaching consequences for Arab Chilean prominence. Rather than breaking down stereotypes, Palestino's entry into professional football fueled negative attacks on Arab Chileans. These increased throughout the 1950s and 1960s when directors from Palestino won offices in national football organizations. For example, the vice president of Colo Colo circulated an anecdote about a trip to his bank.[154] He explained to a sportswriter that he held his accounts with the Bank of Credit and Investments (at that time controlled by the Yarur family) and commented to a group of his friends, "I do not have any complaint. They treat me well. But there is something that disorients me. Each time I go in . . . the employee takes slips from the window and reads in a high voice, 'Ananías! . . . Abumohor! . . . Nazur! . . . Yarur! . . . Abogabir! . . . Musalem! . . . López . . .' Imagine it. I feel sucked dry. I must be the only foreigner in the bank."[155]

The point of the joke was clear: the vice president of Colo Colo, which claimed to represent "the people," had been made to feel foreign by "actual" foreigners. The story also plays upon the "commonsense" idea that a bank is where the Arab community would be found in such large numbers—again playing upon the stereotype that money was the community's sole motivation. Yet the president of Audax Italiano had also been a director of the same bank without facing such comments. Sports journalists heaped praise upon Unión Española and reserved their skepticism for Palestino. For example, in 1961, Unión constructed a club headquarters that cost hundreds of millions of pesos and included several restaurants, clinics, volleyball courts, etc.[156] Sportswriters commented, "They go forward with all the force of established businesses and with the go-getter attitude typical of the Spanish character."[157] Implicit within the description of the Spanish character was the notion that it reflected an essential part of the Chilean identity as well. In the case of the Spanish Chileans, their ambition represented a positive quality, whereas in an Arab Chilean it represented usury.

Despite specific gains made by the Arab Chilean community in social circles, prejudices and discriminatory practices showed an impressive resiliency that grew stronger in the polarized political atmosphere of the 1960s. Spanish and Italian immigrants easily incorporated themselves into the model of Chilean mestizaje. Popular culture, political programs of the Popular Front, and professional "experts" contributed to the acceptance of this model and claims that Chile was a homogenous nation. The persistent emphasis on the harmonious homogeneity of Chilean society hindered discussions of violence against ethnic communities. Civic associations rarely if ever discussed the existence of racial hierarchies. Yet these hierarchies shaped understandings of class differences, national identity, and immigration. They influenced how immigrant civic associations made political claims. In the case of Arab Chilean organizations, these hierarchies made

FIGURE 4.3.   This cartoon caricatured the Arab Chilean leaders of professional football as greedy. The exaggerated noses, earrings, and dress accentuated their foreignness. *Estadio*, 1963. Image courtesy of Zig-Zag.

it difficult to translate economic success into acceptance within cultural, social, and political spheres. Arab Chileans also found their civic rights challenged as a result of being labeled permanently foreign, in contrast to Spanish and Italian immigrants. Spanish and Italian footballers were valued among organizations, while Arabic immigrants faced violent reactions to their participation in both football and politics. Issues of integration, nationalism, and professionalism divided Arab sportsmen. Both European and Arabic immigrant clubs underwent professionalization, which created a growing class division between the directors and members. However, Italian and Spanish Chileans did not face the same criticisms for being materialist that were leveled against Arab Chilean organizations.

The history of football clubs demonstrates the complicated interplay among local, national, and transnational archetypes. It also illustrates the importance of participating in cultural practices and civic associations for the exercise of citizenship. Arab Chilean clubs recognized this from the beginning of the twentieth century but had only limited success in overcoming their status as permanently foreign. The narrative of Chile as a racially homogenous nation of mestizos, with a dominant European heritage, relied upon the exclusion and stereotyping of outsiders such as Arab Chileans and Afro-Brazilians. This narrative was reinforced by the absence of consideration for the contemporary indigenous communities in Chile.

The image of foreign players remained relatively constant. As the century progressed, sportswriters placed less emphasis on players' biological heritage, but they continued to debate whether Chilean football suffered from racial or environmental deficiencies. They consoled themselves that the country's racial unity had produced a stable political system and a spirit of democracy. Amateur sportsman in the 1950s challenged these explanations for the failure of Chilean football internationally, claiming that economic inequality was to blame instead.[158] The narrative of Chile as a homogenous fraternity would remain constant throughout the 1960s and 1970s, reinforcing Chileans' tendency to understand social conflicts as the result of political and economic differences.

"BECAUSE WE HAVE NOTHING . . ."
The Radicalization of Amateurs and the World Cup of 1962

5

In the 1950s, amateur football clubs created a magnetic icon of the popular barrio player. This figure became a symbol of working-class ingenuity and class injustice. Amateurs tore away at the perception of sports as fair by exposing the corruption of professional clubs and the material deprivation of the working class. The influence of the Communist and Socialist parties among amateurs began to supersede that of the Radicals. Historical memory of Popular Front projects, popular clubs from the early 1900s, and the campaign for the National Stadium shaped the construction of the barrio football idol. However, more than any other factor, the relationship between labor unions, leftist political parties, and neighborhood associations encouraged the dissemination of a rebellious icon. The emergence of this hero reflected the process of radicalization that was occurring within and beyond the political sphere. This chapter argues that football clubs, through their creative and organizational practices, contributed to radicalization in working-class neighborhoods. The boom in barrio football clubs became a centerpiece of the Chilean bid to host the World Cup of 1962. Preparations for the event brought to light the ways in which the Cold War shaped relationships within football organizations. Professionals, led by corporate executives with strong connections to the state, sought to depoliticize and delocalize football in order to turn it into a profitable business. Their attacks on the "Marxist" amateurs and the conflicts that ensued shaped how footballers and their fans understood political divisions.

Across Latin America, male archetypes in popular culture celebrated working-class sexual virility and rebelliousness. Despite state efforts to create a unified national identity within popular culture, these icons contained an antigovernment element. The explicitly political nature of the Chilean barrio hero distinguished him from similar figures. One apparent parallel would be the *malandro*, who emerged as a central figure in Brazilian samba beginning in the late 1920s. The malandro was a charming misfit opposed to a regulated schedule of work and home life.[1] He was most comfortable in the poor neighborhoods of Rio de Janeiro, stealthily navigating its dangers. In spite of the disdain of Getúlio Vargas's regime, the malandro's popularity persisted throughout the 1950s. At the same time, some samba musicians criticized the malandro as part of the structure of economic exploitation. They pointed out that rejection of education and the state closed off opportunities for social mobility. Another Latin American icon, the Argentine *pibe*, resembled the Chilean barrio footballer.[2] Sportswriters credited the talented young neighborhood player, or pibe, for the success of Argentine football. His style embodied innovation, spontaneity, and creativity, as opposed to the mechanics of the British style of play. Argentine sports magazines like *El Gráfico* credited the working-class environment, especially the makeshift playing fields, with shaping the pibe's style.[3] In his perpetual youthfulness and rejection of paternal responsibility, the pibe was certainly rebellious. Unlike the Chilean barrio hero, the icon was not connected with a particular political position.

The 1950s, which were crucial years in Chilean politics, saw a tripartite split between the Right, Center, and Left. By the end of the decade, Chile was one of the few countries in the world where Socialists and Communists could realistically hope to take power through electoral means. This was surprising, given what seemed to be two events that worsened the environment for leftist parties: the prohibition of the Communist Party and the dissolution of the Popular Front alliance. In 1948, the Radical president Gabriel González passed the Law for the Permanent Defense of Democracy, which outlawed the Communist Party. The law removed more than twenty thousand members of the Communist Party from the electoral register, effectively barring them from participation in elections for political or trade union offices.[4] Furthermore, the law sent thousands to the Pisagua concentration camp and into exile. Ironically, Communists had provided significant support to González's campaign in 1946. Perhaps his association with the left wing of the Radical Party, combined with the Communist Party's success in the 1947 municipal elections (more than 16 percent of the vote), created strong pressures on González to demonstrate his anticommunism. Since González's predecessors had vetoed similar measures in the late 1930s and 1940s, it is logical to assume that the Cold War created a powerful anticommunist sentiment.[5]

Barrio leaders responded to the collapse of the Popular Front and the persecution of the Communists with renewed attention to local civic associations.[6] Amateur football clubs were among the largest and most politicized of these neighborhood organizations. Santiago's population grew from around five hundred thousand in the 1920s to around two million by the end of the 1950s.[7] Much of this population growth was due to a wave of migration, which intensified struggles over land use and forced many residents into shantytowns. These makeshift neighborhoods appeared so quickly that they were called *callampas*, or mushrooms. Social scientists have identified shantytown residents as key actors in the political radicalization of the working class in Santiago. The study of the politics in shantytowns during the 1940s and 1950s has been neglected, despite a significant body of scholarship that treats the subject under the dictatorship of Augusto Pinochet.[8] Filling this gap has been the image of neighborhoods radicalized by, rather than having given rise to, repression or polarization. In newly formed shantytowns, football clubs provided important spaces for sociability. Clubhouses and football fields, along with plazas and schools, marked the borders of neighborhoods. One director explained, "Without football . . . a group of people cannot be called a community."[9] For many residents, clubs embodied the history of their neighborhood and its character.

The process of creating community identities, albeit changing and unstable, constituted an important political practice in shantytowns. As Verónica Schild explained in her analysis of shantytown movements: "Political learning in this context is a form of cultural production through everyday language that involves competent and creative participants, not passive receivers of preestablished discourses."[10] Few positive images of the poor appeared in newspapers, literature, or movies.[11] Even the descriptions of shantytowns by "sympathetic" social workers were judgmental and sensational. They focused on sexual deviance, alcoholism, and the lack of morality in working-class barrios.[12] While residents frequently agreed with "expert" observers on the need for fundamental change in their barrios, they maintained a sense of optimism and purpose regarding their communities. Whereas mainstream publications portrayed shantytowns as havens of delinquency, local sports clubs stressed that their members, though poor, were healthy, civically conscious, and talented.

THE INDEPENDENT REPUBLIC OF SAN MIGUEL

Just south of the city's center, the sprawling municipality of San Miguel was known for its militant workers and macho footballers. In reference to the neighborhood's distinctive character, the Socialist politician Mario Palestro called it the "Independent Republic of San Miguel." A case study of San Miguel illustrates both the process of radicalization and the effervescence of amateurism in popular neighborhoods. During the 1950s, barrio clubs participated in campaigns to acquire utilities, housing, and public space. In the process, they strengthened their relationships with unions and local politicians. In their appeals for state support, San Miguel's footballers argued that clubs developed young men into future leaders. Their delegates to the Chilean Football Federation warned that without its support for barrio football, civic life would suffer. In an open letter to the director of the State Department of Sports, one leader explained, "The rowdy teens of the barrios protect it and provide for its future. Each neighborhood must have its club, up and running. There, they make snot-nosed kids into machos. And Chile can save itself by believing in its children."[13] Making boys into machos, as the directors phrased their mission, meant teaching young players the proper forms of behavior in social situations with other men, a sense of responsibility, and a commitment to their communities. Instead of embracing the Victorian model of amateurism, barrio clubs rejected restraint and indifference. Barrio footballers criticized class inequalities by claiming to possess a more "honorable" masculinity, based upon manual labor, solidarity with other workers, and political militancy, than upper-class players.[14]

Storytelling, practical joking, nicknaming, drinking, and football playing provided club members with opportunities to build intergenerational relationships and impart neighborhood lore. Older members hoped to generate enthusiasm among youth for their community projects. One director explained, "While [clubs] do not provide adequate means to live, [without them] it would be impossible to ensure the social tranquility of the neighborhood."[15] Clubs created and preserved local histories through yearbooks, trophy cases, and libraries at their social seats. They linked San Miguel's success in sports to its importance in Chilean textiles, metalwork, and meat production.[16] Barrio directors claimed that the physical nature of working in these industries sharpened their players' athletic abilities. Football matches in San Miguel were public performances where players could "prove" their superiority over men who often had power over them in other spheres.[17] Footballers often attributed their skillful dribbling, endurance, and creativity to their working-class upbringing. The notion that workers' barrios cultivated ideal citizens contrasted with prevailing social attitudes toward the urban poor.

According to popular history, the Spanish crown granted the territory that would become San Miguel to Gaspar Banda Aguilar, who came to Chile with Diego de Almagro in the 1530s. During his persecution by the Spanish Inquisition, Banda made a pact with Saint Michael that if he lived, he would construct a church in the saint's honor. Banda successfully raised the church, and the surrounding area became known, after the parish, as San Miguel. San Miguel remained an agricultural area during the colonial and early republican eras. The wealthy Subercaseaux family owned much of the land, cultivating vineyards for wine production and using it as the site for a vacation home. In the mid-nineteenth century, Senator Ramón Subercaseaux donated land to create a public park, a penitentiary, and a slaughterhouse. These three institutions remained important markers of San Miguel throughout the twentieth century. Beginning in the early 1910s, newcomers sought housing in San Miguel; rising real estate prices and inadequate infrastructure drove residents from the city's center. Small industrial ventures peppered the area; however, most residents worked in agriculture until the 1930s, when industries such as metal factories became the primary employers. These industries attracted significant numbers of skilled laborers. In addition, a significant middle-class population moved to San Miguel between the 1920s and 1940s. These residents clustered around the park El Llano.[18]

For urban planners, San Miguel symbolized the problematic development of Santiago. By the 1950s, San Miguel had grown to more than 100,000 residents. The expansion of its boundaries beyond the municipality's control strained the local government's ability to provide services. Urban planners who had hoped to transform Santiago into South America's most modern city were exasperated by the municipality's unruliness.[19] State projects that relocated squatters from the city's center and northern neighborhoods to San Miguel further stretched the municipality's resources.[20] This population increase resulted in severe housing shortages, keeping the quality of housing substandard. According to government census information, the majority of houses in poorer districts lacked running water, electricity, and bathrooms.

UNIONS AND FOOTBALL

Clashes between labor unionists and their employers drew national attention to San Miguel as a hotbed of political conflict. Relationships between the workplace and surrounding communities encouraged the emergence of a militant working-class identity. Union sports clubs and football matches strengthened the connections between members' work and home lives. For example, the football club of MADEMSA, a large metal factory, attracted fans without any affiliation to the company. Approximately thirty metalworkers founded Club Deportivo MADEMSA in 1937; twenty years later, membership had grown to more than one thousand.[21] Although membership was limited to factory workers, thousands of residents followed the club avidly to matches around the city and even in provincial areas. According to one fan, although MADEMSA was "formed exclusively of workers," it was better known as a neighborhood club than a factory club.[22] Female factory workers formed a basketball team in the early 1950s; however, football remained the club's spectator sport. Although club statutes did not specifically exclude women, it was "common knowledge" that women were not invited to play football, and directors recruited players from exclusively male work sections.

Officially, MADEMSA's sports club was autonomous from the union; in practice, however, membership in the union was mandatory for those wanting to participate in the club. Many workers who began as sportsmen in Club MADEMSA went on to leadership positions in the union, and vice versa. The union publicized football club events in its paper, *El Músculo*, which was distributed throughout San Miguel. Union and neighborhood newspapers provided crucial publicity for barrio football matches. Their coverage connected fans, who also met in the stands, around the radio, on the shop floor, and in corner bars. Local media coverage boosted the prestige of standout football players in their communities. Furthermore, in contrast to national publications such as *Estadio*, these papers criticized governmental agencies, professional clubs, and national newspapers for their neglect of amateur sports.[23]

Journalists for union newspapers were attentive to class hierarchies in their writing. They highlighted features of players' lives, such as economic migration, that working-class readers would have likely experienced. Articles about the MADEMSA player Carlos Orrego, for example, described his impoverished childhood at length. Born into poverty in the small town of La Calera, Orrego attended just a year of primary school, which he described as a luxury. The economic distress caused by the death of his father forced Orrego to leave school for work in the limestone mines. *El Músculo* added, "As a good patriot and citizen, he voluntarily presented himself for duty, completing his military service in a regiment at the capital."[24] The poor made up a disproportionate number of those who completed their military duty, and many readers would have identified with Orrego's trajectory. Unions and working-class associations routinely criticized elites for evading military service. Leaders often cited this as evidence that real patriotism flourished among working-class men.

Orrego's economic migration would have been familiar to working-class readers. In the 1920s, he moved from La Calera, lured by salaries at the El Teniente copper mines, and relocated to Santiago in the 1940s. At El Teniente, he served as captain of the football club Unión Cordillera. He also played basketball and ran in track-and-field competitions. *El Músculo* described Orrego's "all-around" athleticism as part of a worker-sportsman tradition, thus rejecting the idea that the attributes of amateurism were intrinsic to British or bourgeois culture. Moreover, the attention given to Orrego's experiences in the copper and limestone mines underscored his connection to the birthplace of the Chilean labor movement. Sports journalists for union papers frequently credited barrio footballers who migrated from mining areas with bringing class consciousness to the city.

El Músculo heaped praise on Orrego for his political activities. This differed from similar accounts in the mainstream press, which lauded football's ability to transcend ethnic, class, and regional differences. Football clubs played a key role in Orrego's integration into union and local politics. Once Orrego arrived in the capital, his reputation as a talented footballer had helped him land a job at MADEMSA. In addition, he joined San Miguel's oldest barrio football club, Carlos Walker Martínez, where fellow members introduced him to local political circles. Orrego was subsequently elected to San Miguel's city council. One writer remarked, "As generals wear medals and decorations for battles won and services rendered to the country, other achievements: secretary-general of the Metalworkers Union, president of Carlos Walker Martínez, president of the Cooperative of Employees and Workers of MADEMSA, director of various sports clubs in the neighborhood, and member of the Central Committee of the Socialist Party."[25] The interlocking relationship between unions, clubs, and local politics made women's marginalization in these arenas all the more difficult to challenge.

Players and trainers drew upon their talent in football to land factory jobs in San Miguel that provided a respectable income. For example, the coach of MADEMSA's premier football squad in the 1950s had played for both Audax Italiano and Green Cross.[26] However, fans and players did not automatically welcome those who moved from professional to union clubs. Thus, sports club directors made efforts to highlight these players' working-class credentials. When Carlos López, previously a professional player for Colo Colo, joined the MADEMSA club, writers introduced him with an anecdote that stressed his humble beginnings. *El Músculo* reported that López had been so poor when he began playing for Colo Colo that he carried his sports clothes in a crate, unable to afford a gym bag. Writers for *El Músculo* clarified that although López had played for Colo Colo, he was "one of them."[27] López attributed his gritty and creative style of play to his modest background. He claimed that before joining MADEMSA, he had never thrived as a "true" sportsman. In the amateur club, he found understanding and respect among teammates. Camaraderie and solidarity were staple characteristics of the ideal barrio footballer.

Despite the frequency with which sports clubs and unions shared members and leaders, sportsmen guarded their independence. They repeatedly voted to maintain distinctions between the two entities.[28] In the case of the paper and ceramics factory El Carrascal, the sports club provided space for workers to organize a union.[29] Union leaders assumed the entities would merge once the union was well established, but the president of Club Deportivo Carrascal campaigned to keep them separate. The sports club president convinced members that the objectives of the sports club were distinct from those of the union, and eventually the club passed a gag measure that applied to union leaders in the club. This conflict resurfaced among factory workers at El Carrascal over a period of twenty years.[30] Football directors feared that if the club merged with the union, it would lose its capacity to collaborate with diverse groups in the community. This helped sports clubs avoid the pitched battles that political parties waged over union positions in San Miguel.[31] A variety of parties from the center-left participated in club directorates.[32] By participating in civic associations, leftist party militants, especially from the proscribed Communist Party, helped ensure their own survival and establish their legitimacy on a local level.

Amateur clubs had insisted on recreation as a right of the working class since the 1910s, but it was not until the 1940s that national labor organizations paid attention to these demands. Clubs like MADEMSA demonstrated that football could become a pillar of neighborhood identity, heighten the union's profile in communities, and bolster a sense of class solidarity.[33] As a result, the national labor confederation, the Confederación de Trabajadores de Chile (CTCh), positioned itself as an intermediary between workers and state agencies at the neighborhood level. It helped clubs obtain modest assistance from state agencies, including the Department of Information and Culture. In addition, the CTCh convened a Commission on Workers' Sports and Culture. This commission collaborated with government officials to build sportsmen's houses, where workers could hold meetings, play games, and relax.[34] Labor leaders attended matches and promoted the construction of stadiums in workers' neighborhoods.[35] In elections for union officers, experience in football clubs proved beneficial. Campaign publicity touted club leadership as a demonstration of candidates' civic concern. For instance, the CTCh supported the candidacy of Alejandro Gallegos for president of the Transportation Workers Union in part because he had directed and played for a barrio football club. Unionists considered his experience in sports as key to his success in building consensus among members.[36]

In their campaigns to control public space and acquire basic utilities in their neighborhoods, barrio clubs welcomed the support of the CTCh and its successor, the Central Única de Trabajadores (CUT). When the Public Housing Corporation (Corporación de la Vivienda, or CORVI) announced its plans to transform stadiums and football fields into housing units, amateur clubs launched a series of protests. The CUT publicly supported the protests: "It is more necessary than ever to strengthen the unity of the Chilean youth in defense of their just right to recreation within their scarce economic means."[37] Football clubs argued that CORVI's plan would create higher-density housing, which would hurt their communities. The Football Association of San Miguel presented a design of alternative sites for the housing projects, one that would protect the public spaces in their neighborhoods. Drawing on decades of experience, barrio clubs circulated petitions, investigated land claims, and met with government officials. Club leaders accused CORVI of not arranging for running water or electricity in the proposed housing units. After nearly a year of wrangling over the plan, CORVI scratched the project.

LOCAL POLITICS

In the 1950s, barrio football clubs broadened their political activities and experimented with new types of organizations. Fifteen clubs in San Miguel formed a lobby group named Footballers of the 8th District.[38] The decision of these clubs to organize according to their electoral district demonstrated their knowledge of politics and their belief in political channels as effective means of addressing community problems. They sought to create new recreational spaces, identify sponsors for poor players, and design an urban plan for San Miguel that would promote "healthier socialization." Ultimately, the clubs hoped to build strong relationships with all the politicians representing the eighth district. They argued that their neighborhoods deserved preferential consideration because working-class residents experienced physical strain from manual labor and high levels of juvenile delinquency. Equally as important, however, was the exceptional sports talent that these clubs claimed could be found in workers' barrios.[39]

In neighborhood associations, Socialists, Communists, Radicals, and Liberals collaborated with one another in ways that would have been unimaginable at the national level. Most of the clubs in the Footballers of the 8th District were affiliated with leftist parties, and the group had declared the Communist Party newspaper *El Siglo* its official publication. The group also publicly endorsed political candidates, usually from either the Socialist or Communist party. During elections, the clubs opened their clubhouses for speeches and debates. Despite this apparent partisanship, the Footballers of the 8th District insisted that it was a multiparty coalition. It even incorporated the Rangers Football Club, which was connected with the Liberal Party.[40] The Liberals had shifted to the right side of the political spectrum by the 1950s. Their participation was remarkable, given the Liberal Party's insistence on the prohibition of the Communist Party and the exile of its leaders. Perhaps out of a lack of interest, conservative parties did not achieve the same success with barrio clubs as their leftist counterparts.[41] Considering the leftist influence in the labor movement, it is probable that the participation of unions in football stymied Conservative, Liberal, and later National parties' influence among barrio clubs.

Following the official ban on the Communist Party beginning in 1948 and the disintegration of national coalitions, leftist party leaders focused on local politics with renewed vigor. This strategy contributed to the growth of the Communist Party's popularity during its ten-year proscription. In San Miguel, the Socialist politician Mario Palestro was one of the men responsible for building ties between parties, the local government, and football clubs. As a young man, Palestro had been a train worker in San Miguel. He participated in the labor union and went on to become a popular politician. His outspoken radicalism and fierce defense of workers' rights drew national attention. Like Elías Lafertte, the Communist leader of a previous generation, Palestro believed in the power of civic associations to change communities and develop workers' consciousnesses. To that end, he organized sports clubs, youth orchestras, and theater troupes. After serving as a city council member and then as the mayor of San Miguel from 1949 until 1953, he was elected to Congress. He was reelected repeatedly until the military coup of 1973. During his campaigns, amateur football clubs mobilized in support of Palestro.[42] Despite their scarce resources, hundreds of football clubs in shantytowns and squatter settlements sent Palestro decorative certificates commemorating his involvement in their organizations.[43]

In his memoirs, Mario Palestro reflected at length on the role of sports in San Miguel's civic life, identity, and politics. For Palestro, barrio clubs were essential for raising young men who would have the confidence to confront the authorities, including patrons and the police. As an adolescent, Palestro had joined the barrio football club Unión Condell. Palestro recalled the importance of the club in shaping his connection to the community and his sense of class solidarity. Most of Condell's members worked in the meatpacking plants and butcher shops that surrounded the public slaughterhouse in San Miguel. He recalled how spectators at football matches sang and chanted insults targeting the opposing team's masculinity, profession, and talent.[44] For Unión Condell's fans, the physical demands of working in meatpacking plants and butcher shops were evidence of their players' superior masculinity. Fans incorporated references to meat, knives, bulls, and other symbols of their industry in chants to underscore the physical fortitude and sexual prowess of their players.

Like unionists, squatters, and leftist militants, club members faced regular harassment from the police. Barrio players' belief in their physical condition shaped their responses to these intimidating experiences. For Palestro, his athleticism enabled him "to escape unscathed from the skirmishes with police that were occurring every day in Santiago. And it was natural that it would be this way since the Greens [a nickname for the *carabineros*] were not in permanent training like me."[45] Athletic agility gave Palestro and his friends the confidence to confront the authorities. As mayor, Palestro opened the municipality's offices to barrio clubs for use as meeting spaces that would be free from the threat of harassment. He also supported their efforts to transform unused lands into public parks and football fields.[46]

The effervescence of amateur football in the 1950s challenges the assumption among scholars and fans that professionalism turned football players into docile spectators.[47] In San Miguel, the popularity of professional football did not end the importance of amateur clubs, numerically or qualitatively. Residents recalled barrio players from the era as "legendary" and "famous." Club members asserted that at any moment, dozens of their players could have joined a professional squad but were too honorable and independent to sell their talents. Palestro recalled, "Marticorena, the Arenas brothers, and so many others could have been stars of any professional team"; however, they were "irrepressible bohemians who could never be subjected to the discipline of the professional club."[48] Barrio clubs had attained such status that Palestro pointed to his relationship with them as evidence of his continued commitment to the working class. He reminisced that after the legislature closed, "I spent the weekends celebrating victories in the neighborhood clubs or at lively parties in celebration of club anniversaries—humble, simple, but full of friendship and warmth."[49]

Campaigns for public space, housing, cooperatives, and utilities strengthened the relationship between football clubs and leftist political parties. For example, in 1957, a devastating fire in San Miguel drew attention to the precarious conditions of shantytowns in the area. Seeking shelter, shantytown dwellers, or *pobladores*, were temporarily housed in the Municipal Stadium of San Miguel. The picture of impoverished families gathered together in a site intended for enjoyment prompted harsh criticism of the Ibáñez government's failure to alleviate the housing crisis. While Ibáñez's opponents were still subject to repression, their vocal objections to his administration highlight the difference between his term as elected president (1952–1958) and his dictatorship, which ended thirty years earlier. Moreover, civic associations organized direct actions with greater frequency than in the past. The stadium provided a central location from which residents planned a *toma*, or illegal land seizure, of terrain in the western part of San Miguel.[50] Thousands set out from the stadium to take part in the toma, which created the community known as La Victoria. The Catholic Church, the Communist Party, the Football Association of San Miguel, and municipal officials supported the squatter movement.

Football clubs in La Victoria served as avenues of integration, storehouses of local history, and centers of organizational experience. The names of clubs commemorated important historical events in the community. Club 30th of October, for example, was named in honor of the date of the La Victoria toma. Abel Ojeda, one of the founding residents, emphasized the importance of football in squatter settlements, where building social solidarity was an urgent task.[51] Ojeda's house had barely been built when he founded the first football club in La Victoria. The establishment of football clubs, local stores, and parishes contributed to residents' sense of their community's permanence. Moreover, Ojeda claimed that through football, La Victoria overcame its reputation as an impoverished neighborhood of delinquents and land thieves. He recalled, "At first [other barrios] beat us, but we began to go every afternoon to the field in the market and practice for about two hours, and with that we began to win, and they respected us."[52] Soon, clubs from La Victoria won the championship of San Miguel, then of metropolitan Santiago. More importantly for Ojeda, players from La Victoria represented the community well through their clean play. Ojeda pointed out that even when opponents refused to pay money they had wagered on the match, players from La Victoria avoided violence and police intervention.[53] Ojeda's anecdotes reveal that players and fans took their behavior during matches seriously.

La Victoria's residents resisted police actions against the community and governmental threats to destroy the settlement. Their success inspired dozens more land occupations in San Miguel. In the context of these tomas, claims to urban space were charged with political meaning. One of La Victoria's football clubs, Deportivo La Posada, launched a project to transform abandoned properties within shantytowns into football fields.[54] This project required research of land ownership records, knowledge of the legal system, and formal petitions to the municipality. Unlike petitions from working-class clubs in the 1920s, which employed narratives of national decline and flagging masculinity, those sent by clubs in La Victoria asserted that the new playing fields would be essential to restoring Chile's reputation abroad. They declared that the national team's honor depended upon a steady stream of talented players from barrio clubs, without whom the team could not hope to win.

Conflicts erupted frequently between barrio clubs and local landowners hostile to land occupations. In 1959, Luis Ochagavía, a member of one of San Miguel's aristocratic families, erected a barrier, manned by armed guards, that blocked La Victoria's access to the municipal stadium.[55] Although the Football Association of San Miguel recognized that the road was within Ochagavía's property boundaries, it cited the barrier as a violation of the public's rights to the stadium. It claimed that Ochagavía's attempt to cut off access to the stadium proved that he did not consider La Victoria residents "human."[56] Moreover, the association argued that citizens' rights

to recreation superseded Ochagavía's property rights. After football clubs
convinced Mario Palestro and members of the city council to intervene on
their behalf, Ochagavía agreed to remove the guards and open the road.

Football clubs linked squatter settlements and established barrios
to agricultural areas undergoing urbanization. In the 1950s, the Football
Association of San Miguel held matches on farmland, in squatter settlements,
and in well-established urban districts. Agricultural workers' clubs sent
delegates to the association's monthly meetings. In the association, delegates worked on projects with firefighters, teachers' associations, and
choral groups.[57] In 1952, association leaders estimated that forty thousand
residents in the south of San Miguel alone belonged to sports clubs.[58] Club
directors may have inflated this number, but since the total population of
the area could not have exceeded one hundred thousand, the director's
estimate illustrates the high profile of clubs in these communities.

Barrio clubs spearheaded efforts to acquire utility services for their
communities. In the shantytown Miguel Dávila, the Cooperative of
Construction Workers, mostly members of the Communist Party, formed
the community's first football club.[59] Drawing upon its members' technical skills and industry connections, the cooperative built an elaborate
headquarters. With the help of the Football Association of San Miguel,
the club attained permits, water, and electricity for its facilities. This
expertise benefited the community's broader efforts to attain public services. For example, the club organized efforts to improve transportation
in the community, which hitherto had been without public bus service.
Backed by the Football Association of San Miguel and the municipality,
the footballers convinced the bus company to extend its routes.

The support of municipal politicians and the success of the clubs' campaigns encouraged barrio clubs to seek resolutions to their problems through
political channels. The clubs from Miguel Dávila launched a letter-writing
campaign that caught the attention of the director of the State Department
of Sports, General Elías Ducaud. Ducaud invited the clubs to his office in
June 1954. This was the dream of thousands of amateur clubs in Santiago,
and the members prepared accordingly. Club directors left the meeting with
promises that Ducaud would help them acquire land where they could
build a modest stadium, that the Department of Sports would present
educational lectures on health and physical education at the club's social
seat, and that two members would receive scholarships to attend physical-
education courses offered by the department.[60] The meeting illustrated
the faith that football clubs had in state education and their confidence in

requesting state aid. For shantytown residents who faced discrimination and police harassment, it must have been gratifying for a state official to treat them as legitimate political subjects.

CROSS-BARRIO BOOMS AND THE RADICALIZATION OF AMATEURS

Amateur football's boom was not a spontaneous occurrence experienced in isolation, but rather a collective event. As in San Miguel, barrio clubs throughout the city organized to acquire urban services, create public spaces, and build relationships with local politicians. In the process, they pushed their unions and political parties to broaden their goals for workers in the realm of recreation and culture.[61] Barrio football clubs celebrated the creativity, civic engagement, and resilience of working-class sportsmen. Professionals attacked amateurs for their "politicization" of the ideal footballer. The effervescence of football in shantytowns and squatter settlements empowered working-class directors in the national Chilean Football Federation. In the federation, amateurs and professionals profoundly disagreed about the role of the state, the market, politics, and women in football. Their arguments reflected both a broader political polarization in Chilean society and the ways in which everyday struggles over football shaped members' understanding of politics.

Amateur club members imagined themselves as a counterpublic, a distinct community among the mass of Chileans interested in football.[62] They claimed their clubs were truly democratic because of their participatory culture, inclusiveness, and roots in the poorest sector of society. They spoke with one another through local media and face to face at organization meetings, bars, and matches. Barrio directors believed that the universal appeal of sports enabled them to overcome the ideological divisions of other civic associations. To their surprise, neither the state agencies that oversaw physical education nor professional clubs were enthusiastic about the growth of barrio football. Professionals reacted with hostility when amateur delegates suggested that public resources should be devoted to encouraging mass participation in sports.

Amateurs took pride in the internal organization of their clubs and the active involvement of rank-and-file members. The ethos that members should be engaged participants meant that club leadership underwent intense scrutiny. Barrio club members demanded that a director be "one of them," in other words, figures who could be approached, criticized, and replaced. Members chastised directors who lapsed in their duties or became estranged from the membership. For example, members accused club directors in the western neighborhood of Las Barrancas of creating a "dictatorship" and removed them from their positions midterm.[63] Cases such as these attest to members' knowledge of club procedures and their willingness to monitor officers. They rejected the paternal figure of the upper-class director, common in the first half of the century. Part of barrio clubs' appeal was their fraternal character. Club histories characterized founders as friends and neighbors and not, for instance, as local business owners.[64]

Amateur club statutes expressed the strong attachment that members felt to their institutions and their commitment to a democratic structure. Since the early part of the century, statutes had become more intricate, reflecting the experiences of barrio clubs. Often numbering more than forty pages, statutes provided procedures for recalling directors or reallocating powers to a general assembly.[65] They laid out the format of meetings in detail (including how many times each member could speak and for how long), the process of elections, and the distribution of assets in the event of the club's demise. The minister of the interior demanded that clubs requesting legal status put their statutes in a standardized form, but most clubs did not elect to file for government recognition. This did not mean, however, that club members objected to rules. Newspaper accounts show that members cared about club rules, and debates over how to interpret them occurred frequently. The formality of clubs reflected members' desire to create lasting institutions that would survive them. Often, founders organized clubs to commemorate deeply personal experiences, such as the death of a loved one.

In the 1950s, amateur clubs from various parts of the city began to coordinate their efforts. Moreover, neighborhood associations from Santiago developed closer relationships with parallel groups in Valparaíso, Temuco, Iquique, and other cities. For instance, when the Football Association of Conchalí sought to construct a stadium, it arranged meetings with the Football Association of Recoleta to find out how it had succeeded in building the Popular Stadium of Recoleta. Delegates from the associations exchanged information during matches, at meetings of the National Association of Amateur Football, and in other civic associations.[66] With the help of directors in Recoleta, the Football Association of Conchalí submitted a proposal to the legislature for the construction of a stadium in its neighborhood.[67]

The neighborhood of Conchalí exemplified the northern barrios, which had been neglected by the state despite their swelling population. Traditional working-class barrios north and west of Santiago's center struggled to repair their decaying neighborhoods while facing competition for land use from shantytowns and squatter settlements. Dominated by a working-class membership, many of the clubs in established barrios sympathized with squatter movements; in fact, many members directly participated in tomas. When squatters on the northern urban periphery encroached on the Football Association of Conchalí's fields, directors negotiated with residents. Instead of attacking the rights of the squatters to the land, the president of the association joined the squatters' call for an urban plan that provided for recreation and housing.[68] In addition, the association demanded the authority to direct projects to revamp unused municipal land.

The Football Association of Conchalí influenced the leftward trend of barrio football in the late 1940s and early 1950s. The association's most prominent sports club, Pedro Aguirre Cerda, or PAC, was among the early supporters of the first Popular Front government. A group of young footballers founded the club on 1 October 1938 to express their enthusiasm for President Aguirre Cerda.[69] PAC, which was well known as an informal affiliate of the Radical Party, collaborated with the Popular Front to implement programs in its community. The sympathies of PAC gradually shifted leftward, especially because of efficient recruitment by the Socialist and Communist parties and alienation from the Radicals. In 1942, it helped form the Football Association of Conchalí with help from the municipality.[70] Despite its modest economic base, PAC was an ambitious club. Its goals included the extension of utilities to shantytowns in Conchalí, public transportation to sports fields, and consumer cooperatives for sports equipment.[71] In addition, it established a form of health insurance for members, providing coverage for injuries suffered while playing sports, a program the professional league had only recently adopted.[72] The club succeeded in convincing the State Department of Sports to arrange a water connection to its sports fields.[73] This provided some parts of Conchalí with their first public access to potable water.

Historical memory figured prominently in the northern barrios' criticisms of governmental inactivity in their neighborhoods. PAC club members complained of the Ibáñez administration's inefficiency in terms similar to those they had used to criticize the Popular Front. Directors recalled decades of governmental agencies' broken promises to construct sports facilities.[74] Civic leaders mobilized nostalgia to illustrate the decay of their neighborhoods. Among the oldest institutions in their neighborhoods, football clubs recalled that during the "golden years" of the 1920s, their communities had been at the forefront of cultural life in Santiago. They reminisced about the clubhouses that had dotted the main thoroughfare, Avenida Independencia, including the one for Colo Colo, which left the area after its transition to professionalism. Photographs, dance cards, and trophies held in clubhouses documented a lively social life. Club members memorialized famous players who played on the association's fields. In editorials to local papers, football directors blamed the lack of civic spirit on economic hardship, government neglect, and alienation among residents.

As in northern Conchalí, the use of public space had long been a contested issue in neighborhoods west of the urban center such as Quinta Normal or Barrio Yungay. During the Ibáñez regime during the 1920s, in one of their first coordinated efforts, football clubs opposed development proposals that would have resulted in the demolition of several residential blocks. Quinta Normal was the home of a great many train workers, as well as a boisterous carnival celebration, which gave the neighborhood a reputation as a center of working-class life.[75] A statue erected in Plaza Yungay in the late nineteenth century became popularly dubbed the "Statue of the Roto" ("statue of the worker") because of its location rather than any intention of the French sculptor. Every January, the neighborhood celebrated the Day of the Roto, with athletic events and festivals. Literature cemented the neighborhood's notoriety—most prominently, the novel *El Roto*, by Joaquín Edwards Bello, which documented the squalid conditions of the barrio. Quinta Normal bore the ill effects of Santiago's first industries, including pollution, labor agitation, and hazardous working conditions.

The increasingly radical politics and organizational skills of football clubs in Quinta Normal shaped their response to land struggles. On the western edges of Quinta Normal, where established working-class neighborhoods and shantytowns were interspersed, the Communist Party organized a dense network of associations. Militants organized several *tomas*, including one to take over fields that belonged to the Football Association of Lo Franco. The directors of the association, some of whom were fellow Communist Party members, voluntarily relinquished the area to the squatters.[76] In another instance, the residents of Lo Franco petitioned the association to cede some football fields for the construction of a school.[77] The association quickly agreed to support the community's efforts to improve education. When CORVI announced plans to create a new housing development on two of the association's last football fields in 1962, the directors announced that their organization stood on the brink of collapse.[78] Club leaders convinced the Communist deputy Julieta Campusano to present a bill that would save the association. The legislation allowed the municipality of Quinta Normal to expropriate abandoned lands. In turn, the association converted the terrain into football fields.

Real estate developers who sought to profit from the housing crisis in the western barrios infuriated local clubs. In 1945, Club Deportivo Roberto Encina, a top club in the Football Association of Quinta Normal, learned that developers had purchased the field that the club had leased for more than a decade.[79] The developers planned to construct a housing complex for low-income residents. The club argued that the project was bad for the community, since the area did not have electricity or running water. They accused the developers of not intending to acquire these services. Furthermore, club members claimed that diminished recreational opportunities would encourage the growth of delinquency. Directors petitioned the municipality to stop the project at least until it had repaired Quinta Normal's municipal stadium. After months of wrangling, the developers persuaded the municipality that their project would alleviate the housing problem. Club members sadly gathered their equipment from the field and locker room. The new owners then sued the club directors, claiming that members had vandalized and stolen property while they were evacuating. The police arrested and incarcerated the club directors. The Football Association of Quinta Normal appealed to the municipal council, which managed to get the charges dismissed.[80] The council promised the club use of municipal land for its matches if it stopped harassing the developers.

Clubs in Quinta Normal learned to negotiate with state agencies while working on local projects. For example, in the 1950s, Club Deportivo Esparta tried to rehabilitate an overgrown lot that had become a dumping site. The club searched in vain for the property owner through state records. Neighbors had complained for years to the police that the lot attracted delinquent behavior. They said that drunks used the lot as a toilet and that local bullies intimidated passers-by. Rather than waiting for the municipality's help, members of Club Esparta transformed the field themselves. The club sent representatives to the Department of Public Works in Santiago's center. Club members promised to clear and prepare the field if the department would send a truck to pave the area. The department agreed; however, when the truck arrived, the driver explained he did not have time to complete the job. Club members convinced the driver to return during his days off. Directors dipped into the club's savings to offer the driver extra money.

AMATEURS VERSUS PROFESSIONALS

The Cold War intensified the acrimony between amateur and professional football clubs. Both sides viewed culture as an opportunity to prove the superiority of either market capitalism or state-directed socialism. Professional club directors and conservative journalists criticized the growth of "Marxist" influences in amateur football. Amateurs, for their part, accused professionals of being driven by materialism. Furthermore, when barrio clubs began to vie for power in the Chilean Football Federation, professionals attacked their leadership abilities and criticized their youth programs for producing undisciplined players. The wealthy businessmen and lawyers who ran the professional clubs felt threatened by amateur football's activities, especially those they defined as "political." However, professionals characterized their own relationships to high-ranking members of the administrations of Carlos Ibáñez (1952-1958) and Jorge Alessandri (1958–1964) as merely social affairs. Officially, amateurs and professionals shared power in the federation equally, but in effect, professional clubs dominated the organization.[81] Professional clubs employed Cold War rhetoric in their attempts to retain control over football.

As discussed in Chapter Four, directors of professional clubs accrued power over clubs' members during the 1950s. In part, the growth of the international market for football heightened expectations of clubs' profitability. Directors justified their increased authority and rosters on this basis. They increased memberships from a few thousand to more than ten thousand. Although, technically, professional clubs remained cooperative in their ownership, directors who invested fortunes in club elections and projects wielded disproportionate influence. The practice of directors offering financial support to professional clubs created a barrier that prevented most members from serving as directors. Instead of analyzing how this changed the nature of club governance, sportswriters uncritically praised professional directors for donating their time and money. *El Mercurio* described the professional director as "a true 'amateur,' in love with his sports' duties. He donates his free time, accepting with pleasure work that would earn a hefty salary under other circumstances. And when the club flounders economically, he supports it with the necessary funds from his own pocket."[82] Directors further empowered themselves by revising statutes in order to consolidate decision making in the directorship.

Professionals and mainstream journalists based their understanding of amateurism on a belief in the interdependence of free-market capitalism, individual liberties, and democracy. They opposed amateurism—a Western, liberal value—to the authoritarian system that Soviet athletes suffered under. Professionals worried that the "naïveté" of working-class footballers left them vulnerable to the appeal of leftist parties. Sportswriters from *El Mercurio* and *La Nación* created frightening caricatures of Soviet sports programs. They warned that the Socialist and Communist parties in Chile would create the same types of institutions if given the opportunity. One journalist described the Soviet Union as "a functional country in which each man is designated for a position; it does not have space for the amateur."[83] The conservative press warned sports fans that the ties between Marxist unions and leftists would destroy football, one of the culture's great spaces of liberty. These warnings reflected the growing polarization among Latin American cultural producers that emerged in the Cold War period. As literary critic Jean Franco has chronicled, artists, journalists, and writers who criticized the authoritarian nature of the Soviet Union defined "freedom" as "freedom of the marketplace."[84]

Professional football's merchandising repulsed many amateur sportsmen. While directors of professional clubs moved their headquarters to upper-class neighborhoods in the northeastern part of the city, they recruited most players from popular barrios and provinces. Their refusal to invest in programs in those areas created resentment among amateurs. According to professionals, the hardships experienced by barrio clubs and working-class neighborhoods more generally were part of an otherwise beneficial process of economic modernization. When amateurs accused professionals of exploiting young barrio talent, professionals responded that amateurs simply misunderstood the market. They explained that the situation had happened "without responsible parties, without anyone proposing that things happen this way. It is this way because the public has its preferences. The incredible thing is that the amateur directors forget the reasons that determine the state of things."[85] Professional directors charged amateurs of creating false class animosity among footballers. They argued that merchandising and increased ticket prices were a healthy part of football's transition to a mass entertainment.[86] One journalist explained, "Money does not stain. On the contrary, it indicates success."[87]

The media played a central role in tensions between amateur and professional clubs. National newspapers and professional clubs shared personnel, economic interests, and social activities. Clubs invited journalists to club events and arranged interviews with star players. Mainstream publications began to focus exclusively on professional or international amateur competitions, such as the Olympic Games. Major dailies like *El Mercurio* had little incentive to cover amateur sports, since the market was geographically segmented, making the reading public difficult to target. Their journalists barely disguised their contempt for the popularity of barrio clubs. *El Mercurio*'s reporters blamed the poor performances of the Chilean national team on the independent and "anarchic" nature of amateur clubs.[88]

Alternative media, particularly the Communist Party's *El Siglo*, were pivotal to the effervescence of barrio football. Founded in 1941, *El Siglo* managed to stay in print for most of the time the party was outlawed. From the paper's inception, its sportswriters worked to publicize events of union,

FIGURE 5.1.   Young football players in Escuela de Fútbol, c. 1960. Youth football programs were central to struggles between amateur and professional directors. Image courtesy of the Archivo Fotográfico Colección, Museo Histórico Archivo, Santiago.

party, and neighborhood clubs. Its sports pages conveyed a collaborative spirit of solidarity with Socialists, despite their fierce partisan competitions. *El Siglo* strengthened the ties between the party and amateur football clubs. Its writers popularized the working-class barrio football icon in cartoons, editorials, and reports on matches. This icon offered all leftists, not only Communists, a positive model of working-class creativity, talent, and honorable masculinity. In addition, the paper fostered interbarrio relationships through its sponsorship of tournaments.[89] Furthermore, amateurs used the publicity provided by *El Siglo* to criticize professionals and state agencies. Party representatives encouraged footballers to understand their conflicts with professionals and the state as part of the class struggle. In turn, footballers pressured party leaders to view recreation and public spaces as central needs of the working class. Barrio clubs drew upon the paper's support to pressure businesses to open their sports facilities to local residents. They also worked with *El Siglo* to create sporting-goods cooperatives and demand tax-exempt status for such goods.[90] Through these activities, barrio clubs influenced a young generation of party militants to see that clubs were bases of political organization.[91]

Amateur clubs created their own neighborhood newspapers and radio programs. Typically strapped for cash, these media outlets pooled resources with local schools, civic associations, and municipalities. These newspapers and radio programs generally lasted less than a year, but they provided a forum for ongoing conversations among amateur clubs and their supporters.[92] The persistence with which clubs began local newspapers and radio shows illustrates the importance of these kinds of media to sportsmen. In these publications, barrio directors publicized their activities, described their matches, and featured local stars.[93] Moreover, they articulated alternative ideas about the relationship between sports and civic participation. Clubs archived these papers in their makeshift libraries, which served to document local history. Finally, local papers gave club members an opportunity to opine as experts on issues such as national legislation pertaining to sports as well as on international football controversies, such as drug use, gambling, and salary limits.

As clubs from working-class neighborhoods began to dominate amateur organizations in the 1950s, conflicts between amateurs and professionals intensified. In 1952, the two groups waged a public battle over the election of the president of the Chilean Football Federation.[94] In previous elections, professional delegates nominated the president and expected to receive the approval of amateur delegates. For the first time, amateurs refused to support the professional candidate and nominated their own, Ernesto Allende. The professional directors were shocked. They complained that their financial importance to the federation justified their wielding greater power within it. Amateurs countered that professionals monopolized state resources for private pursuits, at the expense of the poor. The voting deadlock between amateurs and professionals ended in the victory of Allende, since the rules stipulated (as amateur directors knew quite well) that in the event of a tie, the oldest candidate would win.[95]

Professional clubs that touted the glories of free markets did not let their principles prevent them from seeking state aid. The national government's bailouts of professional clubs infuriated amateurs and pushed them further from the centrist Radical Party, which had mobilized their support since the 1890s. One of the earliest examples took place in 1949, when Colo Colo's stadium project ran into financial troubles. Radical Party politicians introduced legislation to provide the club with substantial funds.[96] Despite its wealthy directors and financial improprieties, Colo Colo carefully managed its image as the club "of the people." Its frequent tours of the provinces and skillful branding of the sixteenth-century Mapuche military leader Colocolo played an important role in building the club's popularity. Colo Colo's membership topped thirty thousand, making it the most powerful club in Chile.[97] Amateurs pointed out that despite the self-proclaimed populism of Colo Colo, its directors came from the highest business circles. Worse yet, the club had befriended "enemies of the people," a reference to its close relationship with President González, who had outlawed the Communist Party.

Amateurs' belief in the superiority of working-class players surfaced in their everyday analyses of style and performance. They described working-class players as more decisive, stronger, and more mentally agile than professionals. Professional players frequently echoed the discourse of amateurs. In interviews, football players linked their athletic skills to their humble beginnings. Daniel Torres, who began playing in the northern city of Antofagasta, attributed his endurance to the necessity of responding to difficult life challenges: "You know how the fields are in the North. . . . The play is hard because the people are hard, because the life is hard."[98] These stories identified material hardships and physical labor as important to the development of rough, powerful men. Their refusal to be dominated by other men was a central feature of their stories and a characteristic of the barrio football icon. The historian Thomas Miller Klubock found a similar connection in the mining communities of El Teniente, where football "contributed to the general construction of a combative masculine identity based on a sense of personal strength and resilience."[99] For amateurs, these qualities produced players with a heightened sense of the game, better dribbling skills, and a physically aggressive style.[100]

Mainstream journalists could not deny that most talented professional players came from working-class clubs. They grudgingly admitted, "It has become something of a tradition that footballers have their start in barrio clubs, which are seedbeds. This situation seems natural if we consider the strikingly popular character of this exciting sport."[101] Instead of applauding barrio sports programs, which typically operated on a minimal budget, journalists complained that they encouraged the "rebellious nature" of players. *Estadio* conceded that working-class players were astute ball handlers, but judged that their lack of discipline hurt the national team. Journalists often described the talent of popular players as natural, rather than the product of strategy or hard work. For example, the magazine wrote of Norton Contreras, a star of Barrio Eugenio, "He played by instinct, without thinking of what he was doing. And it all came easily, without great effort."[102] Rather than celebrating his effective ball handling, the article commented that this natural ability, common among workers, only encouraged his "laziness."

Conservative journalists, critical of barrio clubs, rewrote the history of football to exclude the participation of working-class clubs.[103] Nostalgic articles invited readers to imagine idyllic afternoon matches in which a handful of cultured Europeans and Creoles enjoyed the outdoors in harmony. They romanticized the stoic nature of "old cracks" who never argued with referees or cried at their defeats. In an article that contrasted the popularity of football with its aristocratic past, *Estadio* focused on the life of David Cecil, Lord Burghley, a Conservative Party politician and an avid sportsman. The magazine characterized Burghley as "the first and original model of the British 'sportsman,' correct to the point of exaggeration, stubbornly amateur, gentlemanly."[104] It declared that leftist activism and the divisions it created between professionals and amateurs endangered the values of men like Burghley: "The political agitation of our time threatens to introduce elements unrelated to sport."[105] Furthermore, professional directors blamed the violence of working-class spectators for driving down attendance, rather than higher ticket prices or general alienation from clubs.[106] Complaints of increasing violence in the stands had been a refrain of sports journalists since the 1910s.[107] Although accurate statistics would be impossible to compile, steady increases in fines assessed against players, along with police crowd control, likely decreased violence in football.

When accusations of corruption emerged during the financial crises of professional clubs, directors blamed the materialism of working-class players for driving up salaries. This rhetoric escalated when professional players attempted to organize a union. Fictional serials, articles, and *fotonovelas* were replete with moral tales of footballers who reconciled with their parents, police, and coaches after a misunderstanding.[108] Serial dramas often portrayed a player who had to choose between accepting a lucrative contract with a new club and remaining with his first club. In the end, these characters accepted lower salaries out of obligation to their clubs.[109] Biographical sketches of players conveyed didactic messages about the relationship between workers and their bosses. One such piece featured the star player Juan Toro. Toro worked and lived at the Yarur textile company complex, even after signing with Audax Italiano. Lest any young reader dream of escaping a life of blue-collar employment through sports, the writer bluntly explained that "football is ephemeral and only work endures."[110] Photographs of Toro beaming next to his workstation in the factory conveyed the benevolence of a company known for its staunch resistance to unionization and its exploitation of workers.[111] As discussed in Chapter Four, the Yarur factory owners were also directors of the professional football club Palestino and held high positions in the Chilean Football Federation. Professional club directors used similar antiunion tactics, including fines, sanctions, and propaganda, in their negotiations with factory workers and football players.

WOMEN AND BARRIO FOOTBALL

As the history of barrio clubs illustrates, male sociability was important to the role of clubs as sites where political recruitment occurred and inter-generational relationships were fostered. Barrio clubs constructed a model of masculinity that championed rebellion, class solidarity, and community responsibility. This celebration of hypermasculinity was not accompanied by a heightened fear of women's participation. While the barrio football icon and club leaders were decidedly male, a vocal group of amateur directors who embraced women's participation in football emerged. As early as 1950, one director boasted that women's football had "increased the prestige of our neighborhood."[112] Advances in sports, these directors claimed, would translate into political achievements for women. The position of these directors was at odds with the mainstream press, which blamed feminism and its perceived feminizing effect on male players for the Chilean national team's losses. Professionals and conservative publications were hostile to women's participation in football even as fans, so they questioned the femininity of any woman who would be interested in playing football. This case may be more suggestive than conclusive, but the decidedly "macho" barrio clubs were more open to women's participation than their elite counterparts.

By the mid-1950s, the environment for women's football had improved after the impressive performances of female athletes in the Olympics and the Pan American Games, as well as the activities of the Chilean feminist movement. Barrio footballers were questioning traditional notions of honor, which were often based on men's authority over women and children. Supportive directors saw their encouragement of women's sports as part of a modernized concept of honor. One director explained, "Honorable is he who lives within his economic means, who cares for his dignity . . . who conscientiously fulfills the duties of his profession, whatever they may be, and who works for justice."[113] Furthermore, he advised each player to show "respect and consideration for your wife as a partner in life, not as someone only dedicated to serving the needs of the home." For this group of directors, women's subservience was not necessary to establish men's honor. Their confidence in working-class masculinity and honor contrasted with the doubts of lawmakers and medical professionals who were anxious about the state of workers. In 1953, former Olympian Sergio Ojeda organized a congressional committee to promote sports. He explained in a speech to the legislature that sports would help revitalize the "Latin race," which was threatened by "sexual impotence" and "neurosis."[114] Amateurs showed little interest in working with Ojeda, which resulted in the committee's rapid demise.

Women's participation in neighborhood sports clubs had begun in the 1920s, when young single women created sections of tennis, table tennis, and basketball within clubs. In the 1930s and 1940s, some clubs' statutes outlined sports that could be organized by women, but football was never among them. Often, clubs categorized women's membership with that of children (and just below that of young men age nine to sixteen). This allowed them access to club facilities, but without a "voice" or "vote." Women

created football teams in clubs based in shantytowns and squatter settlements more often than in established working-class neighborhoods. As
participants, women resignified the traditional rituals of clubs. For example, female footballers used the annual election of a Spring Queen as a
fund-raising opportunity for their teams. Others changed the contest,
which was essentially a beauty pageant, to a "Sportswoman of the Year"
competition.[115]

Las Atómicas and Las Dinamítas, the first women's football teams to
capture widespread attention, formed in the early 1950s in the shantytowns
of San Miguel. When sports magazines such as *Gol y Gol* reported on the
matches between Las Atómicas and Las Dinamítas, they received dozens
of requests from women's teams trying to arrange matches.[116] Yet women's
enthusiasm for sports was often met with hostility by Chilean fans. The
idea of women physically occupying the football field and the clubhouse
generated considerable controversy. *Gol y Gol*, a graphic sports magazine
with an amateur bent, received complaints from readers in response to its
coverage of women's sports events.[117] One reader's letter chastised the
magazine for suggesting that the Chilean women's team could "one day"
win the World Cup.[118] The reader, who identified herself as a woman,
claimed that she was shocked at the reporter's pretension and urged women
to leave football to men, adding that female footballers' performances denied
that "a woman should be a woman." For this reader, the suggestion that
women could compete with men's athletic achievements signified such a
transgression that it jeopardized the gender identity of female athletes.

Besides barrio clubs, women participated in union sports clubs more
often during the post–World War II period than before, particularly in
industries where they composed a large part of the labor force, such as
textiles.[119] Female club members enjoyed the collective pleasure of sports
participation and the benefits that their male counterparts enjoyed, such as
prestige among coworkers and access to resources like the club's library,
recreational rooms, and night school. Women participated in union and
neighborhood sports clubs in mutually reinforcing ways. Women joined
union clubs more frequently when they were located in neighborhoods
with a tradition of women's sports. As well, women joined neighborhood
clubs in areas where unions had promoted women's athletics.

Conservative publications discouraged women's presence in clubs, advocated the strict separation of men and women, and stressed the importance of aggression in athletic development. In 1958, *Estadio* published

a letter that blamed the effeminate qualities of Chilean footballers for their poor international standing.[120] The editors praised this as the most salient explanation of losses to neighboring Argentina and Peru. The letter described Chilean players as lazy and passive. To shame them, the writer summarized the national team's play as "feminine football." These analyses equated femininity with indecisiveness and weakness; therefore, while women may have benefited from football, they had nothing valuable to contribute. These journalists connected footballers' loss of masculinity to the blurred boundaries between men and women's activities more generally.

Right-wing journalists were explicitly hostile toward female football fans and players.[121] Women's participation in football clubs threatened men's domination of family resources for recreation, male sociability, and the political capital of sports. Almost weekly, *Estadio* featured comics whose punch lines were based on women's lack of understanding of football rules and terminology or their unreasonable demands on men's leisure time. Violence toward women in these cartoons was intended to be humorous. In Figure 5.2, two women, one the wife of the comic strip's main character, Cachupín, are talking so loudly they interrupt the radio transmission of a football match.[122] Cachupín becomes increasingly agitated and attempts to stop them from talking. Their conversation is transcribed in the cartoon as "bla bla," or meaningless prattle, and accompanied by exaggerated hand gestures. The scene ends with the women silenced—Cachupín has bound their mouths, hands, and feet—and the radio announcing a penalty kick.

Coverage of women's football sparked bitter debates among readers.[123] Amateur club directors wrote to newspapers to defend female footballers and to encourage publications to continue their coverage. One reader sent in photographs of female boxers and football players from the 1920s as a challenge to critics who warned of the potential health hazards of women's sports activity.[124] Barrio directors who advocated for women's football drew on Marxist and feminist arguments to defend their position. For example, one director emphasized that women's improved physical condition could help repair the physical damage that centuries of poverty had inflicted on the poor.[125] He explained that traditional notions of women's domesticity were antiquated ideas used to gloss over exploitation. Furthermore, he pointed out the advantages of women's liberation for men, who needed modern, active companions. His editorial urged women to play sports as part of feminist practice and suggested that men would respect women more if they

FIGURE 5.2.   Frustrated with women's insistent chatter, Cachupín found relief when he
physically restrained them. The cartoon, by "Nato," appeared in *Estadio*, 1952. Image
courtesy of Zig-Zag.

competed on the field. Barrio directors saw the accomplishments of their
own clubs as political milestones for the working class.

THE WORLD CUP OF 1962

The history of barrio clubs and their effervescence in the 1950s has been
overshadowed by the memory of the World Cup of 1962. During their
campaign to host the Cup, professional directors drew upon the magne-
tism and iconography of barrio football clubs while marginalizing them
from leadership roles. Moreover, during the preparations for the event, the

organizers tried to create a less rebellious image of the working-class foot-baller. Professional directors and state representatives co-opted the arche-type of the passionate underdog and used it to characterize the country as a whole. While their campaign succeeded in bringing the World Cup to Chile, their decision to leave out working-class football organizations proved detrimental to the tournament.

Chilean delegates masterfully navigated Cold War politics in order to overcome opposition to their hosting of the cup. In 1956, they presented their case at the FIFA congress held in Lisbon, Portugal. Prospects for Chile's hosting of the Cup seemed bleak, since the national team had never achieved international success, the Chilean Football Federation was nearly bankrupt, and many European delegates admitted that they could not even locate the country on a map.[126] The "Three Musketeers," as the press nicknamed delegates Carlos Dittborn, Ernesto Alvear, and Manuel Bianchi, focused on the state of political tolerance in Chile. To sway Eastern Bloc countries to vote in their favor, the delegates pointed out the activities of leftist parties and labor unions in Chilean football. At the same time, they wooed western European delegates with promises that Chile offered both modernity and a controlled exoticism. In other words, the delegates presented Chile as different, but not too different. Alvear recalled years later that the committee decided to first send a diplomat, Manuel Bianchi (ambassador to Great Britain), instead of a sports club director as a symbol of Chileans' spirit and "governability."[127] The nar-rative of Chilean democracy, firmly rooted in popular culture, created a unifying message that shaped the sense of citizens' responsibility for and involvement in the political process. However, football delegates presented FIFA with a romantic picture that elided the existence of state violence and economic marginalization.

Argentina mounted the greatest challenge to the Chilean bid for the cup. Unforeseen events hurt its case, particularly the turmoil and repres-sion that followed the fall of Juan Perón's government. In addition, Chilean delegates stressed the anticommunism of the Peronists, contrasting it with the close relationship between barrio football and leftist parties in Chile.[128] The antagonistic relationship between Perón and the United States may also have helped to sway the U.S. delegation and their allies in Chile's favor. Despite these developments, most predicted that Argentina would win the bid. Some Chilean journalists went so far as to implore the federation to give up in order to avoid the disillusionment that failure would bring to the public.[129]

Given the pessimistic mood among sportswriters in Chile, most followed the proceedings of the FIFA congress with apprehension. The Argentine presentation lasted more than an hour. The delegation stressed the country's modern infrastructure and undeniable contributions to the development of the game. Emphasizing the country's readiness, the Argentine representative ended by stating, "We can have the World Cup tomorrow. We have it all."[130]

The Chilean federation selected Carlos Dittborn, the charismatic director of the Pontifical Catholic University's club, to deliver the final speech to the FIFA general assembly. Dittborn's rebuttal lasted only fifteen minutes. He built upon three points, including Chile's institutional stability, openness to diverse ideologies, and unique style of sportsmanship. According to Dittborn, Chilean football organizations reflected general characteristics of the country, especially a "considerable tolerance for creeds, races, and other ideologies," which would ensure that every member country would feel welcome.[131] Dittborn claimed that true Chilean sportsmanship resided in the popular classes, which struggled to participate in sports despite their scarce economic resources. He described the vibrant community of amateurs enthused by the prospect of the Cup. Drawing upon the model amateur created in the barrios of Santiago, Dittborn praised the modesty, work ethic, and dedication of working-class footballers. He concluded by praising the "underdog" spirit of Chilean football and connecting it with what he felt was a universal belief in football: that even the humblest deserved the opportunity to play. In a dramatic end that would become the motto of the World Cup, Dittborn declared, "Because we have nothing, we want to do it all." Despite Chile's lack of tourist and sports infrastructure, the emotional appeal, which emphasized the country's humility, touched a chord with delegates.[132] FIFA delegates voted in favor of Chile, 32–10 (with 14 abstentions). Chileans gathered in the National Stadium, crowded around newspaper offices, and waited near radios to hear the decision of FIFA. Euphoric celebrations followed the announcement of the vote. Carlos Dittborn became an instant star, and his famous phrase, "Because we have nothing," headlined reports.

Immediately after the vote, tournament organizers began to mobilize institutions, governmental agencies, and financial resources. Amateur sports clubs participated in the early organization of the tournament in hopes that the increased attention being paid to football would translate into support for their organizations. Although excitement over the Cup

FIGURE 5.3.   Carlos Dittborn (*right*) and other members of the World Cup Organizing
Committee meeting, 1962. Image courtesy of the Archivo Fotográfico Colección, Museo
Histórico Archivo, Santiago.

inspired political speeches, amateurs recognized quickly that they would
receive few benefits directly from Congress. Municipalities with stadiums
large enough to host matches, including the northern city of Arica, Ñuñoa,
and Valparaíso/Viña del Mar, received increased funds from the national
government for structural improvements. The actions of the Cup's organizers
distanced amateurs from the tournament. First, amateur clubs criticized
governmental plans to relocate shantytown residents away from major hotel
areas and the Stadium. Furthermore, amateurs were disappointed that the
committee did not plan to implement measures to prevent the price gouging
of goods and services in response to the influx of tourists. Finally, amateur
club directors were not included in the organizational structure or given
affordable tickets, despite a barrage of petitions.[133]

Sports directors, journalists, and fans sought to construct a historical
narrative of Chilean football in preparation for the Cup. The creation of
nostalgia for preprofessional days conjured a time when Chilean football
had been more successful. Writers sought out football stars from the
1920s and 1930s who could help provide details. The mainstream press
focused on two players from Colo Colo's early years, Waldo Sanhueza and

Guillermo Saavedra. Sportswriters downplayed the men's involvement in professionalism, stating that Guillermo Saavedra was a "true amateur" who "never confused his economic interests with his sporting passion."[134] In fact, Saavedra had signed a professional contract the first year it was possible to do so. Saavedra's teammate Waldo Sanhueza was described as a worker who had the "old-time" values of amateurism. However, Sanhueza had acted as Colo Colo's delegate when the Professional League was organized in 1931. In newspapers, Sanhueza appeared as the emblematic working-class amateur, who writers took care to depict as compliant, happy, and easygoing. After explaining Sanhueza's modest upbringing, *Estadio* summed him up as "likeable, a good friend, without enemies. He was never annoyed."[135] This contrasted with the barrio icon's militancy and passion. Some histories stressed class reconciliation. The Braden Copper Company, which volunteered its stadium in Rancagua for Cup events, commissioned one such work. Braden's history highlighted the support that management had provided to workers' football clubs.[136] The directors hoped to capitalize on the company's participation in the Cup to improve their image while they were in the midst of friction with labor unions.

Chile's reputation abroad was the subject of great anxiety for the official World Cup organizing committee, which consisted of state officials, business leaders, and professional club directors. The committee handled the budget, managed relations with FIFA, and oversaw "official publications." Its magazine stressed the centrality of Chile's liberal democracy to its national identity, informing readers (in several languages) that "[Chile's] political institutions . . . reflect a democracy constantly striving for perfection. Political, social, and racial prejudices are nonexistent. Since 1891, there have been no explosive revolutions in Chile. Chiefs of state walk about the streets and cities as any citizen would."[137] For the committee, this political stability depended upon the country's level of economic development, racial makeup, and modernity.

Sportswriters expressed similar concerns when they warned the public that FIFA officials and international visitors would scrutinize "whether people are white or black, whether Spanish or Portuguese is spoken, whether life is easy or difficult, whether the climate is tropical or temperate."[138] Writers worried that Chile would be confused with Brazil or Colombia, countries that were supposedly less temperate, less white, and subsequently less stable. The committee's publications avoided any references to the country's non-European population. As mentioned in Chapter Four, the committee reported that Chile was "white, of European heritage, without a population of color or mixed races, the population being the most homogenous in the Americas."[139] Generally, the mainstream media supported the committee's assertions, although interviews with "old crack" players sometimes complicated these proclamations. For example, in one interview, Waldo Sanhueza explained that he was nicknamed "the Indian" because of his background. Moreover, he mentioned that players called one teammate "the Jap . . . because that face of his was *so* Chilean, with that something Asian that our race has in the eyes and cheekbones."[140]

The committee's portrayal of Chile as a white, European-derived nation was integral to its image. The committee's publicity on the origins of Chilean football took every opportunity to emphasize the role of Europeans, especially aristocratic British immigrants. Histories in *Estadio*, published throughout the 1950s as part of its campaign against radical, working-class amateurs, provided material for the committee's work. According to these articles, football's golden age began with competition between elite Creoles and British visitors. These histories blamed the political turmoil surrounding Arturo Alessandri's first presidential election, in 1920, with the disintegration of these teams, linking workers' entrance into the political sphere with the decline of genteel football. When governmental officials from the committee mentioned indigenous culture, they often Europeanized it. For example, in 1959, the director of the State Department of Sports, Fernando Renard, addressed a crowd gathered in the National Stadium. Regarding the legacy of the "ancient" Indians, Renard remarked, "We take pride in their spartan habits, their patriotic feeling, and the tenacity that over centuries developed the physical strength of a race that loved the air and sun in the valleys and mountains."[141] When officials included indigenous communities in their discourse, they stressed either the exceptional success of the Mapuche in resisting the Spanish or their European-like features.

Gender constituted the one area in which the committee portrayed tradition, rather than modernity, in a positive light. The committee promised tourists a tranquil paradise where they could enjoy traditional South American culture with the comforts of modern infrastructure. The beauty and subservience of women constituted one of the pillars of "traditional" culture that visitors could enjoy. One government publication explained, "The woman of this country is generally beautiful, possesses a well-formed body, is exquisitely feminine, and knows how to dress with a Parisian simplicity and elegance."[142] The media claimed that Chilean women were as up-to-date as European women were in fashion, but were not influenced

by feminism. In the histories of football featured in the press, women's relationship to sports was presented as a subject for ridicule. In reference to
a "mixed-sex" charity match that took place in 1905, one journalist wrote,
"And to think, fifty-five years later, a match of women's football was prohibited for being considered a circus act!"[143]

A scandal that broke out in the weeks preceding the tournament disrupted the committee's harmonious picture of Chile. A group of Italian
journalists who visited in late 1961 claimed that the organizing committee
had wildly distorted the truth about the modernity of Chile. One journalist
remarked, "The atmosphere is so depressing that some federations have
sent psychiatrists to prevent their players from becoming depressed."[144]
Another writer described Santiago as "a sad symbol of one of the least developed countries in the world, and one affected by all maladies: undernourishment, prostitution, illiteracy, alcoholism, and poverty."[145] They
described the shantytowns and squatter settlements on Santiago's periph-
eries as deplorable and barbaric. These reports so offended readers and
the World Cup committee that the Italian ambassador held a formal press
conference to apologize. Even *El Siglo*, which printed the reports, complained that the journalists had not seen the promise of Chileans, who were
"healthy in spirit, polite, conscious of their problems, and ready to change
the current state of things."[146] While the committee failed to convince most
amateurs that it was organizing the event democratically, they felt that the
Italians had ignored the efforts of common Chileans to create a warm atmosphere for visitors. Chilean fans were still seething the following year when
their team confronted the Italians in the Cup. Journalists dubbed the match
between Chile and Italy the "Battle of Santiago" because of the violence
among players and fans.[147] Even before the match began, spectators shouted insults and threw rocks, food, and other objects onto the field. Referees
threatened to cancel the match if the violent behavior in the stands did not
subside. On the field, a fight broke out between the Chilean player Leonel
Sánchez and Mario David of Italy.[148]

Preparations for the World Cup sparked debate over the leadership
of President Jorge Alessandri. A Conservative politician with a sober de-
meanor, Alessandri inherited the World Cup from Carlos Ibáñez when he
took office in 1958. Alessandri was not the populist his father, Arturo, had
been. Moreover, he had little connection to popular civic associations and
hardly seemed interested in football. Professionals and amateurs criticized
Alessandri's reluctance to commit adequate funds to the event's organization. In 1961, after three years of petitions from amateurs and professionals,

Alessandri passed Executive Order 244, which brought the organization of the Cup under the control of the Ministry of the Interior. The decree ordered state agencies and their personnel to cooperate in every way with the organizing committee.[149] Many club directors doubted that there was enough time to resolve the pending problems. Alessandri delegated most of the responsibility for the Cup to the minister of the interior, Dr. Sótero del Río, who became the government's point man on the committee and Alessandri's chief defender.[150] Sótero del Río and *Estadio* claimed that Alessandri's apparent lack of enthusiasm was in fact a sign of humility. They praised him for dressing modestly and having mild mannerisms.[151] Journalists pointed to Alessandri's habit of walking to work in the morning, unfettered by a security detail, as evidence of this. Alessandri's speech to inaugurate the event was both self-deprecating and brief. Referring to Chile as "this distant corner of the world," Alessandri began with the admission that "our country does not have all of the comforts and advancements that others could have offered."[152]

Despite Conservative support for Alessandri, criticisms of his government mounted as the tournament drew near. A month before the tournament, Chileans were shocked by the announcement that only a small number of tickets had been sold. Amateurs, fans, and some members of the press accused government representatives and professional directors of inflating ticket prices in order to offset the money they had squandered on contracts awarded for architectural improvements.[153] Their suspicions centered on the involvement of Arab Chilean businessmen who sat on the organizing committee, such as Nicolás Abumohor. Initially, Cup organizers promised that the tournament would bring forty thousand to fifty thousand tourists to Chile. In the end, only a fraction of that number arrived. High prices and poor distribution methods hindered Chileans and neighboring Latin Americans from purchasing tickets.[154] Many of the clubs authorized to sell tickets were located far from working-class neighborhoods. Writers for *El Siglo* complained that inflated hotel and transportation rates prevented provincial Chileans from traveling to see the events.[155] Some felt the government had conducted the event so poorly that it would have been better for Chilean fans if Argentina had won its bid to host the Cup.[156]

Amateurs criticized the government's failure to complete projects such as the "World Cup Museum of Carlos Dittborn 1962."[157] In addition, they claimed that the organizing committee had watched idly as amateur associations throughout the country lost three hundred football fields during the five years of preparation for the tournament.[158] Furthermore, football associations had protested the organizing committee's displacement of residents near the National Stadium. After a year of back-and-forth negotiations, hundreds of families that CORVI had ordered to move still refused to do so. Residents had lived in the shantytown for nearly fifteen years without water, plumbing, sidewalks, and other services that *El Siglo* described as "basic to life in a civilized country."[159] Despite such challenges, community members who had made improvements to the neighborhood were reluctant to leave without a firm promise of alternate housing. CORVI claimed that it would provide the families with new housing, but after meetings with the minister of the interior, community leaders were not satisfied. Amateur football associations across the city demonstrated in support of the shantytown residents, but in the end could not prevent the removal of residents.[160]

In its coverage of the World Cup, the newspaper *El Siglo* provided an alternative perspective to that given in the mainstream press. First, it granted extensive interviews to delegations from the Soviet Union and the Eastern Bloc. It also presented a different view of football's history in Chile, blaming the country's poor international performances on environmental factors that stemmed from class inequalities, such as the undernourishment, poor housing conditions, and abusive workloads that plagued the working classes.[161] Moreover, it paid attention to the sacrifices asked of working-class neighborhoods during the tournament, such as power rationings and transportation disruptions. Finally, it highlighted the economic hardships that famous players faced. For example, *El Siglo*'s biography of Raúl Toro described his poor background and truncated education. As one of ten children, "El Chino" had had to leave elementary school after just one year to help his father, who worked as a mechanic on train cars.[162] This biography contrasted sharply with the entirely upbeat profiles that ran in *El Mercurio* and *Estadio*.

Conservative publications like *El Mercurio* interpreted Chile's win over the Soviet Union as proof of the superiority of free-market capitalism and democracy. For others, the event was more akin to David and Goliath than a Cold War parable. The editorial in the centrist *Topaze* stated, "In defeating the USSR, we have not defeated a country or a regime, as some want to believe."[163] Instead, it was about the state of modernity and progress within Chile: "We have defeated our own defeatism, and we have made a demonstration, not to the world, but to ourselves, of what we are capable of. . . . We have a working and a middle class, to which many of these young men belong, that has all the conditions to go forward, not only in the football field, but also in the broadest demonstrations of citizenship." Among the public, the success of the Chilean team validated Dittborn's vision of a small country's chance at greatness. Moreover, many viewed the Chilean team's performance as affirmation of the country's stability and efficiency.[164]

Political parties hoped to benefit from the prestige of football during the World Cup. They recruited retired players to run for political office. This was especially true of the Radicals and the Christian Democrats, whose strongest presence was in professional football.[165] These efforts failed, however, to achieve the desired results. In part, Chileans' party identifications were too strong for celebrities to move voters. Second, these professionals lacked the relationships with civic associations that had enabled the Popular Front to mobilize large numbers of supporters. For example, Eduardo Simián, a legendary footballer for University of Chile, ran for a congressional

FIGURE 5.4.   Advertisement promising that the family could see the World Cup "without lines, without cold, without rain" by watching it on television, in *Estadio*, 1962. Advertisements for the tournament assumed that fans were uniformly male. Image courtesy of Zig-Zag.

seat in San Miguel as a Christian Democrat in 1958.[166] Simián's friends, including the popular player Sergio Livingstone, organized benefits to support his bid. Campaign advertisements drew upon Simián's reputation among sportsmen and referred to him as "the Octopus," a nickname from his football days. Despite Simián's successful career in engineering, it was his "virile and fair play in sports" that the advertisements lauded.[167] Simián promised that if elected, he would be "playing for the future of Chile . . . so that the sports activities of our youth would find the necessary help and support from public officials."[168] In addition, Simián pledged that "amateur sports, perhaps the most abandoned kind, would receive technical assistance, sports fields, equipment, and professors of physical education." Despite hopes that "footballmania" would buoy sportsmen into office, the Liberal Party candidate defeated Simián in his district.

Chileans described the mood during the World Cup of 1962 as festive and carnivalesque. The memory of the Cup among footballers is one of a perfectly executed event that validated the talent of Chileans.[169] The third-place finish of the Chilean team came as a joyful surprise for many fans. Some recalled that the team finished second, rather than that they reached the semifinals. Despite their marginalization from the event's organization, amateur clubs worked hard to raise enthusiasm for the Cup in their communities. Club leaders across Santiago organized fund-raisers to buy tickets to matches. Many directors dipped into club reserves to buy a television, inviting the neighborhood to watch the matches. When they could not afford a television set, clubs tuned in by radio and opened their doors so that neighbors could listen. Vivacious gossip, analysis, and prognosis preceded and followed matches. Many neighborhood clubs organized social events, such as happy hours, in honor of visiting delegations. Amateur directors appeared on radio shows, thereby taking an active role in shaping the public perception of the Cup. Finally, the clubs helped the Chilean Football Federation sell tickets to matches by purchasing group orders and raffling off tickets.

Because of their animosity toward barrio football, the organizers of the World Cup lost an opportunity to tap into the passion of Chile's most dogged football fans. The flourishing barrio clubs throughout the country could have provided a strong organizational base for ticket sales, special events, and travel logistics. Their exclusion from the organization of the Cup likely hurt its success. In histories written outside Chile, the 1962 tournament is considered one of the least exciting World Cup competitions. Unpredictable events, such as the injury of the young star Pelé dampened enthusiasm; the scoring was low, and the violence between players at an all-time high. Many were disappointed to see stadiums only partly full, which detracted from experience of spectatorship. From all accounts, the fun was to be had "offstage" in the local bars and neighborhood clubs, where Chileans gathered around televisions and radios.

In conclusion, it is worth reflecting on a demonstration of barrio clubs that took place in October 1949. Organizers of the demonstration called for the 1950s to be the "decade of the amateur." Observers reported, "The streets and plazas near the Palace of La Moneda remained filled the whole day."[170] Club directors hoped to draw attention to the disparities in recreational opportunities and the quality of life between poor and affluent neighborhoods. Writers for *Estadio* admonished the demonstrators: "Sportsmen do not have a taste for marches of a political nature."[171] Forty years earlier, nearly to the day, sportsmen had held a similar rally, which drew widespread support from even the most conservative sectors of the press. The shift from upper-class to working-class leadership, the barrio directors' leftist politics, and the criticism of socioeconomic inequalities prompted the difference in reaction to the two marches.

As the demonstrators hoped, the 1950s were in many ways a decade of amateurism. Enthusiasm for barrio clubs, along with the numbers of their members, grew steadily. Clubs received increased support from local politicians, labor unions, and leftist parties. Drawing upon their organizing experience, footballers broadened the scope of their activities to participate in struggles over public space, urban services, and housing. They criticized state agencies that had neglected their communities. At the first national congress of amateur clubs, in 1953, economic disparity was a central theme. One leader explained, "We cannot nor should we continue supporting this enormous poverty and the bitter indifference of the authorities."[172]

Battle lines were drawn between those who embraced professionalism as part of economic modernization and the amateur footballers who criticized its materialism. Women's participation in football, the use of state resources, and class inequality were points of contention between sportsmen. Ideas about the proper places for political expression were also at stake. Professionals clung to the notion that sports transcended political differences. For amateur footballers, political activism was not something that had been imposed by Marxist parties, but a legitimate struggle for community improvement and social justice. The popularization of the barrio football icon marked profound changes in the politics of amateur clubs. The idea that the working class was a repository of talent, strength, and ingenuity was a radical one. Politicians from the Socialist and Communist parties and labor organizations lent crucial support to clubs in their campaigns. At the same time, football clubs provided support for leftists and contrib-uted to their influence among civic associations. As the campaign for the 1962 World Cup demonstrated, the barrio footballer had become an important icon on a national scale. However, professional directors used the preparations for the Cup to dominate football.

THE NEW LEFT, POPULAR UNITY, AND FOOTBALL, 1963–1973

6

The atmosphere of the 1960s was charged with tension and excitement for young people in cities around the world. In Latin America, the growth of armed leftist groups, feminism, and indigenous rights movements met with a strong conservative reaction. To further complicate matters, transnational marketing campaigns co-opted various elements of these movements to promote consumption among young people. The political context of the 1960s created new opportunities and challenges for Chilean football clubs. This chapter examines how the emergence of the New Left and the youth culture of the 1960s energized the leftist Popular Unity (Unidad Popular, or UP) government of Salvador Allende, which lasted from 1970 to 1973. The *New York Times* referred to the election of the Socialist Party founder, Salvador Allende, as "cataclysmic" and "without precedent anywhere in the world."[1] U.S. State Department officials speculated that the election was a deathblow to the Alliance for Progress program begun by the Kennedy administration.[2] The United States and, to a lesser extent, the Soviet Union provided support to Allende's opponents and supporters, respectively. Beyond diplomatic wrangling, political debates took place in civic associations, popular-culture venues, and neighborhoods. Amateur football organizations, which were largely in favor of the Allende government, fervently debated how political viewpoints should influence everyday cultural practices. It was an exciting moment for those who hoped to create a socialist society. Amateur clubs that supported Allende's Popular Unity coalition envisioned how sports could develop in new ways under socialism.

Amateur footballers constituted an important base for political mobilization, despite the growth of the professional football industry. According to an informal census conducted by the Department of Sports and Recreation in 1969–1970, around five hundred thousand amateur football players

FIGURE 6.1.   When asked what he most remembered of the Popular Unity period, a worker replied: "I remember that an old man of sixty years hugged me in the street—imagine people hugging one another without knowing who was who—and he said to me, 'I didn't want to die without having seen this moment.' That I have never forgotten" (Gaudichaud, *Poder Popular y Cordones Industriales*, 359). Photograph, "Obreros," by Luis Poirot. Image courtesy of Luis Poirot.

belonged to clubs.[3] Football clubs and other civic associations helped provide resources to working-class neighborhoods in the midst of blockades, hoarding, and threats from paramilitaries. Moreover, they organized public support for Allende's UP government. This type of support was crucial as the administration faced economic sanctions from the United States and a deteriorating relationship with centrist politicians. This chapter argues for the importance of popular culture as a way to understand how people created and understood political identities. It also illustrates the importance of popular culture in shaping the UP agenda at the grassroots level. Footballers interested in reworking the relationship between culture and politics were joined by UP supporters who performed folk music, poetry, and theater. This enthusiasm for a new socialist culture was even more interesting because of the simultaneous emergence of mass advertising. Despite technological innovations that made it easier for multinational corporations to reach consumers via popular culture, they failed to co-opt youthful rebellion and convince their audiences to reconcile with authority.

An analysis of civic associations sheds new light on a well-trodden subject in Chilean history. A key area of research for historical scholarship has been the changes in political parties that contributed to the collapse of the political system in 1973. This perspective has often privileged a top-down perspective on political struggles.[4] In one version of this argument, the refusal of the centrist Christian Democrats to sustain the tradition of building coalitions and brokering negotiations created the climate for military intervention.[5] Others maintain that ideological entrenchment in all political parties rendered the system unmanageable. In this vein, the well-known political scientist Alan Angell summarized the process thus: "Old concepts, like party membership, changed from being seen as a simple expression of party preference to a position in the class war. The general consensus about the validity of the constitutional system was broken. Political violence, until then rare in Chile, grew in intensity and frequency."[6] Angell contends that the system collapsed "probably because neither side was sufficiently committed to that system and because the expectations of all the parties were too high."[7] However, evidence suggests that Allende's support increased during his term and that, at least on a national level, Chileans became less concerned with his Marxist principles.[8] Furthermore, rank-and-file members of leftist political parties, civic leaders, and associations had faith in the political system. These groups operated within institutional channels and took few measures to prepare for a "class war," even as major newspapers and political figures predicted one.

YOUTH AND THE NEW LEFT

The attention paid to the politics of young people made popular culture, of which they were the most important consumers, all the more important as a site of political identity. As previous chapters demonstrated, football had come to be seen as essential for the proper development of young men. Even so, clubs focused on the subject of youth with new intensity in the 1960s. At the same time, young people garnered greater attention as political subjects, both because they participated in politics more frequently than before and because they were the subjects of intense scrutiny generally. Barrio directors in working-class communities hoped to decrease delinquency and build young people's identification with their neighborhoods. Youth clubs, which operated independently or as sections of larger clubs, were points of contention between barrio and professional directors. Since professional clubs drew on the talented players cultivated in youth organizations, amateurs believed that professionals had an obligation to support these programs. This issue arose each time professional clubs sought financial help from the government or public programs.

The emergence of the New Left, part of the broader countercultural movement across the world, pushed the political agenda of parties from the Left and the Center to address sexual practices, drug consumption, gender roles, and appearance. Previous studies of popular culture and youth have stressed the importance of a distinctive generational politics for the broader process of radicalization in Chile. The border between the Old and New Left was more porous at the level of grassroots organizing than these labels convey. Although women were marginalized from leadership of the CUT, local unions considered part of the Old Left were open to feminist demands for women's participation in sports. Nonetheless, the history of football clubs in the 1960s reflects a growing sense of generational segregation. It also indicates a shift in the locus of working-class youth politics from the neighborhoods to the universities. However, a clear ideological chasm among older and younger footballers, especially one that assumes younger members to be more radical, is difficult to establish. In fact, it was the 1964 presidential campaign of the Christian Democrat Eduardo Frei that attracted a new cohort of young people to politics. Frei promised agrarian reform, limited nationalization of the copper industry, and compromises with labor organizations. Despite the reformist nature of Frei's "revolution in liberty," the mainstream media presented an alarmist picture of the politicization of young people.[9]

Historians interested in the radicalization of youth movements around the world in the 1960s have suggested that the counterculture was a reaction against Fordist socioeconomic regulation and the constraints of the bourgeois nuclear family. In addition, events of global importance, notably the Cuban Revolution and anticolonial struggles in Asia and Africa, influenced the emergence of the New Left in Latin America. In Chile, the rapid increase in the availability of formal education and the expansion of state institutions created conditions for youth groups to participate in politics.[10] Advertising and mass media also contributed to the building of a generational identity. Marketing campaigns directed toward young people encouraged them to identify with one another through consumption. Advertisements for sporting goods, makeup, and clothing depicted older people as backward. The lifestyles of grandparents and parents were portrayed as anachronistic in a modernizing world. Often designed for U.S. and European consumers, advertisements glossed over class and ethnic difference among young people. Yet they featured products designed to help young women attract men, encouraging distinct gender roles. Furthermore, advertising campaigns urged young consumers to focus on themselves.

Distinctions between well-established youth organizations like the Socialist Youth, new militant leftist organizations like the Revolutionary Left Movement (Movimiento de Izquierda Revolucionaria, or MIR), and hippies were frequently blurred.[11] While some Socialists and Communists criticized hippies, many appreciated their politics. For example, the Communist *El Siglo* commended John Lennon and Yoko Ono for their charity and antiwar activities. Its depiction of the couple was quite favorable compared with the treatment given them by *El Mercurio*.[12] "Hippie" was often used to characterize one type of bohemian style. For instance, sports clubs in an occupied neighborhood controlled by the MIR sponsored a contest among youth brigades. The contest for community service featured a competition among groups identified as "artists," "hippies," "beatniks," and "gypsies."[13] Their activities included cleaning a garbage incinerator, collecting firewood, repairing a stairwell, fixing a laundry machine, and so on. The inclusion of hippies in this group indicates that among young MIR members, it was not a derogatory term.

Labor historians have shown that changes in the workplace in the post–World War II period encouraged differentiation between generations. In *Weavers of the Revolution*, Peter Winn explained that age differences among textile workers shaped the radicalization of their unions. Younger workers, who knew only the Taylorite system, considered their struggles to be distinct from those of the older generation, which had begun work under the paternal oversight of owner Juan Yarur. For Winn, the consciousness of the workers had changed, along with their expectations regarding working conditions. Social life and political ideologies led many young employees to see work as a liberating experience.[14] Not all sectors of working-class youth felt the same degree of separation from older generations. The leaders of the Communist Youth, such as Gladys Marín, stressed the importance of collaborating with established civic associations in shantytowns and squatter settlements. Their organization encouraged obedience to, respect for, and solidarity with older generations. Although some members of the Communist and Socialist youth sections felt that the hippie ideal of personal liberation was irreconcilable with class solidarity and party discipline, others believed that the party should be open to criticisms from the counterculture. Young Christian Democrats complained vocally that their sections had virtually no institutional spaces from which to influence the party's platform.[15] Centrist parties experienced the strongest divisions between generations, reflecting the radicalization of middle-class youth.

Youth attracted more attention than ever among football fans. The international trend of cultivating young sports stars changed the dynamics of football. In the 1960s, professional clubs began to recruit talented boys when they were ten or eleven. This was a profound departure from the 1930s, when players joined professional clubs in their twenties and played well into their thirties and sometimes forties. In part, interest in younger players was a response to the outstanding performances of players like the Brazilian star Pelé. Many commentators believed the emphasis on young players diminished the strategy involved in the sport. They complained that teams relied more upon speed and strength. Photographic illustrations, close-up televisions shots, and posters highlighted the contours of players' bodies in close detail. The combination of these developments created a virtual cult of the adolescent male body. Marketing aimed at youth presented young men's bodies as unproblematic, whereas young women were told how to hide flaws, cover blemishes, and accentuate the parts of their bodies that young men would find attractive.

Amateur football clubs and other neighborhood associations noted with some dismay that their young members were spending more time with university organizations. This reflected the dramatic increase in the number of working- and middle-class students in higher education, as well as the importance of the university as a site of political activities.[16] Football competition between university clubs (both professional) provided opportunities for student expression. During football matches between the University of Chile and its rival the Pontifical Catholic University, especially the annual Clásico Universitario, students commented on contemporary politics through artistic exhibitions. Students who organized the halftime shows created themes, choreographed dances, wrote musical scores, and built elaborate floats.[17] Leaders of the show tended to come from the wealthier segment of the student body, and tickets were costly.[18] The University of Chile typically presented a theme sympathetic to centrist or leftist causes, while the Catholic University expressed a strong conservative bent. Sportswriters commented that unlike students in any previous years, those who put on the shows during the elections of 1969 and 1970 adopted explicitly political themes.[19]

Whereas members of local voluntary organizations typically worked on one another's projects, university politics drew young people from their communities. Leaders of youth brigades in the universities, particularly for the Christian Democrats and Socialists, encouraged young people to see themselves as part of national movements. They sent students across the country to work in poor communities and raise political consciousness. In addition, the internationalism of leftist causes in the 1960s framed political struggles as global rather than local.[20]

The countercultural movement criticized traditional prohibitions on sex and drug use, religious dogmatism, and conformity.[21] At times, it also encompassed more explicitly political issues such as materialism, ideological rigidity, and wealth inequalities. Most likely, a degree of incompatibility existed between established clubs' reverence for traditions and hippies' inclination to view older institutions with skepticism. The trophy cases, banquets, and formal governance of clubs encouraged respect for tradition. This structure was at odds with the counterculture's challenge to hierarchical relationships and "bourgeois notions" of planning, saving, and obligation. Yet football clubs rarely reported generational conflicts among members. Perhaps there were no confrontations to report, especially if young people either did not seek to join clubs or drifted in and out.

The radicalization of working-class youth and the marginalization of barrio clubs by professionals after the World Cup of 1962 prompted young footballers to create new types of sports organizations. In part, the new organizations flourished because of members' financial constraints. Clubs in shantytowns and squatter settlements had a difficult time collecting the dues required to join established organizations. For example, several youth clubs in the working-class neighborhood of San Gregorio formed a new league after they failed to come up with the dues to pay ANFA. In other cases, youth clubs adopted an explicit political agenda. Some football clubs wanted to adopt a pro-Cuban and pro-Communist stance, which they believed ANFA or other established organizations would shun. In a squatter settlement in La Legua, San Miguel, Club Juventud Rebelde was divided over the decision to declare a political ideology. The club preferred to play other clubs from squatter settlements rather than join the Football Association of San Miguel.[22]

As a result of these financial and political constraints, youth clubs were heavily represented in the National Association of Barrio Sports (Agrupación Nacional de Deportistas Aficionados de los Barrios, or ANDABA) rather than in ANFA. ANDABA was begun in 1952 by sportsmen who sought to connect with other clubs in urban areas across the country. The organization grew rapidly in the 1960s and linked working-class neighborhoods.[23] Young players in ANDABA celebrated barrio football's iconic working-class rebellion and firmly grounded it in local identities. The local nature of the icon may explain why it was not incorporated into the broader countercultural movement.

GENDER, POLITICS, AND AUTHORITY IN MASS MARKETING

Advertisers, journalists, and professional sports directors created ambiguous messages in football publications geared toward young people. On the one hand, the conservative editors of Zig-Zag, which published *Barrabases* (a football magazine for adolescents), *Estadio*, and *El Mercurio*, stressed the importance of discipline and obedience to authority; on the other, advertisements urged young people to identify with their peers. They applauded young people for their modernity. Moreover, they suggested that the consumption of music, clothing, makeup, and other products could resolve adolescents' tensions and insecurities. While mainstream media opined on the need to curb youthful rebellion, some professional clubs sought to capitalize on it. *Barrabases* lent staff artists to corporations to draw comics for ads, which made it difficult to discern between a Falabella department store advertisement, for example, and a serial sports comic strip.[24] In addition, multinational corporations such as Revlon purchased an increasing number of ad spots in Chilean youth magazines. For example, corporations ran spots in *Ritmo*, a magazine that featured interviews with and gossip about stars of sports, television, and movies. To capture the youth market, companies created segmented programming. Sports radio programs encouraged children to join fan clubs and enter contests. This view of adolescents as young consumers marked a significant shift from considering them young athletes.[25] Treating young listeners in this fashion encouraged them to idolize the most talented and famous sports stars rather than to cultivate their own athleticism.

Marketing to young consumers reinforced and created distinct gender roles. In the 1960s, advertisements shifted their focus from trying to establish a good reputation for products and their manufacturers to enhancing the identity of the consumer. The relationship between the content of mainstream media and advertisements became increasingly intimate. Advertisements sent messages about normal gender roles to both male and female audiences. The idea that domestic labor was the sole responsibility of women appeared again and again. For a young male reader, it was clear that any help he provided in the household would reflect poorly on his masculinity.

Women's work was often featured as an extension of their work in the home. Workingwomen were shown as home helpers and as being more concerned than ever with traditional tasks such as laundry. In one issue of the popular magazine *Vea*, an advertisement for laundry soap featured two young nurses in sparkling white uniforms. The copy read, "When a woman worries more, it shows."[26] In the same issue, women who joined mothers' centers, popular neighborhood organizations for women, were described as "working hard like quiet ants."[27]

Although gender roles were changing, the mainstream media portrayed men's and women's natures as unchanging. As the female beauty industry exploited stereotypes of women, particularly their anxiety over skin color, thinness, or hair luster, it also mobilized stereotypes of young men. While less destructive, stereotypes of men circumscribed proper heterosexual male behavior. Advertisements for goods and services as diverse as airlines, deodorant, and tea linked men's success as breadwinners to their appearance. They encouraged men to cultivate a successful persona, which included a close shave and business attire. An advertisement for Williams cologne described the scent as "young, dynamic, and elegant, for [the man] who knows what he wants . . . and gets it."[28] The back cover of the magazine announced that women in the twentieth century had entered fields hitherto closed to them, without "losing their femininity and delicacy." If women were anxious about retaining their feminine charms, the opposite page showed a woman giving her hair a "beauty bath."[29] Just as women were pushing gender boundaries, the beauty industry urged them to take constant stock of the status of their figures, faces, and smells. These messages discouraged women's participation in sports.

A major theme of sports literature directed toward youth pitted the working-class icon that barrio clubs had popularized against a model of obedience. Magazines used a variety of genres, including fotonovelas, comics, articles, and serial dramas, to attract young audiences. Mainstream publications were filled with denunciations of working-class clubs, which they accused of tolerating a poor work ethic among players. Journalists from *Barrabases* and *Estadio* claimed that working-class players needed to curb their rebellious tendencies and lofty dreams of wealth. Repeatedly, stories featured working-class players being punished for trying to use their newly gained status to buy luxuries or pass for a member of high society. Fotonovelas—serial dramas with photographs and captions—blurred the line between fiction and reality by employing real-life stars. In one, Juan Toro played a humble football star from the countryside who used his money to buy designer clothing and a car. Despite promises to his mother to remain humble, Toro's character succumbed to the temptations of nightlife in the city. In a visit to his mother, Toro's character flaunted his wealth in the village and explained he was not "the same *huaso* [peasant] brute as before."[30] Following the conversation, the star suffered a near-fatal crash in his new car when he collided with a horse. The near-death experience brought him to his senses, and he vowed to abandon luxuries.

Sports journalists stressed that obedience to authority was essential for working-class players hoping to achieve their athletic potential. In a biopic on player Fernando Navarro, *Barrabases* explained, "Since childhood, Fernando has had attributes indispensable for quick success in sports, qualities that have often been subsumed by a heightened rebelliousness."[31] Navarro eventually "let his old rebellion sink into the twilight of the past, because in the clear light of day, he saw a smiling horizon and a happy future with his loyal life companion at his side, his good wife." Sportswriters often suggested that marriage could help players overcome their "uppity" tendencies. The writer summarized the lesson to be learned from Navarro: "It is not enough to want to become a superstar. One must sacrifice, strive, and obey." In football magazines, the questioning of authority appeared tantamount to immaturity and laziness.

Didactic pieces like these serial dramas stressed the importance of reconciliation between working-class youth and the authorities, including the police, teachers, and parents.[32] They depicted distrust of the police as the product of a misunderstanding. In a piece by the journalist Mr. Huifa (a writer for *Estadio*), police detained a group of boys from a poor barrio after they broke a window playing football.[33] The leader of the group appealed to the captain, explaining the hardships of life as a poor boy. His moving speech prompted the captain to create a field for the boys, who were so grateful that they named their club for him. The lesson was spelled out for readers: "Things could have been different for the little guys of the barrio, poor, some ignorant, if he had treated them with rudeness, if he had not shown human spirit and understanding." The message was that working-class youth should show deference to authorities and, in turn, the police simply needed to be nicer to the poor.

Along with the image of the police, sports publications also sought to rehabilitate the role of the father, another authority figure that young men needed to respect.[34] In their fiction pieces, the natural bond between father and son suffered because of poor communication rather than young people's legitimate complaints about authoritarianism. The fotonovela "When a Father Is Not Loving" illustrated what could happen when a father acted in an unduly harsh manner and a son questioned his father's opinion. In the story, a young star's career is almost ruined because of problems with his father; unable to play football or sleep properly, he nearly suffers a complete breakdown.[35] Only when he gains his father's approval can his career take off. Sports literature cast football clubs as spaces for young men to develop their own paternal sensibilities, establish their authority over women, and preserve their honor. In this way, clubs served both as public forums where men could prove their physical prowess and as their moral compasses.

In the context of football, boys could express affection toward one another in ways that they could not in other settings. Clubs also offered them the chance to distinguish themselves in the community. Youth magazines portrayed a boy's relationship with his club as a first love affair.[36] Memoirs and testimonies corroborated the intensity of the friendships developed in clubs and the high emotional investment young men placed in their clubs. One protagonist explained, "As we continued winning, the people of the barrio began to take an interest in us, and we began to notice they followed us. They even went to see us play other barrios. They applauded us in a frenzy and fought and argued with fans of rival clubs."[37] These magazines portrayed the club as the center of the world for the boys. Only the gravest offense constituted an acceptable reason to quit. In one serial comic, such a reason arises when a player discovers that his teammate is dating his sister.[38] Joaquín, the wounded brother, "almost cries" when forced to explain that he interrupted his friend and sister in a kiss. The situation is resolved when the offending teammate voluntarily leaves the club, ready to start an adult life with Joaquín's sister.

El Siglo and *Gol y Gol* provided some counterpoint to the heavy-handed parables of mainstream sports journalism. They presented youth as endangered by class inequality rather than moral corruption. Moreover, these publications were more optimistic about young athletes, especially those with leftist ties, like Carlos Caszely. Mainstream journalists criticized Caszely, who premiered for Colo Colo in 1967, for discussing politics. They connected these "nonconformist" dispositions with his play, which they described as "very egotistical, rebellious, and selfish."[39] Caszely frequently gave interviews to *El Siglo* and openly supported leftist candidates. When asked about his support of the Allende government, Caszely responded, "Since I had use of my reason, I have liked the Left and I am not thinking of changing my ideals."[40] In addition, *El Siglo* and *Gol y Gol* offered a much more sympathetic assessment of the players' union than the mainstream press. This came across clearly in their support of the players' strike in 1967. A headline in *El Siglo* read, "Those Who Attack Football Players Are Reactionary *Momios*."[41] The characterization of conservatives as momios, or mummies, further underscored a connection between leftists and youth.

As in the 1950s, it was mostly local papers that paid attention to amateur football. Their approach to young audiences differed markedly from that of large-scale media outlets. For example, beginning in 1960, the magazine *El Campeón* of Quinta Normal organized a contest to honor young standouts from barrio clubs. Their features on players emphasized the positive values intrinsic to their humble backgrounds, such as sincerity and loyalty. These narratives made an effort to reverse the shame associated with poverty. One letter from local club directors lauded young players for acting as mentors and "spark plugs" in shantytown communities.[42] Another letter described a young player as "loved and admired by all for his simplicity and good sportsmanship. He never jokes at someone's fall or at those who are in worse shape than he."[43] The number of such letters from directors overwhelmed the editors of *El Campeón*. Despite their limited experience with formal writing, barrio leaders went out of their way to nominate young sportsmen from their clubs. Many explained that even if their nominees did not win the award, they would be proud to see themselves in print.

Young women's participation in barrio clubs increased steadily throughout the 1960s, but this was not encouraged in the mainstream media. *Barrabases*, for example, considered girls who wanted to play football a "problem." In the serial "Once Corazones," young readers followed the story of an exceptional young female athlete named Quena, who "was a healthy and happy girl, but without feminine tastes."[44] She explained, "Girls bore me. They are really stupid and spend their time thinking of boyfriends and other stupidities." While a male character might have offended the audience with such comments, the editors felt that a female character could freely express animosity toward other girls. When Quena's club entered an all-male tournament, her teammates demanded she cut her hair and pretend to be a boy. Quena protested, but her teammates bluntly replied, "Then you don't play." The incident prompted Quena to quit football. Her physical-education teacher suggested Quena join the track team, where she could compete against other girls. Thus, she could maintain both her athleticism and her femininity.

The story of Quena is an early example of a cautionary tale that was recycled in the mainstream press throughout the 1960s and early 1970s.

Other publications assumed that young women had no interest in sports. For instance, the magazine *Ritmo* advised young women to follow football only to keep their boyfriends' interest.[45] Writers for *Ritmo* portrayed football clubs as young women's rivals for the attention and affection of young men. They counseled readers to manage this rivalry by gently encouraging their boyfriends and learning about the game, but not playing it.[46] The mainstream media was out of touch with, or hostile to, the increase in women footballers in amateur clubs. Yet there was evidence that young women's inclusion had begun to change the practices of clubs. Club Ferrobadminton, for example, contracted with a gynecologist to treat female club members at its family medical clinic.[47]

CHRISTIAN DEMOCRATS AND PROFESSIONAL FOOTBALL

Christian Democrats had successfully mobilized middle-class youth during the early years of Eduardo Frei's administration. However, by the end of his term, many were dissatisfied with his record. On the one hand, proposals for agrarian reform and the nationalization of the copper industry angered the conservative wing of Christian Democrats. On the other, the left wing of the party, especially the youth sections, demanded a greater commitment to those goals. As mentioned earlier, the leaders of youth sections of both the Radical and Christian Democrat parties complained of being ignored by party leaders.[48] As a result of its disenchantment, the left wing of the Young Christian Democrats formed the United Popular Action Movement (Movimiento de Acción Popular Unitario, or MAPU) party in 1969. The Christian Democrats attributed the left turn of their young members to leftist influences in popular culture. They accused Communist and Socialist politicians who supported sports clubs and theater troupes of buying votes.[49]

Despite the effervescence of barrio football, centrist parties focused their energy on professionals. Following its impressive finish in the World Cup of 1962, the Chilean national team returned to its historical mediocrity. Christian Democrats expressed anxiety over the national team's decline during their administration. Legislation written by Radicals and Christian Democrats increased state funds for professional clubs in order to build a better national team.[50] The assumption that professional clubs cared about the national team proved incorrect. In fact, the professional clubs spent significant sums to recruit players from abroad. Professional directors displeased with the supposed Marxism of amateur youth clubs continued to derail projects that would have directed funding to them, as they had done in the 1950s.

Centrist politicians hoped that a larger role for the state in professional football would improve the national team's performance. The Radical senator Humberto Aguirre Doolan was one of the chief critics of the state of Chilean football. His plan to rescue national football called for even greater state intervention than clubs had previously envisioned.[51] A nephew of Pedro Aguirre, Humberto had begun his public service by implementing the Defense of the Race program during the Popular Front. He now sought to replace professional club directors with government officials, whom he believed could end corruption within football. After attempting to launch governmental inquiries into football corruption, Aguirre claimed that professional directors adopted "belligerent positions . . . The treasurer resigns; they blame the trainer. Directors elude responsibility; they criticize journalists. There is bitterness among players, disappointment among fans, and emptiness in the stadiums."[52] Essentially, Aguirre demanded that the government oversee the Central Association's contracts with players, budgets, admission revenue, and international schedule. Furthermore, Aguirre suggested that government officials should help select players for the national team.

The notion that government agencies should help select the national team reflected how important football had become in political circles. Centrist politicians from the generation of the Popular Front, like Humberto Aguirre, drew parallels between the decay of football and the nation. Aguirre explained that true sportsmen "belonged to past eras, distant in history and memory."[53] However, Aguirre rejected leftists' interest in alternatives to professionalism or the conservatives' general disinterest in football. Instead, reform of current institutions was the best solution. This mirrored the broader ideological line of the Radicals and Christian Democrats. Although Aguirre blamed the market for the degradation of values in football, he threw up his hands and proclaimed, "It is natural that it happens this way."[54] Development and modernization programs, Aguirre concluded, would also help provide a better basis for the national team. He explained that players "extracted from humble slums and provincial cities and villages, with low social status, deficient nutrition, and scarce material to develop the sport among its enthusiasts, cannot hope to occupy notable places in the high echelons of sport and will be lost in mediocrity."[55] While this assessment ignored the reality that poor players like Brazil's Pelé dominated the game, it appealed to Radicals who hoped to link the national team's performances with its policies.

The final legislative effort of the Frei administration pertaining to sport proved to be the most controversial, and it reflected important differences in views on sports' role in society. The Sports Law of 1970 increased the tax on alcohol from 24 to 28 percent and used the proceeds to fund sports activities. The law sparked protests from union, barrio, and student organizations that felt the income was distributed in a way that favored professional clubs. These sectors formed the National Sports Front, one of the first national collaborations between barrio directors and physical-education students since the 1940s. First, the group objected to linking funds for sports to alcohol sales. It pointed out the irony of promoting healthy athletic activities by profiting from unhealthy habits. More importantly, it protested the placement of the State Department of Sports within the Ministry of Defense.[56] The group had hoped the law would transfer the department to the Ministry of Education. For members of the National Sports Front, the law identified sports as a priority for military personnel rather than students. In addition, placing sports in the care of the Ministry of Defense allowed conservative legislators to dominate the legislative committees pertaining to sports.[57]

POPULAR UNITY AND CULTURE

The victory of Salvador Allende in the election of 1970 generated tremendous enthusiasm among civic associations, including football clubs, musical troupes, and mothers' centers. The Popular Unity coalition created slogans that put a priority on the needs of young people, such as "In Chile, the only privileged one is the child," which appeared frequently on television and in newspapers.[58] In addition to rhetoric meant to include young people, the UP promoted the idea of *poder popular*, or people power, as an important force in shaping the relationship between culture and the state. Poder popular referred to practices of direct democracy, as distinguished from the liberal democratic structure. Poder popular emphasized the spontaneous and collective action of working-class people. Its relationship to the institutionalized state was a major point of debate during the Popular Unity government. Occupations, or tomas, of factories, urban space, and agricultural land were important components of poder popular. Various figures in folk music, art, film, and, to a lesser extent, sports articulated a notion of poder popular in which workers would become producers of culture rather than consumers. Moreover, the new culture would reflect an "authentic" working-class experience that rejected the individualism of the post–World War II era. Leaders of the UP envisioned workers' organizations, including unions and civic associations, as directors of this process.

Popular-cultural practices such as playing for La Victoria's football clubs or singing folk music became markers of political identity in the 1960s. By the end of the decade, the *nueva canción* was in the process of unseating football as the most popular cultural expression among working-class youth. Nueva canción, or the "new song" movement, offered opportunities for female artists as well as mixed-sex socializing at music festivals. Young people viewed this folkloric style as emblematic of their generation. Talented folk stars emerged, such as Victor Jara, whose strong commitment to social justice contributed to the politicization of the genre.[59] The national labor federation, the CUT, took note of folk singers' sympathies for union struggles and invited stars like Jara to meetings with workers. Many prominent singers campaigned for Allende and bought advertisements in newspapers to support the UP.[60] In response, the mainstream media presented the counterculture as merely a fashion-based identity and dissuaded young people from seeking political messages in music and football, practices that, they claimed, ruined the fun.[61] While tensions sometimes emerged between young people identified as rockers, hippies, and leftists, conservatives grouped them together as part of the broader threat to traditional social mores in Chile.[62] Right-wing papers such as *La Cacerola* frequently attempted to "unmask" secret Communists among musicians and sportsmen.[63]

After the election of Allende, civic associations and cultural producers created a flurry of innovative projects intended to reconfigure the relationship between culture and politics. The reconciliation of different generational experiences surfaced as an important component of the Popular Unity coalition. Young Communists led by the skillful organizer Gladys Marín stressed that members needed to learn from the lessons of an earlier generation of militants who had suffered repression. Many young activists viewed the 1970 election and the creation of the UP as the beginning of a new era, with new possibilities. One activist explained, "I didn't sleep, you understand; I believe that happened to all of us. We understood that for us, to be young meant to be revolutionary, and to be revolutionary twenty-four hours a day, and it meant to deny yourself, renounce everything."[64] The cultural projects of the UP drew upon the experiences of the Popular Front and attempted to move beyond their limitations. As a result, new political actors involved themselves in football. This was particularly apparent after the state became a primary shareholder in Zig-Zag Editorial, which published the mainstream sports magazines.

For UP leaders, sports were among the many practices that needed to be reorganized and rethought under the Socialist government.[65] A few key principles guided the projects of the UP government and shaped its approach to culture. First was the belief that although Chilean poverty had reached a crisis stage, the country was rich enough to provide for everyone. This contrasted with the view that poverty was an inevitable social fact. Culture, then, ought to make workers feel a greater sense of solidarity with one another and a sense of ownership of their labor so that they can participate in economic transformations. Second, UP supporters frequently spoke of democratizing popular culture. While democracy offered protection of individual liberties, the UP needed "to preserve, to make more effective, and to deepen democratic rights and the achievements of workers; and to transform current institutions in order to install a new state where workers and the people truly exercise power."[66] Anti-imperialism was another important part of the UP cultural platform. The UP alliance criticized the intervention of the United States and Europe in the economy, in culture, and in education. Finally, a new emphasis on building ties between the countryside and the city took shape in political rhetoric; however, this often resulted in paternalistic cultural brigades being sent from the city to rural areas to "uplift" working-class culture.[67]

Despite being warmly received by civic associations, not all programs acknowledged the rich organizational experience in working- and middle-class neighborhoods. For example, the State Technical University created new courses for football club directors. The course "Physical Culture and Sports" was part of the series entitled "Social Transformations."[68] In it, young university students of physical education and sociology found themselves in the awkward position of teaching seasoned civic leaders.

In the UP's interpretation of Marxism, it ultimately viewed culture as being at the service of new forms of economic relations. Under socialism, "the triumph of the people will shape a new culture designed to consider human work as the highest value and to express the will of national independence. . . . The deep transformations that will be undertaken require people to be socially conscious and supportive, educated to exercise and defend their political power."[69] Moreover, the new culture would emerge from "the struggle for fraternity rather than individualism; from the valorization of human work rather than its disregard; from national values rather than cultural colonization; from popular access to art, literature, and the means of communication rather than their commercialization."[70]

The outline of physical education in the UP platform was nothing less than utopian. It promised that everyone would have access to exercise and recreation, including homemakers, farmers, and young children. Despite the inclusion of sports in the UP's agenda, physical exercise received far less attention than activities classified as cerebral. Rather than drawing upon mass culture and the grassroots organizations that formed around it, the UP was concerned with democratizing what had previously been considered high culture. This included classical music, art, literature, and dance. As far as popular culture, the UP had a special regard for folk arts, especially the nueva canción.

Football clubs and other civic associations participated in programmatic areas of the UP that went beyond recreation. For example, housing was a high-priority issue for civic associations. This dovetailed with the agenda of the UP. Although the UP could not possibly have implemented the wide-ranging promises of the 1970 presidential campaign, it quickly made progress in urban housing. The Ministerio de Vivienda y Urbanismo (Ministry of Housing and Urban Affairs) contracted for more than seventy-three thousand new housing units, and CORVI contracted for nearly thirty thousand more within the first years of the Allende presidency.[71] To combine public-housing initiatives with quality-of-life programs, the collaboration of civic associations was essential, and they responded enthusiastically. In October 1971, a congress of shantytown residents from eastern San Miguel met to create urban policies that would respond to the urgency of the housing crisis and incorporate the spiritual, educational, and recreational needs of residents.[72] At this meeting were delegates from fifteen cooperatives, eighty mothers' centers, eight women's groups, eighteen sports clubs, four primary schools, and a Christian parish.[73] These groups came together to support the UP's policies and brainstorm on how to effectively implement policies, such as the restriction of liquor licenses in their communities.

In addition to community betterment, leaders of the UP took an interest in sexuality and its relationship to sports. They veered away from viewing sports as an "antidote" to young sexuality, an idea that had been common during previous decades. Influenced by social workers and psychologists, sex experts of the UP era created a less condemnatory discourse, although many continued to consider sex a vice. UP supporters incorporated a criticism of the market into their evaluation of the sexual revolution of the 1960s. The speaker at the inauguration of the Chilean Society for Anthropological

Sexology, which President Allende attended, announced, "It is impossible to ignore the explosion of sex. It appears in adolescents, thwarts their studies and games, drives their conversations, and is converted into an obsession."[74] This increase in the attention paid to sex resulted not from any moral failure but from the fact that "sex is a great selling tool for capitalism." The society's experts warned against heavy repression, which they counseled would only generate more sex among young people.

Whereas physical-education experts earlier in the century had conceived of football as a vehicle for the sublimation of sex, new studies characterized football as a vehicle for channeling homosexuality. Homophobia was rampant among football clubs and crowds, as evidenced by the frequent use of slurs in chants. Right- and left-wing groups accused one another of homosexuality.[75] Recent historical research has suggested that issues connected to sexual liberation and homosexuality created a divide between the Old and New Left.[76] Some suggested that sexuality needed to be understood through the lens of class struggle. For example, the psychologist Regis Marbleu's book *Football: A Homosexual Farce* appeared in Spanish translation (from the French) in Chile in 1968. Marbleu posited that it was natural for men to be attracted to one another and that capitalism was to blame for their frustrated sexuality.[77] Sports channeled aggression, but also generated love between men. It was sensual, explained Marbleu, "Football touched the crudest fibers of homosexuals: the love of the smell of the shirt, sweat, and all the tenderness that is felt for men who struggle for something that belongs to them communally, the club."[78] Drawing upon his reading of Sigmund Freud, Marbleu concluded, "The fan is a perverse and perverted child, a compulsive and cerebral masturbator."[79] However, it was the commercialization of these natural biological impulses that was problematic, rather than sexual practices themselves. While this view of sexuality presented gay men as less pathological than previous literature had done, sports continued to serve as a way to achieve a heterosexual ideal.

In contrast to the view of sexual revolution among UP supporters, those on the far Right blamed permissive popular culture, a lack of religiosity, and the degradation of military power for sexual "perversions."[80] They pointed to the example of the U.S. military, which, they claimed, could not defeat the Vietnamese because of the moral lapses caused by sexual license and pornography.[81] The ultraright organization Patria y Libertad urged parents to take a stronger hand with their children in order to prevent sexual libertinage and to inculcate religious beliefs in the family. One editorial sympathized, "In many Chilean homes, they live a drama . . . The elders look with scorn upon the ignorance, drugs, promiscuity, and scruffiness that appear to be the values of many young people."[82] Patria y Libertad used its press to articulate their view that Siloism (a variety of humanism founded by Mario Rodríguez Cobos), hippies, and Communists were all part of this moral disease.

AMATEUR FOOTBALL AND THE UP

The political polarization leading up to and following the election of the UP worsened relationships between amateur and professional football organizations. Professional directors were appalled when, in the midst of Allende's campaign, amateurs suggested that the government follow the Cuban example of outlawing professionalism in sports.[83] In 1969, the Chilean Football Federation implemented a new policy of alternating between an amateur and a professional president. This policy was a response to amateur directors' complaints of having been marginalized from leadership positions in the federation. However, the policy did not lessen the friction between the two groups. In 1970, ANFA forced the resignation of President Juan Goñi, whom it accused of attempting to limit the influence of amateurs in the federation.[84] Goñi claimed that amateurs misunderstood his intentions. While not part of the amateurs' written complaints against Goñi, his activities aside from football likely increased tensions with them. Goñi worked as a lawyer for the association of bus owners. Barrio directors, who controlled ANFA, battled bus owners who refused to extend routes to shantytowns. Furthermore, the association of bus owners strongly criticized supporters of the UP coalition.[85]

The police had repressed amateur football intermittently throughout the century, but tensions escalated in the late 1960s. Professional directors with higher social status offered little protection to their amateur counterparts. After the election of leftist politicians who took up their cause, amateur clubs may have been emboldened to confront the police and publicize conflicts with them. For example, the Communist senator Volodia Teitelboim denounced police treatment of ANDABA members in the Senate. In March and April 1966, the Ministries of the Interior and National Defense banned the National Football Championship of the Barrios, which was sponsored by ANDABA. According to Teitelboim, "functionaries of the political police have visited the headquarters of the Association of Amateur Sportsmen of the Barrios [ANDABA] and the centers of sports clubs in shantytowns and neighborhoods of Santiago and other important cities, asking for personal information about the directors, carrying out unjustified intimidation, and without any type of legal order. [The sportsmen] request clarification of these declared incidents and guarantee that ANDABA and its members will not continue being victims of harassment and pressure."[86] Teitelboim portrayed the harassment of club members as political persecution that stemmed from ANDABA's ties to Communists, Socialists, and labor unions.

Apart from amateurs' problems with professionals and the police, political differences among them created divisions during the UP period. By 1970, ANDABA had matured into a full-fledged competitor of ANFA, and one with a much more explicit political agenda. ANFA directors sought to maintain the organization's focus on football. While working-class clubs with ties to leftist parties dominated ANFA, many directors valued political diversity within the organization. In addition, they hoped to protect the organization's position as the official voice of amateur clubs. When ANDABA requested to be included in the Chilean Football Federation and the joint state-civil local councils, ANFA campaigned to keep it out.[87] ANDABA protested these exclusions, arguing that it mobilized unaffiliated sportsmen rather than lured players away, as ANFA claimed. Moreover, ANDABA felt that the challenges faced by working-class urban sportsmen needed to be addressed by a separate organization. Its national tournament brought together clubs from Quinta Normal and San Miguel with those from barrios in other major metropolitan areas, including Valdivia and Arica.[88] Despite its organizational isolation, ANDABA flourished throughout the UP period and expanded from football clubs to include cycling, track and field, boxing, and women's basketball.[89] By 1972, ANDABA had registered seventy-six leagues and one hundred eighty thousand players.[90] As ANDABA branched out from football, it complained of hostile reactions from other amateur associations like ANFA, especially the Chilean Boxing Federation.

Women's visibility in civic associations such as sports clubs, JAPs (*juntas de abastecimente y precios*, neighborhood organizations created to ensure that supplies reached barrios), and cultural brigades increased under the UP government.[91] In 1972, ANDABA announced a new emphasis on women's sports, which it hoped would connect it to the women's civic associations that were flourishing in working-class barrios. Sportswomen held more prominent leadership positions in sports organizations. For example, in 1971, Marta Godoy, a young physical-education teacher, became the first woman to head the Communist Youth sports section. Godoy declared the

UP would end "classist" sports, but did not address sexism.[92] Just a few
years earlier, the Socialist congressman Mario Palestro's football club, Unión Condell, had elected Magdalena Quezada as its first female director.[93]
Mainstream media, like *El Mercurio*, and right-wing organizations claimed
that young women's participation in football, as well as in mural painting
and drum circles, threatened to undo traditional culture.[94] While UP supporters frequently praised women's activity in politics and voluntary organizations during the Allende period, in the process they often downplayed
the long history of women's associations. According to one activist, "Another important novelty was the participation of women, which was almost
unknown before the UP. They played an important part in the JAPs, and for
the most part, women organized the health committee. They were also active in education and propaganda, though problems like security remained
very much the domain of men—such changes came slowly."[95]

Women's football continued to make strides during the UP period,
despite a lack of media attention. *Gol y Gol* stopped publication in 1969,
and with a few exceptions, neither *El Siglo* nor *Estadio* took up its interest
in women's football. Based on what can be gleaned from sparse evidence,
such as the lopsided scores of matches, women's football clubs still had
difficulty locating one another. For example, a match between the women's
teams Colo Colo (which does not appear to be related to the professional
men's club) and Mary Clair ended with a score of 16–1.[96] This kind of rout
rarely happened in men's football after the leagues and the requirements to
join them were firmly established. Women's football activity continued to
be most visible in occupied neighborhoods and shantytowns. In 1971, the
población (barrio) Presidente Frei, which was on the periphery of Ñuñoa,
reported that a group of young women had founded Club "Estrella Verde"
three years earlier.[97] The article explained that after playing pickup games
for several years, they started their club in 1968 with 15 members, and by
1971, they had 150 on their rosters, including both young and adult women's
football. Recognizing the growth of interest in women's football and the
importance of including women in sports, local and regional councils created a plan to integrate physical education and sports clubs. These councils
consisted of amateur clubs, municipal officials, and other public figures.[98]
The military coup of 1973 interrupted the projects they designed to promote women's football. Indeed, the reestablishment of traditional gender
roles was central to the right wing's agenda.

Sportsmen who supported the UP government interpreted spectatorship and the authorities differently after Allende assumed office. *El Siglo*

FIGURE 6.2.   Female football players, c. 1968. Image courtesy of the Archivo Fotográfico
Colección, Museo Histórico Archivo, Santiago.

urged fans to see themselves as the "people," who, by extension, represented
the "people's government."[99] It also cautioned fans to approach government
agencies and authorities with new respect rather than fear. *El Siglo* claimed
the police were "not like they were before—an aggressive force and at
times almost provocateurs—but a calm entity that duly complies with its
mission, struggling to impose its presence in order to support the authority
that its power emanates from [that is, the people], not coups or the armed
forces."[100]

Following a violent match between the Chilean club Unión Española
and the Argentine squad Estudiantes de La Plata, which took place at the
National Stadium, the mainstream media reported that workers initiated
fights. Readers who attended the match objected to this portrayal. Some believed that "fascist elements" had instigated violence in order to shame the
Allende administration. Eduardo Olivares wrote to *El Siglo*, "I am a worker
with consciousness, and I do not have homicidal instincts. . . . I belong to
the Stevedores Union of Valparaíso. . . . The violent actions, not only against
the players of Estudiantes but also against the police and against all," were
intended to "create a false image of the Chilean people."[101] The incidents

resulted in one death, twenty-one injured, and seventeen detentions. The columnist Jaime Adaro also believed that right-wing groups had plotted the violence and perpetrated chaos in the stadium: "Day to day Chile lives in an extraordinarily special time, and enemies will not let a single moment pass without taking the opportunity to hurt the country. A football match like the one played on Wednesday was a good opportunity."[102] Adaro's accusations of premeditated right-wing violence may have been hard to substantiate, but conservative newspapers such as *La Segunda* found the clash useful in their criticisms of the UP government.[103] The polarized atmosphere imbued cultural events with a new significance for both supporters and detractors of the UP.

Legislation and state programs surrounding sports provide a window into the mechanics of the UP's efforts to forge a socialist culture. They also reflect a persistent concern with the relationship between the government and the military. In the implementation of the UP's cultural agenda, the Allende administration relied on seasoned sports directors who straddled the amateur-professional divide. Allende appointed Sabino Aguad, the president of the National Olympic Committee, to head the State Department of Sports. Aguad had abandoned a promising law career to pursue his passion for sports. He was well liked, and his thesis on the Israel-Palestinian conflict was highly regarded among Arab Chilean leaders. Aguad served many years as the director of Club Sirio's men's and women's basketball club, during which time he gained experience with amateur organizations. In his new position, Aguad realized the need to negotiate with the military in order to implement any broad plans for sports.[104] To that end, Aguad reached out to Colonel Washington Carrasco from the Sports Confederation of the Armed Forces regarding a new program.[105] The armed forces, still in the process of forming a relationship with the UP government, complained that military sports suffered from economic distress and a lack of good trainers.[106] While amateurs received some help from new programs, particularly in the provinces, the military was the key recipient of funds under new UP legislation. Aguad hoped that his attention to the needs of military sportsmen would be seen as part of a broader improvement in the relationship between the leftist government and military.

Under the direction of Aguad, the State Department of Sports launched a variety of novel projects. One was the creation of a sports-equipment factory, begun on the scale of a workshop, inside the National Stadium.[107] According to Aguad, this workshop could provide jobs, maintain an artisan tradition threatened by large multinational corporations, and provide cheaper alternatives to imported equipment. This fit the UP platform of economic independence perfectly. Another initiative of Aguad and his staff was the "Yo hago deportes" (roughly translated, "I do sports") campaign.[108] On a shoestring budget, a highly motivated group of sports directors and physical-education teachers organized this campaign to get young people out of doors and playing new sports. In the winter of 1972, the State Department of Sports closed fifteen blocks in the center of the city. It contracted with dozens of teachers to instruct children ages six to fourteen in a variety of sports. Sports clubs and public-school teachers brought more than two thousand students from the working-class neighborhood of Las Barrancas alone. The minister of education, Aníbal Palma, referred to the event as "the end of an epoch in which only the elite practiced sports and the people were called upon only when they needed to break records."[109] The department reported that despite the success of the event, it could not convince the children to play anything other than football.[110]

The state actively helped sportsmen take advantage of laws that promoted sports. One of the laws passed by the UP government stipulated that businesses employing one hundred workers or more had to construct sports facilities of a certain size.[111] The government sponsored seminars to help workers and management implement this legislation. Beginning in March 1973, businesses were required to obtain a certificate, procurable from municipalities and the Corporation of Sports Construction, that stated they had complied with the law. The seminars helped empower workers to hold managers accountable and ensure their cooperation with the law.

Many UP officials specifically hoped that female workers would benefit from these laws. One seminar, for example, brought together construction contractors, architects, lawyers, and government officials from the Chilean Economic Development Agency (Corporación de Fomento de la Producción de Chile, or CORFO). A lawyer for the UP, Javier Alsina, explained, "Article 40 is a tool that allows for the democratization of sports activities. ... In no way should we forget the importance of women in the process, and even more so in the case of sports. They must be consulted and considered in the needs of each industry."[112] These efforts were not isolated; the state-directed Corporation of Sports Construction held seminars throughout 1972 with women in civic associations, municipalities, and sports clubs to help them navigate the government bureaucracy and locate resources for their neighborhoods.[113]

The Allende administration looked to other socialist governments for inspiration for its sports policies. In 1972, it organized a series of visits to

Cuba in order to evaluate sports programs there. Cuban athletes' success in international competition inspired other countries in Latin America, even those without a similar political bent. The officials from the State Department of Sports were impressed by the high priority that the Cuban government placed on athletics.[114] The physical-education teachers sent to Cuba studied the country's method of selecting the national team, its policies with regard to acquiring sports equipment, and popular pedagogical methods. State-sponsored trips to Cuba suggested that the UP government was interested in deprofessionalizing football. Sabino Aguad's objections to deprofessionalization appear to have prompted his departure from the department.[115] In public, Aguad explained that he was leaving his position in order to help organize the Pan American Games, but his memoirs and reports indicate it was his objection to deprofessionalization that prompted his resignation.[116]

Aguad was not alone in his skepticism of the Cuban model. The journalist Edgardo Marín, who authored some of the most progovernment editorials in *Estadio* during the UP period, likened professional sports to a sinking ship that Allende should stay clear of salvaging.[117] Marín surmised that the leadership within football rendered it irreparable: "These directors do not have the moral mettle to change the structure of football."[118] Despite these reservations, Benedicto Basly, who had deep roots in amateur football organizations and supported deprofessionalization, replaced Aguad.[119] Basly founded Carrion Star, a working-class club in Barrio Independencia, and served as director of the professional club Green Cross. Basly expressed his political views more explicitly than Aguad, reiterating his support for preferential funding for sports that would benefit the working class.

THE UP IN THE MAINSTREAM: PROFESSIONALS AND QUIMANTÚ

Unlike their amateur counterparts, professional club directors went to great lengths to proclaim their political neutrality during the UP period. The ability of professional clubs to support first the UP government and then the military dictatorship without stirring up any public controversy reflected their corporate sensibilities and public relations experience.[120] On the players' side, the radical nature of labor organizations in the 1960s influenced their union to a certain extent; however, the group did not articulate a cogent political position. The professional players' union leaders criticized the growing number of "experts" and "businessmen" who controlled football, yet they avoided making any proposals for alternative structures.[121]

Leftist sportswriters urged the union to make their internal practices more democratic so that the players who made less money could play a more active role in the union; however, union leaders showed little interest in these proposals.[122] Minor changes took place in some professional clubs pressured by the union. When the Pontifical Catholic University agreed to allow its team captain to attend meetings of the directorate, *Estadio* declared, "Popular participation had come to football."[123] This statement seems exaggerated, since the arrangement did not include a vote for players or other types of integration into club leadership.

Although the players' union expressed gratitude that the UP supported legislation ensuring that football players received social security, it participated minimally in government programs.[124] Carlos Caszely, one of the few outspoken leftist players, warned that professional footballers would not support the Popular Unity government. He predicted, "Among players, a group exists that generally defines itself as apolitical, but at the decisive moment, like most of the 'apolitical,' it will identify with the Right."[125] The union's rhetoric reflected some of the radicalized language of the era, but its actions indicated that players generally cared little either way about the government's programs. For instance, in a meeting of the professional association, the Club Palestino president, Nicolás Abumohor, interrupted a player. In response, Juan Rodríguez, a player, shouted, "You, sir, do not have the right to cut off a compañero that way."[126] Abumohor, however, easily placated the union with a paternalistic style that he used in his textile enterprise.

The sportswriter Edgardo Marín criticized the union for co-opting the language of workers without having a relationship to other labor organizations: "The definition of the football player as a worker has come to dominate the union leadership, has brought some consciousness of the social problem, and is supported by a rank and file that has an exaggerated consciousness of its rights and very little understanding of its duties."[127] Many supporters of the UP hoped that the class background of professional players would eventually push them to sympathize with leftists. The coach of Lota Schwager, Dante Pesce, stated in early 1973: "I cannot conceive of the player as being part of a race that lacks class consciousness or sensitivity toward reality. . . . The players know that children need football, especially proletarian children, and it can't be that the player from a poor background transforms himself into a comfortable bourgeois player only out of a desire for money."[128] Yet there was substantial evidence that this was, indeed, the case.

The UP shaped sports media more than any previous administration through its control of the Zig-Zag editorial house, which it renamed Quimantú. After a labor dispute within Zig-Zag, the publisher of *Estadio*, the state purchased the majority of shares in the company. This placed UP officials in control of the country's most widely disseminated sports magazine. After Quimantú assumed responsibility for *Estadio* in March 1971, the editors published assurances to their readers that the magazine's policies would remain unchanged.[129] While *Estadio* dramatically reoriented its coverage the following year, it continued to focus on professional football. In this sense, *Estadio* worked without a viable precedent. How could a mainstream, glossy sports magazine that covered a billion-dollar industry serve a socialist cause? In interviews and editorials, the magazine expressed its support for the Allende administration and created space for debates about the relationship between sports and politics.

A number of readers expressed their dislike of political themes in the magazine. According to one complaint, "Previously, they ran advertisements in this magazine for businesses selling sporting goods and left politics to the side; it appears that now, unfortunately, it is different, and one can only wait until it returns to its previous policy. No reader of *Estadio* is interested in politics."[130] Presumably, the reader objected to the copious advertisements for other Quimantú titles, many of which had political content. The editors responded by cutting down on think pieces and bringing back some of the journalists from the prenationalization period, such as Julio Martínez.

Interviews in *Estadio* now differed markedly from those published before the takeover. Instead of avoiding political questions, journalists asked for players' opinions.[131] They asked Eduardo Herrera, for example, his opinion of the "new sports politics," the nationalization of copper, and his political affiliations. Herrera offered his enthusiastic support for the UP and the takeover of *Estadio*, since "the traditional sports press, with some exceptions, has always preoccupied itself with elite sports and has not taken into account the significance of mass participation in sports."[132] *Estadio* editors titled the series of interviews "Man Does Not Live by Sport Alone." Not all interviewees were as content as Herrera, however. The player Leonardo Kittsteiner showed reluctance to discuss politics when interviewed.[133] Kittsteiner claimed that both Catholicism and communism "violate the liberty of self-determination in man." In addition to interviews, *Estadio* published pedagogical pieces. A section entitled "Know Your Sport" provided readers with easy-to-understand diagrams, rules, and tips for a different sport each week.[134] Although male models were used for football lessons, those for basketball were women. Sportswriters promoted basketball for women because, in their view, it involved less contact and was not as dominated by men as football. Editors for *Estadio* were inspired by the Cuban state media, which dedicated television and newspaper space to sports instruction.

Editorials in the new *Estadio* suggested ways to approach sports reporting differently. For example, Edgardo Marín made earnest attempts to rethink the national approach to football's failures. His editorial proposed that instead of viewing Chile's losses on the international scene as a national shame, "we should leave with the idea that in sports competitions, everyone participates in the same conditions."[135] Marín urged sports fans not to emulate powerful countries only because they were victorious. They should take pride in themselves, knowing that "we lose, but cleanly; we show who we are, poor still, but dignified without artificially inflating ourselves. This purity of ours (though we lack other virtues) is an excellent foundation to begin to construct better sports on." Beginning in mid-1972, Marín's column was steadily replaced by the noncontroversial and surprisingly nontechnical "Aquí" by Julio Martínez.[136] It is unclear why the editors made the decision to publish more from Martínez.

Apart from periodicals like *Estadio*, Quimantú mass-produced books at affordable prices and commissioned new works on Chile for popular consumption. Shortly after its foundation, Quimantú hired Patricio Manns, a famous musician and writer, to write a series on popular culture. Manns attempted to create an "authentically" Chilean sports history in his book *Grandes Deportistas*. Manns did not depart entirely from other attempts at the history of sports. Like the histories written by journalists and sports clubs, Manns drew upon the ancient Greeks' relish for sports to illustrate the correlation between democratic society and sports. In his discussion of track and field, Manns explained, "The marathon was not invented by the Greeks, but the Greeks imparted it to history. . . . Not by chance is the worker the precursor of athletic tests of endurance. Traditionally, the long-distance runners of our country have come from modest social backgrounds."[137] As government officials during the Popular Front had done previously, Manns emphasized the indigenous contribution to sports. He listed the sixteenth-century Mapuche leader Caupolicán as one of the best athletes in Chilean history.[138] Manns explained that Caupolicán and Lautaro were not only warriors but also sportsmen. Finally, and most dubiously, Manns claimed that the British could merely claim to have "rediscovered" football because Native Americans had played it before.

As evidence, he cited numerous works by ethnographers and anthropologists from the turn of the century.

Manns's work showed an effort to make football more palatable to leftists who may have been skeptical of its didactic power. For example, he compared football to chess. Chess was highly esteemed by intellectuals and received support in the Soviet Union and Cuba. Manns explained that in football, "each movement closes thousands of possibilities. . . . It is not, as many think, the sport of imbeciles."[139] In his defense of football, he argued that its popularity alone warranted it being given serious consideration, since it claimed more fans than jazz, movies, rock music, or television. Manns painted a portrait of class conflict inherent in the sport: "The workers are represented by the players; the patrons, by the professional clubs and the director castes."[140] Moreover, he pointed out that many dangers could befall professional players, as in other working-class jobs. Using the death of David Arellano, who probably died from appendicitis, as proof of the hazards of football, Manns stretched the analogy between manual labor and professional football to extremes. Although Manns did not discuss women's football, he did include prominent female athletes among his all-time greats.[141] The UP period was short and turbulent, but it appeared to coincide with a shift in sports literature toward focusing on women's athletic achievements rather than their family life and domestic skills.

THE COMMUNISTS AND SPORTS

Even before the advent of the UP government, leftist sports enthusiasts had begun to criticize sportswriters more aggressively. *El Siglo* attacked the mainstream media, including the popular daily *El Diario Ilustrado*, for their coverage of the national team's victory over East Germany. Firstly, instead of referring to the country as the Democratic Republic of Germany, journalists from *El Diario Ilustrado* insisted on giving the country new monikers such as "Red Germany."[142] Although Chilean Communists had mobilized sports clubs as part of their political program, the official Communist newspaper complained about others' use of football for ulterior motives: "It is totally dishonest to take advantage of sports in order to mess with fans' heads. These political insults do not have anything to do with what our fans were celebrating; instead, they are lies and fabrications about a country that held a generous reception for our brilliant and triumphant team."[143] *El Siglo* also took a firmer stance on its interpretation of the maladies of

Chilean football. Across the board, its sportswriters expressed frustration with an inadequately trained national team. Their criticisms ranged wildly, from the assertion that Chilean players needed to be more aggressive and attack more frequently to quite the opposite idea that players attempted only to score and knew nothing of defense. From the referees to the trainers to directors, anyone was susceptible to blame. All the sportswriters seemed to agree that Chilean football did not match the leadership of the Chilean nation in other respects and lagged hopelessly behind Argentina and Brazil.[144] While *El Siglo* presented its analysis as completely distinct from that of the mainstream media, it shared with them the notion that science and technology were the proper remedies for the team's ills.

The Communist Party Youth was the most outspoken group, claiming that socialism would improve the national team's poor performance. In October 1971, the National Commission of Communist Youth released a bulletin to its members regarding their sports activities. According to the bulletin, "We know that our sport operates on a very low level, in all branches, compared to the rest of the world. The poor performance of our sportsmen is intimately related to our condition as an underdeveloped country."[145] The bulletin urged party militants to get together to figure out how best to mobilize their clubs in support of the government: "This struggle means that Communist youths will raise the political consciousness of existing sports organizations, making clear the fallacy of sports' apoliticism." To do this, Communist youth needed to volunteer to build sports facilities, work on health campaigns, and organize tournaments designed to show support for the UP, such as those held on the anniversaries of Allende's election. These suggestions were not novel for the Communist Party, as was shown in the previous chapters; however, its position vis-à-vis the state was now completely reversed. Moreover, the bulletin included an urgent message for Communists to cooperate with Socialists and other political rivals within civic associations. Despite the Communists' newly supportive relationship to the state, they continued to criticize government's relationship to professionals and to sports they defined as "elite in nature," such as auto racing.[146]

As part of labor organizations' long-standing relationship with amateur football and their interest in the making of a socialist society, they were very involved in new interpretations of sports during the UP period. In a lengthy editorial, the CUT president and Communist Party leader Luis Figueroa outlined his view of sports under socialism.[147] Figueroa attributed the growth of football among workers to a top-down ideological process spearheaded by labor unions. His 1972 statements contained the CUT's strongest criticism of professionalism to date. The principles of professionalism, he contended, could not be reconciled with socialism. This included the profit-motivated buying and selling of players. Figueroa put forward the concept of sports as fulfilling physical and psychological needs as well as being a right of workers. However, he expressed concern that football could not educate workers as efficiently as choral and folk music, the plastic arts, and theater: "The recent development of folk music, the popular Chilean nueva canción, is a logical consequence of the rising struggle of the people, of workers' organizations, and of students in search of a distinct destiny that is more just, more humane."[148]

The Communist newspaper *Puro Chile*, which shared Figueroa's concerns, at times created patronizing caricatures of football fans. One writer described the football fan as "perhaps the most innocent figure, naïve and lacking in evil. He never thinks that he is deceived: he goes to the stadiums with the passionate dignity of the Stoics and Spartans. He is far from suspecting that football is a business."[149] The article suggested football fans deserved the "Golden Egg" award for their state of ignorance and their faith in the talent of Chilean footballers. These writers failed to offer a more nuanced analysis of fans' enjoyment in sharing adoration of their favorite clubs, admiring the players' talent and skills, and using the social opportunities to discuss shared passions.

CIVIC ASSOCIATIONS IN OCCUPIED FACTORIES

Leaders of factory occupations mobilized cultural practices, including football, to keep workers' spirits up. Moreover, they organized events to ease tensions between factory workers and the volunteers who arrived from universities and political parties to help in the "Battle of Production." The Battle of Production was the struggle by UP supporters to overcome the shortages caused by hoarding and the economic blockade imposed by the United States.[150] New sports leagues sprouted up to connect occupied factories; for example, the Junto a Progreso connected the Andina, Yarur, and Valech factories, among others.[151] The CUT periodicals urged leaders to organize cultural events during the transition to worker-controlled factories so that "the worker feels human and not like just one more bolt or screw in the immense productive machine."[152] The former Hirmas textile factory attempted to put this idea into practice by organizing a music festival held at union headquarters in Barrio Yungay. More than thirty factory workers competed for prizes. Winning songs from the competition, such as "To Work, Compañeros" and "I Sing and Work for Chile," were intended to inspire fellow workers. While labor organizations recommended cultural activities, some party militants objected to spontaneous leisure in occupied factories. Mario Olivares, a twenty-year-old worker in an occupied factory, complained, "The Communists, you know, were terribly disciplined and militant. And we were very young then—*cabros*, as we say in Chile—and part of a toma inside the business. We began to organize, I don't know, some diversion. We danced. They bothered us a lot; they criticized us strongly for that."[153]

Divergent views of *poder popular*, or people power, produced conflicts in neighborhood civic associations.[154] At the same time, young activists who participated in local projects described these years as exciting and productive. While universities may have drawn in young leaders, community work garnered greater respect than in the past. Referring to young shantytown activists, one UP supporter noted, "These young people acquired quite a status with the youth in other *campamentos* [camps]. Their political awareness was much higher. Whenever I was with them elsewhere, at football matches, for example, I noticed the respect this won them and how it influenced other young people to take up similar activities."[155] The notion of workers directing a new national culture generated an enthusiastic response among workers themselves. UP supporters recalled the Allende years as a frenetic time in barrio clubs. In addition, directors of football clubs usually had many other responsibilities and were often in meetings until just before their work shifts began. One club director explained, "We were living with a day-to-day intensity that meant most of us hardly slept. We had our committees in our workplaces, party meetings, the assemblies—we hardly ever saw our families. . . . Yet at the same time, we were all aware of the special nature of this moment."[156]

When creating cultural activities in support of the government, traditional cultural producers sometimes clashed with civic associations. According to "Laura," a resident of the shantytown Nueva la Habana, "It was probably the cultural front that attracted the most participation, although it went through quite a crisis in mid-1971. By this time, Nueva la Habana was something of an attraction to intellectuals and artists, whose influence was almost fatal."[157] According to Laura, residents lost interest when students started talking about theories of underdevelopment. At other times, these discussions turned projects in fruitful directions. For example, while organizing a community preschool, parents pressed for the curriculum to include more hands-on learning and challenged teachers to explain the benefits of classroom education. In the end, a curriculum more oriented to everyday experience was adopted. As Laura explained, "The children went on outings to the nearby foothills of the Andes for botany and biology classes. For mathematics, they visited their parents' workplaces to count the machines and learn about angles—and this taught them to respect what their parents were doing, in itself a minor revolution."[158] Although amateur football clubs mobilized in support of community projects, visiting intellectuals and artists showed little interest in working with them.

Decades of organization among civic associations like football clubs in shantytowns and working-class neighborhoods proved vital to the survival of these communities during the UP period.[159] Threatened by violence, hoarding, and internal divisions, these organizations helped maintain basic services in poor communities. Despite the radicalization of young activists, voluntary organizations sought change through state officials and legal channels. Members with experience in civic associations brought those structures and practices to occupied neighborhoods. One club member recalled, "In the way it handled the election of directors, whether the directors of the campamento or the directors of the base, the civic association was the most democratic popular organization that I have seen in my life."[160] In addition to creating democratic structures, voluntary organizations faced the challenge of procuring supplies amidst hoarding and blockades. Activists drew on decades of organizational experience to successfully run programs like neighborhood food cooperatives. They bragged that through these organizations, they ate better in the shantytowns than in middle-class homes.[161]

The story of football under the Popular Unity government ended abruptly with the military coup led by General Augusto Pinochet. Many of the plans to revamp sports to serve a socialist society could not begin to be implemented. Clearly, however, the groundwork for these projects had been created in amateur organizations during the previous decades. The success of leftist political parties and politicians afforded working-class football clubs greater protection and support than in the past. These sportsmen seized the opportunity to participate in governmental programs and create alternative types of organizations. The polarization of professionals and amateurs shaped how sportswriters, club leaders, and players understood the everyday ramifications of political differences. Many young people who participated in working-class clubs became committed to civic engagement. Because of this, they faced persecution under the military government.

The dictatorship correctly identified civic associations such as football clubs as the nexus between leftist labor, politics, and culture. The belief that institutional channels could absorb the polarization of the moment left civic associations unprepared for the imminent violence and repression.

EPILOGUE

On 11 September 1973, the Chilean armed forces conducted a coup against the government of Salvador Allende. They received support from the U.S. government, especially in the form of covert aid from the Central Intelligence Agency. The bombardment of the presidential palace led to Allende's suicide and the death of many of his closest advisors. Following the coup, the military junta that took control of the country launched a campaign of massive repression. The military detained, tortured, and murdered the supporters of the Popular Unity government. They targeted political party leaders, students, shantytown residents, and union representatives. Putatively nonpolitical citizens were also victims of the military's efforts to eradicate Marxism. Furthermore, around 200,000 Chileans went into exile.[1] This began an era of terror for the civic associations at the center of this study.[2]

Since football clubs and fields constituted important public spaces, the junta sent police to make their presence felt there. The Rettig Report, compiled by the Chilean Truth and Reconciliation Commission, documented cases of military agents arresting young men and detaining them at local fields and in clubs. This continued through the mid-1980s; for example, during government raids in La Victoria in 1985, soldiers turned the San Eugenio football stadium into a torture center. In stadiums, soldiers guarded blindfolded prisoners with machine guns. They stripped, interrogated, and mocked the detainees.[3] The structure of stadiums enabled soldiers to watch over prisoners, who, in turn, were forced to watch the interrogation and murder of others in the center of the arena. Larger stadiums, such as the National Stadium and Estadio Chile, once celebrated by sportsmen as physical manifestations of democracy and progress, became symbols of the military's brutality. Subsequently, these sites have become important

FIGURE 7.1.   The National Stadium shortly after the military coup of 1973. Photograph by
Marcelo Montecino. Image courtesy of Marcelo Montecino.

markers for the human rights movement. In 2003, human rights advocates
succeeded in changing the name of Estadio Chile to Victor Jara Stadium in
commemoration of the singer's execution there in September 1973.[4]

In the year preceding the coup, political violence had disrupted the
activities of football clubs and other civic associations. Despite aggressive
propaganda from right-wing and paramilitary groups, support for the
Popular Unity government grew during the first two years of Allende's
presidency. Members of civic associations, unions, and other activists recall
the period as a time of intense political activity. By the end of 1972, football
club directors found it difficult to maintain club schedules, hold meetings,
or mobilize members for events. Others felt it was inappropriate to play
football in such uncertain times. As one Socialist and CUT (Central Única
de Trabajadores) militant explained, "When we went to cut corn . . . the
workers of that farm played football. . . . I like football, but it was not the
moment to play football, the corn had to be cut to raise more chickens and
to feed more people."[5] Given the political climate, government supporters
focused on production rather than cultural expression. Not surprisingly,
association directors found it nearly impossible to get commitments from
clubs to schedule the 1973 football season.[6] Furthermore, football clubs and

other cultural associations that supported the Popular Unity government were vulnerable to attacks by right-wing groups. For example, the neofascist group Patria y Libertad boasted of its attacks on mural painters and threatened to kill any that it caught.[7] The offices of *Estadio*, which was run by the government publishing house Quimantú, were attacked with Molotov cocktails.[8] Conflicts among university students brought their amateur football clubs to a standstill.

As Carlos Caszely had predicted, "apolitical" professional football acquiesced in the military takeover.[9] Sports journalists and professional directors made every effort to maintain the status quo. The issue of *Estadio* published on the day of the coup did not reflect the chaos that engulfed the country. The cover story, "Plan Moscow," despite its lurid title, updated readers on the national team's preparations for a match with the Soviet Union.[10] There were articles on women's basketball, an interview with Jorge Toro, and reports on European boxing. The next issue appeared nearly a month later, on 2 October 1973, without any explanation for the gap in publication, the changes in staff, or the new publisher. The following week, the head of the military junta, General Augusto Pinochet, sent a telegram to the magazine that accused the player Carlos Caszely of being a traitor.[11] Other than that, it was business as usual for *Estadio* and the Chilean Football Federation. Professional and national football directors ensured that the season continued without a hitch. Meanwhile, the amateur directors they had worked closely with just weeks before faced torture, death, and repression.

In the months after the coup, the junta's use of stadiums as places of torture generated an international controversy. The Soviet Union's federation was alone among football associations in refusing to play in the National Stadium. The Soviets urged FIFA to boycott Chilean football in protest of the human rights abuses taking place in the stadiums, often against amateur football directors, many of whom were also labor leaders. In response, FIFA sent a "fact-finding" mission to Chile in October 1973. It is unclear, given the overwhelming evidence that atrocities were being committed in the stadiums, how FIFA delegates determined that conditions in the National Stadium were suitable for prisoners. Their representative claimed, "Inside the outer fencing everything appears to be normal and gardeners are working on their gardens."[12] FIFA defended its position of neutrality, explaining, "All we want to know is whether playing conditions are right."[13] Delegate René Courte reiterated the desire of FIFA to stay out of politics: "We are not concerned with politics or what regimes are ruling a country."[14] *Estadio* characterized the Soviet Union's actions as part of its game strategy—a type of "psychological warfare" intended to defeat the Chilean team mentally—rather than as a moral objection.[15]

On 11 November 1973, the Soviet team announced its refusal to play in the National Stadium. Although the team offered to face Chile in a different country, FIFA rejected this compromise. As a result, the Soviet Union lost the opportunity to play in the 1974 World Cup in West Germany. This was the first such protest in the history of the World Cup. Frustrated by the attention drawn to atrocities being committed in the stadium, the military government tried, in vain, to force the Soviets to pay for lost revenue from gate fees and television revenue.[16] Few supported the boycott of Chile's National Stadium. For example, the *London Times* called the Soviet delegation's decision a "painful abscess."[17] Certainly, skepticism about the Soviet Union's motives played a role in the international response, but it was also a sign that many viewed the military government as legitimate. Furthermore, it reflected the firm belief, shared by many journalists, that sports should remain apolitical.

In contrast to FIFA's and other football officials' unconcern, exiled Chileans, solidarity groups, and sympathetic fans viewed the appearance of the Chilean national team as a moment to protest the military's repression. In places as distinct as Somalia, Venezuela, New Zealand, Canada, and Scotland, solidarity groups organized in the months after the September coup. West Berlin was a center of such activity, spearheaded by the Chile Solidarity Committee and the Socialist Work Collective (known by its German acronym SAK-JUR) at Berlin's Free University.[18] The Solidarity Committee, composed of Germans and Chileans, used the World Cup to draw attention to the plight of political prisoners and to reach Chilean television audiences. In a competition based around national identity, activists realized the importance of not being characterized as "anti-Chilean." They frequently used the slogan "¡Chile Sí, Junta No!"[19] Despite attempts by the West German police to prevent exiles from reaching television cameras, they managed to appear in several moments of the broadcast.[20] Their most successful protest occurred when they ran onto midfield during Chile's match against Australia with a banner that read, "Chile Socialista."

General Augusto Pinochet hoped to use the World Cup to improve the image of his regime abroad and at home. In June 1974, Pinochet was in the process of consolidating his authority within the military junta. He sent the Chilean delegation with a letter that greeted fellow participants and assured them of the country's "restoration."[21] A key member of the Chilean entourage was Alberto Mela, the new president of ANFA, the National Association of Amateur Football. After the coup, many ANFA directors were persecuted, and at the time of the Cup, they were still in prison, exile, or hiding. The junta sent Mela along with the professional directors to convey the message that amateurs backed the military government. Despite the excitement generated by the delegation's appearance abroad, a dusk-to-dawn curfew throughout Chile, restrictions on public gatherings, and regular police raids at football fields dampened enthusiasm for the tournament. Sportswriters also struck a somber tone leading up to the World Cup.[22]

Chilean players found themselves at the center of the controversy over the military government during the World Cup. Journalists covering the tournament sought out players from Chile and Uruguay, where a military coup had also initiated a repressive wave against leftist groups. Solidarity groups were bewildered that Chilean players either refused to comment on the situation or defended the military dictatorship. They speculated that they had been threatened or brainwashed. After several tense run-ins with journalists, Chilean players decided to charge fifty dollars an interview. Not even superstars like Pelé demanded such fees. The Chilean press hinted that the offensive questions pertained to the Soviet squad's boycott and the repression in Chile.[23] Antonio Martínez, the president of the delegation, supported the decision of the players after witnessing what he considered to be badgering questions. He objected to one journalist's questions about the salaries of Chilean workers. Uruguayan players followed suit, charging two hundred dollars a question.[24] Journalists interpreted this as economic opportunism on the part of the players. Hostility toward the Chilean delegation was such that they traveled in a group with thirty security guards at all times. Despite the trend of celebrity players protecting their worth by remaining politically neutral, it still seems surprising that no Chilean player protested playing for the new regime. Even Carlos Caszely, whose family members were well-known supporters of the Communist Party, continued to play dutifully for the Chilean national team.[25] Later, Caszely explained that he felt very afraid for the safety of his family throughout the dictatorship.[26]

Like General Stroessner in Paraguay and other Latin American dictators in the 1970s, Pinochet served as honorary president of professional football clubs. As the figurehead of Club Colo Colo, Pinochet ensured that it received government money for its long-awaited stadium, Estadio Monumental. Given the popularity of Colo Colo, particularly among the working class, the club's cozy relationship with Pinochet conferred symbolic legitimacy on the dictator. Even with the regime's financial assistance, professional football decayed. In part, the economic austerity program implemented by the regime hurt attendance at matches.[27] Night games were canceled, first because of the curfew, then because of the expense of lighting the field. It was not always clear whether the waning of football, particularly the amateur leagues, was due to economic hardship, police repression, or preemptive measures taken by clubs. In any case, the decline fostered social atomization and drove people into their homes in the evenings. Football associations that did not want to collude with state agencies frequently opted out of national tournaments. In 1974, the Football Association of Arica did not attend the national tournament of barrio football, which was being held in its home city.[28]

In 1975, in an attempt to bolster interest in professional football and generate income for the state, Pinochet legalized a game of chance called *polla gol*, in which players predicted the outcome of football matches. By 1979, polla gol had become a full-fledged craze: one in six Chileans played the game, which brought in $1.5 million a week.[29] Harsh economic times only sweetened the fantasy of winning polla gol, which sometimes paid out one million dollars. Unemployment and inflation increased along with the cost of goods. Moreover, the dictatorship froze workers' wages. For many workers, the likelihood of winning the football lottery seemed equal to their chance of finding steady employment with an adequate salary. Attendance at matches that were important for the football lottery increased; however, over the long term, polla gol altered the practice of spectatorship. It encouraged fans to root for the team that most benefited their individual chances of winning the polla. It also led to further speculation about possible corruption and cheating in professional football.

In 1974, the junta took measures to consolidate its control over professional football, an approach similar to its treatment of other civic associations.[30] Shortly after the coup, the junta banned elections in football clubs as well as in unions and mothers' centers.[31] In 1975, the junta allowed just two elections among civic associations: it permitted Miss Chile to hold a beauty contest, and let the professional football organization, the Central Association, choose officers. When it became clear that the military planned to install its candidate as president, the association's directors objected that elections were outlawed by military decree. The delegate from the city of Antofagasta, Colonel Hugo Moya, assured the association that the junta had given its special permission. The military claimed glibly that as long as the association submitted a list of candidates that did not include Pascal Allende (the nephew of Salvador Allende and leader of the MIR, the Revolutionary Left Movement), it would not interfere.[32]

Father Gilberto Lizano, a sports commentator for *El Mercurio* and supporter of the military government, nominated General Arturo Gordan for the association presidency. The subdirector of the Carabineros, Gordan had not been active in football organizations in the past, but as member number 729 of Club Colo Colo, he was eligible for the post. Once Gordan was on the list, military officers and policemen sent messages encouraging regional authorities to pressure clubs in their jurisdictions to vote for him. One club director who supported Gordan's opponent, Francisco Fluxá, reported that he was taken by the police at four in the morning to vote for Gordan. This was a common trajectory: a member of a civic association sympathetic to the junta would help government agents infiltrate the group, and if the members of the group resisted, the military would pledge to compromise, then follow up with repressive tactics.[33]

POPULAR RESISTANCE

Grassroots organizations were at the forefront of reconstituting social life in poor communities, as well as being integral to the opposition movement. At the same time, some civic associations became surveillance sites. Lucía Hiriart, the wife of Pinochet, encouraged members of mothers' centers to report suspicious activities of fellow members. Activists found it difficult to build new organizations in the hostile environment of the dictatorship. One leader explained that the barrio sports clubs, clinics, firefighters, and feminist groups "disappeared after the coup, because the military, once they took over, removed many people to different neighborhoods and brought many people in from other sectors. With that, they stifled a lot and many directors died and others were detained."[34] The persecution of barrio leaders and the removal of residents to neighborhoods across the city damaged civic associations. In turn, this left working-class communities without important centers of information, conduits to politicians, and vehicles for collective action. Nonetheless, by the early 1980s, women in working-class neighborhoods had created a variety of social organizations, such as soup kitchens, *arpillera* (appliquéd burlap tapestries) workshops, and health clinics.

Leaders who had been active in the years before the coup reemerged and put their experience to work again. However, because of repression, they tended to be isolated, and their work ephemeral.[35] The Catholic Church, through the work of La Vicaría de Solidaridad, played an important role in fostering the rebirth of voluntary organizations. These groups not only criticized the human rights abuses perpetrated by the dictatorship, but also the harsh neoliberal reforms Pinochet and his supporters implemented. By 1976, real wages had fallen to 62 percent of their 1970 levels, and families were desperate to acquire child care, food, and medical treatment.[36] The dictatorship's public announcements of economic success contrasted sharply with life in working-class barrios, and in an atmosphere of economic boasting by the government, the shame of being poor deepened. Without popular-culture venues to articulate this common experience, many working-class Chileans felt isolated, and their identification with other members of the working class weakened. As Temma Kaplan has suggested, shame was a key component in the dictatorship's efforts to break ties of solidarity and feelings of adequacy among citizens.[37] While feminist groups successfully threw shame back onto the dictatorship through their practices, predominantly male organizations, like sports clubs, did not directly confront the shame associated with being economically unsuccessful or subordinate to authorities.

The protests of women gained momentum throughout the 1970s, both from human rights groups like the Association of the Relatives of the Detained-Disappeared and from feminist groups like Women for Life (Mujeres por la Vida). These groups reclaimed public spaces, like stadiums, that had been part of the junta's repressive campaigns. For example, in celebration of International Women's Day in 1979, women's groups gathered in Unión Española's stadium, Santa Laura. The police disrupted the event and drove attendees out of the stadium.[38] In 1984, Women for Life smuggled protest signs into the National Stadium. They hoisted the signs so that they were visible to the large audience. Through their public demonstrations, knowledge of the legal system, and communications network, women's groups prepared their members to become full participants in the transition to democracy.[39] Hundreds of women's grassroots organizations sent delegates to the Civic Assembly, an organization of political parties, unions, and civic associations that spearheaded the campaign against the dictatorship.

While civic associations and cultural groups began to rejuvenate in the late 1970s, barrio football remained in a moribund state. Hardly any football clubs were founded from 1973 until 1978.[40] Among the six thousand civic leaders who gathered to celebrate International Women's Day in 1978— from folklore clubs, unions, religious groups, and dance troupes—no delegates from sports organizations appeared.[41] After a five-year hiatus, clubs organized a barrio football championship in 1978, offering players and their fans an opportunity to claim public space and socialize in the open air. But public space was in high demand, and rents for local clubhouses and fields soared in the 1980s, making it difficult to sustain barrio clubs.[42] Furthermore, La Vicaría de Solidaridad, which became a hub of working-class culture, promoted cultural events other than football.

Football figured more prominently in the actions of solidarity groups abroad than within Chile during the 1980s. Organizations like Casa de Chile (the Chilean House) in Mexico City promoted cultural activities among exiles, including sports.[43] There, exiled Chileans played matches against their counterparts from Uruguay and Argentina. Although football players did not succeed in forming a shadow national team, as happened in Tibet, they provided a vehicle for exiles to form relationships with one another. Football players also used their events to keep attention on solidarity efforts. In Montreal, Mexico City, Brussels, and Rome, amateur clubs played tournaments for the Salvador Allende Cup.[44] In addition, strained relations between the junta and countries with strong solidarity groups prevented foreign sports teams from visiting Chile and hindered Chilean teams' trips abroad. Exiles from Casa de Chile protested matches of professional Chilean clubs that visited Mexico, at least when they could afford to buy tickets.[45]

The decline of barrio football in the 1980s was intertwined with the repression of organized labor. The traditional allies of barrio football clubs, center-left political parties and unions, could not provide resources or protection to clubs during the dictatorship. Labor legislation in the early 1980s severely weakened unions' ability to protect members and negotiate contracts. Despite the obstacles, the workers' movement revived as the decade went on, becoming a formidable opponent of the dictatorship. At the same time, cultural values and expressions promoted by the Pinochet regime undermined positive working-class icons, like the barrio footballer. The government supported artists who promoted individualism, consumerism, efficiency, and commercialization. Through the control of national television, the junta created a vision of a united society in which anyone could achieve economic success through his or her own effort alone. Pride in one's manual labor or working-class neighborhood became anachronistic in Pinochet's Chile.

MEMORY, TRANSITION, AND CIVIL SOCIETY

After a decade of protests and organizational work against the dictatorship, Augusto Pinochet lost a plebiscite in 1988 that would have extended his presidency for eight more years. The "democratic transition" that followed has been the subject of both international celebration and criticism. The Chilean case has been cited as an example of how an authoritarian government successfully implemented a neoliberal economic model and of how a liberal democracy preserved that model, perhaps even with greater efficiency. The Concertación de Partidos por la Democracia—a center-left coalition composed of Socialists, Christian Democrats, the Party for Democracy, and a number of smaller parties—successfully backed Patricio Alwyn for president in 1990, the beginning of its two-decade hold on the executive. Notably, the Concertación excluded the Communist Party. Since the transition, the largest right-wing parties, the Renovación Nacional and the Unión Demócrata Independiente, have garnered nearly half the votes in national elections. The former elected its presidential candidate, Sebastián Piñera, in 2010. This was a major shift away from the Concertación. Piñera, with ideological and institutional ties to the Pinochet regime, presented a challenge to human rights organizations. Despite divesting himself of most investments, Piñera refused to give up his stake in Colo Colo.[46]

The depoliticization of Chilean civil society has been notable since the transition. In part, the notion that "politicization" was to blame for the coup, an idea espoused by prominent members of the Socialist Party and echoed in the media, has discouraged the younger generation from political participation. For example, journalists who covered cases of those arrested and tortured in the National Stadium argued for their subjects' innocence by declaring that they were not "politically committed."[47] The notion that political commitment was responsible for the dictatorship and the atrocities it carried out legitimated the view of political activists as extremists. The Communist Party offered alternative interpretations that blamed concessions to the centrist Christian Democrats and urged the Concertación to focus on structural inequalities.

Struggles over memory of what happened during the dictatorship and the transition period have played a key role in shaping attitudes toward civic engagement over the last two decades. According to historian Steve Stern, the human rights movement forced the Pinochet regime to revise its self-presentation as the savior of the country from Marxist totalitarianism to the engineers of Chilean economic prosperity.[48] Popular culture, especially films, music, and television, has contributed to those debates. Recent ethnographic work, like that of Lessie Jo Frazier, has shown that the history of state violence against workers has been preserved through music and storytelling. In formal education and political discourse, the history of Pinochet's regime has obscured incidents of violence against the workers' movement throughout the twentieth century.[49] Football clubs, at the amateur, professional, or national level, have not contributed to these debates. In part, this reflects a decay of traditional civic associations and their relationship to politics.

Despite the energetic protests of social movements against the dictatorship, voluntary organizations were enervated during the transition to democracy. A number of factors contributed to the weakening of civic engagement. Soon after the transition, many international nongovernmental organizations of considerable stature left Chile.[50] In addition, a sense of profound demoralization among working-class urban residents discouraged activism.[51] Studies have shown that Chileans distrust one another and suffer high rates of depression.[52] The most important factor in stifling civic engagement has been the political climate. During the transition and its aftermath, the Concertación co-opted and marginalized grassroots movements. New methods adopted by political parties across the spectrum limited political discourse to a few "hot" issues. Advised by marketing groups in the United States, the Concertación and its conservative counterparts relied more and more upon polling data and the mass media to win elections.[53] Opinion polls, with the help of the media and social science experts, constructed political perspectives as much as they revealed them. According to Julia Paley, an anthropologist, "Opinion polls have become closely intertwined with elections, operating on a continual basis and nearly supplanting voting as an indication of citizen choice."[54] Given the apathy of Chilean voters, leading political scientists have gone so far as to question the legitimacy of elections.[55]

The debates over the history of Chilean democracy have hardly been able to find their way around continued inequalities and the unfulfilled promises of the transition from the Pinochet dictatorship. The economic disparity in Chile throughout its history, the violent repression of workers and indigenous peoples, and the informal and formal exclusions within the political system severely qualify the labeling of its political system a democracy. Yet football clubs attest to the importance of popular culture and civic associations in creating a vibrant democracy. Amateur football directors viewed the political system as a legitimate arbiter of society, but also as a vehicle for improving their communities and their lives. In the process, they energized local and national politics. Voluntary organizations formed around new cultural practices, such as gaming and free software, show signs of reinvigorating civic associations.

In this age of individual gratification and consumerism, there is nostalgia for a time when it was common for people to belong to social organizations. Without smaller parties or labor unions able to support such groups, it is unclear how the amateur clubs like those of the twentieth century could thrive today. Moreover, the increasingly dominant role of professional football on a global scale means that multinational corporations with control over television contracts shape the discourse around football. Nonetheless, amateur footballers continue to struggle for a place in the national discussion about the politics of sports. In the preparations for the 2010 World Cup, there was a new round of questions about why people love football and what we can glean from its history. But more prevalent were stories of national integration and global understanding, all framed to maximize consumption. One listened in vain for discordant notes, like ones struck by Chilean amateurs, to challenge flattened versions of football's historical significance. The story of their commitment to civic engagement, solidarity, local action, and "making" politics may be the most exciting and threatening of all.

NOTES

INTRODUCTION

Shankly, best known for his management of the Liverpool Football Club, was credited with many quips. I have been unable to find the original source of the oft-cited one that serves as the chapter epigraph. A version appeared in the *Times*: "Football is not just a matter of life and death—it's much more important than that" (Lowe, "Shankly . . . Soccer's True Folk Hero," 30).

    1.   Vallerand and others, "On Passion and Sports Fans."

    2.   Levine, "Sport and Society," 233.

    3.   A virtual cottage industry of edited volumes has appeared over the last twenty years, including Armstrong, Guilianotti, and Toulis, *Entering the Field*; Miller and Crolley, *Football in the Americas*; and Arbena, *Latin American Sport*. Pioneering monographs include Archetti, *Masculinities*; Matta, *Carnival, Rogues, and Heroes*; Lever, *Soccer Madness*; Mason, *Passion of the People?* Santa Cruz, *Crónica de un Encuentro*; and Stein, *Lima Obrera, 1900–1930*. Influential histories of other sports include Dimeo, "'With Political Pakistan in the Offing'"; Bloom and Nevin, *Sports Matters*; and James, *Beyond a Boundary*.

    4.   This diverges from traditional narratives that emphasize sports as part of the political *mis*education of workers; see, for example, Wheeler, "Organized Sport and Organized Labour."

    5.   Quoted in Dreyfus and Rabinow, *Michel Foucault*, 159.

    6.   Uruguay is an important exception to the relative political instability of the region. Its early success in football, including the hosting of the first World Cup, in 1930, makes it a fascinating place to study football and politics. Although relatively little attention has been paid to the history of Uruguayan football, it is an emerging area of research; see, for example, Giulianotti, "Built by the Two Varelas."

    7.   Admittedly, this book represents only a partial engagement with these themes. For example, debates about the importance of political economy for the functioning of civic associations or about people's attitudes toward their governments are hardly

touched upon. For a good overview of disciplinary concerns, see Edwards, Foley, and Diani, *Beyond Tocqueville*.

8.   Putnam, *Bowling Alone*; Tilly, *Democracy*. For an excellent review of this literature in Latin America, see Forment, *Democracy in Latin America, 1760–1900*, and Piccato, "Public Sphere in Latin America."

9.   Weyland, "Neoliberalism and Democracy in Latin America."

10.   Bourdieu, "Sport and Social Class."

11.   Influential studies of the historical relationship between democracy, cultural practices, and civic associations in Latin America, which were especially rich in the nineteenth century, include Guardino, *In the Time of Liberty*; Piccato, "Public Sphere in Latin America"; Sábato, *La Política en las Calles*; and Williams, *Culture Wars in Brazil*. For a critique of the assumption that there is a positive correlation between civic associations and democracy, see Yashar, "Democracy, Indigenous Movements, and the Postliberal Challenge in Latin America."

12.   Arturo Valenzuela, *Political Brokers in Chile*.

13.   Habermas, *The Structural Transformation of the Public Sphere*.

14.   Fraser, "Rethinking the Public Sphere."

15.   Eliasoph, *Avoiding Politics*.

16.   Sábato, *La Política en las Calles*; Forment, *Democracy in Latin America*. Forment has recently studied the politics of contemporary football in Argentina ("The Democratic Dribbler").

17.   The sociologist Seymour Martin Lipset found this function of civic associations to be an indispensable feature of democracy ("The Social Requisites of Democracy Revisited").

18.   Salazar, *Labradores, Peones y Proletarios*; Gazmuri, *El "48" Chileno*. For parallels in Peru, see García-Bryce, "Politics by Peaceful Means."

19.   Posner, "Local Democracy and the Transformation of Popular Participation in Chile."

20.   Ibid., 59.

21.   Posada-Carbó, "Electoral Juggling"; Samuel Valenzuela, "Making Sense of Suffrage Expansion and Electoral Institutions in Latin America."

22.   Asad, *Formations of the Secular*.

23.   Forment, *Democracy in Latin America*; Uribe-Uran, "The Birth of the Public Sphere in Latin America during the Age of Revolution."

24.   Yeager, "Female Apostolates and Modernization in Mid-Nineteenth Century Chile."

25.   As Jeremy Adelman summarized, "The challenge for liberals was how to transform such a coercive engagement with the market into voluntary participation, or at least to create practices that made the metropolitan-colonial relations appear less contrived from above" ("Latin American Longues Durees," 236). As Claudio Lomnitz demonstrated in the case of Mexico, the attempt to create a national culture was mostly an intellectual project that never created the deep fraternal relationships

that Benedict Anderson suggested in his famed *Imagined Communities* (see Lomnitz, *Deep Mexico, Silent Mexico*).

26.   Costa, *Nirvana*, 285. Indeed, Simón Bolívar predicted, "If any American republic is to have a long life, I am inclined to believe it will be Chile" (Bolívar, "Jamaica Letter," 21).

27.   Bryce, *South America*, 223.

28.   Ibid. Bryce flatters Chileans political institutions; the election he observed had been fixed by a backroom arrangement.

29.   Smith, *Temperate Chile*, 15.

30.   For an analysis of the definitions of culture within the social sciences, see Steinmetz, *State/Culture*; and Eagleton, *The Idea of Culture*.

31.   For a review of feminist criticism of Foucault, see Hekman, *Feminist Interpretation of Michel Foucault*.

32.   Bourdieu, *Outline of a Theory of Practice*.

33.   Thanks to Professor Zilkia Janer for this analogy.

34.   Giddens, *Modernity and Self-Identity*, 226.

35.   Euben, *Corrupting Youth*, especially chap. 6.

36.   Morgan, *The Feminist History Reader*.

37.   Winn, *Victims of the Chilean Miracle*.

38.   Leftist movements did not prioritize agrarian reform. See Loveman, *Struggle in the Countryside*. Historical work within Latin American studies has criticized the portrayal of the urban working class as the more "modern" and revolutionary force in national narratives. On women's exclusion, see Rosemblatt, *Gendered Compromises*; Lavrín, *Women, Feminism, and Social Change in Argentina, Chile, and Uruguay, 1890–1940*; and Kirkwood, *Ser Política en Chile*.

39.   Mallon, *Courage Tastes of Blood*, 236. Historian Juan Carlos Gómez suggests that based on property law and electoral reform, democracy existed between 1958 and 1973 and that between 1900 and 1930, when urban working-class men integrated into the political system, state and private landholders collaborated to force Indians into individual landholding (*La Frontera de la Democracia*).

40.   Moulian, *Chile Actual*.

41.   Gramsci, *Prison Notebooks*. Paul Drake presents another critical approach to this process in *Socialism and Populism in Chile, 1932–1952*, which examines how compromise with centrist parties shaped the socialists' agenda.

42.   Foucault, *The History of Sexuality*; Bourdieu, "Sport and Social Class"; Wacquant, "Pugs at Work."

43.   Bourdieu, *The Logic of Practice*, 73.

44.   Gilbert, *Men in the Middle*.

45.   Klubock, *Contested Communities*.

46.   Work remains to be done in regard to how this emphasis on heterosexuality and virility related to homophobia. The written and oral sources are relatively silent on the subject, although they assume a normative heterosexual subject.

47.   Hutchison, "Add Gender and Stir?"; Bliss and French, *Gender, Sexuality, and Power in Latin America since Independence.*

48.   Ibid.; Tinsman, *Partners in Conflict*; Klubock, "Nationalism, Race, and the Politics of Imperialism."

49.   National government archives yield very little information, attesting to the failure of successive governments to formulate a lasting policy on physical education and sports. Municipalities did not keep systematic records in the period under study; however, extant ones were consulted. During the dictatorship, repression and efforts at centralization resulted in the destruction of many municipal documents.

50.   Tragically, Hugo Silva, who was the vice president of the National Association of Amateur Football (ANFA) and director of Puente Alto, and Víctor Sotos, who was the president of the Metropolitan League, died in an automobile accident weeks after my interview with them. I have not used any direct information from those interviews, since Silva and Sotos did not have a chance to review the transcripts. The interviews have, however, shaped my view of the history of the organization. Ten other interviews were successfully conducted. I distributed fifty questionnaires to barrio leaders, but received none back. Several directors openly questioned my sanity and suggested I might be *peinando la muñeca* (a colloquial expression for "crazy," which literally means "combing the doll's hair"). Furthermore, most of the clubs in this study decayed during the 1970s and 1980s. In any case, my powers of persuasion proved lacking.

51.   Mayorga, "Colo Colo," 4. The Chilean journalists Edgardo Marín and Julio Salviat lamented that no archives of ANFA, amateur clubs, or the Chilean Football Federation existed.

CHAPTER ONE

The title of this chapter, "*Rayando la Cancha*," is a colloquial phrase that describes the process of marking a football field and, more generally, of beginning something.

1.   Marín, *Centenario Historia Total del Fútbol Chileno, 1895–1995*; Modiano, "Historia del deporte chileno"; Santa Cruz, *Origen y Futuro de una Pasión.*

2.   Rojas, "El Foot-ball entre los Obreros," *Sport i Actualidades*, 7 July 1912, 2. Note: All translations from the Spanish are my own unless credited otherwise.

3.   The significance, and even the existence, of the middle class in Chile and the rest of Latin America has been debated among historians. See Pike, "Aspects of Class Relations in Chile, 1850–1960"; Villalobos, *Origen y Ascenso de la Burguesía Chilena*; and Barr-Melej, *Reforming Chile.*

4.   Studies of the Chilean social question and how it differed from European and U.S. contexts include those by Berrios, *El Pensamiento en Chile, 1830–1910*, and Grez, *La Cuestión Social en Chile.* For a broader discussion of the relationship between the social question and eugenics, see Stepan, "*The Hour of Eugenics.*" On

new forms of urban culture, see Rinke, *Cultura de las Masas, Reforma, Nacionalismo en Chile, 1910–1930.*

5. Drinot, "Madness, Neurasthenia, and 'Modernity.'"

6. Santa Cruz, *Cronica de un Encuentro.*

7. Bauer, *Goods, Power, History.*

8. Elias and Dunning, *Quest for Excitement.*

9. Bourdieu, "Sport and Social Class."

10. Modiano, "Historia del Deporte Chileno."

11. Organizers of baseball clubs in the United States hoped for similar results. See Bloom and Willard, *Sports Matters.*

12. *El Diario Ilustrado,* 1 August 1918, as quoted in Barr-Melej, *Reforming Chile,* 41.

13. "Dejeneración y Sports," *Sport i Variedades* (Valparaíso), 1 September 1907, 3–4.

14. Marcos Fernández, "Las Comunidades de la Sobriedad."

15. "La Cancha," *El Diario Ilustrado,* 21 July 1913, 1.

16. Ossandón and Santa Cruz, *Entre las Alas y el Plomo.*

17. "Dejeneración y Sports," *Sport i Variedades,* 1 September 1907, 3-4.

18. Ibid.

19. Appelbaum, Rosemblatt, and Wade, *Race and Nation in Modern Latin America,* 32–55.

20. For a detailed study of the image of the mestizo in Latin American national identity, particularly of how romance is employed to resolve tensions of racial hierarchies, see Sommer, *Foundational Fictions.*

21. Guillermo Martínez, *La Organización de los Deportes i el Estadio Nacional,* 10.

22. The visiting Cuban diplomat Roque Garrigó explained, "The injection of foreign elements is so prevalent in the Republic of Chile that the entire nation has lost its Spanish features. . . . Valparaíso, in its beginnings, was almost a British city" (*America para los Americanos,* 161–162).

23. Julio Zegers, *Estudios Economicos,* 75–76.

24. Disagreements over the use of English versus Spanish continued throughout the 1920s; see Oroz, "El Castellano de Nuestros Deportistas."

25. Guillermo Martínez, *La Organización de los Deportes,* 10.

26. "Araucanian" is placed in quotation marks to reflect that this term, although used by Chileans around 1900, is not used today. The indigenous residents of the south-central regions of Chile are now referred to as Mapuche. See Weber, *Bárbaros.*

27. Muñoz, "Necesidad de Fundar una Sociedad que Se Ocupe de Proteger a la Raza Chilena."

28. *Deportes,* August 1917, 10.

29.   "La Criminalidad en las Provincias del Sur," *El Diario Ilustrado*, 24 April 1902.

30.   "En el Paraíso de los Negros," *Sport i Actualidades*, 12 May 1912, 19.

31.   Ibid.

32.   Bederman, *Manliness and Civilization*.

33.   Mangan and Walvin, *Manliness and Morality*.

34.   *Deportes*, 10 December 1917, 10.

35.   Ibid., 26 November 1915, 5.

36.   *El Mercurio*, 5 June 1905, quoted in Josafat Martínez, *Historia del Fútbol Chileno*, 5. Obtaining an accurate count of the number of active club members is complicated by the fact that players often belonged to more than one club, clubs frequently changed names or fizzled out, and many clubs did not use newspapers to communicate.

37.   Grez, *De la "Regeneración del Pueblo a la Huelgo General."*

38.   DeShazo, *Urban Workers and Labor Unions in Chile, 1902–1927*, 88.

39.   "En el Parque Cousiño," *La Reforma*, 26 June 1906, 1.

40.   *La Reforma*, 14 July 1906, 4.

41.   Ibid.

42.   Ibid., 17 August 1906.

43.   Ibid., 15 August 1906, 1.

44.   "A través de los 18 Años de Vida del Morning Star Sporting Club," *Los Sports*, 3 April 1925, 13.

45.   "Asociación Obrera de Foot-Ball," *La Reforma*, 14 August 1906, 3.

46.   *La Reforma*, 14 July 1906, 4.

47.   *El Sportman*, 28 April 1907, 4.

48.   DeShazo, *Urban Workers and Labor Unions*, 78.

49.   *La Reforma*, 30 August 1906, 2.

50.   *Sport i Actualidades*, 14 July 1912, 14–15.

51.   Quoted in ibid., 3 November 1912, 6.

52.   Klubock, *Contested Communities*, 58.

53.   For similar developments in U.S. history, see Bloom and Willard, *Sports Matters*, 86–116.

54.   Lafertte, *Vida de un Comunista*, 40.

55.   Ibid., 45.

56.   Barr-Melej, *Reforming Chile*, 74.

57.   Wheeler, "Organized Sport and Organized Labour," 196.

58.   *La Reforma*, 26 June 1906, 1.

59.   Modiano, "Historia del Deporte Chileno."

60.   Larraín, *Fútbol en Chile, 1895–1945*, 18.

61.   *Revista de Instrucción Primaria* 24 (July and August 1910), 358. Members of the small middle class lived with a modicum of security and cultural capital,

which the working class did not have. See Claudio Arminó, "La Hora Negra," *La Federación Obrera*, 22 August 1921, 6.

62. *La Reforma*, 10 January 1912, 1.

63. *La Revista de Instrucción Primaria* 19 (August 1905): 436.

64. *La Revista de Instrucción Primaria* 24 (July–August 1910): 358.

65. For a study of responses to women's labor outside the home, see Hutchison, *Labors Appropriate to Their Sex.*

66. In a report from 1899, Eloisa Diaz, the medical inspector of public schools, listed the "pernicious" neighbors of the schools, including prostitution houses, bars, and horse stables. At the top of her list of health problems, Diaz cited the presence of water, rodents, and carbon monoxide in classrooms (*La Revista de Instrucción Primaria* 13 (August–September 1899): 645–649).

67. The emergence of youth as a special stage of life, with its own dangers and obligations, has been a topic of academic inquiry in recent years; see Jorge Rojas, *Moral y Prácticas Cívicas en los Niños Chilenos, 1880–1950.*

68. Carlos Fernandez, "De Educación Nacional."

69. Baer and Pineo, *Cities of Hope.*

70. "Memoria del Presidente de La A. de E.N." *La Revista Pedagójica* 5 (April–May 1910): 23. There were actually three precursors to this "first" Pan-American Congress.

71. Guillermo Martínez, *La Organización de los Deportes.*

72. "Liga Chilena de Educación Física," *Sport i Actualidades*, 14 July 1912, 8.

73. "La Mujer i los Sports," *Sport i Actualidades*, 4 May 1913, 1.

74. "El Box entre las Mujeres," *El Diario Ilustrado*, 5 July 1913, 1.

75. Juan Livingstone was the father of legendary Chilean footballer and sports commentator Sergio Livingstone.

76. Livingston and Betteley, *Football*, 5.

77. This was the first South American Cup, held in Buenos Aires in July 1916. Brazil, Uruguay, Argentina, and Chile participated.

78. *La Revista de Instrucción Primaria* 19 (December 1905): 653.

79. Alviz Ovalle, "Gimnasia: La Educación Física," *Deportes*, August 1917, 4–5.

80. These figures are based on a review of newspapers in the first quarter of 1910 and an assumption that clubs averaged forty-five players each. Since clubs were ephemeral and players could have joined more than one, these figures should be considered tentative.

81. Modiano, "Historia del Deporte Chileno," 137–138.

82. "Estadio: Historia de la Federación Deportiva Nacional," *Deportes*, 5 November 1916, 6.

83. "Nuestro Anhelo," *Sport i Actualidades*, 21 April 1912, 3.

84. Bourdieu, "The Social Space and the Genesis of Groups," 724.

85. Bethell, *Chile since Independence.*

86.   Scully, *Rethinking the Center*, 25. It should be noted the number of voters would dip in 1915 and then climb again because of 1914 reforms.

87.   "El Stadium Nacional," *Sport i Actualidades*, 14 July 1912.

88.   *El Mercurio*, 6 January 1921, 5. The club remained linked to the Radicals until its demise in the 1920s.

89.   *Deportes*, 10 September 1915, 3.

90.   Walter, *Politics and Urban Growth in Santiago*.

91.   *Deportes*, 19 May 1917, 2.

92.   For a discussion of this, see Valenzuela, *Democratización via Reforma*.

93.   Scully, *Rethinking the Center*.

94.   "El Stadium Nacional," *Sport i Actualidades*, 4 August 1912, 1.

95.   Ibid.

96.   Cámara de Diputados, *Boletín de las Sesiones Ordinarias*, session 1, 6 June 1918, 74.

97.   Sports publications complained that sportsmen circulated magazines among club members without paying. See *Deportes*, 26 August 1916, 1.

98.   *La Nación*, 18 June 1962.

99.   Rosenzweig, *Eight Hours for What We Will*.

100.   Rojas, "El Foot-Ball entre los obreros," 2.

101.   Baldomero Loyola, "El Sport i Los Obreros," *Sport i Actualidades*, 3 November 1912, 6.

102.   Ibid.

103.   Josafat Martínez, *Historia del Fútbol Chileno*, 45.

104.   *Sport i Actualidades*, 28 June 1912, 1.

105.   "Con Don Guillermo Guzman," *Deportes*, 2 July 1915, 2.

106.   Santa Cruz, *Origen y Futuro de una Pasión*, 84.

107.   "Foot-Ball Jueces i Protestas," *Sport i Actualidades*, 10 August 1913, 1.

108.   "Aficionados i Profesionales," *Sport i Actualidades*, 15 June 1913, 1.

109.   "Foot-Ball," *Sport i Actualidades*, 29 June 1913, 7.

110.   Bowler, "Por qué no Jugamos Cricket," *Sport i Actualidades*, 8 February 1914, 1.

111.   In Argentina, the professional league emerged in 1931, two years before Chile's.

112.   Guillermo Martínez, *La Organización de los Deportes*, 8.

113.   Martínez and his circle's animosity to industrial sporting goods was also a response to the displacement of local artisans from the market; see Salazar, *Labradores, Peones y Proletarios*.

114.   "De nuestra gloriosa retaguardia," *Los Sports*, 30 July 1926, 12. After his football career ended, Próspero González and his family fell on hard times. In the 1930s, football associations all over the country played benefit matches for them.

115.   Waquant, "Pugs at Work."

116.   SAA, "Irregularidad," *Deportes*, 13 August 1915, 2.

262 Notes to Pages 46–55

117. Ibid., 19 May 1917, 2.

118. Ibid., 26 August 1916, 7–8.

119. Klubock, *Contested Communities*; Frazier, *Salt in the Sand*.

120. According to Salazar, "Whereas *externally* it [Marxism] was an instrument of revolutionary opposition, in practice it was simply one more movement among those that operated *within* the system" ("The History of Popular Culture in Chile," 33).

121. "La Popularización de los Sports en Chile," *La Providencia*, 1 July 1918, 2.

122. *El Sportman*, 4 May 1907.

123. *Deportes*, 17 September 1915, 1.

124. Ibid., August 1917, 8–9.

125. *La Palanca*, 1 May 1908, 3.

126. Caviedes, "Los Ejercicios Corporales i Los Juegos."

127. "La mujer i los Sports," *Sport i Actualidades*, 4 May 1913, 1.

128. "En el Paraíso de los Negros," *Sport i Actualidades*, 12 May 1912, 19.

129. *Sport i Actualidades*, 3 November 1912, 5.

CHAPTER TWO

1. The dictatorship of Carlos Ibáñez served as a point of reference for future military movements, including those led by Augusto Pinochet. Historian Margaret Power interviewed one woman who "wished Pinochet had dumped his victims in the ocean, as General Ibáñez had done to the 'homosexuals,' instead of burying them in mass graves where they could be found" ("More than Mere Pawns," 146). See also Valdivia, *El Golpe Despues del Golpe*.

2. "Con El Ministerio del Interior Cornelio Saavedra Montt," *Los Sports*, 6 April 1923, 1.

3. The mobility of cultural practices was reinforced by political efforts to forge stronger relations among the nations in the Americas, or Pan-Americanism (Echevarria, "Chile," 173).

4. Alberto Edwards, *La Fronda Aristocrática en Chile*, as quoted in Montero, *Ibáñez*.

5. Rowe, "The Development of Democracy on the American Continent," 2–3.

6. Mason, *Passion of the People?*

7. DeShazo, *Urban Workers and Labor Unions*, 78.

8. Larraín, *Fútbol en Chile, 1895–1945*, 59.

9. Alessandri marshalled the power of cinema as well, appearing in the 1922 film *El Empuje de una Raza*; see Jara, *Cine Mudo Chileno*.

10. Chalo, *Crónicas del Campeonato Sudamericano de Fútbol de 1920*, 31.

11. Ibid.

12. Iturriaga, "Aunque Ganas o Pierdas."

13. Luís Zegers, *El Football y Su Estilo Moderno de Juego*, 15.

14. *Los Sports*, 16 March 1923, 1.

15. Ibid.

16. Salazar, "Luis Emilio Recabarren y el Municipio Popular en Chile."

17. Walter, *Politics and Urban Growth in Santiago, Chile, 1891–1941*, 101–102.

18. Loveman, *Struggle in the Countryside.*

19. *El Mercurio*, 6 January 1921, 5.

20. *Los Sports*, 22 August 1924, 15.

21. "Deportes," *El Paladin* (Periódico Radical-Yungay), 12 October 1924, 2.

22. *El Paladin*, 9 November 1924, 1.

23. "Deportes," *El Paladin*, 12 October 1924, 2.

24. *Los Sports*, 22 June 1928, 18.

25. "Los Cesantes," *El Obrero Ilustrado*, 30 August 1921, 8.

26. "A Través de los Reportajes," *Deportes*, 23 April 1915.

27. Alfilerito, "Los Deportistas Porteñas," *Los Sports*, 4 April 1924, 6.

28. Rojas, Rodríguez, Fernández, *Cristaleros.*

29. Ibid., 59.

30. "La Fundación Arrieta," *La Comuna*, 12 July 1925, 6.

31. "El Primer Congreso Foot-Ballistico Nacional," *Los Sports*, 4 May 1923, 7.

32. Ibid., 17.

33. Larraín, *Fútbol en Chile*, 42.

34. "El Primer Congreso Foot-Ballistico Nacional," *Los Sports*, 4 May 1923, 7.

35. Luís Zegers, *El Football y Su Estilo*, 22.

36. Acevedo Hernández, "Hacia la Verdadera Democracia," *Los Sports*, 4 April 1924, 2.

37. *El Mercurio*, 21 April 1931, 9.

38. Hugo Grassi, "Un Programa Moderno de Educación Física," *Los Sports*, 18 July 1924, 1.

39. Aleto, "Con José Pardo . . ." *Los Sports*, 21 May 1926, 4.

40. Women received the rights of "voice and vote" in professional clubs during the late 1930s and early 1940s; see Club de Deportes Green Cross, *Estatutos y Reglamentos*, 9. Some clubs had included women in their statutes earlier, in particular those that sponsored sports other than football, such as Colo Colo; see Club Colo Colo, *Estatutos y Reglamentos*, 16. See Chapter Five for a discussion of women's entrance into amateur clubs.

41. Mont-Calm, "La Mujer Debe Cultivar los Deportes," *Los Sports*, 7 September 1923, 3.

42. "Del Album de los Recuerdos," *Gol y Gol*, 28 November 1962, 22.

43. "Los Encuentros," *Los Sports*, 28 August 1925, 10.

44. Humberto Montecinos, "Los Deportes Comunales," *Los Sports*, 2 January 1925, 4.

45. DeShazo, *Urban Workers and Labor Unions*, 4–5.

46. Unión Española, *Bodas de Oro 1897*, 34.

47. Barr-Melej, "Cowboys and Constructions," 37.

48. Ibid.

49. Pedelty, "The Bolero."

50. Rinke, *Cultura de las Masas.*

51. On southern Chile and indigenous movements, see Bengoa, *Historia del Pueblo Mapuche*, and Klubock, "The Politics of Forests and Forestry on Chile's Southern Frontier, 1880s–1940s."

52. Empresa Periodística Chile, *Diccionario Biográfico de Chile.*

53. *Los Sports*, 10 August 1928, 5.

54. "Entrevista," *Los Sports*, 12 July 1929, 9.

55. Ibid.

56. Tonobar, "Nuestros Futbolistas," *Los Sports*, 27 July 1928, 9.

57. "Los Graves Acontecimientos Actuales la Renuncia del Presidente Alessandri," *Justicia*, 10 September 1924, 1.

58. McGee Deutsch, *Las Derechas*, 73–74.

59. On La Coruña, see Rolando Alvarez, "La Matanza de Coruña"; Frazier, *Salt in the Sand*; and Harambour, "Huelga y Sangre Obrera en el Alto San Antonio."

60. Patricio Silva, "State, Public Technocracy and Politics in Chile, 1927–1941."

61. "La Historia de la Federación Deportiva Nacional," *Deportes*, 5 November 1916, 5–6.

62. Dirección Jeneral de Educación Primaria, *Lei No. 3,654 sobre Educación Primaria Obligatoria.*

63. Ibid.

64. Hernández, "Hacia la Verdadera Democracia," 2.

65. Muñoz, *Historia de la Dirección General de Deportes y Recreación.*

66. Nunn, *Chilean Politics, 1920–1931*, 154.

67. Andre, "Carlos Cariola, Deportista," *Los Sports*, November 21, 1924, 1.

68. Ibáñez had used a military sports event to rile his colleague's dissatisfaction with the Altimirano government in 1924 (Nunn, *Chilean Politics*, 71).

69. Homero Aldea, "Sobre el Club Deportivo 'Fábricas del Ejército,'" *El Obrero Industrial*, 18 August 1928, 5.

70. "Gobierno Prestigioso," *El Obrero Industrial*, 7 May 1927, 3.

71. Ibid.

72. Ojeda, *Recuerdos de 80 años*, 93.

73. Ibid.

74. See Walter, *Politics and Urban Growth in Santiago*, and Salazar and Benítez, *Autonomía, Espacio y Gestión.*

75. *Los Sports*, December 1930, 34.

76. Ibid., 24 August 1928, 17.

77. Ibid., December 1930, 34.

78. Ibid., 24 August 1928, 17.

79. Ramón, *Santiago de Chile*, 210.

80. *Los Sports*, 24 August 1928, 17.

81. Ibid.

82. The government had intervened in the Boxing Federation in the previous year; see *Los Sports*, 23 March 1928, 1.

83. Orellano, *La Previsión Social en el Foot-ball Profesional Chileno*, 19–20.

84. Arellano, *David Arellano Moraga*, 21.

85. Sebastián Salinas, *Por Empuje y Coraje*.

86. Teutsch, *Metódo Práctico que Enseña a Jugar Verdadero Foot-ball*, 9.

87. Arellano, *David Arellano Moraga*.

88. Ibid.

89. Vicuña, *Mitos y Supersticiones*.

90. Ibid., 22.

91. Santa Cruz, *Origen y Futuro de una Pasión*, 68–69.

92. Arellano, *David Arellano Moraga*; see also *Los Sports*, 1927–1928.

93. Carlos Zeda, "Togo Bascuñan, que Llego Hace Poco . . ." *Los Sports*, 24 June 1927.

94. Ibid.

95. Arellano, *David Arellano Moraga*.

96. Cámara de Diputados, *Boletín de las Sesiones Ordinarias*, session 32, 6 August 1928, 1445–1446.

97. Cámara de Diputados, *Boletín de las Sesiones Ordinarias*, session 5, June 1928, 191.

98. Ibid.

99. M. Cea O., "Juan Ramsay," *Los Sports*, 25 May 1923, 1.

100. "Conversando con los Presidentes de las Instituciones Footbalísticas Locales," *Los Sports*, 4 April 1924, 10.

101. Ibid.

102. "Manuel Plaza, Campeón Olímpico Latino-Americano," *Los Sports*, 23 March 1923, 4–5.

103. Ibid.

104. Guevara, "El 'Santiago F.C.' Cumple 20 Años de Vida," *Los Sports*, 2 November 1923, 15.

105. Biblioteca del Almanaque, *El Fútbol*, 34.

106. Rabinovitz, *For the Love of Pleasure*.

107. Hutchison, *Labors Appropriate to Their Sex*.

108. "La Mujer, el Gimnasio y el Ejercicio," *Los Sports*, 20 December 1929, 1.

109. "Los Deportes que No Debe Practicar la Mujer," *Los Sports*, 7 February 1930, 1.

110.   Marín, *Centenario Historia Total del Fútbol Chileno 1895–1995*, 92–93.

111.   Interestingly, the historical antecedents of the contemporary *barra* have been lost in popular memory. In interviews, respondents pointed to the 1970s as the era in which the *barras* emerged.

112.   J. Manuel Cea, "Lo que Va de Ayer," *Los Sports*, 23 March 1923, 15.

113.   "Los Domingos," *Los Sports*, 28 October 1927, 9.

114.   "Los Domingos," *Los Sports*, 23 November 1928, 8.

115.   Intendencia Santiago, Archivo Nacional, *Comunicaciones Recibidas*, November–December 1928, vol. 627, no. 1681.

116.   "El Estadio de la Policía," *Los Sports*, 27 April 1923, 4–5.

117.   "Carvajal," *Mister Huifa*, 7 August 1936, 5, 7.

118.   La Nación, *Historia del Fútbol Chileno*, 1:40 (without date or publisher; see the archives of the Comité Olímpico de Chile).

119.   "Nuestro Comentario," *El Diario Ilustrado*, 9 January 1928, 1.

120.   La Nación, *Historia del Fútbol Chileno*, 1:40–49.

121.   *Los Sports*, 15 February 1924.

122.   "Reportajes de Actualidad," *Los Sports*, 3 October 1924, 2.

123.   *Los Sports*, 28 December 1923, 2–3.

124.   Intendencia de Santiago, *Comunicaciones Recibidas*, November–December 1928, vol. 629, 24 December 1928, no. 3747.

125.   *Los Sports*, 22 June 1928, 18.

126.   *Match*, 17 May 1929, 6.

127.   "La Nueva Reglamentación Deportiva," *Los Sports*, 9 August 1929, 1.

128.   "La Nueva Ley sobre Deporte Escolar y Post Escolar," *Los Sports*, 22 November 1929, 1.

129.   Osvaldo Kolbach, "El Director de Educación Física," *Los Sports*, 7 February 1930.

130.   *Los Sports*, 24 August 1928.

131.   Mandujano's speech "The Twenty-two Commandments of Hygiene and Their Observance" was reprinted in Armando Mandujar, "La Educación Física y Higiene," *Los Sports* (n.d., c. 1929–1931).

132.   Martin, *Football and Fascism*.

133.   "Conversando con el Director de Educación Física Señor Alfredo Portales," *Los Sports*, 3 June 1927.

134.   Tonobar, "El Tiro Escolar," *Los Sports*, March 1929.

135.   "Los Encuentros," *Los Sports*, 28 August 1925, 10.

136.   Sepúlveda, *Laborando en Beneficio de la Educación Física de Mi País*, 32.

137.   "Las Instituciones Deportivas Celebrarán las Fiestas Nacionales," *El Mercurio*, 18 September 1931, 16.

138.   *El Mercurio*, 4 December 1931, 5.

139.   Ibid., 19 April 1931, 27.

140.   Ibid., 12 September 1931, 9.

141.   "Frailerismo, Alcoholismo y Prostitucion Son las Armas del Capitalismo," *Justicia*, 15 January 1925, 1.

142.   "El Cisma Footballístico," *Justicia*, 2 September 1925, 2.

143.   Ferrocarriles del Estado, *Reglamento General de Deportes*, 9.

144.   Araya Paz, "Deportes," *El Gancho*, 10 August 1930, 4.

145.   "La Liga Patriótica de Chile y los Deportes," *Los Sports*, 1926. On the patriotic leagues, see McGee Deutsch, *Las Derechas*.

146.   Guerrero, *El Libro de los Campeones*; Rinke, *Cultura de las Masas*.

147.   "Es Lamentable," *El Surco* (Iquique, Chile), 17 January, 1925, 3.

148.   "Somos un Pueblo Feliz," *Verba Roja*, December 1923, no. 2, 2.

149.   Ibid.

150.   "Mucho Músculo . . . pero Poca Cabeza," *La Voz del Chofer* (Valparaíso), 1 May 1924, 5.

151.   For example, the Edwards family, which owned *El Mercurio*, financed workers' football clubs. These clubs organized "spontaneous" celebrations in the family's honor. Directors explained that in football, owners and employees were "perfectly united in mutual understanding" ("D. Agustín Edwards Fué Estejado Ayer por el Club Deportivo 'El Mercurio,'" *El Mercurio*, 14 December 1931, 7).

152.   "Estadio Nacional," *El Mercurio*, 16 April 1931, 3.

153.   Flores and Serrano, *Guillermo Saavedra Tapia*, 6. This seems difficult to believe, given that Saavedra would have been only fifteen during the selection; regardless, he clearly missed opportunities in football because of financial constraints.

154.   "Reorganizar la Fed, los Clubs, y los Hombres," *El Diario Ilustrado*, 27 July 1933, 17.

155.   Larraín, *Fútbol en Chile*, 40.

156.   "Waldo Sanhueza Nos Habla del Football Profesional," *El Diario Ilustrado*, 8 May 1933.

157.   La Nación, *Historia del Fútbol Chileno*, 1:17–18.

158.   "Eduardo da Marcha Atras," *El Diario Ilustrado*, 6 June 1933, 13.

159.   "El Capitán Bate Considera una Insensatez Ir al Profesionalismo," *El Diario Ilustrado*, 9 May 1933, 13.

160.   "Waldo Sanhueza Nos Habla del Football Profesional," *El Diario Ilustrado*.

161.   The original group included Audax Italiano, Badminton, Colo Colo, Green Cross, Magallanes, Morning Star, Santiago National, and Unión Española. The following year, the Professional League admitted three others, all from Santiago: Deportivo Alemán, Ferroviario, and Carlos Walker Martínez.

162.   See *El Mercurio*, 5 June 1933, 11.

CHAPTER THREE

1. Warner, *Publics and Counterpublics*. I rely on Warner's most inclusive definition of a public: a group of strangers who imagine their connections through circulating texts and shared discourse.

2. Héctor Arancibia, the president of the Popular Front, and Pedro Aguirre were the president and vice president, respectively, of the Football Association of Santiago.

3. See Correa and others, *Historia del siglo XX chileno*; Rosemblatt, *Gendered Compromises*; Salazar and Pinto, *Historia Contemporánea de Chile*. In *Socialism and Populism*, Drake argues that the Socialist Party's participation in the Popular Front afforded it power and respectability at the cost of political goals.

4. Drake, *Socialism and Populism*; Knight, "Populism and Neo-Populism in Latin America, Especially Mexico"; Torre, *Populist Seduction in Latin America*; Peruzzotii, "Constitucionalismo, Populismo y Sociedad Civil."

5. Knight, "Populism and Neo-Populism," 223.

6. Germani, *Authoritarianism, Fascism, and National Populism*; Laclau, *Politics and Ideology in Marxist Theory*.

7. In *Resistance and Integration*, James examines Peronism's exaltation of popular culture and its expansion of citizenship to the Argentine working class.

8. Laclau, *Politics and Ideology*, 161.

9. Karush, "National Identity in Sports Pages."

10. "Será Posible Dotar de Campos de Juegos a las Principales Ciudades," *El Mercurio*, 27 September 1931, 15.

11. Cámara de Diputados, *Boletines de Sesiones*, special session 7, 11 November 1935, 412–413.

12. On the exclusion of women from citizenship, see Rosemblatt, *Gendered Compromises*.

13. Cámara de Diputados, *Boletines de Sesiones*, special session 7, 11 November 1935.

14. Ibid., 418.

15. Ibid., 415–416.

16. Ibid., 416.

17. Cámara de Diputados, *Boletines de Sesiones*, special session 4, 4 November 1935, 227–250.

18. Ibid.

19. Ibid.

20. Klein, "The New Voices of Chilean Fascism and the Popular Front, 1938–1942."

21. *La Voz*, October 1935, no. 2, 2–3.

22. Ibid. In this era, the Democratic Party was to the left of the Radical Party.

23. *La Voz*, December 1935, no. 1, 4.

24. Ramón, *Santiago de Chile*, 206–207.

25. Drake, "The Chilean Socialist Party and Coalition Politics, 1932–1946."

26. "Deportes," *La Voz de La Florida*, 19 July 1937, 4.

27. *La Voz de La Florida*, August 1937, 4.

28. Ibid.

29. *La Voz*, November 1935, no. 1, 1.

30. "Nueva Política Deportiva," *La Voz de La Florida*, 28 November 1937, 1.

31. DVA, "Independencia Absoluta del Deporte," *La Voz de La Florida*, 20 February 1938, 1.

32. Residents of working-class neighborhoods resolved disputes among themselves in order to avoid police interference. Their efforts resembled those in the neighborhoods of Mexico City; see Piccato, "Communities and Crime in Mexico City."

33. "Nueva Política Deportiva," *La Voz de La Florida*, 28 November 1937, 1.

34. *La Voz de La Florida*, 26 December 1937, 4.

35. "Estadio Nacional," *Frente Popular*, 24 November 1936, 9.

36. Patricio Silva, "State, Public Technocracy and Politics."

37. Asociación Central de Football, *Memoria, 1933–1941*.

38. *Diccionario Biográfico de Chile*, 4th ed., 1025.

39. Ministerio de Educación, *Tres Miradas al Estadio Nacional*, 120–132.

40. *Zig-Zag*, 15 April 1938, 41.

41. Drapkin, *Historia de Colo Colo*.

42. Mister Huifa, "El Colorin de Iquique," *Crack*, 17 December 1937, 9.

43. Drapkin, *Historia de Colo-Colo*.

44. Sergio Gilbert, "Eduardo Símian: Testigo bajos los Palos," *La Epoca*, 28 November 1988, 16.

45. Ministerio de Educación, *Tres Miradas al Estadio Nacional*. Alessandri claimed that he spent a total of thirty million pesos.

46. Sergio Livingstone, "Testimonio," *La Epoca*, 28 November 1988, 17.

47. "El Estadio y la Educación Física," *La Hora*, 3 December 1938, 3.

48. *Frente Popular*, 28 November 1938, 9.

49. "El Estadio y la Educación Física," *La Hora*, 3 December, 1938, 3.

50. Asociación Central de Football, *Memoria*.

51. Rosemblatt, *Gendered Compromises*.

52. *Crack*, 22 October 1938, 4–5.

53. Ibid., 5.

54. Boizard, *Hacia el Ideal Político de una Juventud*.

55. Arancibia, *La Doctrina Radical: Programa de Gobierno*, 16.

56. "Qué significa el Deporte para el F. Popular?" *Crack*, 4 November 1938, 4.

57. *La Opinión*, 17 November 1938, 6.

58.   See, for example, the *Frente Popular*, 4 September 1936, 9.

59.   *Frente Popular*, 6 November 1936.

60.   "Función Social del Deporte," *Frente Popular*, 10 March 1937, 11.

61.   "Entre dos Martes," *La Opinión*, 15 November 1938, 6.

62.   Rosemblatt, *Gendered Compromises*.

63.   The event even inspired the first athletic tournament among congressmen ("Estamos a Cinco Días," *El Diario Ilustrado*, 29 November 1938, 13).

64.   Quotes in Marín and Salviat, *De David a "Chamaco,"* 36.

65.   *La Opinión*, 18 November 1938.

66.   *Audax*, December 1936, 28.

67.   "Pichangas," *Crack*, 10 June 1938, 10.

68.   "El Football y Basketball Amateur No Participaran en el Desfile," *Diario Ilustrado*, 18 November 1938, 16.

69.   Ibid.

70.   "El Fútbol y la Inauguración del Estadio," *La Opinión*, 30 November 1938, 6.

71.   *La Nación*, 24 November 1938, 11.

72.   *La Opinión*, 2 December 1938, 6.

73.   "El Rincón de los . . . Clubes de Barrio," *La Opinión*, 17 November 1938, 6.

74.   *La Nación*, 2 December 1938, 3.

75.   *Programa Oficial: Inauguración del Estadio Nacional* (Santiago, 1938).

76.   "Como Se Generó la Construcción del Estadio Nacional," *La Nación*, 3 December 1938, 15.

77.   A few female students represented tennis and dancing.

78.   "Estamos a Cinco Días de la Inauguración del Estadio," *Diario Ilustrado*, 29 November 1938, 13.

79.   Ministerio de Educación, *Tres Miradas al Estadio Nacional*, 30.

80.   "Deportistas 'Cargan' con Culpas de Otros," *La Hora*, 4 December 1938, 1.

81.   *Acción Sindical*, 5 December 1934, 4.

82.   "Puño en Alto Saludaron al Sr. Alessandri," *La Hora*, 4 December 1938, 1.

83.   "La Nota Fea del Desfile," *El Diario Ilustrado*, 4 December 1938, 8.

84.   Ibid.

85.   *La Nación*, 4 December 1938, 22.

86.   Ibid.

87.   Ibid.

88.   *La Epoca*, 28 November 1988.

89.   Ibid., 15.

90.   Sergio Gilbert, "Eduardo Símian," *La Epoca*, 28 November 1988, 16.

91.   *La Nación*, 4 December 1938, 21.

92.   See, for example, "Al Día por Espectador," *La Hora*, 5 December 1938, 1.

93.   CZ, "Popularidad," *La Opinión*, 4 December 1938, 3.

94.   Consejo Nacional de Deportes, *Memoria del Consejo Nacional de Deportes*, 5.

95.   Orellana, "El Estadio Nacional."

96.   Ibid, 39–42.

97.   Asociación Central de Football, *Memoria, 1933–1941*, 78.

98.   Consejo Nacional de Deportes, *Memoria*.

99.   Instituto de Información Campesina, *Como Debe Jugarse el Fútbol*.

100.   Rosemblatt, "Charity, Rights, and Entitlement," 561.

101.   Cámara de Diputados, *Boletín de Sesiones*, regular session 72, 13 September 1945, 2823–2825.

102.   Municipalidad de San Miguel, *Memoria de la Labor, 1940–1941*.

103.   Partido Socialista, *Homenaje al 6° Aniversario del Partido Socialista*.

104.   *El Siglo*, 18 September 1940, 13.

105.   Aguirre Cerda, *Defensa de la Raza, 1939–1941*, 2.

106.   Ibid., 3.

107.   Ibid.

108.   *Deporte Popular*, 11 October 1941.

109.   "Deportistas Amateurs," *Deporte Popular*, 18 October 1941, 4.

110.   Asociación Central de Football, *Memorias*, 67.

111.   Juan Moreira, "Oiga Comandante Kolbach," *Barra Brava*, 3 January 1944, 3.

112.   "Los Viejos Cracks Reivindican el Espíritu de Colocolino," *Barra Brava*, 31 January 1944, 7.

113.   Cámara de Diputados, *Boletines de Sesiones Ordinarias*, session 72, 13 September 1945, 2823–2825.

114.   Ibid., session 73, 14 September 1945, 2873. This number includes members of clubs, not only players.

115.   Asociación Central de Football, *Memorias*, 145.

116.   Santiago Morning Club de Deportes, *Homenaje al 40° Aniversario*, 10.

117.   Mouat, *Cosas del Fútbol*, 51-55.

118.   Ibid., 52.

119.   *Frente Popular*, 23 November 1938.

120.   *Voz del Pueblo*, 28 October 1939, 5.

121.   *Frente Popular*, 26 January 1938, 12.

122.   Ibid., 23 January 1939, 7.

123.   Rojas and others, *Cristaleros*, 59.

124.   Ibid., 32.

125.   Ibid.

126.   See, for example, Oscar Guzmán, *La Voz del Cristalero*, 14 April 1944, 4.

127.   Klubock, *Contested Communities*.

128.   *La Voz del Metalúrgico*, 4 October 1940, 4.

129.   *Frente Popular*, 4 May 1938, 7.

130.   Luis Alfaro, "El Partido Comunista Traza las Líneas de Su Clara Política Juvenil," *Boletín de Orientación*, February 1940, 15.

131.   *Boletín de Orientación*, June 1940, 3.

132.   *Línea*, 3 December 1942, 3.

133.   Ibid., 10 September 1943, 3.

134.   *El Siglo*, 25 August 1942, 7.

135.   Ibid.

136.   See, for example, *El Siglo*, 14 September 1942, 8.

137.   "Iquique Deportivo," *Estadio*, 31 July 1942, 24–25.

138.   *El Reporter del Tercer Distrito*, 18 October 1941, 6.

139.   Ibid., 8 November 1941, 6.

140.   For membership and directory information, see *El Reporter del Tercer Distrito*, 30 May 1942, 6.

141.   "Deportistas de la Comuna San Miguel," *El Progreso*, 16 June 1940, 2.

142.   Ibid.

143.   *El Diario Ilustrado*, 5 November 1938, 14.

144.   Club Social y Deportivo "Magallanes," *43°Anniversario*, 6.

145.   *El Blanco* (youth magazine of Club Social, Deportivo y Cultural "Manuel Blanco Encalada"), July 1945, 8.

146.   *El Diario Ilustrado*, 4 November 1938, 15.

147.   See, for example, *Aire Libre*, March 1937.

148.   San Martín, "Nuestra Educación Física y el Deporte Profesional."

149.   Evidently, San Martín was unaware that Saavedra did, in fact, play one professional season before breaking his leg.

150.   Betteley, "Nuestro Deporte Es un Edificio sin Cimientos."

CHAPTER FOUR

1.   *Mundial de Fútbol* 2, December–January 1962, 72.

2.   Rosemblatt, *Gendered Compromises*; Mallon, "Indian Communities, Political Cultures, and the State in Latin America, 1780–1990."

3.   Portes, Guarnizo, and Haller, "Transnational Entrepreneurs"; Orozco, "Globalization and Migration."

4.   Garza and Yetim, "The Impact of Ethnicity and Socialization on Definitions of Democracy"; Pedraza-Bailey, "Immigration Research."

5.   Portes, Guarnizo, and Haller, "Transnational Entrepreneurs"; Orozco, "Globalization and Migration."

6.   A review of journals from 2004 to 2008, including *Historia* (Pontifical Catholic University) and *Revista de Historia Social y Mentalidades* (University of Santiago de Chile), demonstrates the paucity of recent work on immigration, ethnicity, and race.

7.   See, for example, Whyte, *Street Corner Society*.

8. As Lesser demonstrated for Brazil, Middle Eastern immigrants created identities, such as "Sirio-Libanes," that had not existed before their immigration ("(Re) Creating Ethnicity").

9. See, for example, Garza and Yetim, "Ethnicity and Socialization."

10. "Etnografía," *Revista de Instrucción Primaria*, September 1905, 465.

11. Ibid.

12. Rosemblatt, *Gendered Compromises*.

13. Aguirre, *Defensa de la Raza, 1939–1941*.

14. Ibid., 1.

15. Tinsman, *Partners in Conflict*, 38.

16. Applebaum, "Post-Revisionist Scholarship on Race."

17. See Martínez-Echazábal, "*Mestizaje* and the Discourse of National/Cultural Identity in Latin America, 1845–1959."

18. Cadena, *Indigenous Mestizos*.

19. Cachipuchi, "Es Rudimentario el Sistema de Entrenamiento," *Match*, 3 January 1929, 24.

20. Chalo, *Crónicas del Campeonato Sudamericano*.

21. *La Palabra*, 4 April 1944, 21.

22. "Volvemos a lo de antes?" *Estadio*, 6 September 1952, 22.

23. Pichanga, "Hinchas Fanáticos o Histericos," *Pichanga*, 28 August 1948, 1.

24. *Barra Brava*, 5 November 1945, 3.

25. Carlos Rojas, "El Foot-ball entre los Obreros," *Sport i Actualidades*, 7 July 1912, 2.

26. *Barra Brava*, 5 September 1945; 21 and 26 September 1945, 3. Robinson Alvarez, a lawyer who headed the Popular Front's Department of Immigration, served as the president of Colo Colo during this period and obtained millions of dollars in public support for the club.

27. Barr-Melej, *Reforming Chile*.

28. Bauer, *Goods, Power, History*.

29. Palacios, *Raza Chilena*; Encina, *Historia de Chile*, vol. 3.

30. Martínez-Echazábal, "*Mestizaje*," 33.

31. Klubock, "Nationalism, Race, and Imperialism."

32. State records grouped Japanese, Chinese, and Korean immigrants together as *chinos*, which makes it difficult to assess the numbers and origins of Asian immigrants in the first half of the twentieth century; see Lin, *Chile y China*.

33. Klubock, *Contested Communities*.

34. *El Trabajo*, 11 November 1905, 2.

35. "Inmigración Asiática," *El Trabajo*, 24 November 1906, 1.

36. "Mucho músculo . . . ," *La Voz del Chofer*, 1 May 1924, 5.

37. Don Pampa, "Migajes," *Estadio*, 16 February 1945, 32.

38. Ibid.

39. Tatanacho, "Brasil," *Estadio*, 2 February 1945, 23.

40. See *Estadio*, 1945–1955.

41. *Estadio*, 2 February 1945, 2.

42. Stephen, "Gender, Citizenship, and the Politics of Identity."

43. *El Diario Ilustrado*, 5 December 1906, 1.

44. *El Mercurio*, 26 May 1938, 11.

45. Prince of Wales Country Club, *Memoria*.

46. German clubs fractured over National Socialism in the mid-1930s, and Deutscher Sport Verein quickly disintegrated. Its stadium lost its legal recognition during the war (Modiano, *Historia del Deporte Chileno*, 97).

47. Unión Española, *Bodas de Oro*.

48. Ibid., 14.

49. Documentation of the center's early activities was destroyed in a 1923 fire at its headquarters, 838 Merced.

50. Unión Española, *Bodas de Oro*, 19.

51. "Del Album de los Recuerdos," *Gol y Gol*, 28 November 1962, 22.

52. Aguirre, *El Problema Industrial*.

53. Unión Española, *Bodas de Oro*.

54. *Los Sports*, 16 January 1925, 12–13.

55. Josafat Martínez, *Historia del Futbol Chileno*, 23.

56. *Los Sports*, 30 November 1928, 12.

57. "Del Album de los Recuerdos," *Gol y Gol*, 28 November 1962, 22.

58. Ibid.

59. Baggio and Massone, *Presencia Italiana en Chile*.

60. "Adelante!" *Audax*, July 1936, 2.

61. See, for example, the 1937 edition of the *Chilean Who's Who*.

62. Unión Deportiva Española, *Memoria y Balance*.

63. *Audax*, 1936–1939.

64. *Los Sports*, 10 August 1928, 5.

65. *Los Sports*, 12 September 1930, 21.

66. *Estadio*, 29 December 1945, 32.

67. *El Hincha*, 2 October 1943, 2.

68. *Barra Brava*, 3 April 1944, 3.

69. *Audax*, December 1954.

70. Quoted in Mouat, *Cosas del Fútbol*, 74.

71. *Audax*, August 1936, cover.

72. Enzo Fantinati, "Audax en Broma," *Audax*, January 1937, 23–24.

73. See, for example, Unión Española, *Memoria* (1941), 5; Stadio Italiano, *Stadio Italiano*, December 1944, 3.

74. "Pichangas," *Crack*, 10 June 1938, 10.

75. *Frente Popular*, 16 December 1938, 4.

76. *Audax*, July 1936.

77. *Frente Popular*, 22 December 1938.

78. *Audax*, December 1936, 7.

79. Ibid., May–June 1937.

80. Ibid., December 1936, 28.

81. Ibid.

82. Ibid., January 1937, 12.

83. Unión Española, *Bodas de Oro*.

84. Ibid., 5.

85. Presa, *Los Primeros Noventa Años del Círculo Español*.

86. "Nota Editorial," *Stadio Italiano*, January 1947, 1.

87. "Las Colonias y el Deporte," *Barra Brava*, 4 October 1943, 3.

88. Ibid., 14.

89. Unión Española, *Memoria* (1943).

90. *Bollettino Parrochiale*, April 1947, 2.

91. Mouat, *Cosas del Fútbol*, 53.

92. Asociación Central de Football, *Memoria*, 145.

93. Ibid., insert between pages 158 and 159. Employing judges who were also in public service bolstered the authority of the Chilean Football Federation and put players at a significant disadvantage in negotiations.

94. Olguín and Peña, *La Inmigración Árabe en Chile*. For more on Middle Eastern immigration to Latin America, see *Americas* 53 (July 1996), an issue dedicated to the topic, and Klich, "Argentine-Ottoman Relations and Their Impact on Immigrants from the Middle East."

95. Jewish and Muslim clubs existed, but there is much less material on their involvement in sports activities; see the *Anuario del K.K.L. de la Federación Sionista de Chile*. For historical context, see Masters, *Christians and Jews in the Ottoman Arab World*. Jewish civic associations focused on Israeli politics and less on local issues (see *Israel*, January 1959, 14). However, the Jewish community participated in basketball competitions (see the *Tribuna Judía*, 15 May 1953). Also, many Jewish immigrants joined European sports clubs; see Alvarez, "Judíos en Chile de 1930 a 1950," 19.

96. Palacios, *Raza Chilena*. The census of 1920 counted more than 4,000 Palestinans, Syrians, Turks, and Lebanese (Olguín and Peña, *La Inmigración Árabe*, 71).

97. Olguín and Peña, *La Inmigración Árabe*.

98. *El Mercurio*, 13 April 1911, 1.

99. Ibid.

100. Chuaqui, *Memorias de un Emigrante*.

101. Ibid., 413.

102. Ibid.

103. Ibid., 337.

104. *Mundo Árabe*, 16 October 1935, 1.

105. Chuaqui, *Memorias de un Emigrante*, 385.

106.   Sociedad de Beneficia, "Juventud Homsiense," *Estatutos*.

107.   "Elías Deik Nos Narra," *Los Sports*, 21 September 1928, 16.

108.   Ibid.

109.   Ibid.

110.   Club Palestino, *Estatutos*.

111.   Club Sírio Palestino, *Memoria*, 15.

112.   *El Mercurio,* September 20–30, 1931.

113.   Club Sirio Palestino, *Memoria*, 21.

114.   Mattar, *El Guía Social de la Colonia Árabe en Chile*. Mattar estimated that the Chilean Arab population comprised 6,590 Palestinians, 3,520 Syrians, 2,129 Lebanese, and assorted others for a total of 14,890, with nearly two-thirds of them residing in Santiago. Another internal study estimated that the population had grown to 25,000 by 1947 (*Pregones*, November 1947, 5).

115.   Mattar, *El Guía Social de la Colonia Árabe*.

116.   Ibid., 6.

117.   *El Orden*, 18 September 1943, 8.

118.   *El Imparcial*, 1 November 1938, 3.

119.   *El Orden*, 15 October 1943, 6.

120.   Club Sírio Palestino, *Memoria*.

121.   *Mundo Árabe*, 28 September 1935, 1.

122.   Ibid., 5 October 1935, 2.

123.   Ibid., 15 January 1952, 8. The Jewish community in Chile grew at a slower pace than in neighboring Argentina. The head of the Immigration Department, Robínson Alvarez, who was also the president of Colo Colo, was accused of extorting money from Jews fleeing the Holocaust. The investigation resulted in the suspension of Jewish immigration between 1941 and 1944 (*El Mercurio*, January 1940).

124.   *Mundo Árabe*, 31 January 1947, 1.

125.   Ibid., 20 August 1947, 2.

126.   Klich and Lesser, introduction, 7–8.

127.   Rebolledo, "La Integración de los Inmigrantes Arabes a la Vida Nacional."

128.   Pancho Alsina, "Estadio Sociales," *Estadio*, 24 September 1949, 14.

129.   Ibid.

130.   *El Siglo*, 5 February 1953, 7.

131.   *Suplemento Grafico de Oriente en el Microfono*, April 17, 1952, 2.

132.   Aguad, *El Deporte, Pasión de mi Vida*.

133.   Quoted in ibid., 150.

134.   Winn's *Weavers of the Revolution* is a brilliant study of the Yarur family, its anti-union policies, and the politics of the company's workers.

135.   ZZ Jr., "Sentido y Realidad el Estadio Arabe," *Suplemento Gráfico de Oriente en el Micrófono*, 17 April 1952, 2.

136.   Of Club Palestino's professional footballers, only José Sabaj was of Arab descent.

137.   *Suplemento Gráfico Oriente en el Micrófono*, 30 April 1953, 10.

138.   Empresa Periodística Chile, *Diccionario Biográfico de Chile*, 7th ed., 130.

139.   *Suplemento Gráfico Oriente en el Micrófono*, 30 April 1953.

140.   Ibid.

141.   "Elías Musalen e Hijos," *Tribuna Textil*, April 1951, 2.

142.   Ibid.

143.   "Migajas," *Estadio*, 24 September 1970, 50; "La Gran Sorpresa," *Estadio*, 6 May 1971, 49.

144.   *Mundo Árabe*, 27 November 1953, 13.

145.   Ibid., 13 November 1953, 4–5.

146.   The Yarurs were close to Alessandri and his finance minister, Gustavo Ross; see "Entrevistaron a Don Juan Yarur," *Mundo Árabe*, 20 February 1936, 1.

147.   Rebolledo, "La Integración de los Inmigrantes Arabes," 242.

148.   Bray, "The Political Emergence of Arab-Chileans, 1952–1958," 562.

149.   Ibid., 558.

150.   *Mundo Árabe*, 15 January 1952, 13.

151.   EAH, "Hinchas de Palestino," *Mundo Árabe*, 3 July 1953, 4.

152.   *Mundo Árabe*, 28 May 1954, 4–5.

153.   Ibid., 7 August 1952, 4.

154.   *Estadio*, 18 July 1958, 32.

155.   Ibid.

156.   Ibid., 20 April 1961, 22–23.

157.   Ibid., 22.

158.   Pancho Alsina, "Mucha Pasta, pero . . ." *Estadio*, 28 April 1951, 3.

CHAPTER FIVE

Portions of this chapter were first published in Elsey, "The Independent Republic of Football."

1.   Shaw, *The Social History of Brazilian Samba*; McCann, *Hello, Hello Brazil*.

2.   The Mexican wrestler El Santo contains some similar elements; see Rubenstein, "El Santo's Strange Career."

3.   Archetti, *Masculinities*.

4.   Bethell and Roxborough, *Latin America Between the Second World War and the Cold War*.

5.   Maldonado, "AChA y la Proscripción del Partido Comunista en Chile, 1946–1948."

6.   Elsey, "Promises of Participation." According to Ronald McDonald, Santiago represented around 30 percent of the national population by the mid-1960s, but it had only 10 percent of the senatorial representation. From 1947 through 1965, Presidents González, Ibáñez, and Alessandri postponed the publication of

census results that would have forced a redistricting in favor of working-class areas ("Apportionment and Party Politics in Santiago, Chile," 467).

7. This meant that at least one in four Chileans lived in the capital by the end of the 1950s (Collier and Sater, *A History of Chile, 1808–1994*).

8. A notable exception to this dearth of studies is *Tomando Su Sitio* by Mario Garcés. On the role of women in neighborhood organizations, see Schneider, "Mobilization at the Grassroots"; and Valdés, "El Movimiento de Pobladores, 1973–1985."

9. "La Cisterna y el Deporte," *La Tribuna*, 23 July 1950, 6.

10. Schild, "Recasting 'Popular' Movements," 64–65.

11. See Garcés, *Tomando Su Sitio*. On other iconography of the poor and working class, see Barr-Melej, "Cowboys and Constructions"; Klubock, *Contested Communities*; and Pinto, *Trabajos y Rebeldías en la Pampa Salitrera*.

12. Ibid.

13. Juan Moreira, "Oiga Comandante Kolbach," *Barra Brava*, 3 January 1944, 3.

14. Archetti, *Masculinities*; McKay, Messner, and Sabo, *Masculinities, Gender Relations, and Sport*.

15. *El Vocero*, 31 March 1946, 4.

16. On San Miguel's textile workers and class identity, see Winn, *Weavers of the Revolution*.

17. Patricio Piola de Andraca, Hernán Carvajal, and Jaime Nieto, interviews by the author, Santiago, December 2004.

18. Ramón, *Santiago de Chile*, 209.

19. *La Comuna* (San Miguel), 1 November 1947, 1.

20. Social scientists who surveyed shantytowns found that residents were not predominantly rural migrants, but families who had lived in urban settings at least ten years (Handelman, "The Political Mobilization of Urban Squatter Settlements").

21. *El Lucerno*, 21 November 1959, 4.

22. Ibid.

23. See *El Músculo*, 1950–1952, and *El Lucerno*, 1958–1959.

24. *El Músculo*, March 1950, 8.

25. Ibid.

26. *El Músculo*, February 1953, 7.

27. Ibid.

28. "Antecedentes . . . ," *Vida Obrera: Fanaloza Carrascal*, 15 January 1954, 1.

29. Ibid.

30. Ibid.

31. Klubock, *Contested Communities*; Miguel Silva, *Los Sindicatos, los Partidos y Clotario Blest*.

32. *El Músculo*, June 1953, 3.

33. "Informe de la Comisión," *CTCH*, January 1947, 8.

34. Ibid.

35. "La Asamblea de la Juventud Trabajadora," *Vida*, May 1955, 1.

36. "Estampas Sindicales," *CTCH*, February 1948, 2.

37. *Vida*, January 1956, 8.

38. *El Diario Ilustrado*, 23 November 1952, 18.

39. *El Siglo*, 28 April 1953, 7.

40. *La Tribuna* (Sector Sur), 15 October 1950, 2–5.

41. This conclusion is based on a review of newspapers, sports publications, and party documents; see, for example, Prado, *Reseña histórica del Partido Liberal*; *El Paleta* (Juventud Alessandrista) and *Vanguardia* (Juventud Liberal de Chile); and Partido Conservador, *XVI Convención Nacional*. See also Correa, *Con las Riendas del Poder*.

42. Palestro, *La República Independiente de San Miguel*.

43. The Palestro family guarded these certificates carefully. The intricacies of the diplomas are a testament to the affection members had for Palestro.

44. Palestro, *La República Independiente de San Miguel*.

45. Ibid., 111.

46. Concurso de Historias de Barrios de Santiago, *Voces de la Ciudad*; Palestro, *La República Independiente*, 108.

47. On spectatorship, see Santa Cruz, *Origen y Futuro de una Pasión*, and Iturriaga, "Aunque Ganas o Pierdas."

48. Palestro, *La República Independiente*, 110.

49. Ibid., 109.

50. Garcés, *Tomando Su Sitio*.

51. Identidad Grupos Memoria Popular, *Memorias de La Victoria*.

52. Ibid., 17.

53. Ibid.

54. *El Lucerno*, 19 December 1959, 8.

55. Ibid., 21 November 1959, 6.

56. Ibid.

57. *La Hora*, 5 May 1951, 8.

58. *Clarín de la Cisterna*, September 1952, 2.

59. *La Voz del Poblador*, 17 September 1953, 4.

60. Ibid.

61. *Boletín de Resoluciones de la Agrupación de Pobladores de Chile*, December 1957, 1.

62. Warner, *Publics and Counterpublics*.

63. *La Voz de las Barrancas*, November 1949, 3.

64. "El Dirigente Deportivo," *Sector Norte*, 9 September 1950, 5.

65. Only a fraction of the statutes of popular clubs still exist in their entirety; see, for example, Club Atenas, *Revista Aniversario*, and Club Deportivo Subercaseaux, *El Compañero*. A model for statutes was provided by the Asociación

Nacional de Football's *Estatutos y reglamentos de la Asociación Nacional de Fútbol Amateur*.

66.   *La Opinión de Conchalí*, September 1954, 5.

67.   Camara de Diputados, *Boletín de las Sesiones Ordinarias*, session 8, 20 October 1954, 499.

68.   *Clarinadas del Segundo Distrito*, 22 April 1961, 4.

69.   *La Opinión de Conchalí*, July 1954, 6.

70.   *La Voz de Conchalí*, May 1947, 6.

71.   Ibid., 5.

72.   Ibid., 6.

73.   *La Opinión de Conchalí*, August 1954, 2.

74.   *La Comuna*, 8 November 1958, 5.

75.   Maximiliano Salinas, "'¡En Tiempo de Chaya Nadie se Enoja!'"

76.   *El Siglo*, 12 June 1962, 1.

77.   *El Campeón*, 18 September 1959, 3.

78.   Cámara de Diputados, *Boletín de las Sesiones Ordinarias*, session 9, 3 July 1962, 1141.

79.   *Barra Brava*, 15 January 1945, 2.

80.   Ibid.

81.   ANFA reported 100,000 members. If accurate, this figure means that roughly 6.25 percent of adult male Chileans belonged to a club affiliated with the organization; see Asociación Nacional de Fútbol Amateur, *Congreso Nacional de Fútbol Amateur*. This is an estimate, since statistics for the adult male population were calculated in 1950 and classified as adults all males nineteen years or older (Instituto de Estadísticas Chile *Chile: Proyecciones y Estimaciones de Población*, 37). The number of footballers outside ANFA was higher, since many amateur clubs could not afford the dues for affiliation. As previously cited, in 1950, newspapers in San Miguel estimated that 40,000 men belonged to football clubs.

82.   *El Mercurio*, 21 February 1960.

83.   Jr., "Aficionados," *El Mercurio*, 24 June 1958, 3.

84.   Franco, *The Decline and Fall of the Lettered City*, 56.

85.   *Estadio*, 15 March 1962, 1.

86.   Pepe Nava, "Carta a un Viejo Lector," *Estadio*, 13 April 1956, 3.

87.   Ibid.

88.   Jr., "Aficionados," *El Mercurio*, 24 June 1958, 3.

89.   *El Siglo*, 2 February 1953, 1.

90.   Ibid., 6 February 1953, 4.

91.   Juventudes Comunistas de Chile, *Estatutos de las Juventudes Comunistas de Chile*.

92.   The radio program *Voice of Quinta Normal*, directed by Antonio Leiva from 1936 to 1960 on Radio Cervantes, was an exception (*El Campeón*, 25 October 1959, 10).

93.   *El Campeón*, 18 September 1959, 2.

94.   *El Siglo*, 20 June 1958, 11.

95.   *El Mercurio*, 31 December 1953, 23; *El Siglo*, 29 December 1952, 7.

96.   *La Nación*, 9 February 1949, 10.

97.   Club Colo Colo, *Historia del Club Colo-Colo*, 83.

98.   *Estadio*, 10 January 1953, 4.

99.   Klubock, *Contested Communities*, 186.

100.   Mouat, *Cosas del Fútbol*.

101.   Carlos Barahona, "José Donoso," *Barrabases*, 2 September 1958.

102.   Ticiano, "Figuras del Recuerdo," *Estadio*, 14 February 1953, 31.

103.   "El Fútbol Profesional Requiere una Vasta Reforma," *El Mercurio*, 21 February 1960.

104.   Pepe Nava, "Protipo del Sportsman," *Estadio*, 17 February 1951, 4.

105.   Ibid., 6.

106.   *El Mercurio*, 21 February 1960.

107.   *Sport i Actualidades*, 28 June 1912, 1. See also "Los Domingos," *Los Sports*, 23 November 1928, 8; and Intendencia Santiago, Archivo Nacional, *Comunicaciones Recibidas*, November–December 1928, vol. 627, no. 1681.

108.   Guido Vallejos, "Cuando Papa no Quiere," *Barrabases*, 13 June 1961.

109.   See *Barrabases*, 1959–1961; the publication was an affiliate of *Estadio* tailored to a younger audience.

110.   *Barrabases*, 14 July 1959.

111.   Ibid.

112.   *La Tribuna* (La Cisterna) 23 July 1950, 6.

113.   *La Opinión de Conchalí*, September 1954, 6.

114.   Cámara de los Diputados, *Boletín de las Sesiones Ordinarias*, session 27, July 1953, 1310–1312.

115.   *La Voz del Poblador*, December 1953, 1.

116.   *Gol y Gol*, 6 March 1963, 4.

117.   *Gol y Gol* was published by Zig-Zag from 1962 to 1969. It paid more attention to amateurs, women's football, and international competition than did *Estadio*.

118.   *Gol y Gol*, 15 May 1963, 4.

119.   *CTCH*, February 1949.

120.   *Estadio*, 10 October 1958, 1.

121.   *Estadio* was closely related to *El Mercurio*, whose involvement with right-wing parties and the CIA has been well documented; see Kornbluh, "The *El Mercurio* File."

122.   *Estadio*, 26 October 1956, 2.

123.   See, for example, *Gol y Gol*, 15 May 1963, 4.

124.   Ibid., 9 January 1963, 5. This is a suggestive letter; however, from what I was able to find out, only random attempts to organize women's football were made

before 1950. In interviews conducted in October 2004, ANFA directors recalled women's football beginning in the 1970s.

125.   MHS, "El Deporte en la Mujer," *Clarín de la Cisterna*, September 1952, 6.

126.   See coverage of the campaign to host the Cup in *Estadio*, June–July 1956.

127.   "Ernesto Alvear," *Estadio*, 30 Mayo 1972, 24.

128.   *Estadio*, 22 June 1956, 5.

129.   See, for example, Chamanto, "Es Difícil," *Estadio*, 8 June 1956, 3.

130.   *Estadio*, 22 June 1956, 5.

131.   Ibid.

132.   Chamanto, "Es Difícil," *Estadio*, 8 June 1956, 3.

133.   *Estadio*, 27 January 1956.

134.   Ibid., 30.

135.   Pancho Alsina, "Nacido Para el Fútbol," *Estadio*, 31 May 1957, 20.

136.   Hugo Sainz Torres, *Breve Historia del Deportes*.

137.   *Campeonato Mundial de Fútbol*, March 1961, 11.

138.   AVR, "El Contacto Humano," *Estadio*, 29 June 1956, 1.

139.   *Mundial de Fútbol* 2, December–January 1962, 72.

140.   Pancho Alsina, "Nacido Para el Fútbol," *Estadio*, 31 May 1957, 20.

141.   Don Pampa, "Frente a la Realidad," *Estadio*, 15 October 1959, 3.

142.   G. L., "La Mujer Chilena," *El Viaje*, May 1962, 55.

143.   Josafat Martínez, *Historia del Fútbol Chileno*, 12. There is no further information provided on this "prohibited match," and I have not found it referred to in any other sources.

144.   *El Siglo*, 29 May 1962.

145.   Ibid.

146.   Ibid.

147.   Goldblatt, *The Ball Is Round*, 427.

148.   *El Siglo*, 4 June 1962, 5.

149.   *Estadio*, 2 February 1961, 3.

150.   "El Campeonato Mundial de Futbol," *El Viaje*, May 1962, 4. To underscore the Alessandri administration's support for the Cup, Sótero del Río purchased 250 televisions to air the tournament around the country (*Campeonato Mundial de Fútbol*, 4 July 1961, 10).

151.   *Estadio*, 28 June 1962, 64.

152.   Jorge Alessandri, "Discurso del Presidente de la República en la Inauguración del Mundial de Fútbol," 1 (Departamento de Prensa, Archivo Medina).

153.   *El Siglo*, 11 June 1962, 2.

154.   Ibid., 3 June 1962, 13.

155.   Juan De Porte, "Cómo Cubrimos el Mundial," *El Siglo*, 24 June 1962, 12.

156.   *El Siglo,* 3 June 1962, 13.

157.   Ibid., 2 July 1962, 5.

158.   Ibid., 18 June 1962, 2.
159.   Ibid., 22 March 1962, 1.
160.   Ibid., 25 May 1962, 2.
161.   Ibid., 13 June 1960, 2.
162.   "Toro, Ídolo de Sus Padres y de los Cabros del Barrio," *El Siglo*, 30 May 1962, 5.
163.   Profesor Topaze, "Abramos los Ojos," *Topaze*, 15 June 1962, 5.
164.   *Estadio*, 30 May 1972, 24.
165.   Ibid., 16 March 1961, 32.
166.   *El Mercurio*, 5 March 1958, 15.
167.   Ibid., 21 March 1958, 21.
168.   Ibid.
169.   Lamilla, Andrade, and Prieto interviews.
170.   "Ernesto Alvear," *Estadio*, 22 October 1949, 2.
171.   Ibid.
172.   Asociación Nacional de Fútbol Amateur, *Congreso Nacional de Fútbol Amateur*, 11.

CHAPTER SIX

1.   "Chile on the Tightrope," *New York Times*, August 27, 1970, 34.
2.   Ibid.
3.   "Un Diagnostico," *Estadio*, 21 May 1970, 4.
4.   Salazar and Pinto, *Historia Contemporánea de Chile*, 1:67.
5.   Moulian, *Chile Actual*; Scully, *Rethinking the Center*.
6.   Angell, "Chile since 1958," 158.
7.   Ibid., 167. The prominent sociologist Tomás Moulian argued that the political system collapsed in part because the UP proposed a drastic revision of society with at best 43 percent of people's support (Moulian, "La vía chilena al socialismo").
8.   Prothro and Chaparro, "Public Opinion and the Movement of Chilean Government to the Left, 1952–1972."
9.   See, for example, "La juventud de un mundo en crisis," *El Mercurio*, 19 March 1967, 3.
10.   Salazar and Pinto, *Historia Contemporánea de Chile*, vol. 5.
11.   The MIR was formed primarily by students. It supported a policy of armed struggle rather than electoral politics. For a history of the group, see Naranjo et al., *Miguel Enríquez*.
12.   "John y Yoko," *El Siglo*, 7 February 1970, 4.
13.   "Reinas Trabajadoras," *El Siglo*, 26 February 1970, 10.
14.   Winn, *Weavers of the Revolution*, 34.
15.   *Alerta* (JDC [Juventud Demócrata Cristiana]), January 1966, 6.

16.   Salazar and Pinto, *Historia Contemporánea de Chile*, vol. 5.

17.   Jaime Nieto C. and Aníbal Andrede E., interviews by the author, 15 December 2004, Santiago.

18.   Journalists complained of high ticket prices for these matches (*Gol y Gol*, 21 August 1963, 2).

19.   "Migajas," *Estadio*, 12 March 1970, 50.

20.   Young political leaders mobilized to host international meetings, such as the 1964 Congreso Latinoamericano de Juventudes.

21.   Certainly the term "movement" indicates far more cohesion and organization than existed (Barr-Melej, "Revolución y Liberación del Ser").

22.   "Juventud Rebelde," *El Siglo*, 6 July 1969, 15.

23.   "Deporte Entusisma," *La Nueva Aurora*, 14 May 1961, 7.

24.   See, for example, *Barrabases*, 14 July 1959 and 2 September 1958.

25.   Ibid., 20 October 1959.

26.   *Vea*, 13 April 1967, 1.

27.   "La Pobladora Chilena entra en Escena," *Vea*, 13 April 1967, 5.

28.   *Vea*, 13 April 1967, 38.

29.   Ibid., 65–66.

30.   "Mala Senda," *Barrabases*, 18 April 1961.

31.   Carlos Barhahona, "La Vida de Fernando Navarro," *Barrabases*, 10 January 1961.

32.   Mr. Huifa, "Nace un Club de Fútbol," *Barrabases*, 15 July 1959.

33.   Ibid.

34.   Guido Vallejos, "Cuando Papa no Quiere," *Barrabases*, 13 June 1961.

35.   Ibid.

36.   Don Gonzalo, "Bellos Horizontes," *Barrabases*, 29 December 1959.

37.   Ibid.

38.   Ibid.

39.   Sergio Brotfeld, "Así los Veo Yo," *Ritmo*, 1970, 32–33.

40.   "Carlos Caszely Apoya a Gladys Marin," *El Siglo*, 25 February 1973, 9.

41.   *El Siglo*, 25 November 1967, 10.

42.   *El Campeón*, January 1960, 2.

43.   Ibid.

44.   Don Gonzalo, "Once Corazones," *Barrabases*, 20 October 1959.

45.   *Ritmo*, 21 September 1965, 18.

46.   Brotfeld, "Así los Veo Yo."

47.   *Ferrobadminton*, December 1963, 3.

48.   *Alerta* (JDC), January 1966, 6.

49.   *Triunfo Popular*, 30 April 1970, 14. Specifically, they targeted Palestro's support for clubs.

50.   Senado, *Sesiones Extraordinarias del Senado, 1967–1968*, special session 1, 41.

51.   Senado, *Diario de Sesiones del Senado*, session 41, 9 August 1966, 2816–2817.

52.   Ibid., 2817.

53.   Ibid., 2816–2817.

54.   Ibid.

55.   Ibid., 2818.

56.   "Proyecto del Deportes Lesivo al Interés Nacional," *El Siglo*, 7 August 1969, 11.

57.   "El Martes," *Estadio*, 15 July 1971, 18. See the Commission to revise law of professional football. The committee included Juan de Dios Carmona (DC), Jose Musalem (DC), Alberto Jerez (Izquierda Cristiana), Aguirre Doolan (PR), and Fernando Ochagavia (PN).

58.   Rolle, *1973*, 18.

59.   Albornoz, "Cultura en la Unidad Popular."

60.   *El Siglo*, 4 September 1970.

61.   "Estás al Tanto de la Moda Hippie?" *Ritmo*, 4 June 1968, 56–57; "Firme de los Bric a Brac," *Ritmo*, 9 April 1968.

62.   For example, in 1967 at a well-known café, a group of *normales* attacked a group of *rockeros*, forcibly cutting their hair (Salazar and Pinto, *Historia Contemporánea de Chile*, 5:157).

63.   "Del Año que le Piden," *La Cacerola*, November 1972, no. 1, 2–3.

64.   Quoted in Gaudichaud, *Poder Popular y Cordones Industriales*.

65.   Unidad Popular, *Programa Basico de Gobierno de la Unidad Popular*.

66.   Ibid., 15.

67.   The Socialist Youth sent groups across the country. Whereas men were encouraged to travel, women were advised to stay close to home (Eliana Espinoza and Mafalda Galdames, interviews by the author, 23 December 2004, Santiago).

68.   *Central Unica*, July–August 1971, 8.

69.   Ibid., 29.

70.   Ibid.

71.   Garcés, "Construyendo 'Las Poblaciones.'"

72.   Ibid., 72.

73.   Ibid.

74.   *El Siglo*, 12 October 1971, 2.

75.   Power, *Right-Wing Women in Chile*.

76.   Barr-Melej, *Psychedelic Chile*.

77.   Marbleu, *El Futbol*.

78.   Ibid., 68.

79.   Ibid.

80.   Juan Carlos Ossandon, "Sexo y Civilizacion," *Tizona*, September 1969, 4.

81.   Ibid.

82.   "El Problema de la Juventud," *Patria y Libertad* 1 (1972): 5.

83.   "Fútbol Rentado Intenta Desbancar a la ANFA," *El Siglo*, 26 July 1970, 11.

84.   "Renuncia Diplomatica," *Estadio*, 13 August 1970, 22.

85.   *A Toda Maquina*, November–December 1969, 7. The president of the bus owners' union was also the president of the professional football club Santiago Morning.

86.   Senado, *Sesiones Extraordinarias del Senado, 1966–1967*, special session 19, 8 November 1966, 1312.

87.   "ANDABA vs. ANFA," *Estadio*, 24 October 1972, 51.

88.   *El Siglo*, 15 February 1970, 11.

89.   "Según Pasan las Cosas," *Estadio*, 25 May 1972, 18.

90.   Ibid.

91.   For an analysis of how conservatives attacked women's participation in these groups, see Power, *Right-Wing Women in Chile*.

92.   "Dice Marta Godoy," *El Siglo*, 20 June 1971, 14.

93.   "Unión Condell," *El Siglo*, 13 April 1970, 11.

94.   See, for example, *La Cacerola* 1, October 1972.

95.   Quoted in Henfrey and Sorj, *Chilean Voices*, 65.

96.   "Mujeres Tambien se Dieron Festin de Goles," *El Siglo*, 23 November 1972, 15.

97.   "Club Deportivo 'Estrella Verde,'" *El Vecino*, November 1971, 2.

98.   "Plan Sexenal Deportivo," *El Siglo*, 18 October 1971, 11.

99.   "En el Estadio," *El Siglo*, 15 May 1971, 12.

100.   Jaime Adaro, "Es Necesario Terminar con el Futbol Profesional?" *El Siglo*, 18 Mayo 1971, 12.

101.   "En el Estadio," *El Siglo*, 15 May 1971, 12.

102.   Jaime Adaro, "Fueron Provocadores los que Actuaron el Miercoles?" *El Siglo*, 15 May 1971, 12.

103.   Adaro, "Es Necesario Terminar con el Futbol Profesional?"

104.   Senado, *Sesión extraordinaria, 1972–1972*, special session 30, 16 November 1971, 1153–1173.

105.   Carrasco attended the School of the Americas in 1961 and later served as minister of defense (1982–1983) during the dictatorship of Augusto Pinochet.

106.   Senado, *Sesión extraordinaria, 1972–1972*, special session 30, 16 November 1971, 1154.

107.   "Fabrica de Articulos Deportivos Está Comenzando a Producer," *El Siglo*, 23 June 1972, 12; "Implementos Deportivos Made in Chile," *Estadio*, 22 August 1972, 52.

108.   " 'Yo Hago Deporte,' " *El Siglo*, 6 August 1972, 16.

109.   "Yo Hago Deporte Salió a la Calle," *Estadio*, 8 August 1972, 8–9.

110.   "Los Ceros no Respondieron al 'Yo Hago Deporte,'" *Estadio*, 24 October 1972, 15.

111.   "Incorporación de los Trabajadores a la Práctica Activa del Deporte," *El Siglo*, 10 January 1973.

112.   Ibid.

113.   *El Siglo*, 26 June 1972, 1.

114.   "Una Realidad de Fantasía," *Estadio*, 16 January 1973, 48–49.

115.   Ibid.

116.   *Estadio*, 15 August 1972, 43.

117.   Ibid., 26 September 1972.

118.   Ibid.

119.   Ibid., 29 August 1972, 17.

120.   See Iturriaga, "Proletas, Limpios, Cobardes y Burgueses."

121.   *Futbol: Revista Oficial del Sindicato de Futbolistas Profesionales* 1 (1967).

122.   Tio, "Conciencia Gremial," *El Siglo*, 27 November 1971, 12.

123.   "La Declaración con Interpretación Necesaria," *Estadio*, 20 August 1970, 22.

124.   "Jugadores Profesionales Agradecen Promulgacion de Ley de Previsión," *El Siglo*, 7 June 1972, 12.

125.   "Carlos Caszely Apoya a Gladys Marín," *El Siglo*, 25 February 1973, 9.

126.   "Demepelota," *El Siglo*, 13 December 1969, 11.

127.   Edgardo Marín, "No se Trabaja por Ley," *Estadio*, 28 October 1971, 35.

128.   *Estadio*, 28 October 1971, 37.

129.   "A Nuestros Lectores," *Estadio*, 4 March 1971, 3.

130.   *Estadio*, 5 September 1972, 42.

131.   See for example, R. Durney, "Fútbol y Yo," *Estadio*, 17 October 1971, 22.

132.   Ibid.

133.   "No Solo de Deportes Vive el Hombre," *Estadio*, 18 November 1971, 17.

134.   "Conozca Su Deporte," *Estadio*, 15 July 1971, 42.

135.   Edgardo Marín, "Somos que los Somos," 12 August 1971, 35.

136.   "Aquí," *Estadio*, 20 June 1972, 19.

137.   Manns, *Grandes Deportistas*, 43–44.

138.   Ibid., 7–8.

139.   Ibid., 15.

140.   Ibid., 16.

141.   Ibid., 62; see Manns's biography of Ismenia Pauchard, a basketball player and worker for Banco del Estado.

142.   "Fútbol y Política," *El Siglo*, 25 June 1969, 2.

143.   Ibid.

144.   Lautaro Pérez, "Lo que Pasa de Moda," *El Siglo*, 23 July 1969, 11.

145.   "Profesionalismo del Deporte," *El Siglo*, 25 October 1971, 11.

146.   "Redistribución de Fondos de la Ley no. 17.652," *El Siglo*, 8 June 1972, 12.

147.   Luis Figueroa, "Opiniones del Presidente de la CUT," *Central Unica*, February 1972, 15.

148.   Ibid.

149.   "El Huevo de Oro," *Puro Chile*, 16 May 1970, 7.

150.   "Cultura y Expansión," *Central Unica*, October–November 1971, 23.

151.   *Central Unica*, 5 September 1972, 16-17.

152.   "Cultura y Expansión," *Central Unica*.

153.   Quoted in Gaudichaud, *Poder Popular y Cordones Industriales*, 165.

154.   Movimiento de Acción Popular Unitario, *El Primer Año del Gobierno Popular and el Segundo Año del Gobierno Popular*, 23.

155.   Quoted in Henfrey and Sorj, *Chilean Voices*, 140.

156.   Quoted in ibid., 69.

157.   Quoted in ibid., 134.

158.   Ibid.

159.   Gaudichaud, *Poder Popular y Cordones Industriales*.

160.   Quoted in ibid., 128.

161.   Ibid.

EPILOGUE

1.   The military junta formally exiled some, but the majority chose to leave the country, many of whom feared government reprisals (Comisión Nacional de Verdad y Reconciliación, *Informe de la Comisión Nacional de Verdad y Reconciliación*).

2.   *Tortura en Poblaciones del Gran Santiago (1973–1990)*; and Cozzi, *Estadio Nacional*.

3.   *Chile Update: Bulletin of the Chile Committee for Human Rights*, April 1985, 15.

4.   "Revitalizan Legado de Victor Jara," *La Nación*, 11 September 2003, 4.

5.   Quoted in Gaudichaud, *Poder Popular y Cordones Industriales*, 297.

6.   *El Siglo*, 29 June 1973, 15.

7.   Bernardotte, "!Cuidado Brigada Ramona Parra!" *Patria y Libertad* 1, 1972, 10.

8.   *El Siglo*, 20 October 1972, 2.

9.   "Carlos Caszely Apoya a Gladys Marín," *El Siglo*, 25 February 1973, 3.

10.   *Estadio*, 11 September 1973.

11.   *Estadio*, 9 October 1973, 45.

12.   Quoted in Goldblatt, *The Ball Is Round*, 609.

13.   Alex Yannis, "Soccer Storm Brewing in Soviet Bloc," *New York Times*, 4 November 1973.

14.   Ibid.

15.   *Estadio*, 13 November 1973, 54-56.

16.   "No Rubles for Chile Soccer," *New York Times*, 11 January 1974.

17.   Geoffrey Green, "Chile May Yet Move the World Cup Match," *London Times*, 12 November 1973.

18.   Personal communication with the founders of SAK-JUR, Wolfgang Kraushaar (October 2009) and Stefan Saarbach (January 2010).

19.   Kraushaar, "'¡Chile Sí, Junta No!'" The original plan of the Chile Solidarity Committee was to coordinate actions with Joseph Martin "Joschka" Fischer's Putzgruppe, but the future minister rejected the idea (Kraushaar, personal communication with the author, 8 October 2009).

20.   Goldblatt, *The Ball Is Round*; Kraushaar, "'¡Chile Sí, Junta No!'"

21.   The letter accompanied a pamphlet that the football representatives were instructed to distribute (*El Mercurio*, 2 June 1974, 35; page number partially damaged). Unfortunately I have not been able to locate a copy of the pamphlet, only references to its existence.

22.   Ramírez Banda, "'Dudas que Matan' en Equipos Sudamericanos," *El Mercurio*, 1 June 1974, 7.

23.   See, for example, "Tenso Enfrentamiento con La Prensa Tuvo Selección Chilena," *El Mercurio*, 12 June 1974, 10.

24.   "Chilenos Son Criticados," *El Mercurio*, 13 June 1974, 4.

25.   Iturriaga, "Proletas, Limpios, Cobardes y Burgueses," 297.

26.   Ibid., 343.

27.   *El Mercurio*, 7 June 1974, 8.

28.   Ibid., 17 June 1974, 5.

29.   Juan de Onis, "Chileans Absorbed by Soccer Lottery," *New York Times*, 19 May 1979.

30.   *Chile Antifascista* (Berlin), May 1975, 2.

31.   Winn, *Victims of the Chilean Miracle*, 19–20.

32.   *Chile Antifascista*, May 1975, 2.

33.   Ibid.

34.   Quoted in Gaudichaud, *Poder Popular y Cordones Industriales*, 129.

35.   Schneider, *Shantytown Protest in Pinochet's Chile*, 3–4.

36.   Kaplan, *Taking Back the Streets*, 77.

37.   Ibid., 17.

38.   Ibid., 95–96.

39.   Ibid.

40.   "Revista del Campeonato de los Barrios 1978–1979," *La Cancha* (Rancagua), December 1978, 2.

41.   "Día Internacional de la Mujer," *Boletín de la Vicaría de Solidaridad*, March 1978, no. 2, 10.

42.   Treasurer of ANFA, interview with the author.

43.   Yankelevich, *En México, entre Exilios*.

44.   Telephone interviews conducted by author in September and October 2009 under conditions of anonymity.

45.   Anonymous source, interview with the author, 19 October 2009, Santiago, Chile.

46.   Carlos Carrera, "Colo-colo, la pasión de Piñe," *El Economista*, 19 January 2010.

47.   Willy Haltenhoff, "La Gente No Sabe Qué Pasó en el Estadio Nacional el '73," *La Nación*, 8 October 2000, 40.

48.   Stern, *Battling for Hearts and Minds*.

49.   Frazier, *Salt in the Sand*, 124–127, 136–137.

50.   Ríos, Godoy, and Guerrero, *Un Nuevo Silencio Feminista?* 141–143.

51.   Mirko Macari, "De Qué Democracia Nos Hablan!" *La Nación*, 4 September 2004, 9–11.

52.   In addition, increases in personal debt and aggressive methods of debt collection have placed strains on working-class communities. On political distrust, see Posner, "Popular Representation and Political Dissatisfaction in Chile's New Democracy." On the prevalence of depression, see Araya et al., "Common Mental Disorders in Santiago, Chile."

53.   See Paley, *Marketing Democracy*, especially Chapter 4.

54.   Paley, "Making Democracy Count," 137.

55.   Alfredo Joignant, "La Legitimidad Electoral en Cuestión," *La Segunda*, 7 January 2009; Joignant, *Los Enigmas de la Comunidad Perdida*.

BIBLIOGRAPHY

Adelman, Jeremy. "Latin American Longues Durées." *Latin America Research Review* 39, no. 1 (February 2004): 223-237.

Aguad Kunkar, Sabino. *El Deporte, Pasión de Mi Vida.* [no publication information; copy in the National Library, Santiago, Chile]

Aguirre Cerda, Pedro. *Defensa de la Raza, 1939-1941.* [Reel 139, pamphlet 244, Latin American and Iberian Pamphlets, Library of Congress, Washington D.C.]

———. *El Problema Industrial.* Santiago: Universidad de Chile, 1933.

Albornoz, César. "Cultura en la Unidad Popular: Porque Esta Vez no se Trata de Cambiar un Presidente." In Pinto, *Cuando Hicimos Historia*, 147-176.

Alvarez, María José. "Judíos en Chile de 1930 a 1950." Thesis, Pontificia Universidad Católica, Santiago, 1996.

Alvarez, Rolando. "La Matanza de Coruña." *Contribuciones Científicas y Tecnológicas* 116 (November 1997): 77-108.

Aman, Kenneth, and Cristián Parker, eds. *Popular Culture in Chile: Resistance and Survival.* Boulder, Colo.: Westview, 1991.

Anderson, Benedict. *Imagined Communities: Reflections on the Origin and Spread of Nationalism.* London and New York: Verso, 1983.

Angell, Alan. "Chile since 1958." In *Chile since Independence*, edited by Leslie Bethell, 129-202. Cambridge: Cambridge Univ. Press, 1993.

Anuario del K.K.L. de la Federación Sionista de Chile. Santiago: Smirnow, 1945.

Applebaum, Nancy. "Post-Revisionist Scholarship on Race." *Latin American Research Review* 40 (2005): 206-217.

Appelbaum, Nancy, Karin Rosemblatt, and Peter Wade, eds. *Race and Nation in Modern Latin America.* Chapel Hill: Univ. of North Carolina Press, 2003.

Arancibia, Héctor. *La Doctrina Radical: Programa de Gobierno* Santiago: Antares, 1937.

Araya, Ricardo, Graciela Rojas, Rosemarie Fritsch, Julia Acuña, and Glyn Lewis. "Common Mental Disorders in Santiago, Chile: Prevalence and Socio-Demographic Correlates." *British Journal of Psychiatry* 178 (2001): 228-233.

Arbena, Joseph. *Latin American Sport: An Annotated Bibliography, 1988–1998.* Westport, Conn.: Greenwood, 1999.

Archetti, Eduardo. *Masculinities: Football, Polo, and Tango in Argentina.* Oxford: Berg, 1999.

Arellano, Alberto. *David Arellano Moraga: El Deportista Martír.* Santiago: Atenas, 1929.

Arminó, Claudio. "La Hora Negra." *La Federación Obrera,* 22 August 1921.

Armstrong, Gary, Richard Guilianotti, and Nicole Toulis, eds. *Entering the Field: New Perspectives on World Football.* Oxford: Berg, 1997.

Asad, Talal *Formations of the Secular: Christianity, Islam, Modernity.* Stanford, Calif.: Stanford Univ. Press, 2003.

Asociación Central de Football. *Memoria, 1933–1941.* Santiago: América, 1942.

Asociación Nacional de Football. *Congreso Nacional de Fútbol Amateur.* Santiago: San Diego, 1953.

———. *Estatutos y Reglamentos de la Asociación Nacional de Fútbol Amateur.* Santiago: Imparcial, 1954.

Audax: Revista mensual, deportiva y social/Audax Club Sportivo Italiano [monthly magazine]. Santiago: El Club, 1936–1954.

Baggio, Luciano, and Paolo Massone. *Presencia Italiana en Chile.* Santiago: Presenza, 1996.

Baer, James, and Ronn Pineo, eds. *Cities of Hope: People, Protests, and Progress in Urbanizing Latin America, 1870–1930.* Boulder: Westview, 1998.

Barnard, Andrew. "Chile." In *Latin America between the Second World War and the Cold War,* edited by Leslie Bethell and Ian Roxborough. Cambridge: Cambridge Univ. Press, 1992.

Barr-Melej, Patrick. "Cowboys and Constructions: Nationalist Representations of Pastoral Life in Post-Portalian Chile." *Journal of Latin American Studies* 30 (1998): 35–61.

———. *Psychedelic Chile.* Chapel Hill: Univ. of North Carolina Press, forthcoming.

———. *Reforming Chile: Cultural Politics, Nationalism, and the Rise of the Middle Class.* Chapel Hill: Univ. of North Carolina Press, 2001.

———. "Revolución y Liberación del Ser: Apuntes sobre el Origen e Ideología de un Movimiento contracultural Esotérico durante el Gobierno de Salvador Allende, 1970–1973." *Nuevo Mundo Mundos Nuevos,* 18 May 2007. http://nuevomundo .revues.org/document6057.html (accessed 1 October 2007).

———. "Sowing 'Seeds of Goodness' in Depression-Era Chile: Politics, the 'Social Question,' and the Labor Ministry's Cultural Extension Department." *Americas* 59 (2003): 537–558.

Bauer, Arnold. *Goods, Power, History: Latin America's Material Culture.* New York: Cambridge Univ. Press, 2001.

Bederman, Gail. *Manliness and Civilization.* Chicago: Univ. of Chicago Press, 1995.

Bengoa, José. *Historia del Pueblo Mapuche.* Santiago: LOM, 2000.

Berrios, Mario, ed. *El Pensamiento en Chile, 1830–1910*. Santiago: Nuestra América, 1987.

Bethell, Leslie, ed. *Chile since Independence*. Cambridge: Cambridge Univ. Press, 1993.

Bethell, Leslie, and Ian Roxborough, eds. *Latin America between the Second World War and the Cold War*. Cambridge: Cambridge Univ. Press, 1992.

Betteley, Alfredo. "Nuestro Deporte Es un Edificio sin Cimientos." *Boletín de Educación Física* 10 (1943): 22.

Biblioteca del Almanaque. *El Fútbol*. Santiago: Lord Cochrane, 1974.

Bliss, Katherine, and William French. *Gender, Sexuality, and Power in Latin America since Independence*. Lanham, Md.: Rowman and Littlefield, 2006.

Bloom, John, and Michael Nevin Willard, eds. *Sports Matters: Race, Recreation, and Culture*. New York: New York Univ. Press, 2002.

Boizard, Ricardo. *Hacia el Ideal Político de una Juventud*. Santiago: Nascimento, 1931.

Bolívar, Simón. "The Jamaica Letter." In *People and Issues in Latin American History*, edited by Lewis Hanke and Jane Rausch, 15–24. Princeton, N.J.: Weiner, 2006.

Bourdieu, Pierre. *The Logic of Practice*. Translated by Richard Nice. Stanford, Calif.: Stanford Univ. Press, 1990.

——. *Outline of a Theory of Practice*. Translated by Richard Nice. Cambridge: Cambridge Univ. Press, 1977.

——. "The Social Space and the Genesis of Groups." *Theory and Society* 14 (1985): 723–744.

——. "Sport and Social Class." *Social Science Information* 17 (1978): 819–840.

Bray, Donald W. "The Political Emergence of Arab-Chileans, 1952–1958." *Journal of Inter-American Studies* 4 (October 1962): 557–562.

Bryce, James. *South America: Observations and Impressions*. New York: Macmillan, 1912.

Cadena, Marisol de la. *Indigenous Mestizos: The Politics of Race and Culture in Cuzco, Peru, 1919–1991*. Durham, N.C.: Duke Univ. Press, 2000.

Cámara de Diputados. *Boletín de las Sesiones Ordinarias*. Santiago: Nacional.

Caviedes, Victoria. "Los Ejercicios Corporales i Los Juegos." *Revista de la Asociación Educación Nacional* 1 (December 1905–1906): 259–260.

Centeno, Miguel-Angel, and Fernando López-Alves, eds. *The Other Mirror: Grand Theory through the Lens of Latin America*. Princeton, N.J.: Princeton Univ. Press, 2001.

Chalo [pseud.]. *Crónicas del Campeonato Sudamericano de Fútbol de 1920*. Santiago: Talleres Gráficos, 1920.

Chilean Who's Who. Santiago: Nascimento, 1937.

Chuaqui, Benedicto. *Memorias de un Emigrante*. Santiago: Orbe, 1942.

Club Atenas. *Revista Aniversario*. Santiago: La Nación, 1958.

Club Colo Colo. *Estatutos y Reglamentos*. Santiago: Electra, 1930.

———. *Historia del Club Colo-Colo*. Santiago: Deportivas, 1953.

Club de Deportes Green Cross. *Estatutos y Reglamentos*. Santiago: Imparcial, 1940.

Club Deportivo Subercaseaux. *El Compañero*. San Miguel, Chile: Club, 1948.

Club Palestino. *Estatutos*. Santiago: Cervantes, 1940.

Club Sírio Palestino. *Memoria*. Santiago: La Reforma, 1933.

Club Social y Deportivo "Magallanes." *43° Anniversario*. Santiago: La Unión, 1940.

Collier, Simon, and William Sater. *A History of Chile, 1808–1994*. New York: Cambridge Univ. Press, 1996.

Comisión Nacional de Verdad y Reconciliación. *Informe de la Comisión Nacional de Verdad y Reconciliación: Versión Oficial*. Mexico City: La Casa de Chile en México, 1991.

Concurso de Historias de Barrios de Santiago, ed. *Voces de la Ciudad*. Santiago: LOM, 1999.

Consejo Nacional de Deportes. *Memoria del Consejo Nacional de Deportes*. Santiago: La Crítica, 1942.

Correa, Sofia. *Con las Riendas del Poder: La Historia de la Derecha Chilena en el Siglo XX*. Santiago: Sudamericana, 2005.

Correa, Sofia, Alfredo Jocelyn-Holt, Claudio Rolle, and Manuel Vicuña. *Historia del Siglo XX Chileno*. Santiago: Sudamericana, 2001.

Costa, Ángel, *Nirvana: Estudios Sociales, Politicos y Económicos*. Montevideo: Dornaleche y Reyes, 1899.

Cozzi, Adolfo. *Estadio Nacional*. Santiago: Sudamericana, 2000.

DeShazo, Peter. *Urban Workers and Labor Unions in Chile, 1902–1927*. Madison: Univ. of Wisconsin Press, 1988.

Diccionario Biográfico de Chile. 4th ed. Santiago: La Nación, 1942.

Dimeo, Paul. "'With Political Pakistan in the Offing . . .': Football and Communal Politics in South Asia, 1887–1947." *Journal of Contemporary History* 38 (July 2003): 377–394.

Dirección Jeneral de Educación Primaria. *Lei No. 3,654 sobre Educación Primaria Obligatoria*. Santiago: Lagunas, 1921.

Drake, Paul. "The Chilean Socialist Party and Coalition Politics, 1932–1946." *Hispanic American Historical Review* 53 (1973): 619–643.

———. "Corporatism and Functionalism in Modern Chilean Politics." *Journal of Latin American Studies* 10 (1978): 83–116.

———. *Socialism and Populism in Chile, 1932–1952*. Urbana: Univ. of Illinois Press, 1978.

Drapkin, Jaime. *Historia de Colo Colo*. 1952. [no place of publication or publisher given]

Dreyfus, Herbert, and Paul Rabinow. *Michel Foucault: Beyond Structuralism and Hermeneutics*. Chicago: Univ. of Chicago Press, 1982.

Drinot, Paolo. "Madness, Neurasthenia, and 'Modernity': Medico-Legal and Popular Interpretations of Suicide in Early Twentieth-Century Lima." *Latin American Research Review* 39 (2004): 89–113.

Eagleton, Terry. *The Idea of Culture*. Oxford: Blackwell, 2000.

Echevarria, V. "Chile." *Journal of Comparative Legislation and International Law* 2 (1920): 173.

Edwards, Alberto. *La Fronda Aristocrática en Chile*. Santiago: Nacional, 1928.

Edwards, Bob, Michael Foley, and Mario Diani, eds. *Beyond Tocqueville: Civil Society and the Social Capital Debate in Comparative Perspective*. Hanover, N.H.: Univ. of New England Press, 2001.

Elias, Norbert, and Eric Dunning. *Quest for Excitement: Sport and Leisure in the Civilizing Process*. Oxford: Blackwell, 1986.

Eliasoph, Nina. *Avoiding Politics: How Americans Produce Apathy in Everyday Life*. Cambridge: Cambridge Univ. Press, 1998.

Elsey, Brenda. "The Independent Republic of Football: The Politics of Neighborhood Clubs in Santiago, Chile, 1948–1960." *Journal of Social History* 42 (Spring 2009): 605–630.

———. "Promises of Participation: The Politics of Football Clubs in Chile, 1909–1962." PhD diss., State Univ. of New York, Stony Brook, 2007.

Empresa Periodística Chile. *Diccionario Biográfico de Chile*. Santiago: Periodística, 1938.

———. *Diccionario Biográfico de Chile*. 7th edition. Santiago: Periodística, 1951.

Encina, Francisco. *Historia de Chile*. Vol. 3. Santiago: Nascimento, 1970.

Euben, J. Peter. *Corrupting Youth: Political Education, Democratic Culture, and Political Theory*. Princeton, N.J.: Princeton Univ. Press, 1997.

Fernandez, Carlos. "De Educación Nacional." *Revista de la Asociación de Educación Nacional* 1 (September 1905): 120-121.

Fernández, Marcos. "Las Comunidades de la Sobriedad: La Instalación de Zonas Secas como Método de Control del Beber Inmoderado en Chile, 1910–1930." *Scripta Nova* 9, no. 194 (August 2005): item 59. http://www.ub.es/geocrit/sn /sn-194-59.htm (accessed 2 June 2006).

Ferrocarriles del Estado. *Reglamento General de Deportes*. Santiago: Ferrocarriles del Estado, 1925.

Finn, Gerry, and Richard Giulianotti, eds. *Football Culture: Local Contests, Global Visions*. London: Cass, 2000.

Flores, Enrique, and Pancho Serrano. *Guillermo Saavedra Tapia*. Santiago: Alfonsiana, 1957.

Forment, Carlos. *Democracy in Latin America, 1760–1900*. Chicago: Univ. of Chicago Press, 2003.

———. "The Democratic Dribbler: Football Clubs, Neoliberal Globalization, and Buenos Aires' Municipal Election of 2003." *Public Culture* 19 (2007) 85–116.

Foucault, Michel. *The History of Sexuality*. Vol. 1, *An Introduction*. New York: Vintage, 1990.

Franco, Jean. *The Decline and Fall of the Lettered City*. Cambridge, Mass.: Harvard Univ. Press, 2002.

Fraser, Nancy. "Rethinking the Public Sphere: A Contribution to the Critique of Actually Existing Democracy." In *Habermas and the Public Sphere*, edited by Craig Calhoun, 109–142. Cambridge, Mass.: MIT Press, 1990.

Frazier, Lessie Jo. *Salt in the Sand: Memory, Violence, and the Nation-State in Chile, 1890 to the Present*. Durham, N.C.: Duke Univ. Press, 2007.

Garcés, Mario. "Construyendo 'Las Poblaciones': Movimiento de Pobladores durante la Unidad Popular." In Pinto, *Cuando Hicimos Historia*, 57–79.

———. *Tomando Su Sitio: El Movimiento de Pobladores de Santiago, 1957–1970*. Santiago: LOM, 2002.

García-Bryce, Iñigo. "Politics by Peaceful Means: Artisan Mutual Aid Societies in Mid-Nineteenth-Century Lima." *Americas* 59 (2003): 325–345.

Garrigó, Roque. *America para los Americanos*. New York: Garrick, 1910.

Garza, Rodolfo de la, and Muserref Yetim. "The Impact of Ethnicity and Socialization on Definitions of Democracy: The Case of Mexican Americans and Mexicans." *Mexican Studies/Estudios Mexicanos* 19 (Winter 2003): 81–104.

Gaudichaud, Franck. *Poder Popular y Cordones Industriales: Testimonios sobre el Movimiento Popular Urbano*. Santiago: LOM, 2004.

Gazmuri, Cristián. *El "48" Chileno*. Santiago: Universitaria, 1992.

Germani, Gino. *Authoritarianism, Fascism, and National Populism*. New Brunswick, N.J.: Transaction, 1978.

Giddens, Anthony. *Modernity and Self-Identity: Self and Society in the Late Modern Age*. Stanford, Calif.: Stanford University Press, 1991.

Gilbert, James. *Men in the Middle: Searching for Masculinity in the 1950s*. Chicago: Univ. of Chicago Press, 2005.

Giulianotti, Richard. "Built by the Two Varelas: The Rise and Fall of Football Culture and National Identity in Uruguay." In *Football Culture: Local Contests, Global Visions*, edited by Gerry Finn and Richard Giulianotti, 134–154. London: Cass, 2000.

Goldblatt, David. *The Ball Is Round: A Global History of Soccer*. New York: Penguin, 2008.

Gómez, Juan Carlos. *La Frontera de la Democracia*. Santiago: LOM, 2004.

Gramsci, Antonio. *Prison Notebooks*. New York: Columbia Univ. Press, 1993.

Grez, Sergio. *La Cuestión Social en Chile: Ideas y Debates Precursors, 1804–1902*. Santiago: DIBAM, 1995.

———. *De la "Regeneración del Pueblo" a la Huelga General: Génesis y Evolución del Movimiento Popular en Chile, 1810–1890*. Santiago: Biblioteca Nacional, 1997.

Guardino, Peter. *In the Time of Liberty: Popular Political Culture in Oaxaca, 1750–1850*. Durham, N.C.: Duke Univ. Press, 2005.

Guerrero J., Bernardo. *El Libro de los Campeones: Deporte e Identidad Cultural en Iquique*. Iquique, Chile: El Jote Errante, 1992.

Habermas, Jürgen. *The Structural Transformation of the Public Sphere*. Cambridge, Mass.: MIT Press, 1991.

Handelman, Howard. "The Political Mobilization of Urban Squatter Settlements: Santiago's Recent Experience and Its Implications for Urban Research." *Latin American Research Review* 10 (Summer 1975): 35–72.

Harambour, Alberto. "Huelga y Sangre Obrera en el Alto San Antonio: Los 'Sucesos' de La Coruña, Junio de 1925." In *A 90 años de los Sucesos de la Escuela Santa María de Iquique*, edited by Pablo Artaza, Sergio González, and Susana Jiles, 183–208. Santiago: DIBAM-LOM, 1999.

Hekman, Susan. *Feminist Interpretation of Michel Foucault*. University Park: Pennsylvania State Univ. Press, 1996.

Henfrey, Colin, and Bernardo Sorj, eds. *Chilean Voices: Activists Describe Their Experiences of the Popular Unity Period*. Atlantic Highlands, N.J.: Humanities Press, 1977.

Hutchison, Elizabeth Quay. *Labors Appropriate to Their Sex*. Durham, N.C.: Duke Univ. Press, 2001.

———. "Add Gender and Stir? Cooking up Gendered Histories of Modern Latin America." *Latin American Research Review* 38, no. 1 (2003): 267–287.

Identidad Grupos Memoria Popular. *Memorias de La Victoria*. Santiago: Gaudí, 2003.

Instituto de Estadísticas Chile. *Chile: Proyecciones y Estimaciones de Población*. Santiago: INE, 2005.

Instituto de Información Campesina. *Como Debe Jugarse el Fútbol*. Santiago: La Moneda, 1941.

Iturriaga, Jorge. "Proletas, Limpios, Cobardes y Burgueses." In *1973: La Vida Cotidiana de un Año Crucial*, edited by Claudio Rolle, 297–352. Santiago: Planeta, 2003.

———. "Aunque Ganas o Pierdas." Working Paper. Pontifical Catholic University, Santiago, 2005.

James, C. L. R. *Beyond a Boundary*. Durham, N.C.: Duke University Press, 1993.

James, Daniel. *Resistance and Integration: Peronism and the Argentine Working Class, 1946–1976*. Cambridge: Cambridge Univ. Press, 1988.

Jara, Eliana. *Cine Mudo Chileno*. Santiago: Los Héroes, 1994.

Joignant, Alfredo. *Los Enigmas de la Comunidad Perdida*. Santiago: LOM, 2002.

Joseph, Gilbert, ed. *Reclaiming the Political in Latin American History: Essays from the North*. Durham, N.C.: Duke Univ. Press, 2001.

Juventudes Comunistas de Chile. *Estatutos de las Juventudes Comunistas de Chile*. Santiago: Lira, 1961.

Kaplan, Temma. *Taking Back the Streets: Women, Youth, and Direct Democracy*. Berkeley and Los Angeles: Univ. of California Press, 2004.

Karush, Matthew. "National Identity in the Sports Pages: Football and the Mass Media in 1920s Buenos Aires." *Americas* 60, no. 1 (2003): 11–32.

Kirkwood, Julieta. *Ser Política en Chile: Las Feministas y los Partidos*. Santiago: FLACSO, 1986.

Klein, Marcus. "The New Voices of Chilean Fascism and the Popular Front, 1938–1942." *Journal of Latin American Studies* 33 (May 2001): 347–375.

Klich, Ignacio. "Argentine-Ottoman Relations and their Impact on Immigrants from the Middle East: A History of Unfulfilled Expectations, 1910–1915." *Americas* 50 (October 1993): 177–205.

Klich, Ignacio, and Jeffrey Lesser. Introduction to "Turco Immigrants in Latin America." A special issue of *Americas* 53 (July 1996).

Klubock, Thomas Miller. *Contested Communities: Class, Gender, and Politics in Chile's El Teniente Copper Mine, 1904–1951*. Durham, N.C.: Duke Univ. Press, 1999.

——. "Nationalism, Race, and the Politics of Imperialism: Workers and North American Capital in the Chilean Copper Industry." In *Reclaiming the Political in Latin American History: Essays from the North*, edited by Gilbert Joseph, 231–267. Durham, N.C.: Duke Univ. Press, 2001.

——. "The Politics of Forests and Forestry on Chile's Southern Frontier, 1880s–1940s." *Hispanic American Historical Review* 86 (August 2006): 535–570.

Knight, Alan. "Populism and Neo-Populism in Latin America, Especially Mexico." *Journal of Latin American Studies* 30 (May 1998): 223–248.

Kornbluh, Peter. "The *El Mercurio* File." *Columbia Journalism Review* 42 (September–October 2003): 14–19.

Kraushaar, Wolfgang. "'¡Chile Sí, Junta No!': Political Protests at the 1974 FIFA World Cup." *Mittelweg 36* 17, no. 2 (April–May 2008); translated by Toby Axelrod, *Eurozine*, 8 July 2008. http://www.eurozine.com/articles/2008-08-07-kraushaar2-en.html.

Laclau, Ernesto. *Politics and Ideology in Marxist Theory: Capitalism-Fascism-Populism*. Atlantic Highlands, N.J.: Humanities Press, 1977.

Lafertte, Elías. "El Comunismo y la Democracia." In *Los Comunistas, el Frente Popular y la Independencia Nacional: Discursos*, by Elías Lafertte and Carlos Contreras, 11–22. Santiago: Antares, 1937.

——. *Vida de un Comunista*. Santiago, 1961.

Larraín, Fernando. *Fútbol en Chile, 1895–1945*. Santiago: Molina Lackington, 1945.

Lavrín, Asunción. *Women, Feminism, and Social Change in Argentina, Chile, and Uruguay, 1890–1940*. Lincoln: Univ. of Nebraska Press, 1995.

Lesser, Jeffrey. "(Re) Creating Ethnicity: Middle Eastern Immigration to Brazil." *Americas* 53 (July 1996): 45–65.

Lever, Janet. *Soccer Madness*. Chicago: Univ. of Chicago Press, 1983.

Levine, Robert. "Sport and Society: The Case of Brazilian *Futebol*." *Luso-Brazilian Review* 17, no. 2 (Winter 1980): 233–252.

Lin Chou, Diego. *Chile y China: Inmigración y Relaciones Bilaterales, 1845–1970.* Santiago: DIBAM, 2004.

Lipset, Seymour Martin. "The Social Requisites of Democracy Revisited: 1993 Presidential Address." *American Sociological Review* 1, no. 59 (1994): 1–22.

Livingston, J. H., and A. W. Betteley. *Football: Historia, Reglamentos, Comentarios.* Santiago: Cervantes, 1917.

Lomnitz, Claudio. *Deep Mexico, Silent Mexico: An Anthropology of Nationalism.* Minneapolis: Univ. of Minnesota Press, 2000.

Loveman, Brian. *Struggle in the Countryside: Politics and Rural Labor in Chile, 1919–1973.* Bloomington: Univ. of Indiana Press, 1977.

Lowe, Dennis. "Shankly . . . Soccer's True Folk Hero." *London Times,* 30 September 1981, 30.

Maldonado, Carlos. "AChA y la Proscripción del Partido Comunista en Chile, 1946–1948." *Contribuciones FLACSO* 60 (1989).

Mallon, Florencia. *Courage Tastes of Blood: The Mapuche Community of Nicolas Ailio and the Chilean State, 1906–2001.* Durham, N.C.: Duke Univ. Press, 2005.

———. "Indian Communities, Political Cultures, and the State in Latin America, 1780–1990." *Journal of Latin American Studies* 24 (1992): 35–53.

Mangan, J. A., and James Walvin. *Manliness and Morality: Middle-Class Masculinity in Britain and America, 1800–1940.* Manchester, UK: Manchester Univ. Press, 1987.

Manns, Patricio. *Grandes Deportistas.* Santiago: Quimantú, 1972.

Marbleu, Regis. *El Futbol: Una Farsa Homosexual.* Translated by Sergio Guerra. Santiago: Rafaga, 1968.

Marín, Edgardo. *Centenario Historia Total del Fútbol Chileno, 1895–1995.* Santiago: Editores y Consultores REI, 1995.

Marín, Edgardo, and Julio Salviat. *De David a "Chamaco."* Santiago: Gabriela Mistral, 1975.

Martin, Simon. *Football and Fascism: The National Game under Mussolini.* Oxford: Berg, 2004.

Martínez, Guillermo. *La Organización de los Deportes i el Estadio Nacional.* Santiago: Santiago, 1917.

Martínez, Josafat [pseud.]. *Historia del Fútbol Chileno.* Santiago: Chile, 1961.

Martínez-Echazábal, Lourdes. "*Mestizaje* and the Discourse of National/Cultural Identity in Latin America, 1845–1959." *Latin American Perspectives* 25 (May 1998): 21–42.

Mason, Tony. *Passion of the People? Football in South America.* New York: Verso, 1995.

Masters, Bruce. *Christians and Jews in the Ottoman Arab World: The Birth of Sectarianism.* Cambridge: Cambridge Univ. Press, 2001.

Matta, Roberto da. *Carnival, Rogues, and Heroes: An Interpretation of the Brazilian Dilemma*. Translated by John Drury. Notre Dame, Ind.: Univ. of Notre Dame Press, 1991.

Mattar, Ahmad Hassan. *El Guía Social de la Colonia Árabe en Chile*. Santiago: Ahues Hermanos, 1941.

Mayorga, Wilfredo, "Colo Colo: 50 Años de Fútbol." *Las Ultimas Noticias*, 19 April 1975.

McCann, Bryan. *Hello, Hello Brazil: Popular Music in the Making of Modern Brazil*. Durham, N.C.: Duke University Press, 2004.

McDonald, Ronald. "Apportionment and Party Politics in Santiago, Chile." *Midwest Journal of Political Science* 13 (1969): 455–470.

McGee Deutsch, Sandra. *Las Derechas: The Extreme Right in Argentina, Brazil, and Chile, 1890–1939*. Stanford, Calif.: Stanford Univ. Press, 1999.

McKay, Jim, Michael Messner, and Don Sabo, eds. *Masculinities, Gender Relations, and Sports*. Research on Men and Masculinities 13. Thousand Oaks, Calif.: Sage, 2000.

Miller, Rory, and Liz Crolley, eds. *Football in the Americas: Fútbol, Futebol, Soccer*. London: Institute for the Study of the Americas, 2007.

Ministerio de Educación [Chile]. *Tres Miradas al Estadio Nacional de Chile*. Santiago: Andros, 2004.

Modiano, Pilar. "Historia del Deporte Chileno." Thesis, Pontificia Universidad Católica, Santiago, Chile, 1995.

Montero, Rene. *Ibáñez: Un Hombre, un Mandatorio, 1926–1931*. Santiago: Condor, 1937.

Morgan, Sue. *The Feminist History Reader*. New York: Routledge, 2006.

Mouat, Francisco. *Cosas del Fútbol*. Santiago: Pheuén, 1989.

Moulian, Tomás. *Chile Actual: Anatomía de un Mito*. Santiago: LOM-ARCIS, 1997.

———. "La vía chilena al socialismo." In *Cuando Hicimos Historia: La Experiencia de la Unidad Popular*, edited by Julio Pinto, 35–56. Santiago: LOM, 2005.

Movimiento de Acción Popular Unitario. *El Primer Año del Gobierno Popular and el Segundo Año del Gobierno Popular*. Philadelphia: Institute for the Study of Human Issues, 1977. Originally printed in Chile, 1972.

Mukerji, Chandra, and Michael Schudson, eds. *Rethinking Popular Culture*. Berkeley and Los Angeles: Univ. of California Press, 1991.

Municipalidad de San Miguel. *Memoria de la Labor, 1940–1941*. Santiago: Claret, 1941.

Muñoz, Jerman. "Necesidad de Fundar una Sociedad que Se Ocupe de Protejer a la Raza Chilena." *La Revista Pedagógica* 5 (September–October 1910): 201–206.

Muñoz Funck, Cristián. *Historia de la Dirección General de Deportes y Recreación*. Santiago: Chiledeportes, 2001.

Naranjo, Pedro, Mauricio Ahumada, Mario Gracés, and Julio Pinto, eds. *Miguel Enríquez y el Proyecto Revolucionario en Chile*. Santiago: LOM, 2004.

Nunn, Frederick. *Chilean Politics, 1920-1931: The Honorable Mission of the Armed Forces.* Albuquerque: Univ. of New Mexico Press, 1970.

Ojeda, Sergio. *Recuerdos de 80 años.* Santiago: Universitaria, 1986.

Olguín, Myrian, and Patricia Peña, eds. *La Inmigración Árabe en Chile.* Santiago: Universitaria, 1990.

Orellana, Joaquín. "El Estadio Nacional." *Boletín de Educación Física* 7 (1940): 39-42.

Orellano, Wilfredo. *La Previsión Social en el Foot-ball Profesional Chileno.* Santiago: Universitaria, 1964.

Oroz, Rodolfo. "El Castellano de Nuestros Deportistas." *Stadium* 3 (1927): 238-249.

Orozco, Manual. "Globalization and Migration: The Impact of Family Remittances in Latin America." *Latin American Politics and Society* 44 (Summer 2002): 41-66.

Ossandón, Carlos, and Eduardo Santa Cruz. *Entre las Alas y el Plomo.* Santiago: LOM, 2001.

Owensby, Brian. *Intimate Ironies: Modernity and the Making of Middle-Class Lives in Brazil.* Stanford, Calif.: Stanford Univ. Press, 1999.

Palacios, Nicolás. *Raza Chilena.* Valparaíso: Alemana, 1904.

Palestro, Mario. *La República Independiente de San Miguel.* Santiago: LOM, 1998.

Paley, Julia. "Making Democracy Count: Opinion Polls and Market Surveys in the Chilean Political Transition." *Cultural Anthropology* 16 (2001): 135-164.

———. *Marketing Democracy: Power and Social Movements in Post-Dictatorship Chile.* Berkeley and Los Angeles: Univ. of California Press, 2001.

Partido Conservador. *XVI Convención Nacional.* Santiago: Pacífico, 1953.

Partido Socialista. *Homenaje al 6° Aniversario del Partido Socialista.* Santiago, 1939.

Pedelty, Mark. "The Bolero: The Birth, Life, and Decline of Mexican Modernity." *Latin American Music Review* 20 (1999): 30-58.

Pedraza-Bailey, Silvia. "Immigration Research: A Conceptual Map." *Social Science History* 14 (1990): 43-67.

Peruzzotii, Enrique. "Constitucionalismo, Populismo y Sociedad Civil." *Revista Mexicana de Sociología* 61 (1999): 149-172.

Piccato, Pablo. "Communities and Crime in Mexico City." *Delaware Review of Latin American Studies* 6, no. 1 (2005). http://www.udel.edu/LAS/Vol6-1Piccato.html (accessed 1 June 2009).

———. "Public Sphere in Latin America: A Map of the Historiography." Working paper. Columbia University, 2006. http://www.columbia.edu/~pp143/ps.pdf (accessed 2 May 2007).

Pike, Frederick. "Aspects of Class Relations in Chile, 1850-1960." *Hispanic American Historical Review* 43 (1963): 14-33.

Pinto, Julio, ed. *Cuando Hicimos Historia: La Experiencia de la Unidad Popular.* Santiago: LOM, 2005.

———. *Trabajos y Rebeldías en la Pampa Salitrera*. Santiago: Univ. de Santiago, 1998.

Portes, Alejandro, Luis Eduardo Guarnizo, and William J. Haller. "Transnational Entrepreneurs: An Alternative Form of Immigrant Economic Adaptation." *American Sociological Review* 67 (April 2002): 278–298.

Posada-Carbó, Eduardo. "Electoral Juggling: A Comparative History of the Corruption of Suffrage in Latin America, 1830–1930." *Journal of Latin American Studies* 32, no. 3 (October 2000): 611–644.

Posner, Paul. "Local Democracy and the Transformation of Popular Participation in Chile." *Latin American Politics and Society* 46, no. 3 (2004): 55–81.

———. Popular Representation and Political Dissatisfaction in Chile's New Democracy." *Journal of Interamerican Studies and World Affairs* 41 (1999): 59–85.

Power, Margaret. "More than Mere Pawns: Right-Wing Women in Chile." *Journal of Women's History* 16 (2004): 138–151.

———. *Right-Wing Women in Chile: Feminine Power and the Struggle against Allende, 1964–1973*. College Park: Pennsylvania State Univ. Press, 2002.

Prado, José Miguel. *Reseña Histórica del Partido Liberal*. Santiago: Andina, 1963.

Presa, Rafael de la. *Los Primeros Noventa Años del Círculo Español*. Santiago: Fantasia, 1972.

Prince of Wales Country Club. *Memoria*. Santiago: Chile, 1946.

Prothro, James, and Patricio Chaparro. "Public Opinion and the Movement of Chilean Government to the Left, 1952–1972." *Journal of Politics* 36 (February 1974): 2–43.

Putnam, Robert. *Bowling Alone: The Collapse and Revival of American Community*. New York: Simon and Schuster, 2000.

Rabinovitz, Lauren. *For the Love of Pleasure: Women, Movies, and Culture in Turn-of-the-Century Chicago*. New Brunswick, N.J.: Rutgers Univ. Press, 1998.

Ramón, Armando de. *Santiago de Chile*. Santiago: Sudamericana, 2000.

Rebolledo, Antonia. "La Integración de los Inmigrantes Árabes a la Vida Nacional: Los Sirios en Santiago." Thesis, Pontificia Universidad Católica, Santiago, Chile, 1991.

Rinke, Stefan. *Cultura de las Masas, Reforma, Nacionalismo en Chile, 1910–1930*. Santiago: DIBAM, 2002.

Ríos Tobar, Marcela, Lorena Godoy Catalán, and Elizabeth Guerrero Caviedes. *Un Nuevo Silencio Feminista? La Transformación de un Movimiento Social en el Chile Posdictadura*. Santiago: Cuarto Propio, 2003.

Rojas Flores, Jorge. *Moral y Prácticas Cívicas en los Niños Chilenos, 1880–1950*. Santiago: Ariadna, 2004.

Rojas Flores, Jorge, Cinthia Rodríguez Toledo, Moisés Fernández, eds. *Cristaleros: Recuerdos de un Siglo*. Santiago: Artes Gráficas, 1998.

Rolle, Claudio, ed. *1973: La Vida Cotidiana de un Año Crucial*. Santiago: Planeta, 2003.

Rosemblatt, Karin. *Gendered Compromises: Political Cultures and the State in Chile, 1920-1950.* Chapel Hill: Univ. of North Carolina Press, 2000.

———. "Charity, Rights, and Entitlement: Gender, Labor, and Welfare in Early-Twentieth-Century Chile." *Hispanic American Historical Review* 81 (August–November 2001): 555–585.

Rosenzweig, Roy. *Eight Hours for What We Will.* Cambridge: Cambridge Univ. Press, 1983.

Rowe, L. "The Development of Democracy on the American Continent." *American Political Science Review* 16 (February 1920): 1–9.

Rubenstein, Anne. "El Santo's Strange Career." In *The Mexico Reader: History, Culture, Politics,* edited by Gilbert Joseph and Timothy Henderson, 570–578. Durham, N.C.: Duke Univ. Press, 2002.

Sábato, Hilda. *La Política en las Calles.* Buenos Aires: Sudamericana, 1998.

Sainz Torres, Hugo. *Breve Historia del Deportes.* Santiago: Braden Copper, 1961.

Salazar, Gabriel. "The History of Popular Culture in Chile: Different Paths." In *Popular Culture in Chile: Resistance and Survival,* edited by Kenneth Aman and Cristián Parker, 13–39. Boulder, Colo.: Westview, 1991.

———. *Labradores, Peones y Proletarios: Formación y Crisis de la Sociedad Popular Chilena del Siglo XIX.* Santiago: Sur, 1985.

———. "Luis Emilio Recabarren y el Municipio Popular en Chile, 1900-1925." *Revista de Sociología* 9 (1994): 61–82.

Salazar, Gabriel, and Jorge Benítez, eds. *Autonomía, Espacio y Gestión: El Municipio Cercenado.* Santiago: LOM, 1998.

Salazar, Gabriel, and Julio Pinto. *Historia Contemporánea de Chile.* Vol. 1: *Estado, Legitimidad, Cuidadanía.* Santiago: LOM, 1999.

———. *Historia Contemporánea de Chile.* Vol. 5: *Niñez y Juventud.* Santiago: LOM, 2002.

Salinas, Maximiliano. "'¡En Tiempo de Chaya Nadie se Enoja!' La Fiesta Popular del Carnaval en Santiago de Chile, 1880-1910." *Mapocho* 50 (2001): 281–325.

Salinas, Sebastián. *Por Empuje y Coraje: Los Albos en la Época Amateur.* Santiago: CEDEP, 2004.

San Martín, Victor. "Nuestra Educación Física y el Deporte Profesional." *Boletín de Educación Física* 9 (1942): 10–14.

Santa Cruz, Eduardo. *Crónica de un Encuentro: Fútbol y Cultura Popular.* Santiago: ARCOS, 1991.

———. *Origen y Futuro de una Pasión: Fútbol, Cultura y Modernidad.* Santiago: LOM, 1996.

Santiago Morning Club de Deportes. *Homenaje al 40° Aniversario.* Santiago, 1943.

Schild, Verónica. "Recasting 'Popular' Movements: Gender and Political Learning in Neighborhood Organizations in Chile." *Latin American Perspectives* 21 (1994): 59–80.

Schneider, Cathy. "Mobilization at the Grassroots: Shantytown and Resistance in Authoritarian Chile." *Latin American Perspectives* 18 (Winter 1991): 92–112.

———. *Shantytown Protest in Pinochet's Chile*. Philadelphia: Temple Univ. Press, 1995.

Schofer, Evan, and Marion Fourcade-Gourinchas. "The Structural Contexts of Civic Engagement: Voluntary Association Membership in Comparative Perspective." *American Sociological Review* 66, no. 6 (2001): 806–828.

Scully, Timothy. *Rethinking the Center: Party Politics in Nineteenth- and Twentieth-Century Chile*. Stanford, Calif.: Stanford Univ. Press, 1992.

Senado. *Diario de Sesiones del Senado*. Santiago: Senado de la Républica de Chile.

———. *Sesiones Extraordinarias del Senado*. Santiago: Senado de la Républica de Chile.

Sepúlveda Lafuente, Candelario. *Laborando en Beneficio de la Educación Física de Mi País*. Chillán, Chile: Americana, 1931.

Shaw, Lisa. *The Social History of Brazilian Samba*. Austin: Univ. of Texas Press, 1999.

Silva, Miguel. *Los Sindicatos, los Partidos y Clotario Blest: La CUT del '53*. Santiago: Mosquito, 2000.

Silva, Patricio. "State, Public Technocracy, and Politics in Chile, 1927–1941." *Bulletin of Latin American Research* 13.

Smith, William Anderson. *Temperate Chile: A Progressive Spain*. London: Black, 1899.

Sociedad de Beneficia "Juventud Homsiense." *Estatutos*. Santiago: Al-Watan, 1920.

Sommer, Doris. *Foundational Fictions*. Berkeley and Los Angeles: Univ. of California Press, 1991.

Stein, Steve. *Lima Obrera, 1900–1930*. Lima: El Virrey, 1986.

Steinmetz, George, ed. *State/Culture: State-Formation after the Cultural Turn*. Ithaca, N.Y.: Cornell Univ. Press, 1999.

Stepan, Nancy. *"The Hour of Eugenics": Race, Gender, and Nation in Latin America*. Ithaca, N.Y.: Cornell Univ. Press, 1991.

Stephen, Lynn. "Gender, Citizenship, and the Politics of Identity." *Latin American Perspectives* 28 (2001): 54–69.

Stern, Steve. *Battling for Hearts and Minds: Memory Struggles in Pinochet's Chile, 1973–1988*. Durham, N.C.: Duke Univ. Press, 2006.

Teutsch Solar, Enrique. *Metódo Práctico que Enseña a Jugar Verdadero Foot-ball*. Santiago: Instituto Geográfico Militar, 1929.

Tilly, Charles. *Democracy*. New York: Cambridge Univ. Press, 2007.

Tinsman, Heidi. *Partners in Conflict: The Politics of Gender, Sexuality, and Labor in the Chilean Agrarian Reform, 1950–1973*. Durham, N.C.: Duke Univ. Press, 2002.

Torre, Carlos de la. *Populist Seduction in Latin America: The Ecuadorian Experience*. Athens: Ohio Univ., Center for International Studies, 2000.

Tortura en Poblaciones del Gran Santiago (1973-1990): Colectivo de Memoria Histórica. Santiago: José Domingo Cañas, 2005.

Unidad Popular. *Programa Basico de Gobierno de la Unidad Popular.* Santiago: Impresora Horizonte, 1972.

Unión Deportiva Española. *Memoria y Balance.* Santiago: Comercio, 1931.

Unión Española. *Bodas de Oro 1897.* Santiago: Imparcial, 1947.

———. *Memoria.* Santiago: Comercio, 1941.

———. *Memoria.* Santiago: Casa Amarilla, 1943.

Uribe-Uran, Victor. "The Birth of the Public Sphere in Latin America during the Age of Revolution." *Comparative Studies in Society and History* 42 (2002): 425–457.

Valdés, Teresa. "El Movimiento de Pobladores, 1973-1985: La Recomposición de las Solidaridades Sociales." In *Decentralización del Estado: Movimiento Social y Gestión Local,* edited by Jordi Borja, 263-319. Santiago: FLACSO, 1987.

Valdivia, Verónica. *El Golpe Despues del Golpe.* Santiago: LOM, 2003.

Valenzuela, Arturo. *Political Brokers in Chile: Local Government in a Centralized Polity.* Durham, N.C.: Duke Univ. Press, 1977.

Valenzuela, Samuel. *Democratización via Reforma: La Expansión del Sufragio en Chile.* Buenos Aires: IDES, 1985.

———. "Making Sense of Suffrage Expansion and Electoral Institutions in Latin America: A Comment on Colomer's 'Tiger.'" *Latin American Politics and Society* 46 (2004): 59-67.

Vallerand, Robert J., Nikos Ntoumanis, Frederick L. Philippe, Geneviève L. Lavigne, Noémie Charbonneau, Arielle Bonneville, Camille Lagacé-Labonté, Gabrielle Maliha. "On Passion and Sports Fans: A Look at Football." *Journal of Sports Sciences* 26 (October 2008): 1279-1293.

Vicuña, Julio. *Mitos y Supersticiones.* Santiago: Universitaria, 1915.

Villalobos, Sergio. *Origen y Ascenso de la Burguesía Chilena* Santiago: Universitaria, 1987.

Wacquant, Loïc. "Pugs at Work: Bodily Capital and Bodily Labour among Professional Boxers." *Body and Society* 1, no. 1 (1995): 65-93.

Walter, Richard. *Politics and Urban Growth in Santiago, Chile, 1891-1941.* Stanford, Calif.: Stanford Univ. Press, 2005.

Warner, Michael. *Publics and Counterpublics.* New York: Zone, 2005.

Weber, David. *Bárbaros: Spaniards and Their Savages in the Age of the Enlightenment.* New Haven, Conn.: Yale Univ. Press, 2005.

Weyland, Kurt. "Neoliberalism and Democracy in Latin America: A Mixed Record." *Latin American Politics and Society* 46 (2004): 135-157.

Wheeler, Robert. "Organized Sport and Organized Labour: The Workers' Sports Movement." *Journal of Contemporary History* 13 (1978): 191-210.

Whyte, William Foote. *Street Corner Society: The Structure of an Italian Slum.* 4th ed. Chicago: Univ. of Chicago Press, 1993.

Williams, Daryle. *Culture Wars in Brazil: The First Vargas Regime, 1930–1945.* Durham, N.C.: Duke Univ. Press, 2001.

Winn, Peter, ed. *Victims of the Chilean Miracle: Workers and Neoliberalism in the Pinochet Era, 1973–2002.* Durham, N.C.: Duke Univ. Press, 2004.

———. *Weavers of the Revolution: The Yarur Workers and Chile's Road to Socialism.* New York: Oxford, 1989.

Wolfe, Joel. "The Social Subject versus the Political: Latin American Labor History at a Crossroads." *Latin American Research Review* 37 (2002): 244–262.

Yankelevich, Pablo, ed. *En México, entre Exilios: Una Experiencia de Sudamericanos.* Mexico City: ITAM, 1998.

Yashar, Deborah. "Democracy, Indigenous Movements, and the Postliberal Challenge in Latin America." *World Politics* 52 (1999): 76–104.

Yeager, Gertrude. "Female Apostolates and Modernization in Mid-Nineteenth Century Chile." *Americas* 55 (1999): 425–458.

Zegers, Julio. *Estudios Economicos.* Santiago: Nacional, 1908.

Zegers, Luís. *El Football y Su Estilo Moderno de Juego.* Santiago: La República, 1920.

INDEX

CPSIA information can be obtained at www.ICGtesting.com
Printed in the USA
LVOW040452260712

291301LV00005B/8/P